Ford
CHRONICLE

A PICTORIAL HISTORY FROM 1893

BY JAMES M. FLAMMANG, DAVID L. LEWIS,
AND THE AUTO EDITORS OF CONSUMER GUIDE

Publications
International, Ltd.

Louis Weber, CEO
Publications International, Ltd.
7373 North Cicero Avenue
Lincolnwood, Illinois 60712

Manufactured in China.

8 7 6 5 4 3 2 1

ISBN: 0-7853-2509-3

Library of Congress Catalog Card Number: 97-67077

Photography
The editors gratefully acknowledge the photographers who helped make this book possible. They are listed below, along with the page number(s) of their photos:

Cover: Bud Juneau; Mike Mueller; Vince Manocchi; Dan Lyons; Sam Griffith; Mitch Frumkin; Thomas Glatch; Joseph Caro; Scott Baxter

The Henry Ford Museum and Greenfield Village, Dearborn, Michigan: 7, 8, 11, 12, 14, 15, 16, 20, 22, 23, 27, 28, 30, 31, 46, 47, 48, 50, 52, 54, 55, 56, 57, 58, 60, 61, 62, 64, 65, 66, 69, 70, 72, 74, 76, 79, 82, 83, 85, 87, 89, 92, 93, 94, 98, 102, 104, 107 **Jerry Heasley:** 15, 73, 189 **Henry Austin Clark:** 20 **Milton Gene Kieft:** 24, 53, 65, 101, 149, 144, 150, 155, 162, 163, 187 **Vince Manocchi:** 30, 33, 38, 49, 65, 80, 81, 86, 88, 105, 148, 131, 142, 149, 150, 153, 154, 155, 164, 168, 188, 197, 202 **Nicky Wright:** 30, 64, 65, 68, 87, 101, 144, 145, 150, 186, 187, 196, 197, 207, 208, 211, 215, 216, 221, 225, 226, 230, 231, 252 **Bud Juneau:** 34, 35, 38, 58, 83, 90, 96, 112, 160, 181, 191, 216 **Dan Lyons:** 37, 67, 68, 69, 70, 71, 77, 80, 84, 94, 108, 109, 135, 171, 181 **Les Bidrawn:** 40, 41, 63 **Thomas Glatch:** 60, 63, 64, 80, 88, 90, 103, 192, 200, 201, 226 **Doug Mitchel:** 64, 80, 84, 87, 90, 95, 96, 100, 103, 148, 122, 123, 127, 144, 152, 155, 163, 167, 172, 182, 187, 198, 201, 203, 207, 212, 217 **Sam Griffith:** 67, 87, 95, 97, 135, 188, 192, 212, 217, 311 **Eddie Goldberger:** 84 **Rob Van Schaick:** 87 **William J. Schintz:** 91 **Joseph Caro:** 114 **Bob Tenney:** 149, 152 **Alan Hewko:** 110 **Mike Mueller:** 126, 164, 175, 201, 202, 215 **Bert Johnson:** 126 **Lloyd Koenig:** 130 **Doug Dalton:** 139 **Richard Spiegelman:** 150, 202 **David Temple:** 153, 203 **Richard Szczepanski:** 176 **Ken Beebe:** 188 **Studio Image:** 197 **Jim Thompson:** 217 **David Chobat:** 217 **Full Spectrum/Lloyd Grotjan:** 222 **Roland Flessner:** 308

Very Special Thanks To:
Ford Motor Company, Image Library Dept., Dan R. Erickson and Mike Golick; David L. Lewis

Owners
Special thanks to the owners of the Fords featured in this book for their enthusiastic cooperation. They are listed below, along with the page number(s) on which their cars appear:

Cover: **Art Banducci; Vernon A. King, Jr.; Paul Batista; Ed and Debbie Werder; Charles and Mark VanderVelde; Charles Ziska; Larry Ray; Alan Mest; Dells Auto Museum; Wm. Lyon Collection; Dick Pyle**

Panhandle Plains Historic Museum, Canyon, Texas: 15 **Larry O'Neal:** 24, 25 **Kim Dobbins, Crawford Collection Western Reserve Historical Society, Cleveland, Ohio:** 30 **Kim Dobbins:** 33, 81 **Art Banducci:** 34, 35 **Frank Iaccino:** 37 **Bob Fruehe:** 38, 39 **Jim Hearn:** 38 **Edward C. Moody:** 40 **Carl M. Riggins:** 41, 63 **W. Parker Browne:** 53 **Frank Gonsalves:** 58 **Dick and Lance Tarnut, Dells Auto Museum, Wisconsin Dells, Wisconsin:** 60, 88 **Louis Brojanac:** 63 **Richard Bayer:** 64, 80 **Ron Edwards:** 64 **Stan Sokol:** 64 **Jonnie Keller:** 65 **William Lyons Collection:** 65, 80, 86 **Bob and Karyn Sitter:** 65, 68 **Vernon A. King, Jr.:** 67 **Charles Giese:** 67 **Gerard and Lorraine May:** 68, 69, 70 **Richard W. Andrews:** 71 **Sheldon Lake:** 71 **David Patterson:** 73 **Mike Laureno, Jr.:** 77, 80 **Daniel P. Smith:** 80 **Bill Cline:** 83, 96 **Evan and Delores Martin:** 84 **Ted Sattler:** 84 **Louis Grosso:** 84 **Spencer L. Bing:** 87 **Peter A. Spear:** 87 **Carol Nesladek:** 87 **Vance Ferry:** 87 **Gerald Wuichet:** 90 **Douglas Leicht:** 90 **Marc Micale:** 90 **Debbie Colaniro:** 91 **Donald Passardi:** 94, 108, 109 **Dick Pyle:** 95, 96 **Len Vinyard:** 95 **Earl Heintz:** 96 **Thomas Venezia:** 101 **Fred C. Fischer:** 103 **Lloyd Duzell:** 103 **Norman and Joyce Booth:** 105 **Robert Reeves:** 105 **Chip Turtzo:** 110 **John White and Bill Knudsen:** 112 **Alan West:** 114 **Benjamin R. Caskey, Jr.:** 117 **Dan and Barb Baltic:** 122 **Frank C. Guzzo:** 122 **Loren E. Miller:** 123 **William Fink:** 123 **Jim Mueller:** 126 **Donald W. Peters:** 126 **Jim Stewart:** 127 **Henry Patrick, Houston Police Dept.:** 130 **John L. Murray:** 131 **Glen Gangestad:** 135 **John Baker, Sr.:** 135 **Jackie and Shana Cerrito:** 139 **Gail and John Dalmolin:** 139 **Leonard Nowosel:** 142 **Paul Batista:** 142 **Don and Sue Fennig:** 144 **Dick Guess:** 144 **Alan C. Parker:** 144 **Fred and Diane Ives:** 144 **Jim Goldheimer:** 144 **Tom Franks:** 145 **Jerry Charter:** 145 **Lloyd Pettigrew:** 148 **Alan Wendland:** 148 **Edward R. Keshen:** 148 **Ray and Nancy Deitke:** 149 **Don Simpkin:** 149 **Amos Minter:** 149 **Larry Ray:** 150 **David M. Leslie:** 150 **Donald Kish, Sr.:** 150 **Amos Minter:** 152 **Gerry Klein:** 152 **Fred Roth:** 153 **Tom Howard:** 153 **Z. T. Parker:** 153 **Lee Willett:** 154 **Michael Gallagher:** 154 **George Richards:** 154 **Lynn Augustine:** 154 **Charles L. Richards:** 154 **Jerry Retka:** 155 **Frank R. Masyar:** 155 **Gary Richards:** 155 **Ted Maupin:** 160 **William R. Muni:** 162, 163 **Bob Baumgardner:** 163 **Everett Faulkner:** 164 **Henry Alvarez:** 164 **George Holterman:** 167 **Jack and Holly Stewart:** 168 **Howard A. Moore:** 171 **Roger and Gerri Randolph:** 172 **Kenneth and Linda Coleman:** 175 **Ken Boorsma:** 176 **Arnie Addison:** 181 **Ken Leaman:** 181 **Doug and Jimmy Call:** 182 **Gerald King:** 186 **Julie Peters:** 187 **John Breda:** 187 **Roy and Shirley Andrews:** 187 **Frank Spittle:** 188 **Vince and Franca Manocchi:** 188 **Gladys Duzell:** 188 **Quentin Bacon:** 191 **Dick Albrecht:** 191 **Christopher M. Krueger:** 192 **Gary Dickinson:** 192 **Jerry Buczkowski:** 196 **Jason Sauder:** 197 **Alan Nelson:** 197 **Richard A. Emery:** 197 **Alcie Greunke:** 197 **Glenn Eisenhamer:** 198 **Wayne and Terri Warner:** 198 **Tony Begley:** 200 **Rich Neubauer:** 201 **George N. Bowen:** 201 **David Hooten:** 201 **Ron Wood:** 202 **Ed and Debbie Werder:** 202 **David L. Robb:** 202 **T. and K. Shanley:** 203 **David Temple:** 203 **Duane Baker:** 207 **Raymond C. Hamilton:** 207 **Robert and MaryLu Secondi:** 207 **Mike Baker:** 208 **Winfred and Betty Keed:** 208 **Kurt A. Havely:** 208 **Chris Plylar:** 208 **S. Schonegg:** 210 **Tom Haase:** 211 **Chris Dawalt:** 211 **Gary Pahee:** 211 **Edwin Putz:** 212 **Ron Voyles:** 213 **Steve Ames:** 215 **Dixon Polderman:** 215 **Carol Podemski:** 215 **Leroy Lasiter:** 215 **Walter P. Wise:** 216 **Bill Collins:** 216 **Greg and Rhonda Haynes:** 216 **Jim Reilly:** 217 **Steve Engeman:** 217 **Bill Draper:** 217 **Bud Moore:** 217 **Dan and Karen Kerridge:** 221 **Tom and Carol Podemski:** 221, 226, 252 **Doug and Teresa Huidston:** 221 **Thomas E. Rapala:** 221 **Frank Frandsen:** 222 **Clarence E. Gerguson:** 225 **Frank Trummer:** 226 **Ray P. Fisher:** 230 **Ronald Miller:** 230 **Gary M. Gunushian:** 231 **D. L. Bohart:** 252 **Dave Schmerler, Schmerler Ford, Elk Grove Village, IL:** 311

FOREWORD

In the business world, the impact of a single individual tends to fade with time. Not so with Henry Ford. Few businesses have ever exerted as much influence on American—and international—life as the Ford Motor Company that he founded in 1903.

By the time of his death in 1947, Henry Ford had seen his crude but trustworthy Model T blaze a revolutionary trail of transport for the masses. Novelist Aldous Huxley adopted the debut of the Model T as the birth date of his *Brave New World,* with subsequent events taking place "After Ford." Efficient methods of mass production became known as "Fordism."

Largely under Henry's guidance, automobiles evolved from rich men's playthings to machines that ordinary folks could enjoy. After nearly two decades of existence—with amazingly little change—his creation metamorphosed into the Model A and, four years later, the legendary flathead V-8.

Henry Ford was revered not merely as an automaker, but as a symbol of American ingenuity and grit. Like most complex men, he was also mistrusted—indeed hated—often for the same actions that brought praise from other quarters.

Such extreme reactions resulted from what one writer called Ford's "ignorant idealism," and from the polarity of his views. Not everyone appreciated the provincial rural values that he promoted. Henry could be both hateful and compassionate; narrow-minded and visionary; social reformer and cynical reactionary. Ford was a pacifist who nevertheless served the military effort in both world wars. He was an eager innovator, yet also an ostrich who shunned new ideas.

The same man who initiated the $5 workday, launched the Peace Ship, and—long before Equal Opportunity laws—hired the disabled, later issued anti-Semitic statements and let corporate affairs be guided by the likes of Harry Bennett. Under Bennett, the gently named Sociological Department of Ford Motor Company transformed into a network of spies and thugs, helping to keep unions out and Henry insulated.

Mainly because of Henry's resistance to giving up the reins, Ford never turned into a dynasty. Although his only son Edsel was named president in 1919, and gained renown for leadership in design, he stood deeply within his father's giant shadow. That fact contributed to Edsel's premature death in 1943.

Henry Ford II, eldest of Edsel's four children, steered the company from its faltering stance at the close of World War II to a renewed vitality. Far more flamboyant than his grandfather, "Henry the Deuce" earned credit for many achievements, but never achieved public adoration. Brothers William Clay and Benson Ford held corporate posts, but on a secondary plateau.

Along the way, Ford's destiny was tilted by experts from outside the family. A few became famous, notably Lee Iacocca, who led the Mustang's birth. As Ford faltered again in the 1970s and early '80s, a new breed of managers was on hand to usher in the dramatic Taurus. Two fourth-generation Fords—Edsel II and William Clay, Jr.—also have been climbing the corporate ladder.

The fascinating history of this most American of companies is chronicled in a unique format of photographs and informative captions. "Model Breakdown" charts provide each year's weights, prices, and production totals. Also included are "Engine Availability" charts.

While every effort has been made to ensure accuracy, not all factory records—especially in the early years—were precise or complete. Some production figures were recorded for the *calendar* year rather than the *model* year. Prices often changed during the course of a year. Although certain trucks, foreign-built cars, and specialty vehicles are pictured, they are not included in charts.

Most Americans hold fond memories of Fords. Millions learned to drive behind the wheel of a Ford, and shared joyous life experiences in one. Fords carried countless folks on their first dates, their honeymoons, their vacation journeys—and to work each day.

We congratulate Ford Motor Company on its 95th birthday (1903-98), with Alex Trotman at the helm and Ross Roberts heading the Ford Division.

—The Auto Editors of CONSUMER GUIDE

CONTENTS

1893–1902

1863: Henry Ford born

1879: George B. Selden applies for patent on gas motorcar; granted in 1895

1888: Henry Ford marries Clara Bryant

1893: Edsel Bryant Ford born November 6 . . . Henry builds first working engine

1896: Henry Ford drives "Quadricycle" in Detroit

1899: Second Quadricycle finished . . . Detroit Automobile Co. formed

1900: First National Auto Show held in New York

1901: Ford racing car victorious . . . short-lived Henry Ford Co. organized

BEFORE FORD MOTOR COMPANY   BEFORE FORD MOTOR COMPANY   BEFORE F

▲ Young Henry Ford wears a rather formal expression in this early photo. Born on a Michigan farm on July 30, 1863, Henry journeyed to Detroit at age 16. In 1893, when his only son Edsel was born, Henry worked as an engineer at the Edison Illuminating Company. Because of his modest achievements as a young man, few would have predicted the meteoric path Henry's career would follow in middle age. In the popular mind, Henry Ford would become a larger-than-life folk hero: part myth, part reality, thought to blend the pluck of Horatio Alger with the heroics of a Theodore Roosevelt.

◄ As depicted by artist Norman Rockwell in "The Boy Who Put the World on Wheels," America was the land where inventors started their dreams early. Henry Ford's vision of a motorcar for the masses may also have begun to form at an early age, but he was well into his thirties before he began to turn that dream into reality. Not until his 40th birthday neared, in fact, did the Ford Motor Company come into existence. This scene was one of eight painted in 1952 by Norman Rockwell, to mark Ford's 50th Anniversary in 1953. They appeared in the Ford calendar that year, as well as in *Life* magazine and the American Road series of advertisements.

6

◀ The "Square House," or "Honeymoon House," designed by Henry's bride Clara, and partially built by Henry. The Fords lived in the Dearborn home from 1889 until moving to Detroit in 1891. The house, given to Ford look-alike Bob Smith in 1937, was removed in 1952 to Garden City, Michigan.

▼ It doesn't look like much, but Henry and Clara called half of this Detroit duplex home in 1891-92. In this 1979 photo, the Ford's living room was beneath the Money Orders sign; their bedroom upstairs. The structure, at 4420 John R Street, Detroit, was vacated about 1970 and razed in 1991.

▲ Detroit Edison Company's chief engineer, Henry Ford, bottom, third from left, takes delivery of a massive new Worthington vacuum pump in 1895. Henry's salary was $95 per month.

▲ The Edison Illuminating Company stationhouse gang. Henry Ford, top, third from right, sports a mustache, worn until 1903. He may have just learned he would soon be a father.

▲ At Christmastime in 1893, Henry Ford tested his gasoline engine for the first time, clamped to the kitchen sink at home. As shown in this painting, Clara Ford dripped fuel into the intake valve as Henry turned the flywheel. Most of the engine was scrap, costing about a dollar, with a cylinder of one-inch gas pipe. After it ran for about half a minute, Henry went to work on a larger version.

▲ Henry bought this bicycle at the height of a nationwide cycling craze. The frame proved too light, and Henry later rebuilt it. Shortly before acquiring the bike, Ford bought his first camera; this picture and many more to come were taken with it.

▶ Ford's first "better idea"—Henry's Quadricycle. Powered by a two-cylinder, four-cycle engine, the car had a trolley-like electric bell to warn pedestrians. Shortly after this picture was taken, Ford sold his machine to "Chappie" Annesley, who then sold it to A.W. Hall, who on April 11, 1899, wrote Ford a testimonial, perhaps the first automobile testimonial.

◀ "The Revolution That Started in a Shed at Night" was Norman Rockwell's title for this painting, one of eight commissioned for Ford's 50th Anniversary in 1953. Henry is shown tinkering with his first "Quadricycle" in 1896, in the shop behind his Bagley Avenue home, with a proud Clara looking on. An acquaintance, engineer/inventor Charles Brady King, drove the first gasoline vehicle around Detroit on March 6, 1896, while a mustached Henry cycled behind. Three months later, Henry was ready to take the Quadricycle out for a trial. In 1898, *Horseless Age* magazine noted that Ford had built several vehicles, but up to that point there had been only one: this Quadricycle. Another was in the works, but the new century would be well underway before the Ford Motor Company was formed. In the meantime, Henry Ford would be involved in two other automaking ventures.

By the time this Quadricycle was finished, Selden's patent for the gasoline automobile had been granted. By 1901, the Electric Vehicle Company—holder of rights to that patent—began to intimidate automakers into paying royalties for each car built. Ford's subsequent refusal to do so—after being denied a license—cemented his reputation as a maverick.

Henry Ford came across as an idealistic pioneer part of the time, a cynical reactionary at others. He could be selfish, stubborn, and mean—but also open-minded, generous, and compassionate. One biography's subtitle may describe him best: "ignorant idealist." Henry's homespun rural values later played a major role in charting the course of the company.

▲ Most early inventors started small. Inside a brick shed behind his home, Henry Ford began work on a motorized bicycle in 1893. Because the door was too narrow, he had to chop bricks out of the wall to get the Quadricycle out. This replica of the shop can be seen at Greenfield Village in Dearborn.

▲ No publicity at all accompanied the late-night foray of Henry Ford's 1896 Quadricycle, pictured prior to its restoration in the 1950s. Driven by leather belt and chain, the primitive vehicle had two forward speeds—but no brakes or reverse—and could reach about 20 mph.

◄ Driven around Detroit on June 4, 1896, at 2:00 A.M. in the rain, the Quadricycle created little stir. Few knew of its existence. A two-cylinder, four-stroke water-cooled engine developed about four horsepower. The buggy-type chassis rolled on bicycle wheels and tires.

▲ Sometime after his post-midnight run in the Quadricycle, a dapper Henry Ford sits at its tiller. Henry would drive periodically into the countryside, accompanied by Clara and Edsel.

▲ Ford sold the first Quadricycle and finished a second, more refined version by summer 1899. He gave his first interview—with photos—to the *Detroit Journal*. Note bicycle-style wheels.

▲ Built in 1899 by the Detroit Automobile Company, this delivery van was the first Ford-related vehicle intended for sale. That company was formed after several wealthy investors had taken note of Henry's emergence, including Detroit mayor William C. Maybury and businessman William H. Murphy. Henry Ford left his job at Edison and was named superintendent at Detroit, but serious auto production never came to pass. Henry wanted to build a racing car, investors balked, and the company folded in late 1900.

▲ Henry Ford, right, and his younger brother, William, on a country road c. 1899. The day must have been a Sunday inasmuch as Henry is dressed to the nines. Ford, a strong believer in exercise, rode bikes all of his life. Henry never permitted William to join his company, but did set him up as a Ford dealer. William lived on until 1959.

▲ Henry Ford at the wheel of the racing car in which he won his first and only race, defeating Alexander Winton in a 10-mile event at Grosse Pointe, Michigan, on October 10, 1901. Ford's mechanic, Spider Huff, kneels on a shelf-like running board, and on curves hung way out from the hand grips as ballast.

▲ Henry Ford, left, trailed Alexander Winton until the seven-mile mark of their 10-mile race. Then Winton's engine failed, and Ford won handily. "Put Winton in my car," said Ford, "and it will beat anything."

◀ Henry Ford sits at the wheel of his first race car, built in 1901, with a 26-horsepower two-cylinder engine. At the Grosse Pointe track in October, it averaged 43.5 mph to beat a Winton.

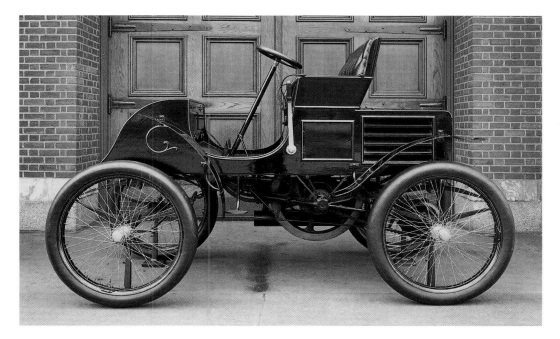

◄ Henry Ford's third car was built by the Detroit Automobile Company while he was superintendent. Note the fancy fenders and curvy dashboard, as well as the use of a steering wheel instead of a tiller. The Henry Ford Company was organized November 30, 1901, following his early race victory. Henry got a one-sixth share and post of chief engineer, but his racing interest didn't sit well with stockholders. He also was displeased when Henry Leland came on board as a consultant. Ford left after three months, taking a $900 settlement, and the firm no longer used his name.

◄ Although Henry Ford focused mainly on auto racing, he built a third Quadricycle in 1901. This one had a steering wheel, not a tiller. Ford and Tom Cooper then built two monstrous 80-horsepower racing cars called "Arrow" and "999," and hired bicycle racer Barney Oldfield as driver. On October 25, 1902, "999" covered five miles in five minutes and 28 seconds.

▼ On August 20, 1902, Henry Ford and Alexander Y. Malcomson, a Detroit coal dealer, agreed to develop a commercial auto. Ford & Malcomson Company Ltd., with 10 investors, led to the Ford Motor Company—ready to build cars in this factory on Mack Avenue in Detroit. Cadillac also emerged in 1902, under Henry Leland, as an outgrowth of the early Henry Ford Company.

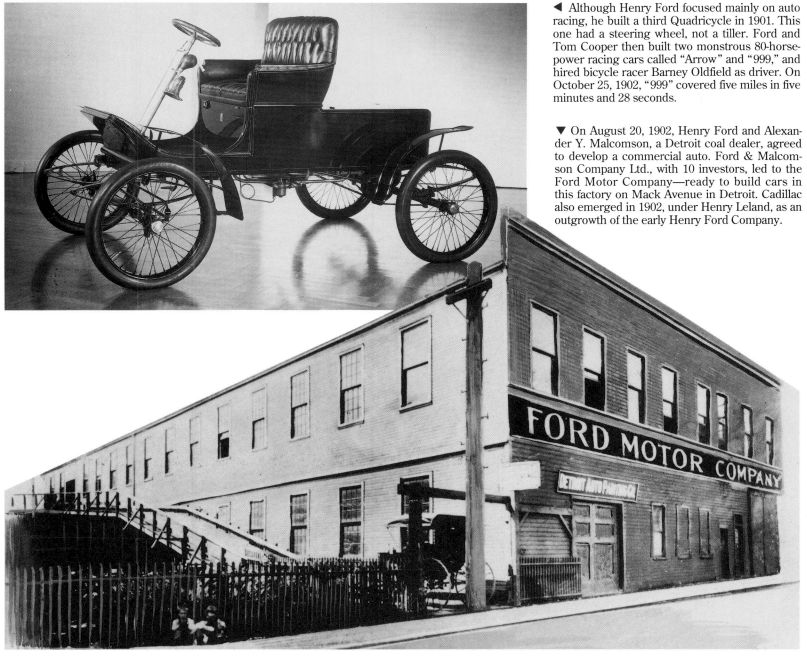

1903

Ford Motor Company incorporated June 16, 1903, with $28,000 capital and little fanfare

Henry Ford gets 25.5-percent interest; named vice president and chief engineer . . . John S. Gray serves as president

Original stockholders include John & Horace Dodge, Albert Strelow, Alex Y. Malcomson, Charles J. Woodall, and James Couzens

Model A runabout launched . . . first car sold in July

Ford earns money from the start, pays 10-percent dividend in November

Selden lawsuit filed; Ford, rejected as licensee, is charged with infringement . . . other automakers join Association of Licensed Automobile Manufacturers and pay royalty

▲ Neither the "Fordmobile" nor "The Fordmobile Co., Ltd.," which were advertised in February 1903, came into existence. But trade paper advertisements such as this one encouraged some C.O.D. orders, which encouraged at least one Detroiter to invest in the future Ford Motor Company.

▲ Ford Motor Company's first car, the Model A. This roadster resembles the Cadillac of the same year, and why not—Henry Ford designed both.

▼ Ford Motor Company's first plant on Detroit's Mack Avenue at Bellevue as it looked at the time of the firm's organization. Ford paid $75 a month rent for the building, soon given a second story.

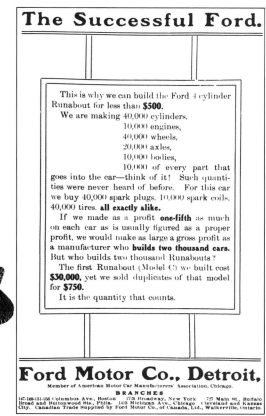

The Successful Ford.

This is why we can build the Ford 4 cylinder Runabout for less than **$500**.
We are making 40,000 cylinders,
10,000 engines,
40,000 wheels,
20,000 axles,
10,000 bodies,
10,000 of every part that goes into the car—think of it! Such quantities were never heard of before. For this car we buy 40,000 spark plugs, 10,000 spark coils, 40,000 tires. **all exactly alike.**
If we made as a profit **one-fifth** as much on each car as is usually figured as a proper profit, we would make as large a gross profit as a manufacturer who **builds two thousand cars.** But who builds two thousand Runabouts?
The first Runabout (Model C) we built cost **$30,000**, yet we sold duplicates of that model for **$750**.
It is the quantity that counts.

Ford Motor Co., Detroit,
Member of American Motor Car Manufacturers' Association, Chicago.
BRANCHES
147-149-151-158 Columbus Ave., Boston   1728 Broadway, New York   727 Main St., Buffalo
Broad and Buttonwood Sts., Phila.   1413 Michigan Ave., Chicago   Cleveland and Kansas City.   Canadian Trade Supplied by Ford Motor Co., of Canada, Ltd., Walkerville, Ontario.

▲ Even as the first Model As rolled out of the Mack Avenue plant, Ford was planning additional models like this Model C with a rear-entrance tonneau. Introduced late in 1904, its two-cylinder engine developed 10 horsepower. A Model C weighed about the same as the Model A, but had a front hood. The familiar Ford script, derived from the type used by Childe Harold Wills as a boy printer, was the company's trademark from the start.

▲ Even before the Model T era, Ford could boast that its volume production reduced costs, and that the company passed on the savings to its customers. As this ad states, "It's the quantity [not quality, as today] that counts."

The
Latest
and
Best

THE FORDMOBILE with detachable tonneau, $850

Boss
of
the
Road

▲ Simple, light, and efficient, the Model A two-seat runabout rode a 72-inch wheelbase. Under the seat, a two-cylinder, 100.5-cubic-inch opposed-twin engine, with four-inch bore and four-inch stroke, developed eight horsepower at 1000 rpm. A planetary transmission—to see service on two decades of Model Ts—had two forward speeds. Note the lack of doors and the right-hand steering wheel.

▲ No false modesty here—Ford's "Fordmobile," which actually went to market as the Model A, is advertised as "The Latest and Best" and "Boss of the Road." Almost half of the A's engines were made by the Dodge brothers, all of the bodies by C.R. Wilson Carriage Company.

▲ Ford ads boasted of the exploits of the mighty "999." Driven by daredevil Barney Oldfield on July 25, 1903, the mammoth racing car covered one mile in 55⅘ seconds to set a world record at 64.5 mph. Henry Ford himself sometimes took the tiller, having beaten a Mr. Winton at the Grosse Pointe track in 1901.

▶ Barney Oldfield at the tiller of 999, Henry Ford, and Ford's monstrous racing machine in the winter of 1902-03. The photo is one of the few showing Barney, a former star cyclist, without a cigar in his mouth. Oldfield later joked that he and Ford had made each other, "but I did much the best job of it."

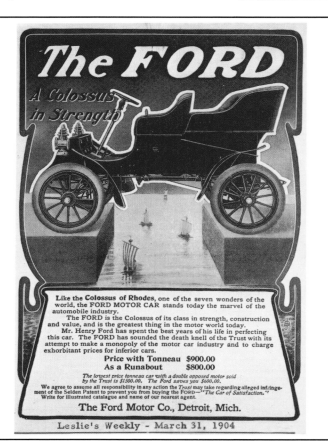

▲ Here, a restored 1903 Model A stands in front of the general store at Greenfield Village, Ford's bountiful paean to early American life at Dearborn, Michigan. Passengers climbed aboard the high-off-the-road Model A by way of a small carriage step. A detachable rear tonneau, with seating for two extra people and back-door access, cost $100 extra.

◀ Ford advertised both its product and its defiance of the Selden Patent Trust, as in in this 1904 advertisement, which promised buyers both high value and protection from lawsuits threatened by the Selden forces. Ford's prices, although low by the day's standards, still were much higher than those to come with the Model T. It would take both volume and mass production to lower prices appreciably.

Model Breakdown Chart

Model A—wb 72.0		Wght	Price	Prod
A	runabout 2P	1,250	850	*
A	tonneau 4P	na	950	*

*Early production totaled 670, according to Ford; 1,708 units were sold in the first 15 months.

1903 Engine Availability

Engines	bore × stroke	bhp	availability
H-2, 100.5	4.00 × 4.00	8	S-Model A

▶ This tiller-steered experimental car differs considerably from the production Model A of 1903, which used a steering wheel. Even the earliest ads for the "Fordmobile" (a name that never was used) showed steering wheels, not tillers. After production began, ads described the first Model A as a "new, light touring car [that] fills the demand for an automobile between a runabout and a heavy touring car." Capable of 30 mph, the Model A Ford was immodestly proclaimed to be "positively the most perfect machine on the market."

◀ Dressed in their Sunday finery, a trio of adventurous Americans looks ready to brave the dusty roads of the day in their Model A runabout. Ostensibly a two-seater, the runabout could squeeze in three friendly folks if need be. Early production Fords had a hand throttle, and ignition came from two sets of six dry cells. Frames for the first Ford automobiles came from the Dodge brothers' machine shop.

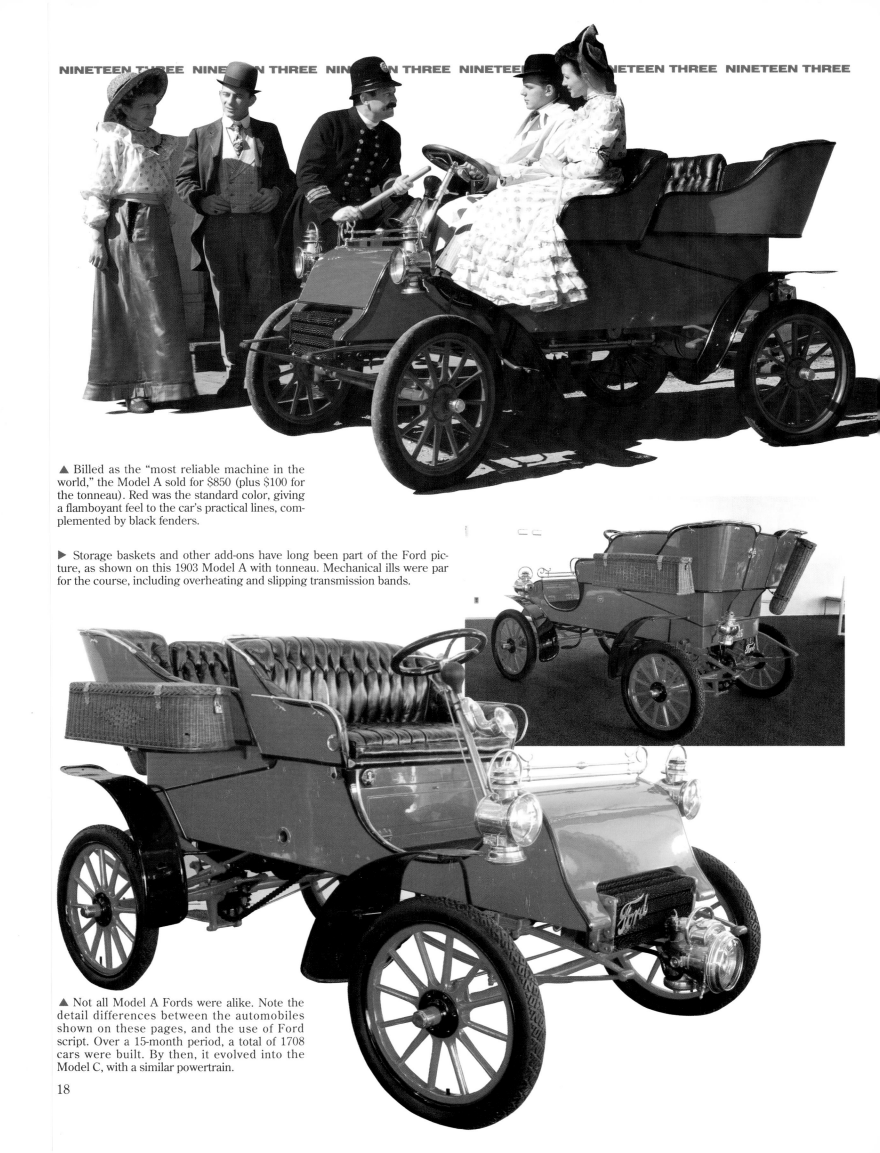

▲ Billed as the "most reliable machine in the world," the Model A sold for $850 (plus $100 for the tonneau). Red was the standard color, giving a flamboyant feel to the car's practical lines, complemented by black fenders.

▶ Storage baskets and other add-ons have long been part of the Ford picture, as shown on this 1903 Model A with tonneau. Mechanical ills were par for the course, including overheating and slipping transmission bands.

▲ Not all Model A Fords were alike. Note the detail differences between the automobiles shown on these pages, and the use of Ford script. Over a 15-month period, a total of 1708 cars were built. By then, it evolved into the Model C, with a similar powertrain.

18

1904

January 12: Henry Ford drives "Arrow" racer to world record of 91.37 mph, on iced-over Lake St. Clair

Detroit Tribune describes Ford's feat as "the wildest ride in the history of automobiling," but it's soon topped by William K. Vanderbilt in a Mercedes

Ford launches three new cars: Models C, F, and B

1695 Fords built in calendar year . . . Ford takes 7.7 percent of industry production

Ford Motor Company of Canada Ltd. founded

Ford opens first branch, on Detroit's Jefferson Avenue

Fords displayed at auto shows in seven cities, and at Louisiana Purchase Exposition in St. Louis

▲ This *Field and Stream* ad pushed the new Model F touring car, on an 84-inch wheelbase with 127.2-cid two-cylinder engine. Ford boasted that it "climbs hills on high speed" and "rides like a Yacht."

▲ An improved Model C runabout replaced the Model A, on a longer (76-inch) wheelbase. A modified horizontal-twin engine yielded 10 horsepower. The "Doctor's" runabout initially cost $850; this rear tonneau added $100.

▲ Henry Ford's dream of a $500 "family horse" wasn't furthered by the debut of the Model B, a $2000 touring car on a 92-inch wheelbase. Its four-cylinder engine was rated 24 horsepower. Sales never took off.

▶ After the arrival of the three new models during 1904, with their "modern" front hoods, the old Model A seemed primitive. Mechanically, however, the new Model C wasn't quite as different as it looked, with a similar two-cylinder engine.

1904 Engine Availability

Engines	bore × stroke	bhp	availability
H-2, 100.5	4.00 × 4.00	8	S-Model A
H-2, 100.5	4.00 × 4.25	10	S-Model AC, C
L-4, 251.3	4.00 × 5.00	24	S-Model B
H-2, 127.2	4.50 × 4.00	16	S-Model F

Model Breakdown Chart

		Wght	Price	Prod
A	runabout 2P	1,250	850	*
A	tonneau 4P (wb 72.0)	1,250	950	*
AC	runabout 2P	1,250	850	*
AC	tonneau 4P(wb 76.0)	1,250	950	*
C	runnabout 2P	1,250	850	*
C	tonneau 4P (wb 76.0)	1,250	950	*
B	tour 4P (wb 92.0)	1,700	2,000	*
F	tour 4P (wb 84.0)	1,400	1,000	*

*Ford reported total production was 670 model A and 1,230 model AC. but other sources give total of 1,695 units for calendar year. Model F was later advertised at $1,200.

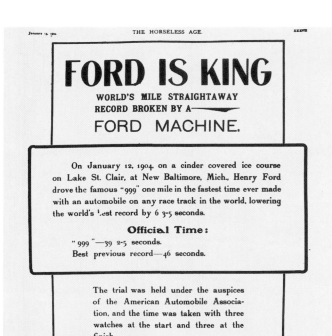

An ad trumpeting Henry Ford's record-setting mile run. The record stood for seven days, being broken on Florida sands by W.K. Vanderbilt.

▲ Henry Ford at the wheel of 999, prior to setting a world's speed record.

▲ On January 9, 1904, on Lake St. Clair (northeast of Detroit), Henry Ford covered the flying mile in 36 seconds—an unofficial world's record.

▲ Henry Ford, center, poses with 999 and associates on the ice of Lake St. Clair on January 12 when he sped 91.37 mph—an official mile record.

1905

Models B and C improved . . . Model E commercial fails to sell well

24,250 cars built in U.S.; only 1599 are Fords

Ford moves to bigger plant on Piquette Avenue . . . joins new Society of Automotive Engineers

Ford Manufacturing Company formed to build powertrains

Auto racing criticized, due to rise in accidents

Cars sold on installment plan—but not by Ford

▲ Customers weren't clamoring to pay $2000, but the elegant Model B touring car returned with a slightly different radiator and larger four-cylinder engine. Model F wasn't a hot item either.

▲ The Model C's engine and wheelbase grew. A windshield, headlamps, and top cost extra.

▲ In addition to the Model C tonneau (shown) and runabout, a Model E panel-delivery debuted.

Model Breakdown Chart

wb—C 78.0, B 92.0, F 84.0		Wght	Price	Prod
C	runabout 2P	1,250	850	*
C	tonneau 4P	1,250	950	*
B	tour 4P	1,700	1,200	*
F	tour 4P	1,400	1,200	*

*Total production was 1,599 Fords of all models.

1905 Engine Availability

Engines	bore × stroke	bhp	availability
H-2, 113.4	4.25 × 4.00	10	S-Model C
H-2, 127.2	4.50 × 4.00	16	S-Model F
L-4, 283.6	4.25 × 5.00	24	S-Model B

▲ Model C tonneau

1906

Modestly priced, four-cylinder Model N debuts: forerunner of Model T

Cycle and Automobile Trade Journal hails N debut as "most important mechanical traction event of 1906" . . . Henry Ford calls it his "crowning achievement"

Model F dropped; two-cylinder cars out

Big, plush six-cylinder Model K replaces Model B—guaranteed to go 60 mph

Ford production soars to 8729 cars . . . total of 33,200 built in America

Ford's market share reaches 26.3 percent

1906 Engine Availability

Engines	bore × stroke	bhp	availability
H-2, 127.2	4.50 × 4.00	10	S-Model F
L-4, 134.2	3.63 × 3.25	15	S-Model N
L-6, 405.4	4.25 × 4.25	40	S-Model K

Ford Times

Vol. II   FEBRUARY 1, 1909   No. 9

3½"

What Vanadium Does

DUTEE WILCOX FLINT, Providence, R. I., Ford Dealer, wanted to demonstrate to a skeptic that his claims for the superiority of Vanadium Steel were backed by facts, so he requested Mr. A. W. Burch, a man who weighs 208 pounds, to stand on the front fender. The picture shows how little the weight deflects the fender out of normal position, less than one-half inch, and there was no permanent set, the fender returning to original position when Mr. Burch stepped off.

▲ Ford endlessly touted the advantages of vanadium steel over ordinary steel, saying that it alone could withstand the strain of poor American roads. Much of the bragging about vanadium proved unjustified, and Ford eventually returned to older steels, using scientific heat treatment.

▲ As mechanics work on a Model K, Henry Ford, in goggles, awaits his chance to lower the world's mile speed record at Cape May, NJ. He failed.

▲ Despite Henry's eagerness, Ford would soon ease out of racing. A racing version of the Model K set a new 24-hour record: 1135 miles at 47.2 mph.

Model Breakdown Chart				
		Wght	Price	Prod
wb—F 84.0, K 114.0/120.0, N 84.0				
F	tour 4P	1,400	1,200	*
K	tour 4P	2,000	2,500	*
K	runabout 4P	2,000	2,500	*
N	runabout 2P	1,050	600	*
*Total production for calendar year was 8,729 Fords of all models.				

◀ Signaling the soon-to-arrive Model T, the dashing yet low-priced "boattail" Model N runabout found eager acceptance. A front-mounted 134.2-cid, four-cylinder engine, developed 15 bhp at 900 rpm—good for 45 mph.

▲ Henry Ford in 1906, the year he moved from the vice presidency of Ford Motor Company. That year Ford, deferring to fellow stockholders, also introduced a big car, Model K.

◀ The Model N runabout, seen here with the top down, rode a short 84-inch wheelbase. Its low price, just $600, made it attractive to potential buyers, as did a quickly established reputation for reliability. The cowl-mounted headlamps were nickel plated.

▲ Biggest and plushest Ford yet, the Model K touring car (or roadster) rode a 114/120-inch wheelbase and weighed a full ton. Under its stretched-out hood sat a huge 405.4-cid six-cylinder engine, churning out 40 bhp.

▲ Henry Ford (at the wheel) wasn't fond of the elephantine Model K. Transmission bands often failed, due to excess weight. This car helped trigger the split between Ford and Alexander Malcomson.

1907

Models R and S join the Model N as final right-hand-drive Fords

Ford production zooms 59 percent, to 14,887

Ford grabs nearly 35-percent market share

U.S. auto registrations pass 140,000 mark

Ad slogan, "Watch the Fords Go By," becomes one of most famous phrases ever

Ford branches open in Paris, France, and Hamburg, Germany

Dow Jones average drops 8.3 percent on March 14—largest loss to that time

Despite recession, Packard and Ford post profits over $1 million

Ford departs from auto racing; many dealers displeased

▲ As if its opening price of $2500 wasn't enough to keep customers at bay, Ford boosted the Model K by $300, without offering any notable changes. The massive roadster with "mother-in-law" seat had a dashing look, to be sure, with plenty of brass, pretty pinstriping, and handsome running boards.

▲ Big headlights and a bold radiator gave the Model K roadster an assertive appearance, but that didn't help sales. Near the end of its 1906-08 run, prices were slashed by $1000 to get rid of them all.

1907 Engine Availability

Engines	bore × stroke	bhp	availability
L-4, 149.0	3.75 × 3.38	15	S-Models N, R, S
L-6, 405.4	4.25 × 4.25	40	S-Model K

Model Breakdown Chart

wb—K 114.0/120.0, N/R/S 84.0		Wght	Price	Prod
K	runabout 4P	2,000	2,800	*
K	tour 4P	2,000	2,800	*
N	runabout 2P	1,050	600	*
R	runabout 2P	1,400	750	*
S	rdstr 2P	na	750	*
S	runabout 3P	1,400	700	*

*Total production for calendar year was reported as high as 14,887 (including approximately 2,500 Model R); 6,398 cars were sold in 1907-08 season.

▲ Anyone who could pay $2800 for a Model K roadster got a motorcar that was guaranteed to hit 60 mph—provided that person was brave enough to attempt such a feat on the roads and tires of the day. By waiting, the potential customer could get a K for $1000 less, as Ford tried to clear out the stock in favor of a car "for the multitudes" rather than the rich.

◄ First seen in 1907, "Watch the Fords Go By" became one of the best-known auto slogans of the century. Ford used it sporadically, right up to the early 1940s. *Ford Times* credited traffic manager W.S. Hogue for the phrase, claiming he'd shouted out the words during a race, as Fords zipped past. Some believe that advertising manager E. LeRoy Pelletier composed the words. The phrase appeared on a huge electric sign atop Detroit's Temple Theater in 1908, and was seen all over the country on Ford-carrying trains. Naturally, far more people watched Model N Fords go by—and the new Model R and S—than the mammoth Model K.

▶ A Model K touring car looked much taller, more ponderous, and ordinary than the spirited roadster. Henry Ford was glad to see Model K go, now that the Model N had shown that a $500 car for the masses was feasible, and the Model T was soon to arrive. Competition was keen in the luxury automobile league, with rivals on the order of Packard and Cadillac, not to mention such mammoths as the Oldsmobile Palace Touring Car, the Mitchell, Pope-Hartford, and Haynes. Emergence of the Model T Ford, on the other hand, found few competitors—and fewer yet once the selling price started to fall.

▼ Plenty of elbow room was needed around the Model K Ford's inline six-cylinder engine, as revealed on this bare chassis. With a 4.25-inch bore and 4.25-inch stroke, the big six displaced 405 cubic inches and drew its fuel through a Holley carburetor. Meanwhile, the low-budget Model N continued to attract buyers with its $600 price tag—which even dropped as low as the $500 mark. On the competition front, Frank Kulick earned ample publicity by beating eight cars in a 24-hour speed-endurance contest. Ford claimed the world record for one, eight, and 24 hours, before abandoning racing.

▲ Though not exactly a common sight on American roads in 1907, women took up driving early in the century. Even fewer female automobilists were likely to be spotted at the wheel of a massive Model K Ford touring car.

▲ Billed as "a car of more pretentious appearance," this costlier Model R joined the N, followed by a less-equipped Model S. Each had a 15-bhp, 149-cid four. The last right-hand-drive Fords, they carried running boards.

1908

Experiments begin with rope-and-pulley system for final Model Ns—will lead to mass-production, moving assembly line

Model T catalog goes to dealers in March; public debut October 1 as a 1909 model . . . Henry finally has his car for the masses

Early Model Ts have two-pedal operation; later switches to three-pedal

Industry produces 63,500 cars; Ford turns out 10,202 (all models) . . . 6398 sold in 1907-08 fiscal year

Model Breakdown Chart

wb—K 114.0/120.0, N/R/S 84.0		Wght	Price	Prod
K	runabout 4P	2,000	2,800	*
K	tour 4P	2,000	2,800	*
N	runabout 2P	1,050	600	*
N	landau 4P	na	na	*
R	runabout 2P	1,400	750	*
S	rdstr 2P	na	700	*
S	runabout 3P	1,400	750	*

*Total production for calendar year was 10,202 Fords of all models.

1908 Engine Availability

Engines	bore × stroke	bhp	availability
L-4, 149.0	3.75 × 3.38	15	S-Models N, R, S
L-6, 405.4	4.25 × 4.25	40	S-Model K

▲ Mr. and Mrs. Jos. Holle and a Model C jounce over ties to the top of Mt. Tamalpais, California.

▲ Until the arrival of the Model T in October 1908, Ford cars continued with little change. The two-passenger Model S roadster shown here sold for $700, or $750 with a single-seat rear tonneau. In bad weather, that back-seat rider might not praise the seating arrangements. Of course, even with the top up (if one had been ordered), front passengers weren't exactly cocooned from the elements. Models R and N also carried on, as did the remaining Model Ks.

◄ Millions of motorists in the 1908-27 era learned to drive by mastering these three pedals in a Model T Ford cockpit. Pressure on one pedal made the car move out, another caused it to stop (one hoped), while the third put it into reverse. "Complete control of the Ford car," the company insisted, "may be had without removing the hands from the steering wheel." The first 800 Model Ts built, however, had only two foot pedals and two control levers.

27

▲ Like the low-priced Model N, this Model S roadster helped pave the way for the creation of the Model T—Henry Ford's long-awaited car for "everyman." By this time, Ford already had produced nine distinct car models, but those would be virtually forgotten once the T-Bone captured the public imagination.

▶ This three-seat Model T Runabout sold for $825 ($25 less than the touring car), with a separate one-passenger back seat. Early models came in several colors, with black fenders. The 22-bhp, 176.7-cid four-cylinder engine had a removable head and a magneto. Early engines had a water pump, but that would soon be deleted.

▲ C. Harold Wills, along with Henry Ford, was the Model T's principal designer. He later built the Wills Sainte Claire car.

▲ Most popular of the early Model T bodies was the $850 touring car. A massive publicity campaign let the whole country know about the homely but appealing Model T by late 1908, though only a few hundred were sold that year.

1909

Model T modifications included three-pedal transmission . . . conversion kit sold for early models

Formal debut of Model T at Grand Central Palace, New York, on December 31, 1908

By May 1, production lags far behind demand; no orders taken for nine weeks

Tourabout model added at mid-year

17,771 Fords built in calendar year; industry produces 123,900

Ford enters two cars in New York-to-Seattle race; one wins, but is disqualified

FORD MOTOR CARS

Illustrating Four Positions of the Model T Touring Car with Top

Serviceable and of very pleasing appearance from every view point

WATCH THE FORDS GO BY

Model Breakdown Chart

Model T—wb 100.0		Wght	Price	Prod
T	runabout 2P	na	825	2,351
T	tour 5P	1,200	850	7,728
T	twn car 7P	na	1,000	236
T	landaulet 7P	na	950	298
T	cpe 2P	na	950	47

Note: Figures above are for 1908-09 fiscal year. Total production for calendar year was 17,771.

▲ Catalogs described the Model T as "Serviceable and of very pleasing appearance from every view point." Not everyone agreed, as the tall touring car looked ready to tip over. Visibility suffered with side curtains in place. Ads described the T as "the one reliable car that does not require a $10,000 income to buy, a $5000 bank account to run and a college course in engineering to keep in order."

▲ Added in mid-1909, the four-passenger Tourabout (also called Tourster) came with a standard windshield, top, lights, and horn. Never popular, partly because it lacked rear doors, the Tourabout lasted only a year.

▲ The touring car gave rear passengers some security, but had no front doors. Windshields and tops cost extra at first, but soon became standard. Green was the standard color by late 1909. Note the neat pinstriping.

▲ Ford's famous slogan, "Watch the Fords Go By," appeared for many years in a mammoth electric spectacular atop Detroit's Temple Theater.

▲ Formal-bodied Model Ts looked especially top-heavy. Most expensive was the $1000 Town Car. The Landaulet had a fabric rear roof.

▲ Thermo-syphon cooling replaced the water-pump setup used in early T engines. Three-point engine mounting helped on rough roads.

▲ Wings alongside the "Ford" radiator script were deleted on most models this year. Heat-treated vanadium steel was used extensively.

1909 Engine Availability

Engine	bore × stroke	bhp	availability
L-4, 176.7	3.75 × 4.00	22	S-Model T

▲ Model Ts were loaded with innovations, including left-hand steering, transverse leaf arc springs, and an integral magneto.

▲ Oil-filled brass cowl and taillamps were standard on the Model T touring car. Headlamps, speedometers, and other accessories cost extra.

▲ Henry Ford proudly poses with the racing car that was assumed to have won the 1909 New York-to-Seattle race. Drivers are C.J. Smith (with goggles) and B.W. Scott. Race sponsor M. Robert Guggenheim is at left.

▲ Even a Model T occasionally mired down in the mud, and the "winning" Ford in the New York-to-Seattle race, on its return to Detroit, was no exception. Here, at an unknown site a dejected Bert Scott awaits help.

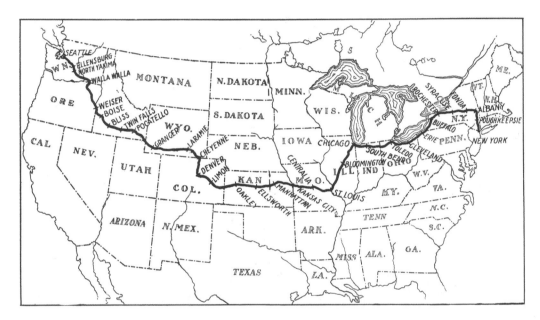

▲ The route of the New York-to-Seattle race. Ford No. 2 "won," but later was disqualified because one of its crewmen illegally changed the engine. First prize then went to Shawmut. Ford reclaimed "victory" in a 1959 race reenactment.

▲ The *Seattle Daily Times* trumpets the story of New York-to-Seattle race. Alas, the winning car was disqualified five months later.

▲ Ford's twin entries approach Cleveland in the New-York-to-Seattle race. The drivers of Ford No. 1, right, Frank Kulick, at wheel, and Advertising Manager H.B. Harper became lost, costing them a nine-hour lead. First-place finisher was Ford No. 2, with Bert Scott, at wheel, and C.J. Smith.

▲ Ford No. 2, "winner" of the New York-to-Seattle race, in an unknown city on its 6000-mile return trip. The vehicle was trumpeted in Ford advertising and displayed at hundreds of dealerships before its victory drums were silenced because its engine had been changed for part of the race.

1910

Ford's output leaps to 32,053—enough for market share of 17.8 percent

Ads note that 40,000 Fords have been built

Total industry output rises 57,100, to 181,000 units

Model T carries more equipment . . . Landaulet, Tourster/Tourabout dropped

Torpedo and Commercial runabouts debut, the latter with removable rear seat

Ford markets $700 chassis that accepts bodies from outside suppliers

▲ Except for a shuffling of models, the 1910 Model Ts showed few changes. Touring car and Runabout prices rose, but a windshield, top, and headlamps were now standard. Open-car tops looked bulky and awkward when down, as shown here. Fords had flat-topped fenders and used plenty of wood and brass.

▲ This Model T participated in the Munsey Tour, with a dapper gent occupying the "mother-in-law" seat. By summer, Ford resumed full-scale racing, boasting that Frank Kulick could beat anyone.

1910 Engine Availability

Engine	bore × stroke	bhp	availability
L-4, 176.7	3.75 × 4.00	22	S-Model T

Model Breakdown Chart

Model T—wb 100.0		Wght	Price	Prod
T	tour 5P	1,200	950	16,890
T	tourabout 4P	na	950	*
T	runabout 3P	na	900	1,486
T	torpedo 2P	na	725	—
T	comm rdstr 3P	na	650	—
T	cpe 2P	na	1,050	187
T	twn car 7P	na	1,200	377
T	landaulet 7P	na	1,100	2
T	chassis	900	700	108

*Production included in Touring figure. Figures above are for 1909-10 fiscal year. Total output for calendar year was 32,053.

▶ A sleek new Torpedo Runabout (roadster) emerged in 1910, with a more rakish windshield angle than usual to suggest speed. Torpedos also had a lower seating position, longer steering column, and longer hood. Instead of the customary under-seat gas tank, the Torpedo's was mounted on the rear deck. Looks weren't deceiving in this case, as a Torpedo was indeed faster than other Ford models.

▲ Like other Model Ts, the $950 touring car rode a 100-inch wheelbase and had 56-inch front/rear tread (60-inch optional).

▲ Tinkering with the rear axle was the only mechanical change for this year's Model T. Note the transverse-mounted, arced rear spring.

▲ Once again, the touring car was top seller. New this year: a no-frills $650 Commercial Roadster, with rear seat that removed to carry cargo.

1911

Model Ts get new body, cut prices; sales double, share hits 35 percent

Branch-plant assembly begins, at Kansas City

William S. Knudsen joins Ford—later to head Chevy

Ads tout Ford ownership by celebrities

Model Ts score major wins in hillclimbing events

Selden Patent declared "valid but not infringed"

Model Breakdown Chart

Model T—wb 100.0		Wght	Price	Prod
T	tour 5P	1,200	780	26,405
T	tourabout 4P	na	725	na
T	runabout 3P	na	680	7,845
T	torpedo 2P	na	725	*
T	rdstr 2P	na	680	*
T	cpe 2P	na	840	45
T	twn car 7P	na	960	315
T	landaulet 7P	na	1,100	na
T	chassis	940	700	248

*Production included in basic Runabout figure. Figures above are for 1910-11 fiscal year. Total output for calendar year was 69,762.

▲ This year's touring car body used sheet steel over wood framing, instead of the former wood construction. Other models soon followed. New metal running boards were stamped with "Ford" script.

▲ Long-distance touring was popular in the teens. Here, a dusty driver in a Model T Runabout participates in the famed Glidden Tour. Steering wheels grew an inch, to 15-inch diameter, for greater leverage when parking.

▲ Only a handful of the startlingly tall Model T coupes were built in 1911, including this one with a New York license. This closed body style, which used plenty of glass and wood, then was phased out for a couple of years.

◄ Model T touring cars were slashed in price from $950 to $780 (fully equipped). A person could buy any open Ford without the usual windshield, top, headlights and horn, saving $80, bringing a touring car down to $700 or a Runabout/roadster as low as $590. Many body panels came from the Briggs Manufacturing Company, which had contracted with Ford in 1910. Though body panels were new, this year's Fords closely resembled the earlier models.

1911 Engine Availability

Engine	bore × stroke	bhp	availability
L-4, 176.7	3.75 × 4.00	22	S-Model T

▼ Like other Model T styles, the touring car gained a handful of mechanical improvements during 1911—a pattern that continued through the car's long life. The engine added a removable connecting-rod pan, and the steering wheel grew larger. A bigger access door eased adjustment of the oft-troublesome transmission bands. A new front axle used spindles with separate steering arms. This year's price cut also set the stage for many future reductions.

▲ Sport-minded Model T buyers in 1911 had the option of a Torpedo Runabout, capable of 45 mph but with no doors at all, for as little as $590. Fully equipped Runabouts dropped from $900 to $680. Two-seat roadsters had a rear-deck 16-gallon fuel tank, instead of the under-seat 10-gallon tank on three-seaters. Torpedo styling touches included curved fenders, lower seating, and a lengthened hood. The Commercial Roadster converted into a cargo carrier.

► Only 315 of the luxurious six-passenger Town Cars were built this year, despite a price cut. The fact that it existed at all was a surprise in view of Henry Ford's distaste for luxury automobiles. Late in 1911, a Delivery Car joined the Model T line, wearing an "official" factory panel body or offered as a bare chassis alone ($700 either way). Bodies actually came from various suppliers, and the commercial vehicles could haul as much as 750 pounds.

Claiming every $1 price cut attracts 1000 new buyers, Henry slashes $80 from most models

Though hard-pressed to meet demand, Model T output increases 12.4 percent to 78,440 units

Ford market share drops from 35 percent to 22 as industry sales jump 33 percent to 356,000 units

The Model T is restyled early in 1912, but its appearance changes little

A "Fore-Door" option closes in the front seat—but only three doors actually open

In a Ford-sponsored survey, 84 percent say they bought a Model T on the recommendation of other owners

▲ The sportiest of the production 1912 Model Ts was the Torpedo Runabout, but less so than before because it was now based on the standard Runabout. It was quite a bargain, too, as the price was cut from $680 in 1911 to just $590. Output of both Runabouts came to 13,376 units for the year.

◄ Henry Ford is seen here posing at the wheel of a $690 "Fore-Door" Touring, though in fact the driver's "door" didn't open. With 50,598 built, it accounted for about two-thirds of 1912 output.

► Take a 1912 Runabout, install a "monocle" windshield, wire wheels, and oval gas tank; remove the panel between running boards and body; and paint it bright yellow. Now what do you have? A Speedster! The Touring weighed 1200 pounds, the chassis 940, with "others in proportion."

Model Breakdown Chart

Model T—wb 100.0		Wght	Price	Prod
T	tour 5P	1,200	690	50,598
T	runabout 2P	na	590	13,376
T	rdstr 2P	na	590	*
T	cpe 2P	na	na	19
T	twn car 7P	na	900	802
T	delv car 2P	na	700	1,845
T	chassis	940	na	2,133

*Production included in Runabout figure. Total output for calendar year was 78,440.

1912 Engine Availability

Engines	bore × stroke	bhp	availability
L-4, 176.7	3.75 × 4.00	22	S-Model T

◀ New for this year's Model T was availability of what we'd now call an option: separate front doors for the ubiquitous Touring, making it a Fore-Door. However, the left front "door" was just a solid panel painted to *look* like it opened. Both the dummy and genuine front door could be removed if desired to create the familiar "open-front"-style Touring seen here.

▲ This Runabout sports a rectangular gas tank on the rear platform and an ornate bulb horn. Compare how this windshield and Henry's (opposite page) are folded.

▲ If a more dashing Runabout than the one to the left was desired, that could be remedied by foregoing the windshield and doors. Note the round gas tank.

1913

Mass-production begins . . . Model T is first car assembled on moving line

Chassis assembly time halved, to six man-hours; by year-end, near 1½ hours

Annual output more than doubles, to 168,220 cars

Prices cut, down to $525 for Runabout, as mass production reduces costs

Henry Ford turns 50

Assembly of Model T from kits begins in France

Short-lived cyclecar fad begins; no threat to Ford

Model Breakdown Chart

Model T—wb 100.0		Wght	Price	Prod
T	tour 5P	1,200	600	126,715
T	runabout 2P	na	525	33,129
T	cpe 2P	na	na	1
T	twn car 7P	na	800	1,415
T	delv car 2P	na	625	513
T	chassis	960	na	8,438

Note: Production for calendar year was 168,220.

▲ "Fore-Door" touring cars lacked a working left front door. Sheetmetal now encircled the entire passenger compartment, from cowl top to rear, unlike the prior separate-tonneau style. The 20-bhp engine got internal modifications. Model T nicknames ranged from Bone Crusher and T-Bone to Tin Lizzie and Passion Pot.

◄ Sporty gents didn't have to be content with an ordinary Runabout—not when a racy, low-slung Speedster could mount a Model T chassis. Special lightweight bodywork offered little weather protection, but brightly colored, with wire wheels, it cut a dashing figure. Note "monocle" windshield and fuel tank behind seat.

▲ With mass production about to emerge, the number of Model Ts headed to dealers soon would grow to startling numbers. Here, a winter parade of cars enroute to a New York dealer pauses for a quick photo. Brass was now almost extinct except for light bezels, and door panels switched from leather to leatherette. The Torpedo Runabout was dropped, while the regular one got a "turtleback" rear end.

1913 Engine Availability			
Engine	bore × stroke	bhp	availability
L-4, 176.7	3.75 × 4.00	20	S-Model T

▶ Again the most upscale—and expensive— Model T, the elegant Town Car dropped in price during the year. The '13 version had smoother lines and slim glass windows on each side of the front compartment. That didn't help sales much, as only 1415 went to buyers; but taxi owners were taking close notice. Note the Landau bars at rear, and the two-piece windshield that opened to let breezes flow in.

▲ Used by a Ford agent, this special pickup rode a Runabout chassis. Many Model Ts were fitted with custom "Closed-Cab" pickup bodies, *sans* doors.

▲ Model T conversions by outside firms proved capable of a wealth of commercial tasks. Farmers often loaded their Ts to capacity—and beyond.

1914

$5 a day minimum wage announced on January 5; work day cut from 10 to eight hours—news draws worldwide acclaim

Goals of $5 day: reduce worker turnover, keep IWW out, boost productivity

Of that $5 wage, $2.66 is profit-sharing, given only to qualified workers

Sociological Department formed to see that workers make "proper" use of wage

Output of 308,162 (56 percent of industry total) sets calendar-year record

Model T sold "in any color so long as it's black"

Ford promises rebates if sales exceed prescribed level—$50 paid in 1915

▲ Despite fresh styling, appearance of the Model T touring car didn't change dramatically. Doors were now inset into side panels and had rounded bottom corners, setting the trend for the next decade. This was the final year for straight-topped rear fenders, acetylene headlamps, and a cherry wood dashboard. Touring-car production rose by almost 40,000, to 165,832. Prices were cut again, but only about $50. All Fords included a windshield, top, and horn. Late in the year, a new "Coupelet" body emerged.

▲ Black was now the sole Ford color, though wheels came in blue or natural wood. Touring cars outsold Runabouts by five to one.

▲ Ford wasn't about to ignore women customers, like this early Runabout driver accompanied by an eager gentleman. Note the "turtle deck" rear-end.

▲ Station wagons would not be part of the official Ford picture for some time, but forerunners like this Depot Hack came from outside bodybuilders. Some Hacks had removable seats, and could also be used to haul cargo.

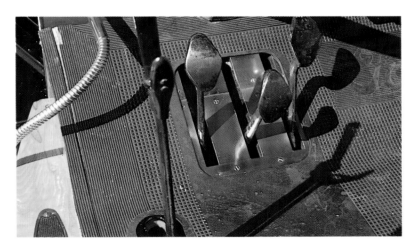

▲ Passengers in a Depot Hack got a stylish ride and plenty of fresh air.

▲ Initials became extinct, but the familiar three-pedal layout remained.

▲ In addition to the upmarket Town Car offered by Ford, custom builders could deliver special closed bodywork atop a touring-car chassis. Note sidemounted spare tires. Regular Town Cars had tall windows at the rear of the cockpit.

Model Breakdown Chart

Model T—wb 100.0		Wght	Price	Prod
T	tour 5P	1,200	550	165,832
T	runabout 2P	na	500	35,017
T	twn car 7P	na	750	1,699
T	chassis	960	na	119

Note: Total production for calendar year was 308,162.

1914 Engine Availability

Engine	bore × stroke	bhp	availability
L-4, 176.7	3.75 × 4.00	20	S-Model T

▲ Wheel hubs on this Depot Hack leave no question as to the Model T's national origin. Factory-built bodies came only in quick-drying black, but wooden bodywork and natural-tone wheels gave the Ford a fresh personality.

1915

Model T restyled with curved rear fenders

Coupelet and Center Door Sedan arrive

Prices continue to drop: Runabout dips to $390

Over half-million Fords built: 56 percent of industry total

Electric headlights made standard on Model T

One-millionth Ford built; 100,000 visit Ford plant

Ford exhibit at the Panama-Pacific Exposition draws huge crowds

Prototype Ford tractors demonstrated

Ford buys 1000 acres along Rouge River for new plant

Henry Ford Hospital takes first Detroit patients

Model Breakdown Chart

Model T—wb 100.0		Wght	Price	Prod
T	tour 5P	1,500	490	244,181
T	runabout 2P	1,380	440	47,116
T	cpelet 2P	1,540	750	2,417
T	sdn 2d 5P	1,730	975	989
T	twn car 7P	na	690	na
T	chassis	980	410	13,459

Note: Total output for calendar year was 501,462.

1915 Engine Availability

Engine	bore × stroke	bhp	availability
L-4, 176.7	3.75 × 4.00	20	S-Model T

▲ Most Town Cars went to taxi fleets rather than private owners, partly because the once-luxurious upscale version of the Model T looked rather dumpy in comparison to mid-teens rivals. Taxis were advertised as separate models, and differed slightly in upholstery and details from the Town Car, which dropped in price from $690 to $640. Rounded rear fenders were part of this year's freshening.

▲ Introduced late in the 1914 model year, the two-seat "Coupelet" had a folding top and replaced the fixed-roof coupe. Unlike the Runabout, its doors contained windows. The windshield was sedan-like, and the Coupelet wore a larger "turtle deck." All Model Ts now had a hand-operated Klaxon horn and magneto-powered brass electric headlamps, instead of the old bulb horn and acetylene lights.

▲ Only a few Coupelets emerged in 1914, but the body became widely available this year. Side windows instead of primitive curtains made it comparable to latter-day convertible coupes, suitable for top-down fun or cozy top-up weather protection. Prices began at $750, but dropped to $590 later in the year. Fewer than 2500 were built in 1915, despite Henry Ford's reputed claim that this was the most practical two-passenger model ever built by Ford.

◄ Hood louvers and an unbraced rear-folding windshield were features of most 1915 Fords, including the popular touring car. Steel replaced cherry wood on dashboards, which sloped down sharply to the aluminum hood. Pedals were ribbed instead of lettered. Close to a quarter-million touring cars were built this year, and as the price fell to $440, it became an even better value. Oil cowl and tail lamps were retained, with rounded lenses.

▲ Some Model T owners, including the occupants of this no-frills racer, were content with the most rudimentary, home-crafted bodywork. Touring, Runabout, and Town Car bodies stuck to the old style until mid-year, including gas headlamps. Wire wheels became available from Ford this year.

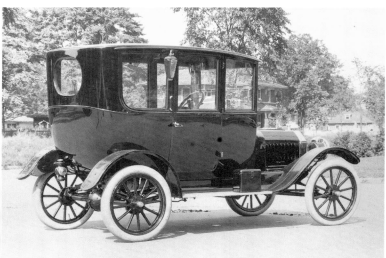

▲ In addition to the Coupelet, Ford launched a "Center Door Sedan" late in 1914. As the name suggests, doors on this tall, upright body were just behind the center point of the wheelbase, with three windows on each side. At $975 this was the most costly Model T, but the price soon fell to $740.

▲ Aluminum panels were used initially on the Center Door sedan, which required special rear fenders and splash aprons. The gas tank went under the rear seat. Reworking during the year included adoption of steel panels, as well as repositioning of the tank under the front seat. Note the gracefully shaped rear fenders, following the contour of the tires.

▶ Ford's price leader, once again, was the two-seat Runabout, which started at $440 but then dipped to $390—fully equipped. Open cars had leatherette upholstery; closed bodies used cloth. Rear fenders were curved, but fronts kept their flat, lipped shape. Ford options included a toolbox for the running board. The new electric headlights were magneto-powered.

44

1916

734,811 Fords built

Prices cut again in August: Runabout drops to $345, Touring car to $360

Chicago Tribune **calls Henry Ford an anarchist after Mexican border war flap; libel suit initiated**

James Couzens gone now due to Henry Ford's mixing of pacifism with company policy

28 branch plants assemble Ford cars in U.S.

More than 1.5 million cars built in America this year, 48 percent of them Fords

Henry's name surfaces on first ballot at Republican National Convention

1916 Engine Availability

Engines	bore × stroke	bhp	availability
L-4, 176.7	3.75 × 4.00	20	S-Model T

Model Breakdown Chart

Model T—wb 100.0		Wght	Price	Prod
T	tour 5P	1,510	440	363,024
T	runabout 2P	1,395	390	98,633
T	cpelet 2P	1,540	590	3,532
T	sdn 2d 5P	1,730	740	1,859
T	twn car 7P	na	640	1,972
T	ambulance	na	na	20,700
T	chassis	1,060	360	11,742

Note: Total output for calendar year was 734,811.

▶ Stylish "Ford" script adorned Model Ts from the start. The company halted all advertising in 1917, but required dealers to include the symbol in their own ads. In 1919, C. Harold Wills, who'd designed the script within an oval for the 1903 Model A, left Ford for the Wills Sainte Claire firm. The symbol was used on Fords into the 1940s, and returned again—with blue oval—in 1982 on the two-seat EXP.

▲ Only 3532 Coupelets were built, and the model would be dropped during 1917, after slashing the price to $505. Note the tiny "portholes" added to the "convertible" top, behind the landau bars.

▲ Opening price for this year's touring car was $440, but that slid to $360 as output passed the 360,000 mark. Only the first 800 Model Ts for 1916 had brass radiators; then, all were black. Horns and head-lamps, too, switched to black steel. Instead of aluminum, hoods were now steel, transmission covers cast iron. As part of this year's cost-cutting, a speedometer no longer was standard. Optional 60-inch tread widths, popular on southern roads, were dropped; all Fords now had 56-inch tread.

1917

Model T gets modern facelift: larger radiator and hood, crowned fenders

Ford production slips to 622,351—share sinks to 36 percent as industry rises

America enters "Great War" in Europe on April 6

First true Ford truck launched . . . 39,000 go to Allied forces by the time World War I ends

Henry Ford II born to Edsel and Eleanor, September 4

1917 Engine Availability

Engine	bore × stroke	bhp	availability
L-4, 176.7	3.75 × 4.00	20	S-Model T

Model Breakdown Chart

Model T—wb 100.0		Wght	Price	Prod
T	tour 5P	1,480	360	568,128
T	runabout 2P	1,385	345	107,240
T	cpelet 2P	1,580	505	7,343
T	sdn 2d 5P	1,745	645	7,361
T	twn car 7P	na	595	2,328
T	ambulance	na	na	1,452
T	chassis	1,060	325	41,165
TT	trk chassis	1,450	na	3

Note: Total output for calendar year was 622,351.

▲ Like all Fords, the Runabout had a fresh, surprisingly streamlined look. The newly rounded hood swept back gracefully into a shapely cowl. The larger, higher-set radiator had a pleasing contour, with separate pressed-steel shell. Fenders were crowned; hubcaps and radiator cap nickel-plated.

▲ Model Ts often transported animals, giving rise to such nicknames as "cattle hack" and "Noah's Ark." A handmade crate on the running board was handy for carrying a pet goat, as shown here, or a pig, calf, or sheep. Chickens and rabbits usually rode in the back seat.

▲ The Model T frequently was used as a stationary power plant as well as over-the-road. Here, the Tin Lizzie provides power for a hoist on a building project.

▲ The Model T had a well-earned reputation for "getting you there and getting you back." This specially equipped runabout not only could maneuver over snow; it could climb "rugged terrain."

1918

Despite Henry's pacifism, Ford military production begins May 7; civilian volume drops to 436,000 as war sends prices upward

Model Ts serve valiantly in European battlegrounds

Military output includes aircraft engines, armored vehicles, sub chaser

Industry production falls by nearly half, to 943,436

Town Car phased out; closed coupe replaces Coupelet

Armistice signed November 11, 1918

1918 Engine Availability

Engine	bore × stroke	bhp	availability
L-4, 176.7	3.75 × 4.00	20	S-Model T

HENRY FORD
For UNITED STATES SENATOR

▲ Ford's Senate bid failed by only 4337 votes.

▲ Despite government orders to cut car production after U.S. entry into the war, Ford sent its wares to the nation's auto shows. After changing amply in 1917, this year's Model T had few modifications.

▲ Despite touring-car popularity, enthusiasm for open cars was fading. A revived closed coupe featured removable window pillars.

▲ This one-ton stake-body truck, used by the Ford company, could be bought for $600. Ford trucks helped in final months of World War I.

▲ Police departments soon saw the utility value of a tough screen-sided Ford truck.

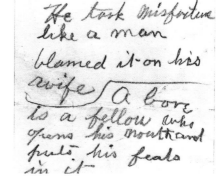

▲ Entries from one of Ford's many "jot" books.

Sails begins on the drawing board

▲ Henry Ford was a notoriously poor speller and grammarian, but few would argue with his logic, as exemplified by this jotting.

Model Breakdown Chart

Model T—wb 100.0		Wght	Price	Prod
T	tour 5P	na	360	432,519
T	runabout 2P	na	345	73,559
T	cpe 2P	1,685	650	14,771
T	sdn 2d 5P	1,715	645	35,697
T	twn car 7P	na	595	2,142
T	ambulance	na	na	2,136
T	chassis	1,060	325	37,648
T	delivery	na	na	399
TT	trk chassis	1,450	600	41,105

Note: Total output for calendar year was approximately 436,000.

1919

"High-tech" hits Flivver: electric starter (with battery) available on closed cars—and on open cars late in model year

Trucks keep hand crank—offered on cars until 1925

Optional demountable rims simplify tire-changing

Three-millionth Model T built as output doubles, to nearly half of U.S. total

Libel suit against *Chicago Tribune* goes to court . . . Henry snorts words heard 'round the world: "History is more or less bunk"

Benson Ford born July 20

Ford wages reach $6 a day

▲ Edsel Ford, second from left, and his wife, Eleanor, left, enjoyed yachting and water sports, and built their mansion on the shores of Michigan's/Ontario's Lake St. Clair.

▲ Henry Ford sits in a wheat shock near Mt. Clemens, Michigan, locale of his libel suit against the *Chicago Tribune,* which had described him as an anarchist. Ford won the suit.

COLEMAN C. VAUGHAN
SECRETARY OF STATE

FRANK D. FITZGERALD
DEPUTY SECRETARY

MICHIGAN
DEPARTMENT OF STATE
LANSING

MO 1 4 '19

Operator's License No. 120565   Date................19........

Henry Ford ....residing at

Dearborn ....Michigan

........................St.
Twp.   is hereby licensed

to operate a motor vehicle in accordance with the provisions of Act No. 368, Public Acts of 1919.

DESCRIPTION OF PERSON LICENSED

Age .... 56 ....Years;   Color of Hair.......... Gray ....;

Height .. 5 ..ft. 8½..Inches;   Color of Eyes.......... Blue ....;

Sex.... M ....; Color.... W ....;   Weight .... 138 ....lbs.

Coleman C. Vaughan
Secretary of State.

Not valid until endorsed by licensee.

Signature of Licensee.

▲ Henry Ford's driver's license attests that he stood 5 feet 8½ inches and weighed 138 pounds.

Model Breakdown Chart

Model T—wb 100.0		Wght	Price	Prod
T	tour 5P	1,500	525	286,935
T	runabout 2P	1,390	500	48,867
T	cpe 2P	1,685	750	11,528
T	sdn 2d 5P	1,875	875	24,980
T	twn car 7P	na	na	17
T	ambulance	na	na	2,227
T	chassis	1,060	475	47,125
T	delivery	na	na	5,847
TT	trk chassis	1,477	550	70,816

Note: Total output for calendar year was 820,455.

▲ Engines were modified for electric starting.

◀ Added standard equipment boosted the price of a Center Door sedan, with oval rear window.

▲ Not the most svelte of Model T Fords, the tall closed coupe lured its share of buyers. Instrument panels went into cars with electric starters.

▲ The Rev. Branford Clarke, of New York City, and his Model T "chapel on wheels."

◀ Based on the two-seat Runabout, this Model T roadster pickup, owned by the Ford company, carried a cargo box with side rails. Commercial bodies were crafted by outside firms, even after trucks became a standard Ford item. Note the oversize toolbox mounted on the running board. Trucks of this sort often were used as service vehicles at Ford factories.

1919 Engine Availability

Engine	bore × stroke	bhp	availability
L-4, 176.7	3.75 × 4.00	20	S-Model T

49

1920

Ford output drops by half, despite industry gain . . . share skids to 22 percent

Nation endures recession in winter 1920-21

Model T prices cut drastically—averaging $148—on September 21, but sales fail to respond

Plants shut from Christmas to February 1, 1921

Rumors of Ford financial plight spread . . . recovery comes as Ford dealers pay for cars received

1920 Engine Availability			
Engine	bore × stroke	bhp	availability
L-4, 176.7	3.75 × 4.00	20	S-Model T

▲ Henry Ford and his grandsons, Henry II, left, and Benson, gardening on Ford's estate.

▲ Henry Ford and three-year-old grandson, Henry II, at the "blowing in" of a company blast furnace.

▲ Edsel was named the Ford Company's president the last day of 1918, but his father called the shots throughout the remainder of their careers.

▲ Henry and Clara Ford stand beside the Rock Garden of their Dearborn estate, Fair Lane.

▲ On summer days in Oakland, California, a Model T Ice Cream Truck hawked its wares. Commercial Fords were familiar sights by the '20s.

▲ Model T motorists could keep their hats on, even if the top was erected. This Runabout sold for $650 with starter and demountable rims.

▲ Some high steppin' was required to climb into a tall Ford coupe, but a new oval fuel tank allowed lower seating. Output boomed, topping five times the 1919 total.

Model Breakdown Chart				
Model T—wb 100.0		**Wght**	**Price**	**Prod**
T	tour 5P	1,500	575	165,929
T	tour 5P*	1,650	675	367,785
T	runabout 2P	1,390	550	31,889
T	runabout 2P*	1,540	650	63,514
T	cpe 2P	1,760	850	60,215
T	sdn 2d	1,875	975	81,616
T	chassis	1,060	525	18,173
T	chassis*	1,210	620	16,919
TT	trk chassis	1,477	640	135,002

*Price included starter and demountable wheels. Total output for calendar year was 419,517.

▲ Long before the snowmobile craze of the 1970s, an enterprising company fitted Fords for winter duty. Model Ts could handle the rigors of even a northern Michigan winter, with rear treads and front ski runners.

▲ A Model TT truck chassis with the usual 20-bhp engine sold for around $600, and could accept a breathtaking variety of bodies from outside firms. This panel delivery truck kept its driver well protected from the elements.

1921

Big price cuts again stimulate sales, helped by upturn in U.S. economy

Ford production more than doubles, to record-setting 903,814 units

Ford's market share triples, to 61.5 percent, as industry declines

Model T bodies sit slightly lower, but show little other change

William S. Knudsen leaves Ford for Chevrolet

1921 Engine Availability

Engine	bore × stroke	bhp	availability
L-4, 176.7	3.75 × 4.00	20	S-Model T

Model Breakdown Chart

Model T—wb 100.0		Wght	Price	Prod
T	tour 5P	1,500	440	84,970
T	tour 5P*	1,650	535	647,300
T	runabout 2P	1,390	395	25,918
T	runabout 2P*	1,540	490	171,745
T	cpe 2P*	1,760	745	129,159
T	sdn 2d*	1,875	795	179,734
T	chassis	1,060	360	13,356
T	chassis*	1,210	455	23,436
TT	trk chassis	1,477	545	118,583

*Price included starter and demountable wheels. Total output for calendar year was 903,814.

▲ Henry and Edsel Ford pose with a Fordson tractor at a midwestern fair in 1921. The nation's best selling tractor, the Fordson was priced at $625 in 1921, $395 in 1922.

▲ A whopping $180 price cut dropped the Center Door Sedan to $795—then lower yet. This year's Model T body looked similar to 1920's, but the rear quarter panel was an integral element of the bodyside, no longer split in two sections. Mechanical details included the use of pressed-steel muffler heads rather than cast iron. Front engine supports and spring clamps were forged in a single unit.

▲ As usual, bodies for the handsome woody Depot Hack came from outside suppliers. Prices for a Model T chassis alone began at $360 (or $455 for a heavy-duty edition).

▲ By year's end, the Model T Runabout dropped from $395 to $370, then hit $325. Once again, sales lagged well behind the touring car, partly due to the roadster's two-seat capacity.

▲ To combat the recession, some Ford dealers resorted to stunts to attract new business. This Center Door Sedan conquers the steps of a Portland, Oregon, high school.

52

1922

Model T earns another round of price cuts: touring car dips as low as $298

Output nears 1.2 million—over half of U.S. total

Exports account for eight percent of Fords built

Hoodless Model T wins Pikes Peak hillclimb

"Lizzie Label" craze takes hold: pranksters paint funny phrases on Fords

73 percent of cars bought on time—Henry Ford still disapproves

▲ Henry Ford was a devotee of the great outdoors, and loved his camping trips with famous friends. Here, Ford and fellow inventor Thomas Alva Edison enjoy an outdoor outing.

1922 Engine Availability

Engine	bore × stroke	bhp	availability
L-4, 176.7	3.75 × 4.00	20	S-Model T

▼ Ford trucks came with no end of specially built bodies, including this "Fire Chief Runabout." The "B" on the hood stands for the initial of the vehicle's latter-day owner. A record-setting number of Model TT chassis went to customers this year. Steel-covered wood frames enhanced Ford durability.

Model Breakdown Chart

Model T—wb 100.0		Wght	Price	Prod
T	tour 5P	1,500	355	80,070
T	tour 5P*	1,650	450	514,333
T	runabout 2P	1,390	325	31,923
T	runabout 2P*	1,540	420	133,433
T	cpe 2P*	1,760	595	198,382
T	sdn 2d*	1,875	660	146,060
T	snd 4d*	1,950	725	4,286
T	chassis	1,060	295	15,228
T	chassis*	1,210	390	23,313
TT	trk chassis	1,477	445	135,629
TT	trk chassis*	1,577	475	18,410

*Price included starter and demountable wheels. Total output for calendar year was 1,173,745.

1923

NINETEEN TWENTY-THREE NINETEEN TWENTY-THREE NINETEEN TWENTY-T

Model T restyled: lower, more streamlined stance

Advertising resumes after six-year lapse

Ads push price—as low as $295 for touring car—and Ford as "quality product"

Over 1.8 million Ford cars built—half industry total

"Fordor" and "Tudor" sedans debut—names coined by Henry and used for decades

Doors now front-hinged

1923 Engine Availability

Engine	bore × stroke	bhp	availability
L-4, 176.7	3.75 × 4.00	20	S-Model T

Model Breakdown Chart

Model T—wb 100.0		Wght	Price	Prod
T	tour 5P	1,500	298	136,441
T	tour 5P*	1,650	393	792,651
T	runabout 2P	1,390	269	56,954
T	runabout 2P*	1,540	364	238,638
T	cpe 2P*	1,760	530	313,273
T	sdn 2d*	1,875	595	96,410
T	snd 4d*	1,950	725	144,444
T	chassis	1,060	235	9,443
T	chassis*	1,210	330	42,874
TT	trk chassis	1,477	380	197,057
TT	trk chassis*	1,577	475	64,604

*Price included starter and demountable wheels. Total output for calendar year was 1,817,891.

▲ First Ford to wear new styling was the touring car. Bodies sat lower on the chassis, the split windshield sloped, and a "one man" top was used. Over 929,000 were built (including foreign).

▲ Henry Ford, right, and son Edsel, left, entertained celebrities including Charlie Chaplin.

▲ Still popular, the touring car got a taller radiator and hood for a more modern look.

▲ Side curtains cut vision—and looked lumpy.

▲ "Fordor" sedan had front and rear doors.

▲ Henry Ford, outfitted as a Western desperado, clowns with Thomas A. Edison on a camping trip.

▲ Stake-body trucks could have a closed cab.

▲ A Fronty Ford finished fifth in the Indy 500.

1924

10-millionth Model T built in June—leads parades on Lincoln Highway, Route 66

Prince of Wales given 11-millionth Ford, in October

Production slips to 1.75 million, yet Ford hangs onto half of market

Prices drop to $265 for Runabout, $295 for Touring—average employed worker earns $1293 yearly

In two-year period, over 300,000 Fords sold under weekly purchase plan

Ford earns record $100 million profit in 1923-24

▲ In a milestone-car ritual, Henry Ford poses on his estate with the 10-millionth Ford and his 1896 Quadricycle. The Model T was driven cross-country for publicity purposes.

1924 Engine Availability

Engine	bore × stroke	bhp	availability
L-4, 176.7	3.75 × 4.00	20	S-Model T

▲ Driver Alfred Moss in a Ford-powered Fronty Ford at the Indy 500. The car finished 16th.

Model Breakdown Chart

Model T—wb 100.0		Wght	Price	Prod
T	tour 5P	1,500	295	99,523
T	tour 5P*	1,650	380	673,579
T	runabout 2P	1,390	265	43,317
T	runabout 2P*	1,540	350	220,955
T	cpe 2P*	1,760	525	327,584
T	sdn 2d*	1,875	590	223,203
T	snd 4d*	1,950	685	84,733
T	chassis	1,060	230	3,921
T	chassis*	1,210	295	43,980
TT	trk	na	490	38,840
TT	trk*	na	555	5,649
TT	trk chassis	1,477	370	127,891
TT	trk chassis*	1,577	435	32,471

*Price included starter and demountable wheels. Total output for calendar year was 1,749,827.

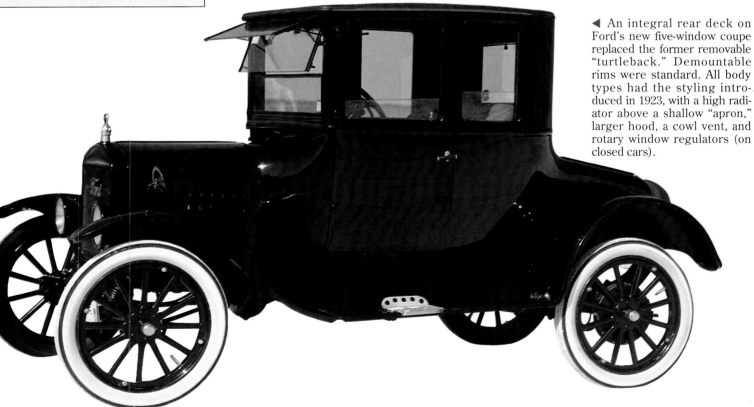

◄ An integral rear deck on Ford's new five-window coupe replaced the former removable "turtleback." Demountable rims were standard. All body types had the styling introduced in 1923, with a high radiator above a shallow "apron," larger hood, a cowl vent, and rotary window regulators (on closed cars).

▶ Not everyone was satisfied with an ordinary Model T body style, no matter how diverse the lineup had become. Even with the top up, this Speedster—a specially built two-passenger roadster—looked quick and ready. With their sloped windshields, in fact, all the open models displayed a sporty demeanor, reminiscent of the long-gone Torpedo. Bright colors, on the other hand, had not yet returned to "factory" cars. Note the fuel tank behind the seat.

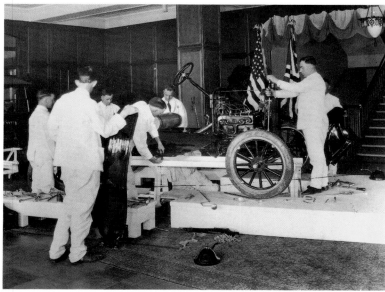

▲ Workmen assemble the 11-millionth Ford on October 24, 1924. The car was presented later in the day to the Prince of Wales, then visiting Detroit.

▲ The Prince of Wales, later the Duke of Windsor, is seen here between Edsel and Henry Ford, at Edsel's estate.

▲ This closed van with sliding-door entry and accessory Bi-flex bumper delivered flowers in Detroit. Truck bodies often varied in detail, even if they appeared similar at a glance.

▲ A rugged Model T or TT chassis was available with a cab or stripped, ready to hold a vast selection of special bodies. Output in U.S. plants dipped to 172,221 for the calendar year.

▲ Roll-down side curtains turned a canopied express truck into a $520 screenside delivery. Ford's own steel bodies were now sold. Note the "half moon" cab shape and tiny oval window.

1925

Prices cut again, to all-time low: $260 for Runabout and $290 for Touring car

Output slides down to 1,643,295 cars—market share dips to 44 percent

Ford truck output sets record at 268,411

Ford ads push safety and affordability

During 1925, Model T earns its second major facelift

Ford opens Mexican plant, starts sales in Japan

William Clay Ford born March 14—third son of Edsel and Eleanor

▲ A romantic 62-year-old Henry Ford prepares to carve his and his wife's initials in a tree on their Dearborn estate, Fair Lane. Ford often credited his success to "sticking to one model," referring both to his wife and the Model T, and once said, "If I were to die and come back to another life, I would want the same mate." He called Clara "The Believer" because she recognized his abilities when few others did. Mrs. Ford outlived her husband by three years, dying in 1950.

1925 Engine Availability

Engine	bore × stroke	bhp	availability
L-4, 176.7	3.75 × 4.00	20	S-Model T

◄ As Chevrolet and other rivals grew stronger, demand for the Model T was skidding steadily downward. Dealers were losing faith. Ads still claimed that Fords were "within the means of millions," at least when bought via weekly advance payments, but dealers had a rough time meeting their quotas. Edsel Ford argued for a new model. Many wanted a sliding-gear gearbox. For now, all that Henry would agree to was a restyling of the familiar flivver for mid-1925.

▲ All Fords, including this $520 coupe, got a touch up in 1925 with larger fenders. Two new options arrived: a nickel-plated radiator shell and a factory-installed, hand-operated wiper.

▲ A Fordor sedan offered a cozy ride for the family, but at $660 it cost twice as much as a touring car. This was the last year that open cars without electric starters were sold.

▲ Priced lower than ever, this Runabout wears the new optional 4.40×21 balloon tires. Priced at an eye-opening $25 (each), the reduced-pressure rubber improved style and handling.

▶ Henry Ford shouts into the ear of his closest friend, Thomas A. Edison. Henry, 16 years Edison's junior, idolized the inventor from the time (1896) Edison encouraged Ford's gasoline-car experimentation. Ford later named the Edison Institute (Henry Ford Museum/Greenfield Village) for his idol.

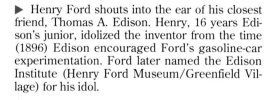

Model Breakdown Chart

Model T—wb 100.0		Wght	Price	Prod
T	tour 5P	1,500	290	64,399
T	tour 5P*	1,650	375	626,813
T	runabout 2P	1,390	260	34,206
T	runabout 2P*	1,536	345	264,436
T	cpe 2P*	1,760	520	343,969
T	sdn 2d*	1,875	580	195,001
T	snd 4d*	1,950	660	81,050
T	chassis	1,060	225	6,523
T	chassis*	1,210	290	53,450
T	pickup	1,471	281	33,795
TT	trk	na	485	192,839
TT	trk chassis	1,477	365	186,810
TT	trk chassis*	1,577	430	62,496

*Price included starter and demountable wheels. Total output for calendar year was 1,643,295.

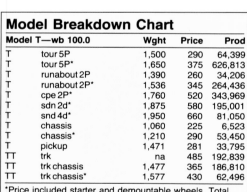

▲ America's first light-duty pickup resembled Ford's regular roadster-pickup, with a fixed cargo box replacing the usual "turtleback" deck. Priced at $281, it found 33,795 buyers.

▲ Ford's new "closed cab" Model TT truck with roll-down glass windows cost $20 more than the $65 "open cab" shown here. This truck carries an express-type body and heavy-duty rear tires.

▲ Modifications to screenside trucks in the 1920s didn't impair their popularity with police departments—one of many special applications. Note the tough-looking tires.

1926

NINETEEN TWENTY-SIX NINETEEN TWENTY-SIX NINETEEN TWENTY-SIX NIN

Model T nears end: volume drops 17 percent, Ford share dips to 36 percent

Customers have more money—and modern cars to buy . . . women's influence and low-cost used cars cited as factors in slow sales

Tin Lizzie comes in colors

Starter now standard on open Model Ts . . . prices cut twice during year

Wild rumors of Model T replacement denied by Ford

1926 Engine Availability

Engine	bore × stroke	bhp	availability
L-4, 176.7	3.75 × 4.00	20	S-Model T

THE FORDOR
$660
F.O.B. DETROIT

BEAUTY, COMFORT, CONVENIENCE, UTILITY

▲ With the exception of this Fordor sedan, Model T bodies this year sat 1½ inches lower, running boards were wider, and headlights moved to the fenders. Closed cars came in a choice of colors.

▲ Despite Henry Ford's protests, an all-new model was under development by the time the 15-millionth Ford was built, in May 1927. Edsel sits at the touring car's wheel, with his father alongside.

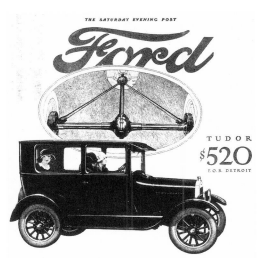

THE SATURDAY EVENING POST

Ford

TUDOR
$520
F.O.B. DETROIT

"The Torque Tube Drive"—An Original Ford Idea

One of the notable features of Ford car design since 1903 is the torque tube drive, a method of applying and controlling the driving and braking forces which has definitely and conclusively established its superiority.

This is accomplished simply and effectively by means of a single torque tube surrounding the driving shaft. Not only are the torque reactions taken up, but the driving thrust is carried to a point well forward on the

chassis—giving the most efficient application of the car's motive power. Moreover, this driving thrust is carried on a line almost parallel with the ground, relieving the car from vertical thrusts.

With this construction, two diagonally attached radius rods are used, assuring alignment of the rear axle and leaving the springs free to act solely as flexible supports for the load. FORD MOTOR COMPANY, Detroit, Michigan

▲ "Torque Tube Drive," as described in this *Saturday Evening Post* ad, was nothing new to Ford. Fuel tanks were moved to the cowl (except on Fordors), and the Tudor adopted a one-piece windshield. Fenders and hood were new for '26.

▲ A nickel-plated radiator shell was now standard on closed models. Fordor colors included Black, Fawn Gray, Highland Green, and Royal Maroon—possible because of new quick-drying lacquers.

59

▲ A racy Runabout might be painted Phoenix Brown or Gun Metal Blue, but fenders were black, wire wheels optional. The steering wheel grew to 17 inches, and pedals were rectangular.

Model Breakdown Chart

Model T—wb 100.0		Wght	Price	Prod*
T	tour 5P	1,738	375	364,409
T	runabout 2P	1,655	345	342,575
T	cpe 2P	1,860	520	288,342
T	sdn 2d	1,972	580	270,331
T	snd 4d	2,004	660	102,732
T	chassis	1,272	290	58,223
T	pickup	1,736	366	75,406
TT	trk chassis	1,577	430	228,496
TT	trk body	na	na	142,852

*Price included starter and demountable wheels (available without those options). Total output for calendar year was 1,368,383.

▲ Accessories, whether from Ford or the aftermarket, added "Jazz Age" pizzazz to the Runabout. This one sports mirrors and a winged radiator cap, as well as a windshield wiper.

▲ For the first time since 1911, touring cars got a driver's door. In addition to their sporty appeal, open cars cost less. Note the optional bumpers, side curtains, and top boot.

▲ Henry Ford and Henry M. Leland stand behind sons Edsel and Wilfred, as Ford purchases the Lincoln Motor Company—then in receivership—in February 1922. Custom bodies came from LeBaron, Dietrich, and other coachbuilders. Lincoln output peaked in 1926, then began to decline.

▲ Henry Ford laces up his skating shoes on a pond near Wayside Inn, South Sudbury, Massachusetts. Ford told reporters that he had made the skates from a Model T axle in 1919. The magnate bought the inn, one of the nation's two oldest hostelries, in 1923 and restored it handsomely. It is still open to the public.

1927

NINETEEN TWENTY-SEVEN NINETEEN TWENTY-SEVEN NINETEEN TWENTY-SI

Legendary era ends: Model T grinds to a halt, after 19 years with minimal change

Flivvers recalled with affection, but could no longer compete . . . Model T's impact on American life rarely—if ever—matched by any product

15,007,033 Lizzies built through May (plus 477,748 that summer)— record stands until Volkswagen Beetle

Wire wheels become standard

1927 Engine Availability

Engine	bore × stroke	bhp	availability
L-4, 176.7	3.75 × 4.00	20	S-Model T

Model Breakdown Chart

Model T—wb 100.0		Wght	Price	Prod
T	tour 5P	1,738	380	81,181
T	runabout 2P	1,655	360	95,778
T	sdn 2d	1,972	495	78,105
T	snd 4d	2,004	545	22,930
T	cpe 2P	1,860	485	69,939
T	chassis	1,272	300	19,280
T	pickup	1,736	381	28,143
TT	trk chassis	1,577	375	83,202
TT	trk body	na	na	41,318

▲ Henry Ford, left, and his son, Edsel, pose with the 15-millionth Ford and Henry's 1896 Quadricycle in front of the company's Dearborn Engineering Laboratory on May 26, 1927, announcement day of the Model T's discontinuance. The Tin Lizzie's life span exceeded that of any other car until the 1960s and its production record stood until 1972, when surpassed by the Volkswagen Beetle.

▲ At a glance, this touring car didn't look much different from its 1909 predecessor, but a lot had changed. Neatly crowned fenders were bolted to the body, with wire wheels standard.

▲ Least costly of the final Model Ts at $360, the Runabout was a snazzy item, if not quite graceful. Bumpers added $15, but this two-seater lacks the nickel-plated radiator shell.

▲ One of scores of cartoons that mourned the Model T's passing. The perspective of time has served only to increase affection and respect for the Tin Lizzie, generally regarded as "the world's greatest car."

▲ Henry Ford greets Charles A. Lindbergh in Dearborn on August 11, 1927. The aviator took both Henry and Edsel aloft in the Spirit of St. Louis, in which he had soloed the Atlantic in May. The flight was Henry's first.

1928

Model A creates frenzy; has regular gearbox, 40-bhp engine, four-wheel brakes

10 million people see Model A within 36 hours of debut

Model A designed by Edsel Ford and Joe Galamb, akin to scaled-down Lincoln

Safety glass standard on Model A—first in industry

Ford assets near billion dollars . . . switch over to Model A costs $250 million

Model Breakdown Chart

Model A—wb 103.5		Wght	Price	Prod*
A	RS rdstr 2-4P	2,106	480	30,129
A	bus rdstr	2,050	480	51,807
A	phaeton 4P	2,140	460	47,255
A	RS cpe 2-4P	2,265	550	70,784
A	bus cpe 2P	2,225	550	37,343
A	spec bus cpe	na	525	—
A	spt bus cpe	na	525	79,099
A	Tudor sdn	2,340	550	208,562
A	Fordor sdn	2,386	585	82,349
A	taxi 4d	na	600	264

*Figures shown are for calendar year; total of approximately 633,500 Ford passenger cars.

▲ First Model A built was the Tudor sedan, with a sweeping hoodline, high beltline, and nickeled radiator shell. Crowned fenders matched the wire wheels. Bodies came from Briggs, Murray, and Budd.

▲ Four coupes made the early Model A lineup: Standard business (shown), with fabric top; Business, with rubberized roof; leather-topped Special; and rumble-seat Sport Coupe.

▲ Most popular of the lower, prettier bodies was the Tudor sedan, complete with visor. A Model A could hit 65 mph, versus 43 mph for the boxy Model T, which rode a shorter wheelbase.

▲ Competent and respected, Edsel Ford gained responsibility for styling and marketing, but never for labor, engineering, or manufacturing.

▲ Henry Ford listens as his son, Edsel, pumps away on a player piano. Both Fords enjoyed music, although Henry's tastes ran to old-fashioned fiddling and songs like "Turkey in the Straw," "Uncle Remus," and "Jeanie with the Light Brown Hair," while Edsel preferred more serious fare.

▲ Roadsters came with or without a rumble seat, for the same $480. Step plates aided rear access. This car has optional trunk, stone guard, and spare tire cover. Gravity sent fuel from the tank, which was part of the cowl.

▲ An all-new, 200.5-cid L-head four had twice the power of the Model T's, yielding 40 horsepower on 4.22:1 compression, due to Harold Hicks. Battery ignition replaced the magneto, and a water pump was installed.

1928 Engine Availability

Engine	bore × stroke	bhp	availability
L-4, 200.5	3.88 × 4.25	40	S-Model A

◀ André Citroën, founder and head of the French auto firm bearing his name, confers with Henry Ford during a visit to Dearborn. In 1919, Citroën unsuccessfully offered Ford a partnership in his firm for $10 million. Ford, however, preferred to go it alone in France. Citroën's visit to Ford's River Rouge Plant, like that of many other automakers of his day, is reminiscent of latter-day Americans' visits to Japanese plants in pursuit of the latest in production techniques.

▲ Two truck groups went on sale: light-duty 70-Series derived from the passenger cars, and heavier 80-Series on a 131.5-inch wheelbase. Stake-side was one of several factory bodies.

▲ One nifty commercial was the roadster-pickup, continuing a Model T idea. Open- and closed-cab pickups had Model A front ends and carryover TT cargo boxes, for $395 or $445.

▲ Light trucks used the Model A passenger-car drivetrain, hood, and cowl, but with a painted radiator shell. This one, with a tall cargo box, served the Wisconsin Telephone Company.

1929

Model A little changed; Ford continues policy of running improvements rather than annual revisions

Open Fords get external door handles

Four new body styles debut during 1929

Millionth Model A built; then two-millionth in July

Ford car production and market share double, to 32 percent of cars built

▲ Glamour entered the Model A domain as the $670 cabriolet arrived—the first true convertible since the Model T Coupelet. Bright hues and accessories made it spiffier yet. All fenders were black.

1929 Engine Availability

Engine	bore × stroke	bhp	availability
L-4, 200.5	3.88 × 4.25	40	S-Model A

▲ With its top up a cabriolet looked like a rumble-seat sport coupe, but landau bars were functional. Note the external trunk, a popular add-on. Interiors were upholstered in imitation brown leather.

▲ Edsel Ford at his winter home in Hobe Sound, Florida. His summer home was on Seal Island, Maine.

▲ At a glance, this looks like a Tudor sedan, but the missing rear side windows mark it as a $595 Deluxe Delivery. A swing-out back door gave access to the 35×42×43-inch cargo area.

▲ Best-selling Model A, once again, was the $525 Tudor sedan. Note the neat pinstriping. Most customers took kindly to the three-speed gearbox, clutch, and floor-mounted gas pedal.

▲ Winged radiator caps were popular extras—more so if they contained a useful gauge. This cap decorates a "leatherback" sedan. Bumpers, wiper, and a tail/stop light were standard.

◄ Leather (or leatherette) was installed on the back and top of the Briggs-built Fordor "leatherback" sedan. Regular Fordor bodies came from both Briggs and Murray, selling for the same $625. Model As were far more complex than the primitive Model T, thus more costly, but were seen to offer greater value. At the factories, Model T bodies had slid by gravity to a chassis driven underneath, whereas the "A" body dropped by power crane to a moving line.

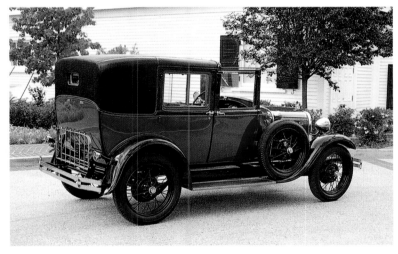

▲ Created by Edsel Ford, the Town Car aimed at those who favored formal style, but didn't wish to flaunt their wealth. At $1400, with an open chauffeur's compartment and covered roof, it cost $775 more than a Fordor.

▲ As Henry Ford looks on, President Herbert Hoover, at the dedication of Greenfield Village, starts a "perpetual fire" in the courthouse in which Abraham Lincoln practiced law. The fire did not prove to be perpetual.

▲ This five-window coupe with rumble seat offered better over-the-shoulder visibility than companion coupes. Note the tool box and step plate.

▲ Small rear side windows identified the $695 Murray-bodied Town Sedan, with standard cowl lights. Ordinary Fordors had blank rear quarters.

1929 Selected Colors

Bonnie Gray

Rocky Moss Green

Seal Brown

Rose Beige

Chelsea Blue

Andalusite Blue

Vagabond Green

Duchess Blue

Balsam Green

Medium Cream

Thorne Brown

Cigarette Cream

Lawn Green

Aragon Ruby Light

Valley Green

▲ Equivalent to the old Model T touring car, the phaeton delivered open-air motoring for a modest price—for anyone willing to wrestle with side curtains. Open cars now had outside door handles.

▲ Only $450 bought a Model A roadster, with either a trunk or rumble seat. The "flying quail" ornament adorned many a Ford.

▲ A Standard business coupe, with trunk, sold for $525. Some coupes lacked the oval quarter windows. Also available: a dapper Sport Coupe.

▲ With a closed cab, the workhorse pickup went for $445. Heavier trucks got a four-speed 'box.

▲ Maple/birch bodies for the new Murray-built woody wagon came from Ford's lumber mills.

◀ Three generations of Fords—Edsel, left, Henry, in derby, Benson, being held by his grandfather, and Henry II—in front of a Model A. The boys sport highboots. Henry doted on his grandsons, and had them over to his estate far more than his son and daughter-in-law might have wished.

Model Breakdown Chart

Model A—wb 103.5	Wght	Price	Prod
sta wgn 4d	2,500	650	4,954
RS cabr 2-4P	2,339	670	16,421
RS rdstr 2-4P	2,106	450	191,529
phaeton 4P	2,203	460	49,818
RS spt cpe	2,250	550	134,292
bus cpe 2P	2,216	525	37,644
cpe 2P	2,248	550	178,982
Tudor sdn	2,348	525	523,922
Murray sdn 4d	2,497	625	53,941
Murray twn sdn	2,517	695	84,970
Briggs 2W sdn	2,419	625	146,097
Briggs sdn 4d	2,497	625	*
Briggs LB sdn	2,500	625	*
Briggs twn sdn	2,517	625	*
twn car 4P	2,525	1,400	913
taxi 4d	na	800	4,576

*Included in sedan figures above. Totals shown are for calendar year.

1930

Modified Model A attracts considerable attention after January debut

Ads promote "The New Beauty of the New Ford"

Cowl stanchions are gone, hood-to-body lines taller, fenders more sweeping

DeLuxe two-door phaeton and Victoria two-door arrive during year

First use of stainless-steel brightwork, including radiator shell

Model As gain favor with early California "hot rodders," as add-on speed equipment becomes available from aftermarket firms

Production falls as nation's economy sags into Great Depression, but Ford grabs 41-percent share

▲ DeLuxe roadsters came with cowl lights and twin taillights, as A-Bone earned a beauty treatment.

▲ Smaller (19-inch) wheels, but bigger tires, gave the popular Tudor sedan a modern stance.

▼ Roomier interiors held a central instrument panel with "cyclops-eye" speedometer.

1930 Engine Availability

Engine	bore × stroke	bhp	availability
L-4, 200.5	3.88 × 4.25	40	S-Model A

Model Breakdown Chart

Model A—wb 103.5	Wght	Price	Prod
rdstr 2P	2,155	435	122,703
rdstr 2-4P	2,230	460	
phtn 5P	2,212	440	39,886
Standard cpe 2P	2,257	495	232,564
spt cpe 2-4P	2,283	525	72,572
cabriolet 2-4P	2,273	625	29,226
Tudor sdn 5P	2,375	495	425,124
Fordor sdn 2W 5P	2,441	600	7,838
Town sdn 5P	2,475	660	122,534
town car 5P	2,525	1,200	96
Standard sdn 3W 5P	2,462	600	53,958
DeLuxe rdstr 2-4P	2,230	520	11,629
DeLuxe phtn 5P	2,285	625	4,635
DeLuxe cpe 2P	2,265	545	29,777
victoria 5P	2,265	625	6,447
DeLuxe sdn 5P	2,488	640	13,710
wgn 4d	—	650	3,799
bus cpe 2P	—	—	110

67

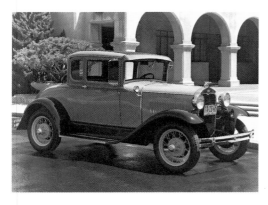

▲ Handy vent wings were optional on this DeLuxe coupe, which shows off the restyled Ford's more generous fender contours.

▲ As revealed by this rakish dual-cockpit phaeton, believed to be a LeBaron creation, the Model A lent itself to custom bodywork.

▲ A $625 DeLuxe two-door phaeton joined the four-door this year, with left sidemount spare tire, trunk rack, and leather upholstery.

▲ Five-window coupes came in standard or DeLuxe trim, the latter costing $50 more. Far more of the lower-cost coupes, with trunk, went to buyers.

▲ Owners of a ritzy cabriolet got roll-up windows and sturdy A-pillars, for $190 more than the cheapest roadster. Note cowl lights and mirrors.

▲ Fondly known as the "Tin Goose" because of its metal construction, the Tri-Motor evolved from the Stout plane, after Ford bought that company in 1925. In 1928, the 5-AT Tri-Motor adopted 420-bhp Pratt & Whitney engines.

◄ Carrying the mail was a major duty, but the Tri-Motor was best known for coast-to-coast passenger service. Riders sat on wicker seats. In 1930 it was the mainstay of Transcontinental Air Transport (forerunner of TWA).

1931

Model A returns with modest appearance updates

Town Sedan debuts during year, followed by convertible sedan with fixed window frames

Broad variety of "factory" truck bodies added to line, including Town Car Delivery

20-millionth Ford built in April; that Town Sedan tours the nation, then goes on display at Ford Museum

Ford production tumbles to 541,615 cars, as industry suffers Depression woes

Chevrolet edges Ford in model-year production

Rumors of V-8 Ford heard, as four-cylinder engine loses popularity fast

75,000 Ford workers laid off in July; 25 U.S. plants shut down; daily wage sliced to $6 in October

Model Breakdown Chart

Model A—wb 103.5	Wght	Price	Prod
rdstr 2P	2,155	430	7,793
rdstr 2-4P	2,230	455	
phtn 5P	2,212	435	11,060
Standard cpe 2P	2,257	490	82,885
spt cpe 2-4P	2,283	500	21,272
cabriolet 2-4P	2,273	595	13,706
Tudor sdn 5P	2,375	490	170,645
Standard sdn 3W 5P	2,462	590	25,720
DeLuxe rdstr 2-4P	2,230	475	56,702
DeLuxe phtn 5P	2,285	580	2,875
DeLuxe cpe 2P	2,265	525	23,653
victoria 5P	2,265	580	36,830
DeLuxe Tudor sdn 5P	2,388	525	23,490
DeLuxe Fordor sdn 5P	2,488	630	4,967
DeLuxe town sdn 5P	2,475	630	65,447
conv sdn 5P	2,360	640	5,072
wgn 4d	—	625	3,018

▲ Henry and Clara Ford in the living room of their home. Mrs. Ford loved to redecorate, and Henry acquiesced, philosophizing, "peace at any price."

▲ An accessory trunk tags behind this DeLuxe coupe with rear quarter window panes, which sold for $525. A standard coupe with trunk went for $35 less. Updates included a restyled radiator shell with body-color indentation, revised instrument panel, and one-piece running-board splash aprons.

▲ Most costly '31 was the $640 all-season convertible sedan, whose top rolled back on tracks above the windows. A tailored boot hid the folded roof. Only 5072 were built.

▲ Introduced late in 1930, the close-coupled Victoria had a slightly lower roofline than a basic Tudor sedan. Price was $580, with or without the snappy canvas-covered top and back.

▶ Priced at $630, the DeLuxe Town Sedan that debuted in March 1931 came with standard cowl lamps. Regular Fordor sedans, which cost $40 less, lacked such niceties—though all Model A buyers had an ample selection of extra-cost accessories to choose from. More distinctive than former Town Sedans, this one wore a rather racy slanted windshield, similar to that used on the Victoria. This trick was accomplished by trimming back the front roof header a bit, and moving the windshield base slightly forward. Ford's 200.5-cid four developed 40 horsepower—10 less than Chevrolet's 194-cid six-cylinder engine. Chevy's Independence series rode a 55-inch-longer wheelbase than Ford's 103.5 inches.

1931 Engine Availability			
Engine	bore × stroke	bhp	availability
L-4, 200.5	3.88 × 4.25	40	S-Model A

◀ Henry Ford, center, visits his privately financed high school in tiny Macon, Michigan, where the auto king ran a sawmill powered by water and steam. Second from left is William J. Cameron, Ford's principal spokesman. Macon, surrounded by thousands of acres of Ford-owned soybean fields, also served as the "capital" of Ford's rural Michigan empire; and the magnate had a country home there. The former high school and sawmill now is part of a home for wayward youths.

▲ Henry Ford drove this milestone Town Sedan off the line, before it toured the nation.

▲ Both the DeLuxe roadster and the no-frills version could have a trunk or rumble seat.

▲ On sunny days, this side-curtained roadster looked spiffier than a windowed cabriolet.

▲ Cargo space grew by 5.4 cubic feet for the Model AA pickup, with bodywork from Briggs. DeLuxe versions had an integrated box/cab.

▲ Nearly 100,000 pickups were sold, including a few DeLuxe editions.

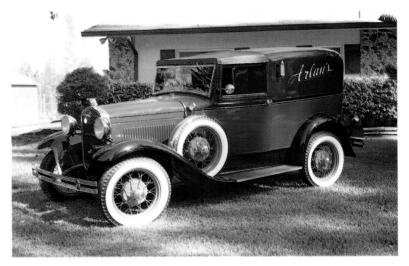

▲ Only 196 Town Car Deliveries emerged, at $1150 with lined cargo area.

▶ Heavy-duty AA commercials, like this brawny dump truck, used the same engine as cars and proved their worth as tireless workhorses. A chassis sold for $340, with open or closed cab.

1932

NINETEEN THIRTY-TWO NINETEEN THIRTY-TWO NINETEEN THIRTY-TWO NINETE

Flathead V-8 arrives . . . 221 cubic-inch engine packs 65-horsepower wallop

Fords gain streamlined look—exposed radiator gone

Charles Sorensen earns "Cast Iron Charlie" moniker for engine-casting work

First V-8 assembled March 9; unveiled March 31; seen by public April 2, 1932

Four-cylinder Model B sold alongside V-8 Model 18

Chevrolet ends year well ahead . . . calendar-year volume lowest since 1914 . . . Ford loses $75 million

▲ Edsel Ford, left, and his father, Henry, check out the new eight-cylinder V-shaped (V-8) engine, often described as the senior Ford's "last mechanical triumph." The motor offered quick acceleration, as attested to by both John Dillinger and Clyde Barrow of Bonnie and Clyde fame. It also required lots of oil after 1000 miles, and thus acquired a reputation as an "oil burner."

◀ Henry Ford, right, visits Orville Wright, second from right, in Dayton, Ohio. Ford later moved from Dayton to Greenfield Village the house and cycle shop in which Orville and his brother, Wilbur, had lived, designed, and built their first airplane. The dedication ceremony brought together more than 200 plane designers and manufacturers, Army Air Force officers, and pioneers.

▲ Cabriolets with fixed windshield pillars came with either a trunk or rumble seat, for $610—a hot value even in Depression '32. The slightly vee'd grille now lacked an exposed radiator. Edsel Ford and Joe Galamb joined forces on styling, just as they had for the Model A, using the sculptured lines of the big Lincoln as their focal point. Eugene Farkas and Emery Nador handled chassis engineering; bodies came from Briggs, Murray, and Budd.

▶ Roadsters carried fold-down windshields. The V-8 emblem marks this beauty as a Model 18.

◀ Credit for the ingenious, low-cost flathead V-8 goes to Emil Zoerlein, Carl Schultz, and Ray Laird, who secretly built upon old Henry's ideas. Starting with a fresh slate, the three created a complex 90-degree block that could—amazingly—be cast in a single unit. In a reliability trial held to counter early negative publicity, a Ford V-8 traveled 33,301 miles in 33 days, across the Mojave Desert.

Model Breakdown Chart

Model 18 V-8—wb 106.5	Wght	Price	Prod
rdstr 2P	2,077	410	520
rdstr 2-4P	2,119	435	
phtn 5P	2,213	445	483
cpe 2P	2,236	440	28,904
spt cpe 2-4P	2,261	485	1,982
Tudor sdn 5P	2,353	450	57,903
Fordor sdn 5P	2,388	540	9,320
DeLuxe rdstr 2-4P	2,153	450	6,893
DeLuxe phtn 5P	2,243	495	923
DeLuxe cpe 2P	2,339	525	20,506
victoria 5P	2,319	550	7,241
cabriolet 2-4P	2,370	560	5,499
DeLuxe Tudor sdn 5P	2,373	500	18,836
DeLuxe Fordor sdn 5P	2,407	595	18,880
conv sdn 5P	2,324	600	842
wgn 4d	—	—	1,400*

Model B—wb 106.5			
rdstr 2P	2,217	460	948
rdstr 2-4P	2,258	485	
phtn 5P	2,344	495	593
cpe 2P	2,387	490	20,342
spt cpe 2-4P	2,397	535	739
Tudor sdn 5P	2,487	490	36,553
Fordor sdn 5P	2,524	590	4,116
DeLuxe rdstr 2-4P	2,283	500	3,719
DeLuxe phtn 5P	2,350	545	281
DeLuxe cpe 2P	2,477	575	968
victoria 5P	2,463	600	521
cabriolet 2-4P	2,390	610	427
DeLuxe Tudor sdn 5P	2,497	550	4,077
DeLuxe Fordor sdn 5P	2,543	643	2,620
conv sdn 2-4P	2,455	650	44
wgn 4d	—	600	—

*Incl. 4-cylinder.

1932 Engine Availability

Engines	bore × stroke	bhp	availability
L-4, 200.5	3.88 × 4.25	50	S-Model B
V-8, 221.0	3.06 × 3.75	65	S-Model B

▲ Henry Ford reading a brief speech at the dedication of Ford Field, a Dearborn park, in 1936. A poor speaker, Ford never looked up once, for fear of losing his place. The magnate, priding himself on his eyesight, was reluctant to be seen wearing his glasses. This photo is one of the few showing the industrialist with his spectacles; even so, he's holding, not wearing, them. Later in this speech, Ford bowing to necessity, donned his glasses.

◄ Henry Ford supports President Herbert Hoover's 1932 reelection bid. Ford's comments were read perfunctorily, and upon concluding them he threw up his hands as if to say, "Thank God that's over." The auto king spoke to groups unfamiliar to him only 16 times in his life. Four speeches were radio addresses, two were phone talks to dealers. He often said that his first speech was to Sing Sing prisoners, to whom he said, "I'm glad to see you all here."

▲ This DeLuxe Fordor had the 65-bhp V-8. Fuel tanks were now in the rear; 18-inch wheels improved handling and gave a road-hugging stance.

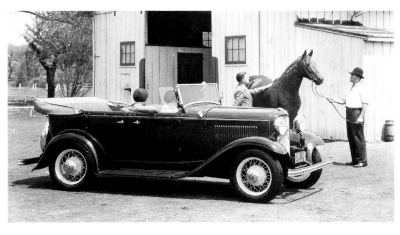

▲ At $545, a DeLuxe V-8 phaeton with cowl lights and pinstripes cost $50 more than a Standard. Four-cylinders started at $410. Note the vent wings.

▲ Landau bars on sports coupe had no function, since the top stayed put. Wheelbase was longer than Model A, with similar transverse springs.

▲ Only a trunk was available at the back of the V-8 DeLuxe three-window coupe, which held two passengers. Windshields had no visor.

▲ Model B Fords, like this upright station wagon, had the same styling as V-8 cars, but the improved Model A four developed 50 bhp.

▲ One body style carried over from the Model A was the Victoria DeLuxe two-door, which showed even cleaner lines in V-8 form. Price tag was $600. Note the single wiper and fully crowned fenders. Only a handful of V-8s went into commercial vehicles at first, and many early engines suffered from cracks or overheating.

◀ Not all '32 Ford V-8s spent their lives in such serene settings. "Deuce" roadsters and coupes became instant hits with "speed demons." Open cars weren't selling so well anymore, as only 8996 roadsters went to buyers—standard and DeLuxe, with or without the rumble seat. Steering columns contained an anti-theft lock.

1933

Competition forces Ford to adopt annual model changes

Graceful, low-slung design stems from British Ford

Four-cylinder Model C Fords still sold; few ordered

V-8 boosted to 75 bhp

Ford debut delayed until February, partly due to strike at Briggs body plant

Fords turn to "suicide" (rear-hinged) doors

Ford calendar-year car production again trails Chevrolet—334,969 to 481,134—with Plymouth a solid third

Reo has self-shifter (semi-automatic transmission)

▲ Henry Ford and actress Mary Pickford at the Ford Exposition of Progress in New York City.

▲ Racers could strip running boards, fenders, top—and beat nearly anything. At an Illinois stock-car event, Fords took top seven spots.

▼ Edsel and Henry Ford review a lineup of Ford cars ranging from the 1903 Model A, left, to the 1933 V-8 on the company's 30th Anniversary.

▶ New Fords, including this DeLuxe roadster with "suicide" doors, rode a longer (112-inch) wheelbase. Note the elegant grille shape.

Model Breakdown Chart

Model 40 V-8—wb 112.0	Wght	Price	Prod
rdstr	2,021	425	126
rdstr 2-4P	2,064	450	
phtn 5P	2,124	445	232
cpe 3W/5W 2P	2,147	440	6,585
cpe 3W/5W 2-4P	2,202	465	31,797
Tudor sdn 5P	2,418	450	106,387
Fordor sdn 5P	2,465	510	19,602
DeLuxe rdstr 2-4P	2,264	460	4,223
DeLuxe phtn 5P	2,154	495	1,483
DeLuxe cpe 3W/5W 2P	2,196	490	15,894
DeLuxe cpe 3W/5W 2-4P	2,202	515	11,244
victoria 5P	2,230	545	4,193
cabriolet 2-4P	2,181	535	7,852
DeLuxe Tudor sdn 5P	2,435	500	48,233
DeLuxe Fordor sdn 5P	2,505	560	45,443
wgn 4d	—	—	1,654
Model 46 Four—wb 112.0			
rdstr 2P	2,337	475	107
rdstr 2-4P	2,420	500	
phtn 5P	2,435	495	457
cpe 3W/5W 2P	2,448	490	189
cpe 3W/5W 2-4P	2,380	515	2148
Tudor sdn 5P	2,536	500	2911
Fordor sdn 5P	2,590	560	682
DeLuxe rdstr 2-4P	2,376	510	101
DeLuxe phtn 5P	2,444	545	241
DeLuxe cpe 3W/5W 2P	2,453	540	24
DeLuxe cpe 3W/5W 2-4P	2,450	565	28
victoria 5P	2,510	595	25
cabriolet 2-4P	2,460	585	24
DeLuxe Tudor sdn 5P	2,540	550	85
DeLuxe Fordor sdn 5P	2,599	610	179
wgn 4d	—	640	359

1933 Engine Availability

Engines	bore × stroke	bhp	availability
L-4, 200.5	3.23 × 4.25	50	S-Model 46
V-8, 221.0	3.06 × 3.75	75	S-Model 40

▶ Smooth rear contours, wide-skirted fenders, and stylish bumpers made the roadster one of the prettiest '33s. Wire wheels slimmed to 17-inches. A stiffer X-frame still carried transverse springs.

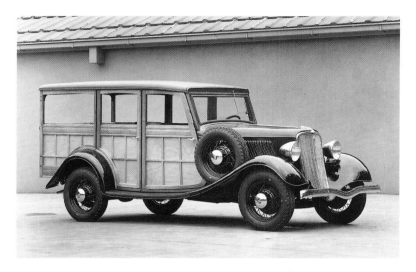

▲ With new streamlined front styling, the V-8 wagon, with rear-hinged doors, looked less vertical. Fords had an engine-turned instrument panel.

▲ Best-seller was the Tudor sedan, which found well over 150,000 buyers. For $550, the DeLuxe version sported cowl lights and dual horns.

▲ Though Henry still ruled the company with an iron fist, son and president Edsel Ford was largely responsible for some of the finest Ford styling. Working with such artists as Joe Galamb and Eugene T. "Bob" Gregorie, he helped create Ford's new look for '33, just as he'd done for the Model A.

▲ Beautiful then and now, the V-8 cabriolet came with a trunk or rumble seat. Four-cylinder models cost less, but never grew popular.

▲ Less popular than Tudors, the DeLuxe Fordor came with a four or V-8. Aluminum heads and higher compression added 10 bhp to the V-8.

▲ New Era Motors created the $995 Fordor taxi, based on a LeBaron custom body. Rear doors extended up into the roof for easy entry.

▲ Light weight helped the Standard Tudor excel in economy runs, averaging 18.3 to 22.5 mpg, dispelling doubts about V-8 economy.

1934

Updated Fords debut—with Prohibition over, press preview serves alcohol!

Mild facelift includes new hood, radiator, grille—"clear vision" ventilation

Body-color fenders standard for first time—black available on request

Enamel paint replaces hand-buffed lacquer on Fords

Intake revisions raise V-8 output to 85 bhp

Ads push V-8's economy, as well as performance

Fords take top 10 spots in Gilmore Cup Race ... V-8s going strong in competition

Admiring letters arrive at Ford headquarters from "folk hero" criminals John Dillinger and Clyde Barrow

1934 Engine Availability

Engines	bore × stroke	bhp	availability
L-4, 200.5	3.88 × 4.25	50	S-Model 40A Four
V-8, 221.0	3.06 × 3.75	85	S-Model 40A V-8

Model Breakdown Chart

Model 40A—wb 112.0	Wght	Price	Prod*
Standard cpe 5W 2P	2,448	505	47,623/20
Standard cpe 5 2-4P	2,534	530	
victoria 5P	2,670	600	20,083/—
conv cabriolet 2-4P	2,460	590	14,496/12
Tudor sdn 5P	2,536	520	124,870/185
Fordor sdn 5P	2,590	575	22,394/405
DeLuxe rdstr 2-4P	2,376	525	6,863/—
DeLuxe phtn 5P	2,444	550	3,128/412
DeLuxe cpe 3W 2-4P	2,453	545	26,348/7
DeLuxe cpe 5W 2-4P	2,450	570	26,879/3
DeLuxe Tudor sdn 5P	2,540	560	121,696/12
DeLuxe Fordor sdn 5P	2,599	615	102,268/384
wgn 4d	2,695	660	2,772/83

*V-8/4-cylinder

▲ Henry Ford, a McGuffey Reader collector, speaks at a ceremony honoring William Holmes McGuffey.

▼ Henry Ford shone at press conferences (as opposed to giving speeches). Here he talks V-8s with newsmen.

▲ Styling touch-ups for the $615 DeLuxe Fordor sedan included a thicker grille surround, and a new hood with twin latches on each side. DeLuxe bodies had triple pinstripes (formerly two), plus dual taillights, cowl lights, and outside horns. This year's window mechanism moved front door glass to a "vent" position before it lowered vertically. Note the graceful greyhound hood ornament—a popular '34 option. Of the 124,662 Fordor V-8s built, 102,268 were DeLuxe.

▼ Nine could ride merrily in a woody wagon, which cost $660. All but 83 of the 2855 built had a V-8. A single sidemount was included.

▲ Headlamp shells were shallower on '34 Fords, including the luscious DeLuxe V-8 three-window coupe. A total of 26,348 were built.

▲ Only two folks fit inside a DeLuxe five-window coupe, but a parcel shelf added utility. A rumble seat made room for two outsiders.

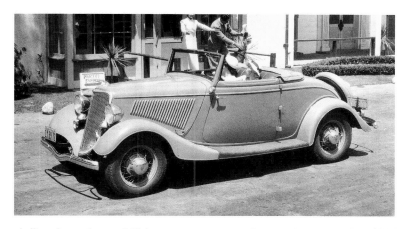

▲ Top-down fun and V-8 go-power were orders of the day with a $525 DeLuxe roadster. Hood louvers were straight this year.

▲ Closed cabs were virtually standard for the $470 V-8 pickup, with only 347 open cabs built. Fewer than 192,000 Ford trucks were made in the U.S.

▲ Most customers again chose a Tudor sedan. Just over half of the 246,763 built were $520 Standard models, as shown here. Note the hood ornament.

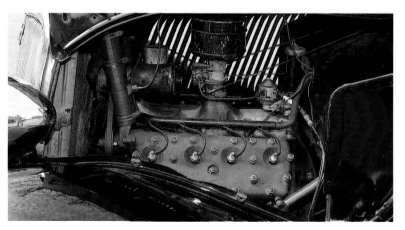

▲ A Stromberg two-barrel carburetor atop a new manifold helped boost V-8 output by 10 bhp. The cast-alloy steel crankshaft was an industry "first."

▲ Richer upholstery graced the bucket-like Tudor seats, inside "suicide" doors. A painted dash replaced the former engine-turned panel.

1935

'35 is fastest Ford yet, with totally new look

Ford bodies longer, wider, sleeker with narrower grille and 16-inch wheels

Styling credited to Phil Wright at Briggs company

Front doors front-hinged . . . last year for outside horns and wire wheels

Ad theme is "Greater Beauty, Greater Comfort, and Greater Safety"

New DeLuxe "trunkback" sedans outsell fastbacks

Revived V-8 convertible sedan paces Indy 500

Edsel Ford forms design group under "Bob" Gregorie . . . Ford test track opens

1935 Engine Availability

Engine	bore × stroke	bhp	availability
V-8, 221.0	3.06 × 3.75	85	S-all

▲ Henry Ford attended few athletic events, but here he and Mrs. Ford are seen at Detroit's Briggs Stadium following a World Series game between the Detroit Tigers and St. Louis Cardinals.

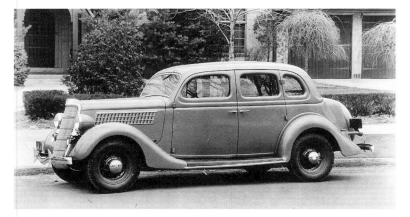

▲ Built-in trunks were new, as on this Fordor sedan, but loading from the top wasn't easy. "Center-Poise Ride" put riders within the car's wheelbase. External radiator caps were gone, and parking lights sat inside headlamps.

▲ Unlike the old Model A version, the revived DeLuxe convertible sedan had four doors and removable B-pillars. Ford's most costly model, it went for $750. Only 4234 were built. Fords still rode on transverse leaf springs.

▼ Rumble seats weren't exactly the rage anymore, but still available on the DeLuxe five-window coupe. The rear-mounted spare tire and protruding taillamps add a jaunty air.

▶ With its shorter roof and curved upper door, the DeLuxe three-window coupe had a more sporting flair than the five-window. This one has a trunk instead of optional rumble seat.

Model Breakdown Chart

Model 48—wb 112.0	Wght	Price	Prod
cpe 5W 2P	2,620	495	111,542
DeLuxe cpe 5W 2P	2,643	560	
conv cabriolet 2-4P	2,687	625	17,000
Tudor sdn 5P	2,717	510	322,575
DeLuxe Tudor sdn 5P	2,735	575	
Tudor touring sdn 5P	2,772	595	87,326
Fordor sdn 5P	2,760	575	124,984
DeLuxe Fordor sdn 5P	2,767	635	
Fordor touring sdn 5P	2,787	655	105,157
DeLuxe rdstr 2-4P	2,597	550	4,896
DeLuxe phtn 5P	2,667	580	6,073
DeLuxe cpe 3W 2P	2,647	570	31,513
conv sdn 5P	2,827	750	4,234
victoria	—	630	235
wgn 4d	—	670	4,536
sdn 7P	—	—	182

▲ Always good copy, Henry Ford is surrounded by reporters at the debut of his 1935 models.

83

▲ Most expensive Ford of the year, at $750, was the new convertible sedan. Roll-up windows kept passengers cozy if the weather turned sour. When the collapsible top was lowered, the B-posts could be removed and stored in a bag beneath the boot. Curb weight was 2827 pounds.

▶ More practical in sunnier climates, the DeLuxe four-door phaeton cost $170 less than a convertible sedan, and 6073 were produced. Side curtains stowed beneath the rear cushion and took a little while to install on the doors. Standard Fords had painted grilles.

▲ Cabriolet convertible owners got both style and the convenience of roll-up windows, for $625. Note the large driving lights and curved-base mirror.

▲ With the top up, rumble-seat passengers in a cabriolet tended to feel a tad isolated from the front-seat folks. A total of 17,000 were built.

1936

Gracefully touched-up Fords get long, pointed hood above sharply vee'd grille

'36 a favorite of Ford fans

Steel artillery wheels replace wire; horns hidden

Fords with integral trunks called Touring Sedans

Six open Fords, including DeLuxe club cabriolet and "Trunkback" Touring Sedan

Ford again surges ahead of Chevy in model-year output, but lags in truck sales

Chevrolet regains calendar-year lead, 975,238 to 791,812 . . . hydraulic brakes cited as reason

1936 Engine Availability

Engine	bore × stroke	bhp	availability
V-8, 221.0	3.06 × 3.75	85	S-all

▲ Henry Ford heartily disliked President Franklin D. Roosevelt, which made it all the easier for him to support Kansas Gov. Alfred E. Landon, left, in the 1936 Presidential election.

▲ Celebrities didn't always stick with domestically built autos. Here, actor Clark Gable drives a strikingly streamlined British Jensen-Ford custom cabriolet. Rakish "suicide" doors had been abandoned on U.S. Fords.

▼ Henry Ford, left, presents Dearborn with Ford Field, a 40-acre natural amphitheater, and one of Henry's boyhood retreats. At right are Dearborn notables, including Miss Dearborn.

▲ An evolving Ford company is showcased by old-era Lincoln K (right) and new Lincoln-Zephyr (left), flanking a contemporary Ford.

▲ Fast, open-air fun for two or four came in the form of a DeLuxe V-8 cabriolet, priced at $625.

Model Breakdown Chart

Model 68—wb 112.0	Wght	Price	Prod
cpe 5W 2P	2,599	510 }	78,534
cpe 5W 2-4P	2,641	535 }	
Tudor sdn 5P	2,659	520	174,770
Tudor T/B sdn 5P	2,728	545	165,718
Fordor sdn 5P	2,699	580	31,505
Fordor T/B sdn 5P	2,771	605	39,607
wgn 4d	3,020	670	7,044
Model 68 DeLuxe—wb 112.0			
rdstr 2-4P	2,561	560	3,862
phtn 5P	2,641	590	5,555
cpe 3W 2P	2,621	570 }	21,446
cpe 3W 2-4P	2,656	595 }	
cpe 5W 2P	2,641	555 }	29,938
cpe 5W 2-4P	2,666	580 }	
cabriolet 2-4P	2,649	625	14,068
club cabriolet 2-4P	2,661	675	4,616
Tudor sdn 5P	2,691	565	20,519
Tudor T/B sdn 5P	2,786	590	125,303
Fordor sdn 5P	2,746	625	42,867
Fordor T/B sdn 5P	2,816	650	159,825
conv sdn 5P	2,791	760 }	5,601
conv sdn T/B 5P	2,916	780 }	

▲ Nothing could be sleeker in '36 than a cabriolet with the top and rumble seat down, and the auxiliary trunk rack folded. Fenders, hood, and grille were new. Horns hid behind small grilles.

▲ Second most popular model was the Fordor Touring Sedan, which cost $25 more than a slantback. Fordors got pivoting rear-quarter windows.

▲ Early '36 convertible sedans were fastbacks. Because buyers wanted luggage space and a hidden spare tire, it became a "Trunkback" at mid-year.

▲ Aftermarket skirts accented the quick look of a Tudor Touring Sedan.

▲ Space was tight in the back seat of the new DeLuxe club cabriolet.

▲ Only the late convertible Touring Sedan had its spare tire inside the trunk, which had a full-size, top-hinged lid. Center posts were removable.

▲ Many considered the open phaeton more appealing than a convertible sedan, even if it lacked roll-up windows. Cheaper, too, at only $590.

▲ Spencer Tracy, left, Henry Ford, and Ford's chief aide, Harry Bennett.

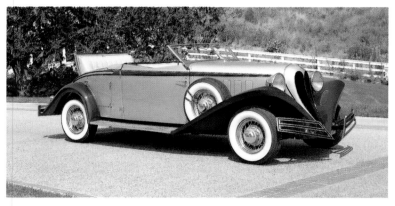

▲ By the time the Brewster coachbuilding firm finished its task, this tapered-grille roadster bore little resemblance to its Ford origin.

▲ Coachbuilders ordinarily worked with classics, but the Brewster firm of New York created one of its most stunning bodies atop the Ford chassis.

▲ Handsome it was, but a DeLuxe convertible sedan was far beyond reach of most—even with Ford's $25 per month financing plan.

▲ Rare even in its day, this specially bodied Brougham Town Car with open chauffeur's compartment came from the Cunningham Motor Car Company of Rochester, New York. Though Ford-based, it was identified as a Cunningham.

▲ Aimed at small business, the sedan delivery was basically a Tudor sedan with rear door and blanked windows. Load space was protected by steel skid strips. Some 7801 were built.

▲ Unlike a standard panel truck, this DeLuxe edition had twin chrome horns, body-color wheels, and more body insulation. The aluminum-finish grille had a different shape than on passenger cars.

▲ Ford V-8 pickups were favorites on America's farms. Half-ton trucks rode the same chassis as passenger cars and adopted the same revisions.

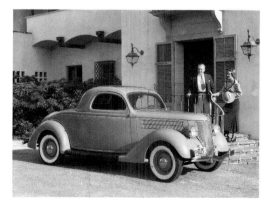

▲ A DeLuxe two-passenger, three-window coupe sold for $570 with a trunk, or $595 with rumble seat. Whitewalls accented its sporty shape.

1937

Streamlined Fords get steel roofs . . . pointed nose inspired by Lincoln-Zephyr

Final year for roadster, first for DeLuxe club coupe

Ford offers choice of 60- or 85-horsepower V-8

25-millionth Ford built

"Battle of the Overpass" on May 26— union leaders beaten by thugs from Harry Bennett's "Service Dept."

1937 Engine Availability

Engines	bore × stroke	bhp	availability
V-8, 136.0	2.60 × 3.20	60	S-74
V-8, 221.0	3.06 × 3.75	85	S-78

Model Breakdown Chart

Model 74—wb 112.0*	Wght	Price	Prod
cpe 5W 2P	2,275	529	43,866
Tudor sdn 5P	2,405	579	*
Tudor T/B sdn 5P	2,415	604	51,332
Fordor sdn 5P	2,435	639	18,541
Fordor T/B sdn 5P	2,445	664	13,976
wgn 4d s/curtains	2,691	744	} 193
wgn 4d glass windows	2,776	764	
Model 78 Standard—wb 112.0*			
cpe 5W 2P	2,496	586	46,481
Tudor sdn 5P	2,616	611	308,446*
Tudor T/B sdn 5P	2,648	638	78,895
Fordor sdn 5P	2,649	671	30,521
Fordor T/B sdn 5P	2,666	696	31,555
wgn 4d s/curtains	2,906	754	} 9,111
wgn 4d glass curtains	2,991	775	
Model 78 DeLuxe—wb 112.0			
rdstr 2-4P	2,576	694	1,250
phtn 5P	2,691	749	3,723
cpe 5W 2P	2,506	659	26,783
cabriolet 2-4P	2,616	719	10,184
club cpe 5W 5P	2,616	719	16,992
club cabriolet 4P	2,636	759	8,001
Tudor sdn 5P	2,656	674	33,683
Tudor T/B sdn 5P	2,679	699	73,690
Fordor sdn 5P	2,671	734	22,885
Fordor T/B sdn 5P	2,696	759	98,687
conv sdn 5P	2,861	859	4,378
sdn 7P	NA	NA	521

*Combined production.

HIGH MILEAGE, LOW PRICE AND A CHOICE OF TWO V-8 ENGINES

Ford V-8 FOR 1937

FORD is making motoring history in 1937 by offering a choice of two V-type 8-cylinder engine sizes in the same big modern car. They give you top performance or top economy, according to your needs.

The 85-horsepower engine provides flashing power and pick-up at low prices, plus greater fuel economy than ever.

The 60-horsepower engine, first developed for Europe, delivers smooth V-8 performance at

speeds up to 70 miles an hour and more miles per gallon than any Ford ever built. It comes in five body types at the lowest Ford prices in years.

Because more than 25 million Fords have been built, because of familiar Ford ideals, people always expect more of a Ford car—and get it.

The 1937 Ford V-8 is unmistakably THE QUALITY CAR IN THE LOW-PRICE FIELD.

▲ Ads touted the "flashing power and pick-up" of the 85-bhp V-8, but praised economy of the V-8/60.

▲ Henry Ford and camera enthusiast Edsel at a new-car press preview at the Dearborn test track.

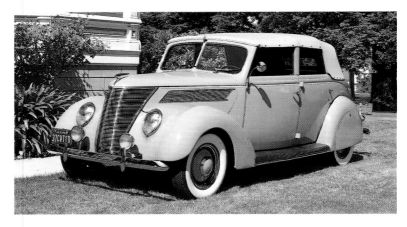

▲ This DeLuxe Convertible Sedan shows off Ford's swept-back vee grille, fuller fenders with faired-in headlamps, and two-piece vee windshield.

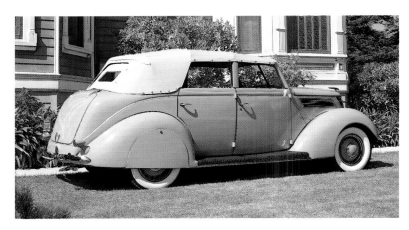

▲ President Roosevelt bought one of the 4378 convertible sedans, with roll-up windows, for his Georgia retreat. Rear ends were curvier for '37.

▲ Tudor "Trunkback" touring sedans came in Standard or DeLuxe trim, with a 136- or 221-cid V-8 engine. Slantback models also had a trunklid.

▲ A Standard woody wagon could have roll-down front windows and sliding glass rear panels, or be equipped with side curtains in back for $20 less.

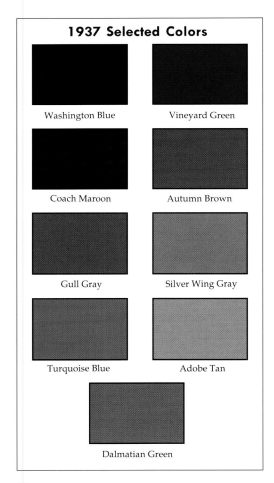

1937 Selected Colors

Washington Blue	Vineyard Green
Coach Maroon	Autumn Brown
Gull Gray	Silver Wing Gray
Turquoise Blue	Adobe Tan
Dalmatian Green	

▲ Standard Fords, like this two-seater coupe, had painted windshield surrounds and a single wiper.

▲ "Factory" skirts added to the speedy look of this DeLuxe Fordor Trunkback sedan, priced at $759.

"Don't worry, lady—we couldn't make the road rough enough to be risky for a Ford!"

BYWAYS ARE HIGHWAYS IN THE NEW FORD V-8

Ford V-8 FOR 1937

THE famous old Ford Model T actually made roads where none existed. And today's handsome Ford V-8 has the same rugged dependability built into every inch of it.

Confidence makes cross-country miles more fun in a Ford. You know you have plenty of responsive power for any situation. You know you'll ride safely and comfortably. So you drive relaxed and arrive rested.

Many factors contribute to Ford comfort. . . . The Center-Poise principle, by which passengers are cradled

near the center of the car and even the back seat is seven inches ahead of the rear axle. . . . High steering ratio. . . . Low center of gravity. . . . Flexible springs and adjustable shock absorbers. . . . Wide seats. . . . And the extra body room made possible by a compact V-type 8-cylinder engine.

With a choice of two sizes of this modern power plant—with new operating economy, the lowest price in years and distinctive features all around—the 1937 Ford V-8 is very definitely THE QUALITY CAR IN THE LOW-PRICE FIELD.

"But officer—when I told you I was just going to get a hat pretty enough for my new Ford, you said yourself THAT wouldn't be easy!"

DISTINCTIVE BEAUTY BORN OF USEFULNESS

Ford V-8 FOR 1937

TODAY's world wants beauty born of usefulness . . . form that follows function . . . lines both pleasing and practical.

By such modern standards, the 1937 Ford V-8 is unmistakably beautiful. It's wide, low, roomy. No horns, headlamps or spare tires break its smooth, clean curves. Every detail, inside and out, contributes to its simple, distinguished design.

There's beauty of another kind in its fine

materials, precision workmanship, faithful service. And there's beauty in its budget figures too!

Both the improved 85-horsepower V-8 engine and the new 60-horsepower V-8 engine provide smooth performance with economy. In fact, the "60" engine, optional in five standard body types, makes possible the lowest Ford price in years and the greatest gas mileage ever built into a Ford car.

▲ Ads pushed this Ford's tie to the "rugged dependability" of the Model T. Hoods now opened "alligator-style," and closed models got all-steel roofs.

▲ Speeders beware! With the bigger V-8 underfoot, a Standard Tudor (Model 78) sedan proved formidable when equipped for police duty. Mechanical brakes now had cable linkage, promoted as "all steel from pedal to wheel."

▲ Pickup truck adopted a two-piece windshield, horizontal-bar grille, and four-inch-longer cargo box (now 73 inches). A rod-actuated tailgate latch replaced the three-strap setup. Price was $470 with the smaller V-8.

▲ Coal was still king, and had to be delivered. Dump trucks came only with an 85-bhp V-8, but other models with 131-inch wheelbase could have either engine. Half- and 1½-ton trucks got a barrel grille and lower headlamps.

1938

Sharp recession sinks economy, after modest recovery in mid-1930s

Ford output tumbles by more than half, to 410,048; Chevrolet again Number One

Industry production falls 40 percent

Ford adopts twin-tier styling policy: DeLuxe models revised, Standard cars keep former DeLuxe body with altered grille

Slantback bodies gone

Henry Ford continues to resist such advances as hydraulic brakes

Henry Ford turns 75 and suffers stroke . . . accepts Grand Cross of the Supreme Order of the German Eagle, from Adolf Hitler

Henry Ford II elected to board on December 19

▲ Henry and Edsel Ford at a River Rouge Plant building site in 1938. The company would have been better off if the elder Ford had passed the reins to Edsel by the 1930s; instead he hung on.

Model Breakdown Chart

Model 82A (wb 112.0)	Wght	Price	Prod
cpe 5W 2P	2,354	595	13,712
Tudor sdn 5P	2,455	640	30,850
Fordor sdn 5P	2,481	685	5,878
Model 81A (wb 112.0)			
cpe 5W 2P	2,575	625	20,347
Tudor sdn 5P	2,674	665	75,267
Fordor sdn 5P	2,697	710	24,409
wgn 4d	2,981	825	6,944
DeLuxe phtn 5P	2,748	820	1,169
DeLuxe cpe 5W 2P	2,606	685	22,225
DeLuxe conv cpe 2-4P	2,679	770	4,702
DeLuxe club cpe 5P	2,688	745	7,171
DeLuxe Tudor sdn 5P	2,742	725	101,647
DeLuxe Fordor sdn 5P	2,773	770	92,020
DeLuxe conv sdn 5P	2,883	900	2,743
DeLuxe sdn 7P	NA	NA	449

▲ Henry Ford interviewed by newsmen at the historic Wayside Inn, South Sudbury, Massachusetts.

◄ Henry Ford, hat to face, leaves the White House after a two-hour luncheon conference with President Franklin D. Roosevelt. Ford's son, Edsel, and spokesman, William J. Cameron, also attended. Ford told the press corps that his meeting with the President was "very pleasant" and the U.S. is "all right and will continue to be all right." Ford and Roosevelt held strongly opposing views, and each usually was quick to criticize the other.

1938 Engine Availability			
Engines	bore × stroke	bhp	availability
V-8, 136.0	2.60 × 3.20	60	S-82A
V-8, 221.0	3.06 × 3.75	85	S-81A

▲ Like other DeLuxe Fords, the fading-away convertible sedan got a longer sloping hood, a heart-shaped grille with rounded corners, and more rounded fenders. Only 2743 were built.

▲ Setting a trend, Standard Fords like this two-seat coupe got a rehash of the prior year's DeLuxe front end. Upper grille bars swept back almost to the cowl, eliminating hood louvers.

▲ Updated in design, a DeLuxe V-8 Fordor cost $60 more than the Standard model. This year's cars looked—and were—heavier. Knobs were recessed, and windshields still cranked out.

▲ Henry and Clara Ford on their patio. Clara for many years annually sat for a photo in this dress.

▲ Every public figure has had a "dingbat" photo taken of himself; here is Henry Ford's.

93

1939

At last, Fords gain hydraulic brakes

Phaeton, club coupe, and convertible club coupe disappear . . . final year for convertible sedan

DeLuxe Fords get bright vertical-bar grille below pointed nose

More than 487,000 '39 Fords built—nearly 90,000 behind Chevrolet and not too far ahead of restyled Plymouth

Chevy leads by 21 percent—648,471 to 532,152—in calendar-year output

Fords displayed at New York World's Fair, in elevated "Road of Tomorrow"

Six-millionth Ford V-8 engine built . . . also 27-millionth vehicle

▲ Dedication ceremony for the "Road of Tomorrow," part of Ford's exhibit at the New York World's Fair. Left to right, Grover Whalen, New York City's official greeter, Henry Ford II, Edsel Ford, Henry Ford, former New York Governor Alfred E. Smith, and New York Mayor Fiorello H. LaGuardia. Henry II recently had been named a company director, and would join the firm next year.

▲ Close to the costliest '39 was the DeLuxe woody wagon—now classed as a car instead of a truck. Only 6155 were built, plus 3277 Standard wagons.

▲ Ford coupes were common sights on the nation's race courses—and in the victory circles. Sponsors were important, even in the 1930s.

▲ Who wouldn't covet a '39 convertible coupe—with skirts yet! Teardrop headlamps sat deep in fenders. Hoods also were deeper and lacked louvers.

▲ Rumble seats were nearly extinct by 1939, and the DeLuxe convertible was the final Ford to have one. Body contours were smooth and sleek.

◄ Everyone knew those twin hoses led to a flathead V-8. A new Ford-built dual-downdraft carburetor helped boost torque of the 221-cid V-8 to 155 lbs/ft, but horsepower stayed at 85. Internal components were strengthened. DeLuxe models got a lower radiator with larger cooling area. Biggest tech news was the Lockheed hydraulic braking system—a Ford "first."

▼ Nearly all other makes had a column-mounted gearshift available, but Ford stuck to the floor lever a little longer. A taller gearbox tower permitted shorter "throws." DeLuxe drivers faced a dashboard with golden grain mahogany finish, twin round gauges, a glove box clock, and grasped a "banjo" steering wheel. Convertibles had Russett leather upholstery.

1939 Selected Colors

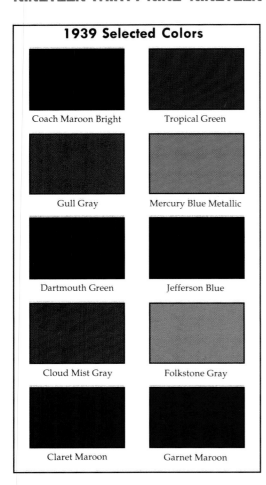

Coach Maroon Bright	Tropical Green
Gull Gray	Mercury Blue Metallic
Dartmouth Green	Jefferson Blue
Cloud Mist Gray	Folkstone Gray
Claret Maroon	Garnet Maroon

▲ Nothing dowdy about Ford's DeLuxe Tudor sedan, which looks ready to pounce. Headlamps were farther apart for '39, no longer alongside the grille. Slim trim strips enhanced the car's graceful profile.

▲ DeLuxe Fords, including this $702 two-seat, five-window coupe, came only with the 221-cid, 85-bhp V-8 standard. Luggage was reached by raising the seatback cushion, or opening the trunklid.

Model Breakdown Chart

Model 92A V-8/60—wb 112.0	Wght	Price	Prod
cpe 5W 2P	2,463	599	*
Tudor sdn 5P	2,608	640	*
Fordor sdn 5P	2,623	686	*

Model 91A V-8/85—wb 112.0	Wght	Price	Prod
cpe 5W 2-3P	2,710	640	38,197
Tudor sdn	2,830	681	124,866
Fordor sdn	2,850	727	28,151
wgn 4d	3,080	840	3,277
DeLuxe cpe 5W 2-3P	2,752	702	37,326
DeLuxe conv cpe 2-4P	2,840	788	10,422
DeLuxe Tudor sdn	2,867	742	144,333
DeLuxe Fordor sdn	2,898	788	90,551
DeLuxe conv sdn	2,935	921	3,561
DeLuxe wgn 4d	3,095	916	6,155
DeLuxe sdn 7P	—	—	192

*Incl. with Model 91A Standard.

1939 Engine Availability

Engines	bore × stroke	bhp	availability
V-8, 136.0	2.60 × 3.20	60	S-92A
V-8, 221.0	3.06 × 3.75	85	S-91A

▲ Ideal for family duties, a DeLuxe Fordor sedan was the choice of 90,551 Ford buyers. Standard Fords also sold well, despite their completely different 1938-style front ends, with smaller hood louvers.

▲ Fender skirts added pizzazz, while flipping the quarter windows allowed plenty of air to breeze through a DeLuxe Fordor. Notice the graceful rear.

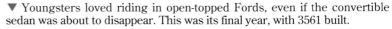

◄ Twin fog and spotlights cost extra on this handsome DeLuxe Fordor, which sold for the same $788 as a convertible coupe. Deep-set headlamps existed this year only. Standards were similar from the windshield back.

▼ Youngsters loved riding in open-topped Fords, even if the convertible sedan was about to disappear. This was its final year, with 3561 built.

▲ Heavy trucks served a variety of duties. This well-equipped engine with "barrel" grille" was ready to fight fires at Ford's own River Rouge plant.

▲ Separately mounted headlamps and a tall barrel-style grille gave Ford trucks little kinship with passenger cars, but both had hydraulic brakes.

1940

War buildup underway . . . Ford starts new Rouge plant to build aircraft engines

European auto branches turn to military output; German Ford under Hitler's control

Striking Ford facelift penned by "Bob" Gregorie, under Edsel Ford

Ford claims 22 "Important Improvements" including "finger-tip" column shift and sealed-beam headlamps

Only 599,175 Fords built in calendar year, versus 895,734 Chevrolets

Last year for V-8/60 engine

Lincoln Continental debuts

Modern Cars for Modern Highways

Watch the FORDS go by!

Through crowded city canyons . . . down busy small-town Main Streets . . . past pleasant country cross-roads . . . *the 1940 Fords are going by!*

Big cars, these—with long, low hoods and flowing lines. . . . *Colorful* cars—with lustrous, lasting enamel baked into the body metal and rustless steel shining bright. . . . *Comfortable* cars—with rich appointments, deep, soft seats and a quiet, restful ride.

 Ten years ago, you couldn't have bought cars so fine at *any* price—

and you would have paid several hundred dollars more for a smooth, sweet-running V-8 engine!

More than 27,000,000 Ford cars—far more than any other make—have gone out to serve the world. The experience gained in building nearly one-third of all the cars ever built contributes to the excellence of today's Ford cars.

The low-priced 1940 Ford V-8 has all the honest value Ford owners have come to expect plus many modern features that make it more than ever The Quality Car in the Low-price Field.

▲ Borrowing a slogan dating from 1907, Ford pushed the '40 model's quality, size, color—and the fact that more than 27 million Ford cars had been built. DeLuxe Fords had sealed-beam headlamps.

▲ Henry Ford cycling on his Dearborn estate, Fair Lane, on his 77th birthday, July 30, 1940.

▲ Wind-in-the-hair fans loved the convertible coupe's racy styling. Ford's $849 ragtop was rather popular when new, with 23,704 built. Note the chevron taillamps. No other open Fords were sold.

▲ Despite American mobilization in case the European war should take an expanded turn, Ford's assembly lines ran at a normal pace in 1940. Here, three Tudors near completion.

▼ Assembled in New Jersey, the 28-millionth Ford was seen at the New York World's Fair.

28,000,000th FORD CAR

ASSEMBLED AT EDGEWATER, N.J.
APRIL 8, 1940

▲ Replacing the club coupe, the five-window business coupe included fold-up jump seats. This DeLuxe sold for $762, while Standards started at $681.

▲ Not quite the snazziest, Ford's $765 DeLuxe Tudor sedan was the most popular model. Styling touches included a crisply pointed hood atop a vee'd grille of delicate horizontal bars, flanked by painted grilles. Vent wings let breezes flow, and their divider strip lowered with the door window.

▲ Business coupes with jump seats soon became known as "opera coupes." Whitewalls gave some extra sass. Hot rodders adored either coupe style, for their lovely body curves and long deck as well as their V-8 potential.

▶ Ads for 1940 focused on the V-8's smoothness, quiet running, and low operating cost. This would be the final year for the unpopular 136-cid V-8. Drivers now grasped a column gearshift and new two-spoke steering wheel.

▲ The promise of an engine that needed no break-in period was no small matter in 1940. Ford claimed the 85-bhp V-8 could be driven 60 mph "the day it's delivered," and need not be "babied." Other ads touted the Gilmore-Yosemite Economy Run, where a Ford V-8 topped its class at 24.92 mpg.

◄ Highest-priced '40 was the DeLuxe station wagon, with only 8730 built. Joints between the maple segments fit snugger this year and displayed more graceful pattern contours, and corner posts had a more rounded look. Both front and rear doors hinged at the front.

▲ Spare tires on the DeLuxe (shown) and Standard wagons moved to the tailgate, tucked within a body-colored cover. Roofs were fabric-topped. Standard wagons had simulated leather interiors, while DeLuxes wore the real thing. Standards kept the 1939-style grille, with painted headlamp housings.

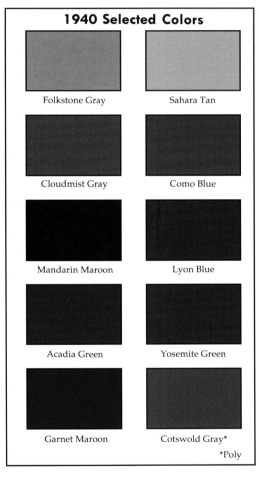

1940 Selected Colors

Folkstone Gray	Sahara Tan
Cloudmist Gray	Como Blue
Mandarin Maroon	Lyon Blue
Acadia Green	Yosemite Green
Garnet Maroon	Cotswold Gray*

*Poly

▲ This handsome sedan delivery shared front-end sheetmetal with DeLuxe passenger cars, whereas pickups adopted Standard fronts. Larger Ford trucks received fresh cab styling, as well as open "Hotchkiss" drive to replace the old torque-tube setup. Many had parallel-spring front suspensions.

Model Breakdown Chart

2A V-8/60—wb 112.0	Wght	Price	Prod
cpe 2-3P	2,519	619	*
bus cpe 4-5P	2,549	640	*
Tudor sdn	2,669	660	*
Fordor sdn	2,696	706	*
01A V-8/85—wb 112.00			
cpe 2-3P	2,763	660	33,693
bus cpe 4-5P	2,801	681	16,785
Tudor sdn	2,909	701	150,933
Fordor sdn	2,936	747	25,545
wgn 4d	3,249	875	4,469
DeLuxe cpe 2-3P	2,791	722	27,919
DeLuxe bus cpe 4-5P	2,831	742	20,183
DeLuxe conv cpe	2,956	849	23,704
DeLuxe Tudor sdn	2,927	762	171,368
DeLuxe Fordor sdn	2,966	808	91,756
DeLuxe wgn 4d	3,262	947	8,730

*Incl. with Model 01A.

1940 Engine Availability

Engines	bore × stroke	bhp	availability
V-8, 136.0	2.60 × 3.20	60	S-02A
V-8, 221.0	3.06 × 3.75	85	S-01A

101

1941

End of Depression in sight—partly due to war buildup

Ford boasts of roomier bodies; wheelbase grows two inches, cars gain weight

Evolutionary redesign features tall grille, minimal running boards

Six-cylinder engine debuts

Three trim levels: no-frills Special, DeLuxe, and Special DeLuxe

Chevrolet's model-year production lead grows even larger—1,008,976 cars to Ford's 691,455

After violent strike, Henry allows union vote—first closed shop in industry

Henry Ford II appointed ensign in Naval Reserve

This is not "A Man's World" by a long shot!

IT MAY BE ENGINEERS with their blue-prints who make the plans to which we build our cars. But more and more it is the women of this country who determine what needs the engineers must meet.

Their influence, of course, is not new to us. It merely grows more and more pronounced.

Women took a hand in car design early in this century, when we shifted the steering wheel from right side to left where it is now.

Women hurried the change along, because until we changed, they sat at the left and had to get out into the street instead of on the curb.

Today more than ten million women in this country have licenses to drive. And it seems fair to state that most of what you see as you walk toward a new car—and much of what you feel as you ride in it or drive—was put there for women, or put there sooner than it would have been without their influence.

It is certain that the changes and improvements made for this year in our Ford cars show the influence of women very clearly.

Check them off and see.—A much bigger car. A much softer ride. A much quieter car. Bigger windows. Easier driving. Increased style. Finer appointments.

No, this is not a man's world, by a long shot. And nothing makes that more clear than the Ford cars at your dealer's right this minute!

Some Ford Advantages for 1941:

NEW ROOMINESS. Bodies are longer and wider this year, adding as much as seven inches to seating width.

SOFT, QUIET RIDE. A new Ford ride, with new frame and stabilizer, softer springs, improved shock absorbers.

GREAT POWER WITH ECONOMY. Ford cars are the most powerful in their price field, and hold records for economy as well as for performance.

BIG WINDOWS. Windshield and windows increased all around to give nearly four square feet of added vision area in each '41 Ford Sedan.

LARGEST HYDRAULIC BRAKES in the Ford price field, give added safety, longer brake-lining wear.

GET THE FACTS AND YOU'LL GET A FORD!

▲ Women's influence on auto design was growing, so Ford hyped roominess, soft ride, and style.

▲ The world's first plastic car, unveiled by Henry Ford at a Dearborn community festival. The vehicle generated nationwide publicity.

▲ Henry Ford takes a hefty whack at the trunklid of his "soybean" sedan (actually plastic), which evolved from experiments with soybeans.

▲ Sportiest Ford was the Super DeLuxe convertible, with powered top.

▲ Gauges sat in a narrow strip, and passengers had plenty of hip room.

▲ Headlamps on this Super DeLuxe Tudor fit flush, with separate parking lights above.

▲ Wider bodies *sans* running boards allowed the Fordor's front seat to widen by seven inches.

▲ Half-ton pickups borrowed front-end styling from the Standard '40 and cost $605 with a V-8.

Model Breakdown Chart

1GA Six—wb 114.0	Wght	Price	Prod
Special cpe	2,870	684	*
Special Tudor sdn	2,975	720	*
Special Fordor sdn	3,020	761	*
DeLuxe cpe	2,947	715	*
DeLuxe cpe, A/S	2,970	746	*
DeLuxe Tudor sdn	3,065	756	*
DeLuxe Fordor sdn	3,100	797	*
DeLuxe wgn 4d	3,395	946	*
Super DeLuxe cpe	2,934	761	*
Super DeLuxe cpe, A/S	2,974	792	*
Super DeLuxe sdn cpe	3,030	833	*
Super DeLuxe conv cpe	3,145	931	*
Super DeLuxe Tudor sdn	3,096	802	*
Super DeLuxe Fordor sdn	3,131	843	*
Super DeLuxe wgn 4d	3,400	998	*
11A V-8—wb 114.0			
Special cpe	2,878	700	9,823
Special Tudor sdn	2,983	736	27,189
Special Fordor sdn	3,033	777	3,838
DeLuxe cpe	2,953	730	33,598
DeLuxe cpe, A/S	2,981	761	12,844
DeLuxe Tudor sdn	3,095	772	177,018
DeLuxe Fordor sdn	3,121	813	25,928
DeLuxe wgn 4d	3,412	962	6,116
Super DeLuxe cpe	2,969	777	22,878
Super DeLuxe cpe, A/S	3,001	807	10,796
Super DeLuxe sdn cpe	3,052	849	45,977
Super DeLuxe conv cpe	3,187	946	30,240
Super DeLuxe Tudor sdn	3,110	818	185,788
Super DeLuxe Fordor sdn	3,146	859	88,053
Super DeLuxe wgn 4d	3,419	1,013	9,485

*Incl. with 11A.

1941 Engine Availability

Engines	bore × stroke	bhp	availability
L-6, 226.0	3.30 × 4.40	90	S-1GA
V-8, 221.0	3.06 × 3.75	85	S-11A

▲ ▶ In theory, six people could squeeze into the new Super DeLuxe sedan coupe, which differed slightly in roofline from the three-passenger coupe shown here. They'd better be friendly, however.

Fords get mild touch-up . . . painted parts replace chrome in "blackout" '42s

Customers clamor for cars, worried that war may come

Within three months of Ford debut, U.S. is at war

Ford visitors' center shut

Civilian car production halted February 10 . . . only 160,432 Fords built

Car rationing begins on March 2 . . . civilian trucks cease production March 3

Gas rationing ordered, effective December 1

▲ President Roosevelt, left, and Henry Ford motor through the Willow Run Bomber Plant.

▲ General "Hap" Arnold, commander of Army Air Forces, and Henry at Willow Run.

◀ Harry Bennett, Henry Ford's chief lieutenant and crony. Picaresque and colorful, Bennett over time became a substitute son to Ford. By the early 1930s he was one of the company's most powerful men, and after Edsel's death in 1943 he all but ruled the firm in the founder's name. Bennett was fired by Henry Ford II in his first act as president on September 21, 1945. The strongman spent the remainder of his life in retirement in Desert Hot Springs, California, and Las Vegas, dying in 1979.

▼ The Ford clan, minus Henry's second and third grandsons, Benson and William Clay, in wartime. Seated are Clara and Henry with Henry II's first daughter, Charlotte, on Mrs. Ford's lap. Standing are, left to right, Henry II, Mrs. Edsel (Eleanor) Ford; an unidentified nonfamily girl; Mrs. Henry Ford II (Anne); Henry's granddaughter, Josephine; and Edsel, already looking wan because of his terminal illness. The photo was taken in Edsel's residence, now a suburban Detroit landmark.

▲ Super DeLuxe wagons used mahogany paneling; DeLuxes wore maple or birch. Rear doors got roll-up glass. Note wide grille and ungainly visor.

▲ A reduced-height frame gave this DeLuxe Fordor a lower stance, while softened springs improved the ride. Both the V-8 and Six rated 90 bhp.

► Half-ton pickups got a new flat-front look with squared-up fenders and vertical-stripe grille—far removed from Ford's passenger cars. Cargo boxes were a little wider, with parallel leaf springs installed. Price: $675 with V-8.

► A longer rear roofline on the still-popular $825 sedan delivery body allowed a 92.5 cubic-foot cargo area. Access was through the rear door. Styling and chassis were taken from '42 passenger cars, with side panels blanked.

▲ Golden Tan leather upholstery went into the Super DeLuxe wagon. Dashboard grain patterns varied by trim level. Note under-dash heater.

Model Breakdown Chart

2GA Six—wb 114.0		Wght	Price	Prod
70C	Special Tudor sdn	3,053	815	3,187
73C	Special Fordor sdn	3,093	850	27,189
77C	Special cpe	2,910	780	1,606
70A	DeLuxe Tudor sdn	3,122	840	*
72A	DeLuxe sdn cpe	3,045	865	*
73A	DeLuxe Fordor sdn	3,141	875	*
77A	DeLuxe cpe	2,958	805	*
79A	DeLuxe wgn 4d, 8P	3,405	1,035	*
70B	Super DeLuxe Tudor sdn	3,136	885	*
72B	Super DeLuxe sdn cpe	3,109	910	*
73B	Super DeLuxe Fordor sdn	3,179	920	*
76	Super DeLuxe conv cpe	3,218	1,080	*
77B	Super DeLuxe cpe	3,030	850	*
79B	Super DeLuxe wgn 4d, 8P	3,453	1,115	*

21A V-8—wb 114.0		Wght	Price	Prod
70A	DeLuxe Tudor sdn	3,141	850	27,302
72A	DeLuxe sdn cpe	3,065	875	5,419
73A	DeLuxe Fordor sdn	3,161	885	5,127
77A	DeLuxe cpe	2,978	815	5,936
79A	DeLuxe wgn 4d	3,420	1,090	567
70B	Super DeLuxe Tudor sdn	3,159	895	37,189
72B	Super DeLuxe sdn cpe	3,120	920	13,543
73B	Super DeLuxe Fordor sdn	3,200	930	24,846
76	Super DeLuxe conv cpe	3,238	1,090	2,920
77B	Super DeLuxe cpe	3,050	860	5,411
79B	Super DeLuxe wgn 4d, 8P	3,468	1,125	5,483

*Incl. with 21A.

1942 Engine Availability

Engines	bore × stroke	bhp	availability
L-6, 226.0	3.30 × 4.40	90	S-2GA
V-8, 221.0	3.06 × 3.75	90	S-21A

1943-1945

Ford contributes mightily to war effort, building planes, Jeeps, trucks—and cars for authorized use

Edsel Ford dies of undulant fever, ulcers, and stomach cancer on May 26, 1943

Henry Ford re-elected president June 1, 1943 . . . Henry II released from Navy July 26, elected vice president December 15—but Harry Bennett is in charge

Several top Ford staffers depart in 1943 . . . Charles Sorensen leaves March 1944

Anne Ford born in 1943

Old Henry finally resigns . . . Henry II is president on September 21, 1945

48 percent of cars in use are seven years old or more

▲ At the huge Willow Run complex, 30 miles west of Detroit, B-24 "Liberator" bombers were built by the hundreds. By the time the plant closed on June 23, 1945, it had turned out 8685 bombers.

▲ Henry Ford looks in charge in this portrait, but the iron hand he'd exercised had weakened.

▲ Forever in his father's shadow, Edsel died at age 50, having revitalized Ford styling.

▲ Even before the U.S. entered the war, Ford was producing war materiel—including gliders that could carry 30 men and their gear. During the war, Ford facilities turned out armored and amphibious vehicles, tanks, gun carriers, and a variant of the Jeep, as well as aircraft.

◀ Edsel's burial at Detroit's Woodlawn Cemetery, May 29, 1943. Left to right are Edsel's parents, Clara, heavily veiled, and Henry, daughter Josephine and her husband, Walter B. Ford, daughter-in-law Edith and Benson Ford. Edsel, the company's president and head in name only, was fully capable of running the firm had he been given the chance. His death from stomach cancer prompted his 80-year-old father to resume the company's presidency.

▲ Both Henrys look pleased as they study a model of the Rouge plant.

▲ After Edsel's death, company leadership was in question. Henry Ford resumed the presidency, but some feared the influence of Harry Bennett, his long-time right-hand man. Worrying that Ford might be unable to honor its wartime contracts, the U.S. Government sent Henry Ford II home from Navy duties. Clara Ford threatened to leave her husband unless he relinquished the corporate reins to his grandson. Grudgingly, the old fellow did so—but not until 1945.

▲ Henry Ford and Vice President Henry A. Wallace before a B-24 "Liberator" bomber.

▲ Henry chats with N.Y. District Attorney Thomas E. Dewey at a publisher's dinner.

Civilian production resumes July 3, 1945, with warmed-over '42 models—a month before V-J Day signals end of war in Pacific

New Fords shown to public on October 26, 1945

Henry Ford II is company president, after failed bid by Harry Bennett

Henry II hires team of "Whiz Kids" to help boost sagging company

Car-starved Americans eagerly grab first postwar Fords, despite $300-$400 price hikes over 1942

Ford builds 70,000 more cars than Chevrolet, yet posts $8.1 million loss

▲ Super DeLuxe Sportsman woody convertible was the sole new model, topping the line at $1982. Styled by Eugene T. "Bob" Gregorie, billed as "two cars in one," it rivaled Chrysler's Town & Country. Maple or yellow birch paneling, with mahogany-veneer inserts, was grafted to steel convertible body. A total of 1209 were built in 1946 (plus 205 Mercury editions).

There's a *Ford* in your future

▶ Henry Ford II needed more than a crystal ball to influence Ford's shaky future. To make a fresh start in this crucial era, he hired 10 Army Air Corps officers, known as the "Whiz Kids." Two of them—Arjay Miller and Robert McNamara—later became Ford presidents; McNamara also served as U.S. Secretary of Defense. Various GM people also moved to Ford.

▲ Frisky even in stock form, Fords gained easy popularity in police fleets. They also attracted the growing pack of hot rodders, who took advantage of the countless hop-up possibilities of the bigger flathead V-8. Parts suppliers soon offered a wonderland of goodies, from dual exhaust headers and twin carbs to high-compression heads and full-race cams.

◀ To get the first postwar Fords to customers as quickly as possible, revisions were kept to a minimum. A new grille wore red stripes in its horizontal bars, and rear deck trim was modified. Instead of the prewar 221-cid V-8, Fords borrowed Mercury's 239.4-cid mill, rated 100 horsepower.

▲ Offered in two trim levels instead of the prewar three, Fords rode a 114-inch wheelbase and carried either the V-8 or a 226-cid L-head six, the latter developing 90 bhp. Far more customers took their Fordor sedans in Super DeLuxe trim than in lower-cost DeLuxe level (92,056 versus 9246). With a V-8 under the hood, the Fordor cost $1322 as a Super DeLuxe, or $1248 in DeLuxe guise. Choosing six-cylinder power saved about $50.

▲ Wearing its fastback body with a bit more grace than Fordor counterparts, the Tudor sedan was the most popular body style, selling for $1260 in Super DeLuxe form. An impressive 238,324 rolled off the line—more than half the total Ford production in a long model year. Nearly four out of five Fords sold were Super DeLuxe, including the $1488 convertible.

▲ While steel remained in short supply, wood for the Sportsman convertible was abundant in Ford's Upper Peninsula forests near Iron Mountain, Michigan, where bodies were built. Fittings included hydraulic window lifts and visor mirrors. Rear fenders and taillights came from the 1941 sedan delivery—necessary to attain proper panel fit. Solid wood blocks were precisely mitered, fitted, and varnished. No two were exactly alike, and all carried a V-8.

◄ Customers for the first postwar Fords faced a familiar symmetrical instrument panel, with below-the-dash heater, matching clock, and easy-to-grasp three-speed column gearshift. Chassis revisions improved ride and braking slightly. Modifications to the V-8 included new pressurized cooling, revived aluminum pistons, and silver alloy bearings for longer life.

109

▲ Six-passenger "coupe sedan" (sometimes known as a close-coupled sedan) came only in upper-rung Super DeLuxe trim, priced at $1307 with V-8 power. Fewer shoppers were interested in single-seat business coupes after the war. Only 22,919 of those were built in 1946, starting at $1074.

▲ Three could squeeze into the front seat of a '46 Ford without pain. Note the pull-out handbrake, a common sight on postwar domestic cars. Ford was one of the first manufacturers to fire up its assembly lines, after the government authorized a return to civilian production in July 1945.

Model Breakdown Chart

6GA Six—wb 114.0*		Wght	Price	Prod
70A	DeLuxe Tudor sdn	3,157	1,136	—
73A	DeLuxe Fordor sdn	3,187	1,198	—
77A	DeLuxe cpe	3,007	1,074	—
70B	Super DeLuxe Tudor sdn	3,157	1,211	—
72B	Super DeLuxe cpe sdn	3,107	1,257	—
73B	Super DeLuxe Fordor sdn	3,207	1,273	—
77B	Super DeLuxe cpe	3,007	1,148	—
79B	Super DeLuxe wgn 4d	3,457	1,504	—
69A V-8—wb 114.0*				
70A	DeLuxe Tudor sdn	3,190	1,185	—
73A	DeLuxe Fordor sdn	3,220	1,248	—
77A	DeLuxe cpe	3,040	1,123	—
70B	Super DeLuxe Tudor sdn	3,190	1,260	—
71	Super DeLuxe Sprtsmn conv	3,340	1,982	1,209
72B	Super DeLuxe cpe sdn	3,140	1,307	—
73B	Super DeLuxe Fordor sdn	3,240	1,322	—
76	Super DeLuxe conv cpe	3,240	1,488	—
77B	Super DeLuxe cpe	3,040	1,197	—
79B	Super DeLuxe wgn 4d, 8P	3,490	1,533	—

*Model Year Production by Body Style (Six/V-8):

DeLuxe

Tudor sdn	74,954
Fordor sdn	9,246
cpe	10,670
chassis	86

Super DeLuxe

Tudor sdn	163,370
Fordor sdn	92,056
sdn cpe	70,826
conv cpe	16,359
cpe	12,249
wgn 4d	16,960
chassis	37

1946 Engine Availability

Engines	bore × stroke	bhp	availability
L-6, 226.0	3.30 × 4.40	90	S-Six
V-8, 239.4	3.19 × 3.75	100	S-V-8

▲ A total of 70,826 Super DeLuxe coupe sedans went to dealers. Twin trim strips decorated '46 trunks. Like Chevrolet, Ford planned a lightweight car. That goal was shelved, but it evolved into the French Vedette.

▶ Panel trucks on 114- or 122-inch wheelbase were slow to emerge, due to shortage of steel panels, but 5539 half-tons were built. Body striping on this 7½-footer wasn't standard.

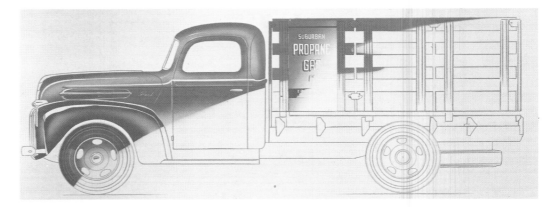

▶ Truck production resumed at the start of 1945. By V-J Day, most models were available (except the ¾-ton). Styling mimicked prewar trucks, and Ford beat Chevrolet in output.

110

1947

Ford announces in March 1946 that no 1947 model will appear that year

Prices rise about $100 due to postwar inflation, then drop— but soar in summer

Auto industry mourns death of Henry Ford I on April 7, 1947, at age 83

Passenger cars facelifted for mid-year debut

Truck production resumes at Highland Park for first time in two decades

Development underway of all-new '49 Ford; light-car project abandoned

Ford earns $64.8 million profit for the year

Groundbreaking for new Research and Engineering Center at Dearborn

Ford's Finer in '47!

Spring's smartest styling... inside and out!

With all these new style features . . . A newly styled instrument panel with big new dials for easy reading . . . new body colors . . . new front-end appearance . . . new stainless steel body molding . . . new hood medallion . . . newly fashioned door handles . . . new wheel rims and hub caps . . . new heavier bumper guards—And many other new features!

Listen to the Ford Show starring Dinah Shore on Columbia Network stations Wed. evenings.

Any way you look at it, today's Ford is by far the smartest car in the low-priced field. One look and you know it's got style . . . from stem to stern . . . inside and out!

There's a FINER *Ford* in your future

▲ "There's a finer Ford in your future," the ads declared. Early '47 Fords changed not at all, but a modest restyle arrived in spring. The horizontal-bar grille lost its red striping, round parking lights went below the headlamps (replacing inboard rectangular units), and decklid trim included a broad plate with Ford lettering. Ford's L-head six was still rated at 90 horsepower, the V-8 at 100.

▶ Much of the world mourned the death of Henry Ford, who earned a permanent spot in the history he'd once described as "more or less bunk." Far more than an industrialist, Ford had become a folk hero—an icon of American culture. In the popular mind, he was virtually credited with "inventing" the automobile. He died on April 7, 1947, at the age of 83.

▶ No one could mistake a wood-paneled Sportsman for an ordinary convertible. Production rose to 2250, despite a $300 price hike to $2282.

▲ This Sportsman wears the facelifted front end introduced at mid-year, as well as a selection of accessories. All 1946 models had used the same wood pattern; for '47, three styles were used. The cheaper ($1740) all-steel ragtop sold at nearly 10 times the rate of its wooden mate.

▲ Woody wagons remained part of the Ford lineup, all in Super DeLuxe trim. Priced at $1972 with a V-8 ($1893 with the six), the four-door wagon held eight passengers. A total of 16,104 were built, slightly under the 1946 figure. Today, they rank among the most popular Ford collectibles.

◀ Henry Ford II stood squarely at the helm, but he faced a formidable job in reviving the company's fortunes. A fresh model was desperately needed. After a flurry of interest in touched-up '42s, shoppers were eager for something different—especially after eyeing the all-new Studebakers and Kaisers.

Model Breakdown Chart

7GA Six—wb 114.0*	Wght	Price	Prod
DeLuxe Fordor sdn	3,213	1,270	—
DeLuxe Tudor sdn	3,183	1,212	—
DeLuxe cpe	3,033	1,154	—
Super DeLuxe Fordor sdn	3,233	1,372	—
Super DeLuxe Tudor sdn	3,183	1,309	—
Super DeLuxe cpe sdn	3,133	1,330	—
Super DeLuxe cpe	3,033	1,251	—
Super DeLuxe wgn 4d, 8P	3,487	1,893	—
79A V-8—wb 114.0*			
DeLuxe Fordor sdn	3,246	1,346	—
DeLuxe Tudor sdn	3,216	1,288	—
DeLuxe cpe	3,066	1,230	—
Super DeLuxe Fordor sdn	3,266	1,440	—
Super DeLuxe Tudor sdn	3,216	1,382	—
Super DeLuxe cpe sdn	3,166	1,409	—
Super DeLuxe conv cpe	3,266	1,740	22,159
Super DeLuxe Sprtsmn conv	3,366	2,282	2,250
Super DeLuxe wgn 4d, 8P	3,520	1,972	—

*Model Year Production by Body Style (Six/V-8):	
DeLuxe	
Tudor sdn	44,523
Fordor sdn	20
cpe	10,872
chassis	23
Super DeLuxe	
Tudor sdn	136,126
Fordor sdn	116,744
cpe sdn	80,830
wgn 4d, 8P	16,104
chassis	23

1947 Engine Availability

Engines	bore × stroke	bhp	availability
L-6, 226.0	3.30 × 4.40	90	S-Six
V-8, 239.4	3.19 × 3.75	100	S-V-8

1948

Ford lingers in financial chaos—but odds for survival look better than in 1945-46

Production slumps in short model year, as company awaits redemption by all-new '49 model

Chrysler ranks second in car production, behind GM

"Bonus Built" trucks debut in January with fresh frontal appearance and simpler F-1 (½-ton) to F-8 (3-ton) nomenclature

Truck production reaches record daily rate

▶ F-1 pickup displays the 1948 restyling. Front fenders were broader and squared-off (matched by back fenders). Door vent windows and one-piece windshields were new.

▲ Financial wizard Ernest R. Breech had been hired from GM's Bendix division in 1946 to become executive vice president. Breech, a mentor to Henry II, was the chief architect of the Ford Company's postwar revival.

▶ Passenger-car changes were few for the short 1948 model year, following Ford's mid-1947 facelift. Ads pointed out the "Lifeguard" body and "Rest-ride" springs, plus availability of either the 95-bhp six or 100-bhp V-8.

▲ Captives of the San Diego police faced a tight fit in the back of this coupe sedan. A civilian version of the close-coupled six-seater cost $1330 with a six or $1409 with the V-8. A total of 44,826 were built.

▲ Man and his "best friend" appear ready for the great outdoors once this '48 Super DeLuxe convertible reaches its destination. One of 12,033 built, the ragtop listed for $1740. Also sold: 28 leftover Sportsman models.

▲ Production of the Fordor sedan still lagged behind Tudors, with 71,358 rolling off the line. That contrasted with 82,161 Super DeLuxe and 23,356 DeLuxe Tudors. Offered only in Super DeLuxe trim, a Fordor sold for $1440 with V-8.

◄ Not everyone realized it at the time, but the era of the wooden-bodied station wagon was drawing to a close, though the body style was ideal for postwar suburban life. Following a flirtation with partly-wood 1949-51 models, Ford's wagons would wear all-steel bodies. Shown here is a 1948 Super DeLuxe four-door wagon, which seated eight and sold for $1972. A total of 8912 wagons were built during the abbreviated model year.

Model Breakdown Chart

87HA Six—wb 114.0*		Wght	Price	Prod
70A	DeLuxe Tudor sdn	3,183	1,212	—
77A	DeLuxe cpe	3,033	1,154	—
70B	Super DeLuxe Tudor sdn	3,183	1,309	—
72B	Super DeLuxe cpe sdn	3,133	1,330	—
73B	Super DeLuxe Fordor sdn	3,233	1,372	—
79B	Super DeLuxe wgn 4d, 8P	3,487	1,893	—
89A V-8—wb 114.0*				
70A	DeLuxe Tudor sdn	3,216	1,288	—
77A	DeLuxe cpe	3,066	1,230	—
70B	Super DeLuxe Tudor sdn	3,216	1,382	—
71B	Super DeLuxe Sprtsmn conv	3,366	2,282	28
72B	Super DeLuxe cpe sdn	3,166	1,409	—
73B	Super DeLuxe Fordor sdn	3,266	1,440	—
76B	Super DeLuxe conv cpe	3,266	1,740	12,033
79B	Super DeLuxe wgn 4d, 8P	3,520	1,972	—

*Model Year Production by Body Style (Six/V-8):

DeLuxe

Tudor sdn	23,356
cpe	5,048

Super DeLuxe

Tudor sdn	82,161
Fordor sdn	71,358
cpe sdn	44,826
wgn 4d, 8P	8,912

1948 Engine Availability

Engines	bore × stroke	bhp	availability
L-6, 226.0	3.30 × 4.40	95	S-Six
V-8, 239.4	3.19 × 3.75	100	S-V-8

▲ From the front, styling of this F-1 eight-foot panel truck was identical to the pickup. Longer, wider, and roomier, it offered 160-cubic-foot cargo capacity and sold for $1412. The sedan delivery, with passenger-car styling, was gone but would reappear in 1952. Not until the 1948 restyle did ¾-ton (F-2) models arrive.

▲ Even higher-rated Ford trucks displayed front-end styling similar to the half-ton F-1 series. Extra-heavy-duty F-7 and F-8 (2½- and 3-ton) models finally joined their smaller brethren, powered by a huge 336.7-cid flathead V-8 that would soon see service in Lincolns, yielding 145 bhp and 225 pounds/feet of torque.

1949

Stunning restyle earns credit for saving Ford Motor Company

New design goes from drawing board to production in just 19 months

By June 1948 debut, Ford has 1.3 million orders for the new model

Tooling claimed to cost three to four times as much as in 1939-40, prompting price hike

Changeover costs $72 million, but Ford ends year with $177 million profit

Ford Division established

Model-year production beats Chevrolet by more than 100,000, topping 1.1 million

Industry production hits record high at 6,253,651

Cutaway views to show "Mid Ship" Ride . . .

. . ."Hydra-Coil" Springs . . .

. . ."Deep Deck" Luggage Locker

Any way you look... inside and out...it's The Car of the Year!

We think you'll agree the '49 Ford has "the look of the year"! Many people say: "It looks like a custom-built automobile!" But the inside will thrill you, too! Seats are sofa-wide! Big "Picture Windows" all around! 57% more luggage space. Two new engines...V-8 and Six! Gasoline savings up to 10% . . . with new Overdrive, optional at extra cost up to 25%. 59% more rigid "Lifeguard" Body. New "Hydra-Coil" Springs. New "Mid Ship" Ride. See the new Ford. It's "the car of the year." At your Ford Dealer's now.

White side wall tires available at extra cost.

There's a New Ford in your future!

'49 Ford

See it today at your Ford Dealers!

▲ Slab-sided in profile, three inches lower, slightly shorter and narrower, the '49 Ford marked a dramatic change from prior models. Ads boasted of "Mid Ship" ride, "Picture Window" visibility, and "Hydra-Coil" front springs. Credit for the car that "saved" Ford goes to design consultant George Walker and engineering vice president Harold Youngren, though early clay rendering (with vertical taillights) came from Holden "Bob" Koto.

▲ Engine changes were subtle, if welcome. In the V-8's cooling system, water now ran directly to the back of the block from a larger radiator—but that didn't cure all of the flathead's cooling ills. New valve guides were meant to cut oil consumption, intake and exhaust systems improved their "breathing," and locked-in main bearings replaced floating units. The L-head six remained, with five fewer horsepower (95) than the V-8.

▲ Lab testing was becoming vital. Here a '49 Ford undergoes cold-weather tests to ensure easy winter startups. The 1949 model sported a host of mechanical revisions. Most notably, the chassis finally switched from antiquated transverse leaf springs with beam axles to independent front coil/parallel leaf rear suspension. Optional overdrive replaced Ford's outmoded two-speed axle, promising fuel savings of up to 25 percent.

115

► Partly because of the rush into production, build quality of the 1949 Ford suffered—despite the efforts of these body-drop workers. Doors, hoods, and trunks tended to fit poorly, prone to dust and water leakage. Squeaks and rattles taunted early buyers. Even the foam seat cushions were flawed. Because customers were so eager, sales didn't suffer, but Ford made a series of running changes to cure the troubles. By 1950, quality was far better.

▼ What a difference a couple of decades can make, as revealed by this shot of a 1949 Custom Fordor sedan posing next to a Model T Ford. A total of 248,176 Custom Fordors were built, priced at $1559. Studebaker influence is evident in the "bullet-nose" grille spinner, though Ford's version floated on a full-width horizontal bar, below F-O-R-D on the hood.

▲ Crowds gathered around a Custom club coupe during the new Ford's press debut at the Waldorf Astoria Hotel in New York City, starting June 8, 1948. The general public saw it 10 days later. In the first three days, more than 28 million folks thronged dealerships for a look. By season's end, 150,254 such coupes would be built, selling for $1511 apiece. Note the external trunk hinges and shortened greenhouse, with extended deck.

▲ A revolving turntable at the Waldorf highlighted four Custom models: station wagon, Tudor, convertible, and club coupe. Preview visitors could not only gape at Ford's flush-fender body, but also inspect the underside. Except on convertibles, the X-member chassis was gone, replaced by a ladder-type frame. Lighter in weight, the new model was livelier, able to scamper to 60 mph in as little as 15 seconds (with overdrive).

The '49 Ford has been awarded the Fashion Academy Gold Medal as the 'Fashion Car of the Year'

It's a Dream Wagon...this '49 FORD
with its heart of steel and the new FORD "FEEL"!

It's steel, steel, steel.

Yes, it's all steel—even under that gleaming molded plywood paneling. It's Ford's famous all-steel "Lifeguard" body, welded into a rigid unit for even greater strength and safety. Truly a heart of steel, wrapped in luxury!

It's sealed against dust.

The convenient easy-opening tailgate—as well as the doors—is completely weather-sealed to guard against annoying dust and water leaks. Here's a feature you'll certainly appreciate, especially when you're touring.

Feel that safety!

This new Ford "Dream Wagon" has two wide doors instead of four narrow doors, a blessing to parents of small children. There's more visibility all around, and the safer, surer stopping of King-Size brakes that are 35% easier acting.

And feel that comfort!

There's plenty of room for eight big people, plus a ride that's in a class by itself—thanks to new "Hydra-Coil" front springs and new "Para-Flex" rear springs that smooth out the roughest roads!

Feel that power!

You'll love this great car's performance . . . it's powered with the famous 100 h.p. Ford V-8, the same type of engine used in America's costliest cars. Why not see the new Ford Station Wagon today? Take the wheel—try the new Ford "Feel"!

"Take the Wheel try the new Ford Feel" There's a New Ford in your future

White side wall tires, optional at extra cost.

▲ Real wood reappeared on the wagon, but the molded plywood adorned an all-steel body. Two "wide" doors instead of four were termed "a blessing to parents of small children."

▲ Still able to carry eight passengers, the Custom wagon sold for $2119 (V-8 only). A total of 31,412 were built.

▲ Ford proclaimed the virtues of the new wagon's "heart of steel," playing down the presence of wood paneling.

◀ Suburban life was becoming a vital element of the American scene, so Ford offered a "Dream Wagon" for that future. Ads touted its Gold Medal as "Fashion Car of the Year."

▲ Taking earlier ads a step further, this year's copy promised "a NEW Ford in your future." Moving the engine forward five inches brought more leg room, with the rear seat pushed ahead of the axle. "Sofa-wide" seats actually were six inches broader, and trunk capacity grew by 57 percent. New "Magic Air" temperature control proved superior to the heaters of many rivals. An "aircraft-inspired" dashboard held gauges in a single backlit unit, while upholstery came in only one hue: medium gray.

▲ Far more customers chose a Custom club coupe at $1511 over the standard edition, which cost $96 less. A total of 150,254 Custom coupes went to dealers, versus only 4170 of its cheaper mates. In addition to a more rakish profile, the '49 had slimmer roof pillars and better visibility.

▲ Most popular of the '49 models was the Custom Tudor, with 433,316 built. Price tag was $1511. George Walker was responsible for rotating the taillights 90 degrees, inserting them into "pods" that merged with a character line along fenders. That helped give the car its distinctive look.

▲ Even though the 1946-48 Sportsman had sold only a few thousand copies, Ford was reluctant to give up the idea of a specialty model. Executives considered a 1949 Sportsman coupe, and possibly a matching ragtop.

▲ At least one club coupe was mocked-up as a potential Sportsman, and a convertible version weighed, but the concept was shelved. Bodyside trim was decorative, not structural, foreshadowing the 1951 Crestliner.

▶ Naturally, an invigorated Ford company needed a fresh convertible. Sportiest of the lot, this Custom ragtop attracted 51,133 customers with its $1886 price tag. A new Chevy arrived several months later than Ford's '49, helping Ford hold its own in sales.

▼ Dropping the top was an eagerly sought facet of the driving experience, especially by the teenagers who were becoming car buyers. Many a teen craved a 1949-51 ragtop, later to be immortalized—along with '49 Mercury coupe—in the James Dean film, *Rebel Without a Cause.*

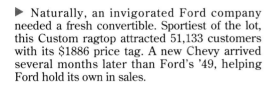

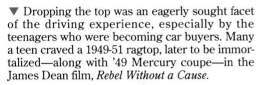

▲ Fully redesigned for 1948, Ford's truck line carried on with little change (as did commercials from Chevrolet and Dodge). This F-3 parcel delivery chassis was new for '49. Most were ranked ¾-ton to 1½-ton with a 104-inch wheelbase and 7800-pound GVW rating, but a 122-inch was available.

▲ This step-van's chrome grille is the only clue to its vintage, as few changes were evident between the 1948 and '49 models. Ford's "Bonus-Built" truck line added 25 models during the year, bringing the total to a whopping 164. Even so, truck output sunk to a three-year low.

▼ Stake trucks came in a number of series. This F-5 was rated 1½ tons, and usually carried the V-8. Like other trucks, it was essentially a carry-over from the 1948 restyle. F-4s were likely to have a six-cylinder engine.

▶ F-1 trucks could now get a heavy-duty three-speed transmission instead of the four-speed. Grille bars lost their earlier red striping, and wheels came in body color. Like passenger cars, the small trucks could have new "Magic Air" heating, drawing fresh air through a cowl vent.

Model Breakdown Chart

Standard—wb 114.0		Wght	Price	Prod
70A	Tudor sdn	2,965	1,425	126,770
72A	club cpe	2,945	1,415	4,170
72C	bus cpe	2,891	1,333	28,946
73A	Fordor sdn	3,010	1,472	44,563
—	chassis	—	—	1
Custom V-8—wb 114.0				
70B	Tudor sdn	2,968	1,511	433,316
72B	club cpe	2,948	1,511	150,254
73B	Fordor sdn	3,013	1,559	248,176
76	conv cpe	3,254	1,886	51,133
79	wgn 2d, 8P	3,543	2,119	31,412
—	chassis	—	—	18

1949 Engine Availability

Engines	bore × stroke	bhp	availability
L-6, 226.0	3.30 × 4.40	95	S-Six
V-8, 239.4	3.19 × 3.75	100	O-V-8

1950

Still lacking a pillarless "hardtop convertible" body style, Ford launches specially trimmed Crestliner

Industry car sales set record—more than 6.33 million for calendar year

Ford slips to second place in car volume at 1.2 million; Chevrolet builds nearly 300,000 more

Ford's market share reaches 24 percent—highest since the mid-Thirties

Interceptor police package debuts, with 110-bhp Mercury engine

FoMoCo name adopted for Ford parts

Clara B. Ford, wife of founder, dies in September

What makes a fine car FINE, Ford HAS !

"Compare Ford with the most expensive car on the road"

Ride for ride, it doesn't take its hat off to anybody! From the new front seat with non-sag springs and buoyant foam rubber cushion, to the hushed "Mid Ship" ride in the "sound-conditioned," heavy gauge steel "Lifeguard" body, you get comfort that's in a class by itself!

"That V-8 whispers while it works"   *"You can hardly hear it"*

Power per pound, ah, there's the secret of that sweet Ford "feel"! The '50 Ford has a new 100 horsepower V-8, the same type engine used in America's finest cars and it runs so very quietly you'll say: "It whispers while it works!"

Safety for safety . . . Ford takes the cup here, too, with those "King Size" Brakes that gentle you down to a full stop with 35% less pedal push! And those big windows give you a "look see" 'fore and 'aft, that's really something to cheer about!

"Nothing touches Ford for looks either"

Fine, yes, fine at low dollar price. Just add up the things you call "fine"—style, comfort, performance, safety—you get 'em all in the '50 Ford plus another little item big cars can't even claim, and that's economy!

"TEST-DRIVE" A '50 FORD before you buy *any* car!

There's a Ford in your future   with a future built in

▲ Billed as "Fifty Ways New . . . Fifty Ways Finer" because of its 50 new features, the 1950 model displayed only a few visible revisions. Most significant improvements lurked beneath the skin, including new "king size" brakes that were claimed to need 35 percent less pedal push. As in 1949, Ford promoted the fact that New York's Fashion Academy again named it "Fashion Car of the Year."

▲ Convertibles continued to use an X-braced frame after other Fords had switched to a ladder-style chassis. Offered only with V-8 power, the Custom soft-top listed for $1948. An impressive 50,299 were produced. Strength and quality of all 1950 models were far better than equivalent '49s, a result of extensive tinkering in the course of the car's first season. Bodies, hoods, doors, and trunklid were tighter and better sealed.

▲ Fordor sedans came in both DeLuxe and Custom trim, priced at $1472 and $1558, respectively. More than three times as many Custom sedans were built. Handling on all models got a boost this year, due to reduced weight up front and the installation of a torsion-bar stabilizer. Road testers managed 21-mpg fuel economy on the highway, with a V-8 and overdrive. As before, Ford proclaimed the comfort virtues of its "Mid Ship" ride.

121

◄ Ford boasted in 1950 that "What makes a fine car FINE, Ford HAS!" And indeed the custom Fordor did have a number of nice features, among them vent windows in the rear doors. This car, which has extra cost whitewalls, grille guard, and exterior sun visor, weighed 3078 pounds.

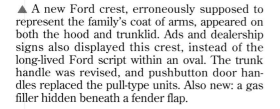

▲ A new Ford crest, erroneously supposed to represent the family's coat of arms, appeared on both the hood and trunklid. Ads and dealership signs also displayed this crest, instead of the long-lived Ford script within an oval. The trunk handle was revised, and pushbutton door handles replaced the pull-type units. Also new: a gas filler hidden beneath a fender flap.

▲ Front-end appearance differed little from 1949, except for the new Ford crest at the front of the hood, which replaced the '49 F-O-R-D block letters. Topping that hood was a more stylish ornament. Lowered parking lights sat in chrome housings that wrapped around the front fenders. Inside, the upgraded Ford held a restyled handbrake lever, larger defroster vents, higher-capacity heater, and wider sun visors. Foam seats were more durable, too—less likely to collapse before their time.

▲ Tudor sedans were the sales leaders in 1950, with 275,360 DeLuxe models and 398,060 Customs built. This contrasted with 35,120 DeLuxe business coupes and 85,111 Custom club coupes. Each weighed a tad over 3000 pounds. Hard to believe, but the 1949-51 cars rode the same 114-inch wheelbase as the far different 1941-48 Fords. Two engines were available again: the 95-bhp, 226-cid six and the 100-bhp, 239.4-cid V-8, both continuing with L-head construction. Overhead valves would not arrive until '52.

▲ Despite inflation, prices changed little for 1950, again starting at $1333 for the DeLuxe business coupe. A Tudor sedan went for $1424 in DeLuxe trim, as shown here, or $1511 in the Custom series. Custom sported a thicker trim piece with C-U-S-T-O-M lettering just behind the front wheels. The 1950 Fords went on the market in November 1949. Though well behind Chevy, Ford's increased car volume was laudable since this model year was four months shorter than 1949's.

▲ Introduced late in the season, the Crestliner was Ford's interim answer to the pillarless hardtop, now sold as a Chevrolet Bel Air. Styling was influenced by famed designer Gordon Buehrig, who dubbed the dashing two-tone scheme akin to the "LeBaron" sweep of the Thirties.

▲ Crestliner's matching vinyl roof accented its convertible look. Rear skirts were standard. A total of 17,601 were built, with standard V-8 and $1711 price ($200 more than a regular Tudor sedan). Chevrolet, meanwhile, sold 76,662 copies of its new hardtop. Crestliners would continue into 1951.

▲ Crestliners came in three body-color combinations: Sportsman Green (chartreuse) with black, maroon/black, and bronze/brown. Matching plush interiors also were two-toned. Front fenders displayed gold-anodized script, and special wheel covers were installed.

▲ Ford officials doubtless were eager to get a true pillarless hardtop onto the market to compete against Chevrolet's Bel Air, but the ladder frame couldn't withstand the strain of topless life. The convertible's X-frame had to be used, and Ford wasn't quite ready for that step.

▲ Ads proclaimed that the V-8 engine "whispers while it works," and it was indeed quieter this year. Improvements included a composition timing gear, revised pistons to cut cold-start "slap," and a new cam to reduce tappet noise. A three-blade fan ran slower than its four-blade predecessor.

▲ Sedans like this Custom Fordor may seem a trifle ordinary now, but were the prize sellers in 1950. Whitewalls added a little flash to the car's profile, and a variety of factory accessories could be added. Ford also continued to offer a two-door station wagon with part-wood paneling. The Country Squire wagon introduced later in the season had a "stowaway" back seat instead of the fully removable version, and sold for $148 less.

1950 Engine Availability

Engines	bore × stroke	bhp	availability
L-6, 226.0	3.30 × 4.40	95	S-all exc C70C, C76
V-8, 239.4	3.19 × 3.75	100	S-C70C, C76; O-others

▲ Canadian Fords, like this Meteor convertible, differed in appearance from U.S. models. A total of 94,161 Ford cars were built in Canada.

Model Breakdown Chart

DeLuxe—wb 114.0		Wght	Price	Prod
D70	Tudor sdn	3,007	1,424	275,360
D72C	bus cpe	2,949	1,333	35,120
D73	Fordor sdn	3,064	1,472	77,888
Custom—wb 114.0				
C70	Tudor sdn	3,015	1,511	398,060
C70C	Crestliner sdn 2d	3,050	1,711	17,601
C72	club cpe	2,981	1,511	85,111
C73	Fordor sdn	3,078	1,558	247,181
C76	conv cpe	3,263	1,948	50,299
C79	Country Squire wgn 2d	3,511	2,028	22,929

▲ Younger enthusiasts may be mystified, but older folks will immediately recognize the F-1 Ford trucks from which Good Humor ice cream bars were sold. Engine improvements were similar to those on passenger cars. Truck output approached the record set in 1929, at 345,801 for the calendar year.

1951

Korean War intensifies; production cutbacks ordered by Washington

Government limits civilian use of zinc, tin, nickel

Passenger-car facelift is more extensive than in 1950, on same basic body

Victoria pillarless coupe joins Ford lineup, attains instant popularity—the only low-price hardtop with a standard V-8

Ford-O-Matic joins the options list

Both Ford and Chevrolet slip in production

Thanks to 1949-51 models, Ford weathers its worst financial crisis since 1921

▲ Custom Fordor sedan gets final inspection. Twin grille "spinners" instead of bigger center unit led the year's changes. Headlamps were slightly "Frenched." Chrome trim strips atop rear character line merged into new twin-point taillights. Side trim on Custom models now wrapped around the rear.

1951 Engine Availability

Engines	bore × stroke	bhp	availability
L-6, 226.0	3.30 × 4.40	95	S-all exc 60, 70C, 76
V-8, 239.4	3.19 × 3.75	100	S-60, 70C, 76; O-others

▼ Over a million Fords were shipped for '51, including these three Customs: convertible, Victoria, and Tudor. Output sunk by some 200,000 units in a slow year for the industry. The "seller's market" was fading fast.

Model Breakdown Chart

DeLuxe—wb 114.0		Wght	Price	Prod
70	Tudor sdn	3,043	1,417	146,010
72C	bus cpe	2,979	1,324	20,343
73	Fordor sdn	3,102	1,465	54,265
Custom—wb 114.0				
60	Victoria htp cpe	3,188	1,925	110,286
70	Tudor sdn	3,043	1,505	317,869
70C	Crestliner sdn 2d	3,065	1,595	8,703
72	club cpe	3,015	1,505	53,263
73	Fordor sdn	3,102	1,553	232,691
76	conv cpe	3,268	1,949	40,934
79	Country Squire wgn 2d	3,530	2,029	29,017

▲ Styled by Gordon Buehrig, the dashing Custom Victoria hardtop sold for $1925 ($24 less than a convertible). Rivaling Chevy's Bel Air and Plymouth's Belvedere, 110,286 were built. Note wraparound back window.

▲ A V-8 again was standard in the convertible, which sold for $1949. A total of 40,934 found customers, even in this sluggish year.

▲ Handsome "Safety Glow" dashboard featured an asymmetrical layout and key-type starter. No-sag springs offered "Automatic Posture Control."

▲ For its final season, the Crestliner's chrome and two-tone color break were revised. Only 8703 were built, priced at $1595, its role having been usurped by the Victoria. Five colors were listed, including all-black.

▲ Participating in the 1951 Mobilgas Economy Run proved to be a test of endurance as well as frugality, as the contestants trekked through the desert southwest. Even with Ford-O-Matic, a V-8 could manage 18 mpg.

▲ "Country Squire" script in the doors identified the sole Ford station wagon, priced at $2029 and again wearing wood paneling. Output climbed to 29,017 for the model year. Engines had the same ratings, but enjoyed various internal modifications. Optional three-speed Ford-O-Matic had been developed with Warner Gear and cost an extra $159 (about $70 more than overdrive). Testers ranked it smoother than Chevy's two-speed Powerglide. Starting in Low shaved a second from 0-60 mph.

▲ Custom club coupe and DeLuxe business coupe (shown) weren't the most popular models, but continued to attract cost-conscious customers.

▲ DeLuxe models lacked the Custom's chrome bodyside spear and windshield moldings. This Fordor cost $1465 and sold 54,265 copies.

▲ Fordors were at home in suburbs, but a sedan could zip to 60 mph in 18.9 seconds with Ford-O-Matic—faster than a manual-shift Chevy.

▲ Both appearance and utility of light-duty trucks got attention, for the first time since 1948. In addition to aggressive styling, a wider cargo box with wood floor went into this F-1 pickup, which sported a tighter-sealed tailgate and larger back window. A total of 117,414 were built.

▲ Dual wipers became standard on F-1 models, including this panel truck. Flanked by headlamps, a bold triple-bullet grille sat within a full-width opening in reshaped fenders. New bumpers went on F-1 to F-3 trucks. "Five Star Extra" options added chrome moldings and upgraded interiors.

1952

Fords get second restyle in three years—Chrysler and GM field facelifted '51s

Wheelbase grows an inch, to 115

Overhead-valve, 215.3-cid "Mileage Maker" six-cylinder engine debuts

New Fords come in three series, 11 models

Crestline series includes Victoria hardtop, Sunliner convertible, Country Squire wagon—all with V-8

All-steel station wagons join lineup, including Courier sedan delivery

Ford drivers face new "Power-Pivot" suspended brake and clutch pedals

Korean conflict limits auto production

Only 671,733 cars built, down from 1,013,381—but Chevrolet suffers similar drop

New higher compression! You get it in both the new 101-h.p. Mileage Maker Six, with free-turning overhead valves, and in the famous 110-h.p. Strato-Star V-8. Both engines have the Automatic Power Pilot, so they deliver all their "go" on regular!

New Flight-Style Control Panel—one of the many quality features of Ford's Coachcraft Bodies—blends into the doors in a sweeping curve. Controls are easier to reach and instruments are easier to read.

New Power-Pivot Pedals are suspended from above! They're easier to operate. They give the driver much more foot space—eliminate drafty holes in the floor.

New Full-Circle Visibility really lets you see where you're going and where you've been. You have the safety advantages of a huge one-piece windshield and a car-wide rear window plus side windows that are picture-window big.

Ford's first with the newest!

It's the Ablest Car on the American Road

That rear window is as wide as the car. Makes it easier to park.

"Test Drive" it today at your Ford Dealer's.

Once again Ford's *first* . . . first with the newest in its price class . . . first to meet the widest range of motorists' needs. The 1952 Ford is available in more models and in more color and upholstery combinations than any other car in its field. In addition, it is the only low-priced car to offer three drives: Fordomatic, Overdrive, and Conventional. Your Ford Dealer invites you to "Test Drive" a '52 Ford today. You'll agree it's the ablest car on the American road! Yes, you can pay more, but you can't buy newer or better!

White sidewall tires (if available), Fordomatic, and Overdrive optional at extra cost. Equipment, accessories and trim subject to change without notice.

Ford's new Center-Fill Fueling cuts down spillage.

New Center-Fill Fueling makes gassing-up convenient from either side of the pump. With no long filler pipe in the way, the luggage compartment is a suitcase bigger. And the rear license plate is spring-mounted to conceal the gas cap!

▲ Billed as "Ablest car on the American road," the fully restyled '52 Ford featured a "Flight-Style" instrument panel, "Full-Circle" visibility with curved one-piece windshield, and "Coachcraft" body. The 101-bhp, 215.3-cid "I-Block" six could nearly keep up with a Strato-Star V-8, now rated 110 bhp.

▲ All-new styling and some tempting engineering innovations helped give Ford a leg up on the competition. Star of the '52 lineup was this Sunliner convertible, part of the new upper-rung Crestline series. Cutbacks due to the Korean War helped keep production down to only 22,534.

▲ Portraits of Henry Ford I and son Edsel over-look a meeting of top decision-makers (left to right): J.R. Davis (vice president), T.O. Yntema, Benson Ford (general manager, Lincoln-Mercury), J.S. Bugas, E.R. Breech (executive vice president), Henry Ford II (president), D.S. Harder, L.D. Crusoe (general manager, Ford Division), and W.T. Gossett (general counsel).

▲ Ford had come a long way since Henry the elder created his Quadricycle (pictured here with grandson William Clay Ford) in 1896. Even more changes would be arriving soon. The two-decade-old flathead V-8, so beloved by hot rodders, was about to expire, replaced by a cutdown of the overhead-valve V-8 that went into '52 Lincolns. Henry I's eldest grandson, Henry Ford II, now served as president. His brother Benson headed Lincoln-Mercury.

▲ A 1952 Customline Tudor sedan appears to pass inspection, ready to be whisked off to a dealer. This Tudor was one of 175,762 built, making it the second best seller behind the Customline Fordor. Clean, fresh styling helped conceal the new model's rather boxy, upright profile. A single spinner was installed in the new grille, at the center of a slotted horizontal bar. Parking lights had a similar shape, so onlookers could be excused for considering it a triple-spinner front end. Deeply "Frenched" headlights (a notion borrowed from hot rodders and customizers) were another detail that added pizzazz. Fordo-matic ($170) went into nearly one-third of Fords. Overdrive added an extra $102.

▲ One of the most popular '52 Fords—then and now—was the Crestline Victoria hardtop, of which 77,320 were produced. Offered only with V-8 power, this Victoria exhibits an intriguing selection of accessories, including dual spotlights, fender skirts, and full-disc hubcaps. Chrome strip atop the rear side sculpture could be dealer- or owner-installed.

▶ Clean, trim styling was evident on Ford's front end as well as its profile. As in 1949-50, the grille consisted of a center "spinner," but it now rode a slotted bar. Priced at $1925, the Victoria hardtop cost $102 less than a real convertible. Like other '52 cars, Fords were criticized for "Korean War chrome," which wore through after a few polishings.

1952 Engine Availability

Engines	bore × stroke	bhp	availability
I-6, 215.3	3.56 × 3.60	101	S-all exc 79C, Crestline (ohv)
V-8, 239.4	3.19 × 3.75	110	S-79C, Crestline; O-others

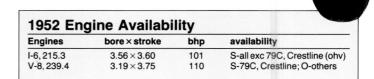

◀ Police fleets had long been partial to Fords. This '52 "Radio Patrol" car (V-8 powered, naturally) did its duty for the Houston police. Strangely enough, it was a Tudor rather than a Fordor, and a mid-range Customline instead of the usual cheaper Mainline. Police Fordors, logically enough, typically contained a mesh screen between front and back seat, to keep captives secure. Mainline sedans for civilian use sold for $1485 and $1530, but weren't nearly as popular as better-trimmed Customlines.

▲ Ford owners had plenty of opportunities to dress up their cars, both before and after purchase. This '52 Sunliner ragtop sports chromed rocker panel moldings and wheel trim rings. No doubt about the underhood contents with that big V-8 emblem circling the decklid's Ford crest. Overdrive was still popular, evidenced by script in the decklid's corner.

▶ Without all the doodads that decorated this example, a Crestline Sunliner convertible sold for just $2027, and 22,534 were built. Styled by Bob Maguire and staff, the '52 displayed a boxy lower body, with fenders roughly the same height as hood and deck. Modestly bulged rear fenders relieved the slab-sided look and, on upper models, carried airscoop-like trim.

Model Breakdown Chart

Mainline—wb 115.0		Wght	Price	Prod
59A	Ranch wgn 2d	3,212	1,832	32,566
70A	sdn 2d	3,111	1,485	79,931
72C	bus cpe	3,035	1,389	10,137
73A	sdn 4d	3,190	1,530	41,277
Customline—wb 115.0				
70B	sdn 2d	3,111	1,570	175,762
72B	club cpe	3,116	1,579	26,550
73B	sdn 4d	3,190	1,615	188,303
79C	Country Sedan wgn			
	4d, 6P	3,617	2,060	11,927
Crestline—wb 115.0				
60B	Victoria htp cpe	3,274	1,925	77,320
76B	Sunliner conv cpe	3,339	2,027	22,534
79B	Country Squire wgn			
	4d, 8P	3,640	2,186	5,426

◀ Only the Customline Fordor sold better than its Tudor mate, pictured here. A total of 175,762 Tudors were produced, versus 188,303 Fordors. The price difference between the two was only $45. A nicely appointed club coupe also was part of the Customline series. Many Customlines (and Mainlines) were sold with the new ohv 215.3-cid six, rated at 101 bhp. Ford's new "K-bar" frame had five cross members welded to box-section side rails, for added rigidity.

131

▲ Though called the "Big '52," the freshly styled Ford actually looked a trifle smaller than its predecessor, despite adding an inch to the wheelbase (now 115 inches). Ads described the car as "new from the road up," promoting its longer rear springs, wider tread, and stronger K-bar frame.

▲ Station-wagon volume jumped sharply, to 49,919 units, with new all-steel bodies. Pictured here is the mid-level, six-passenger Customline Country Sedan. The Country Squire, with simulated-wood decal inserts, was the most costly Ford but could carry eight. Cheapest: the two-door Ranch Wagon.

Model Breakdown Chart

Mainline—wb 115.0		Wght	Price	Prod
59A	Ranch wgn 2d	3,212	1,832	32,566
70A	sdn 2d	3,111	1,485	79,931
72C	bus cpe	3,035	1,389	10,137
73A	sdn 4d	3,190	1,530	41,277
Customline—wb 115.0				
70B	sdn 2d	3,111	1,570	175,762
72B	club cpe	3,116	1,579	26,550
73B	sdn 4d	3,190	1,615	188,303
79C	Country Sedan wgn			
	4d, 6P	3,617	2,060	11,927
Crestline—wb 115.0				
60B	Victoria htp cpe	3,274	1,925	77,320
76B	Sunliner conv cpe	3,339	2,027	22,534
79B	Country Squire wgn			
	4d, 8P	3,640	2,186	5,426

▶ This 1952 rendering demonstrates that Ford designers were looking ahead, in this case with a van-type vehicle. Note the lack of A-pillars, the headlights tunneled into the "bumper," the windshield-mounted crest, and the step plate for entry into the cab. The air scoop just ahead of the rear wheel suggests that this was meant to be a rear-wheel-drive vehicle.

▲ Middle-of-the-road choice for a Ford shopper in '52 might have been this Customline club coupe, but it sold far fewer copies than Customline sedans. Only 26,550 were built, versus 364,065 sedans. With no extra-cost accessories, the price was a modest $1579. Options included whitewall tires, windshield washers, an electric or spring-wound clock, DeLuxe or Custom radio, rocker panel trim, and a MagicAire heater. Ford promised more color combinations, inside and out, than any other low-price car. As hardtops gained popularity in the 1950s, the pillared coupe body—once a popular selection for couples and small families—rapidly lost favor.

▲ Bargain hunters who weren't enthralled with chrome could elect the Mainline Tudor, with bare rubber moldings and an alluring $1485 price tag.

▲ Round taillights in square deck were a Ford hallmark through 1957. These initial versions were solid. Fuel filler behind license plate was new.

▲ Changed little this year, the F-1 pickup—with heavy-looking painted grille—sold for $1425 and could have either the ohv six or flathead V-8.

▲ Ford offered no equivalent to Chevrolet's Carryall, but Marmon-Herrington converted F-1 panel trucks into the four-wheel-drive Ranger.

133

1953

Ford celebrates 50th anniversary in June—promoted on TV's Ed Sullivan Show

Ford completes one of most dramatic comebacks ever

Flathead V-8 enters its final season

Cars get modest facelift

Korean truce signed—government eases auto production allocations

"Blitz" begins: To build sales against GM, factory forces cars on dealers, whether ordered or not

Ford production comes within 100,000 of Chevy's—nearly 1.25 million built

Ford six with overdrive wins class in Mobilgas Economy Run, at 27.03 mpg

Trucks get biggest change in two decades, including available automatic transmission

▶ The styling process in the '50s was a long and arduous one, inevitably beset with numerous detours before the final lines were firmed up. This is evident in the posted drawings and partial clay model of the next Ford. Sketches and pen-and-ink renderings started off the procedure, which progressed to clay scale models, larger models, and full-size prototypes. "Lead time," the period from idea to finished product, typically ran three years.

▲ Both automakers and the public loved their "dream cars," and these futuristic 1953 editions strongly influenced Ford styling. Henry Ford II (foreground) stands next to the black Continental "Nineteen fifty X" (195X), which stood 56.7 inches tall on a 123-inch wheelbase and contained a phone and dicta-phone, as well as automatic jacks. Brothers William Clay and Benson show off the red Mercury XL-500 with similar-size fiberglass body, featuring pushbutton transmission controls and an all-glass roof. By now, Henry II had gained a firm reputation as a manager—partly as a result of his top-notch staff.

▶ Most glamorous of the '53 offerings was the Crestline Sunliner convertible, which cost $2043 with standard V-8. Fordomatic added $184. Even though changes were limited to details, the new Ford seemed to have a fresh face. Revisions included a new bullet-style grille on a slimmer, notched crossbar; rectangular parking lights; and twin-section taillights. Horizontal spears went on rear fender bulges of Crestlines and Customlines.

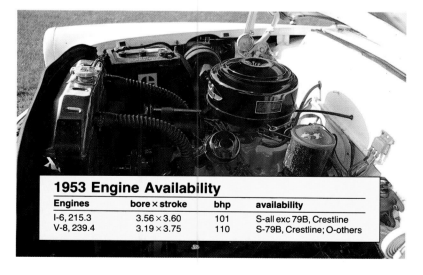

▶ In its Golden Anniversary year, Ford was chosen to pace the Indianapolis 500 race. William Clay Ford, youngest grandson of the founder, drove this specially trimmed Sunliner Pace Car. A limited number of Pace Car replica convertibles were offered for sale. This one sports two popular add-ons: rear fender skirts and a "Coronado" dummy continental kit.

▼ After more than two decades under Ford hoods, the flathead V-8 was about to fade into history. Standard on Crestlines and the Country Sedan, it again developed 110 horsepower. Engines were nearly silent beneath fiberglass-insulated, newly counterbalanced hoods. Two notable options appeared: "Master Guide" power steering ($125) and power brakes ($35).

1953 Engine Availability

Engines	bore × stroke	bhp	availability
I-6, 215.3	3.56 × 3.60	101	S-all exc 79B, Crestline
V-8, 239.4	3.19 × 3.75	110	S-79B, Crestline; O-others

▲ Except for extra trim around the knobs that flanked the semicircular speedometer, Ford's dashboard showed no change. All steering wheel hubs held a "50th Anniversary 1903-1953" commemorative horn medallion.

135

▲ Chrome grille "teeth" identify the DeLuxe cab on this F-700 dump truck, which also had extra comfort features. This year's "Driverized" cabs had taller greenhouses with greater glass area. Note the squared-up hood and fenders, and the double-bar grille with outboard headlamps.

▲ Ford didn't overlook its heavy-duty-size truck line, including ... g Job" C-700, which displayed a front end similar to light-duty models. Cab-forward trucks had a stubby, boxy hood, with a functional air slot above the grille. All manual transmissions now had synchronized gears.

1954

"Y-Block" overhead-valve V-8 replaces long-lived flathead—horsepower race begins in earnest

Ford becomes first low-price car with ball-joint front suspension

Skyliner debuts with tinted Plexiglas roof panel

Model-year production of 1,165,942 beats Chevrolet by 22,381—new V-8 engine gets the credit

Trucks gain sales, earn 29 percent market share

Nash and Hudson merge; so do Studebaker and Packard

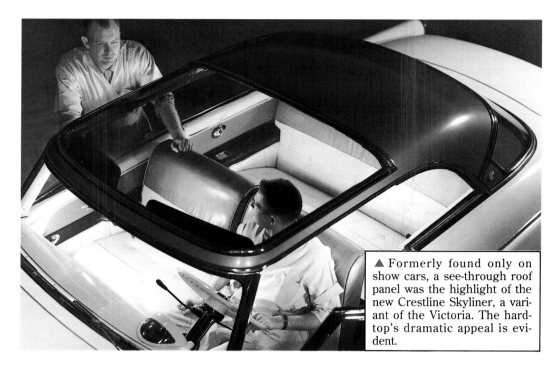

▲ Formerly found only on show cars, a see-through roof panel was the highlight of the new Crestline Skyliner, a variant of the Victoria. The hardtop's dramatic appeal is evident.

The Ford Sunliner

Nearly twice as many people buy Ford Sunliners as any other convertible. Why? Because they appreciate that extra "something" that a Ford Sunliner gives them. Part of this extra "something" is sheer beauty. Part is the instant response... the smooth silky "Go" of Ford power. Ford, you know, is the only car in its field that offers a V-8 engine. Then, too, there's the roadability and "solid" feel that only Ford's Ball-Joint Front Suspension can provide.

These FORDS top the Best-Seller list

Worth More when you buy them ...
Worth More when you sell them

The Ford Skyliner

For the first time ever in Ford's field, you can own a "hardtop" with a transparent roof! And the sweeping beauty of this new type of car is only a clue to what lies within! Interiors are either nylon or nylon-vinyl combinations ... tailored to a decorator's taste. And you can have the most advanced optional power assists. Only Ford in its field offers power steering, power brakes, power windows *all around*, a 4-way power seat and Fordomatic Drive.

The 4 Ford Station Wagons

More people buy *Ford* station wagons than any other make! One reason is Ford's choice: two 6-passenger Ranch Wagons, and the 8-passenger Country Sedan and Country Squire. But, more important, Ford has proved that station wagons can be beautiful and comfortable—as well as completely *practical*. All Ford station wagons are noted for the ease with which they can be converted from "utility" cars to passenger cars. V-8 or Six—Ford is your best station wagon buy.

Your Ford Dealer cordially invites you to come in for a Test Drive

▲ Ford's crest fronted hoods of all passenger models, which gained a subtle facelift. Inside, "idiot lights" replaced oil and amp gauges.

▶ Hot sellers or not, dealers often received more '54 Fords than they bargained for. To move them, many advertised prices "below cost" and adopted tactics that prompted investigation.

▶ Though green-tinted, the Skyliner's roof brought complaints of excess heat on sunny days. A snap-on sunshade helped. Ford ads praised it immodestly, promising "freshness of view" and "vast new areas of visibility." The see-through sold for $2164, with 13,344 built.

Model Breakdown Chart

Mainline—wb 115.5		Wght	Price	Prod
59A	Ranch Wagon 2d	3,399	2,029	44,315
70A	sdn 2d	3,147	1,651	123,329
72C	bus cpe	3,082	1,548	10,665
73A	sdn 4d	3,203	1,701	55,371
Customline—wb 115.5				
59B	Ranch Wagon 2d	3,405	2,122	36,086
70B	sdn 2d	3,160	1,744	293,375
72B	club cpe	3,141	1,753	33,951
73B	sdn 4d	3,216	1,793	262,499
79B	Country Sedan wgn			
	4d, 6P	3,574	2,202	48,384
Crestline—wb 115.5				
60B	Victoria htp cpe	3,245	2,055	95,464
60F	Skyliner htp cpe	3,265	2,164	13,344
73C	sdn 4d	3,220	1,898	99,677
76B	Sunliner conv cpe	3,292	2,164	36,685
79C	Country Squire wgn			
	4d, 8P	3,624	2,339	12,797

◀ Dubbed "Y-Block" because of its cross-sectional shape, the overhead-valve V-8 stemmed from a project that mandated a single basic design for all corporate engines. Displacing 239.4 cid (same as the flathead), it developed 130 bhp.

▲ Ragtops now sold for $2164—exactly the same as the "bubble-top" Skyliner. All grilles, hubcaps, and minor trim were revised slightly. The tri-spinner grille/parking light setup was similar to 1952's, along a more complex slotted bar.

▲ Sunliner convertible displays some of the touch-ups granted to the top-ranked Crestline series, namely new badges on rear quarters and triple hashmarks ahead of rear wheels. Output slipped a bit to 36,685, but stood far ahead of the new Skyliner hardtop. Sunshine fans obviously preferred their rays *sans* filtering. Power windows and seats were now optional.

▲ Top seller for 1954 wasn't a fancy Skyliner or Sunliner, but this practical Customline Tudor sedan, which lured 293,375 buyers. Both Customlines and Crestlines displayed a nearly full-length stainless steel bodyside molding, with a triangular dip to the rear of front doors. Ford shoppers got a lot of value for $1744 (with the 115-bhp six).

▲ Ranch Wagons now came in two trim levels: Mainline and Customline. Ball-joint front suspension eliminated a dozen grease fittings.

▲ This Victoria hardtop sold almost as many copies as the new Crestline sedan, despite $2055 price. Wheelbases grew half an inch.

▲ With whitewalls and a radio, a Courier could make delivery chores a pleasure. The standard six grew to 223 cid, adding 14 horsepower.

▲ Mainline Tudor was available as a sedan with back seat, or a no-frills business coupe.

▲ Country Squire prototype shows elements of '55 models, but lacks wraparound windshield.

▲ This 1954 "trim sample car" shows some of the design ideas under consideration by Ford. Note the hood scoop and side trim.

1954 Engine Availability

Engines	bore × stroke	bhp	availability
I-6, 223.0	3.62 × 3.60	115	S-all exc 79B
V-8, 239.4	3.50 × 3.10	130	S-79B; O-others (ohv)

▶ Even at the height of Fifties excess, no production auto wore fins nearly as tall as those on Ford's FX Atmos show car. Dual spears protruding from the front looked terribly threatening.

▼ FX Atmos

▲ Is it a fighter plane? A spaceship? Ford's bubble-topped "Future Experimental" FX Atmos could seat three, but contained no engine. Central driver would steer with handgrips, watching a radar screen. Ford claimed engineering had not been permitted to interfere with Atmos styling.

1955

Two-seat Thunderbird bows—sells 16,155 first-year copies to Corvette's 674

Full-size Fords get major facelift, rakish look

Fairlane replaces Crestline as poshest Ford

Crown Victoria adopts "basket-handle" roofline

Tubeless tires standard

Industry sales hit record 7.17 million— Ford tops 1.4 million

Model-year car output highest since 1923, yet ¼ million below Chevy

Ford earns record $437 million profit

Trucks get 30 percent of market—a postwar high

Robert S. McNamara becomes Ford general manager

▲ In June 1953, stylist William P. Boyer submitted this drawing of a "Ford sports car" with "competition windscreen." For 1955, it would evolve into the Thunderbird two-seater, whose grille and overall appearance wound up surprisingly similar. Corvette's debut in 1953 spurred production.

▲ Ford never called its instantly successful T-Bird a sports car. Unlike Corvette with its drafty side curtains, this "personal" two-seater had roll-up windows and a selection of power extras, aimed at luxury-minded buyers.

◀ Henry Ford II appears happy with the Thunderbird he needed to match Chevy in every market segment. A wood mock-up appeared at the Detroit auto show early in 1954, and production began in September. Some 300 names were considered, including Sportsman and Coronado.

▲ T-Bird's mesh grille and hooded headlamps were related to big Fords, as were taillights and the shape of upper rear fenders, though the two-seater rode a 13.5-inch shorter wheelbase. A removable hardtop was standard. Twin exhausts exited through bumper guards. Note wire-pattern wheel covers.

▲ Thunderbird's 292-cid V-8 with 8.5:1 compression and four-barrel carburetor developed 193 bhp with a stick, or 198 with automatic.

▲ Main instrument pod on the Thunderbird's dash was flanked by tachometer and clock. Manual and automatic transmissions used a floor selector. A total of 16,155 first-year 'Birds were built, priced at $2944.

▲ This early prototype looks close to final production T-Bird. Along the way, stylists discarded such features as a bolt-on hardtop (patterned on the coming Continental Mark II), canted fins, and an eggcrate grille.

▲ Marketers sometimes get overly eager. Two early Thunderbird ads showed sweepspear side moldings—kin to those on the new Fairlane—but those were dropped in production. Early prototypes wore chromed headlamp bezels.

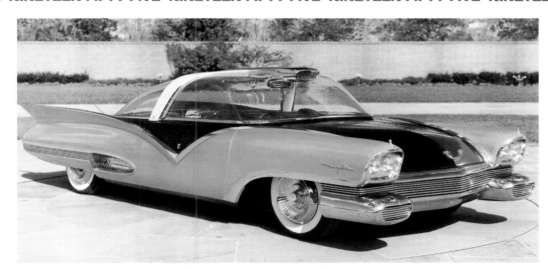

◄ Ford delayed the auto-show appearance of its Mystere dream car, so rivals wouldn't get any ideas. A gas-turbine rear engine was to provide the power. Variants of the roof band, sweepspear and two-toning were used on '55s. The vast lift-up windshield never happened.

▼ The eight-passenger Country Squire was Ford's most costly wagon at $2392, and sold in smallest numbers. The lineup also included twin Ranch Wagons and Country Sedans, of which more than 106,000 were built. Ford beat Chevy in wagon volume. Fuel mileage could disappoint.

▲ Chrome "basket handle" across the new Crown Victoria's roof concealed its origin as a two-door hardtop. Crown Vics had a flatter roof, longer sloped pillars, and less rear-window curvature than regular Victorias.

▼ The forward-raked band over the roof gave a Crown Vic the appearance—but not the structure—of a rollbar. Price was $2202 plain, or $70 more with a Plexiglas roof insert.

▲ A Fairlane Club Sedan cost $113 more than a comparable Customline two-door, and sold considerably fewer copies. Ford's standard I-Block six added five horsepower (now 120). Optional Fordomatic added a "speed-trigger" kickdown into Low gear, which cut three seconds from 0-60 times.

▲ Most Fairlanes, like this $1914 Club Sedan, came with the 272-cid "Trigger-Torque" Y-Block V-8, which whipped up 162 bhp. Bold moldings curved down from above the Fairlane headlamps, dipping at A-pillars before continuing straight back. With automatic, 12 mpg was likely around town.

▲ Fairlane usurped the Crestline as top-dog series—and became the hottest seller, with 626,250 built. Victoria hardtop volume came to 113,372. These Fords were plagued by squeaks, rattles, ill-fit doors, and water leaks.

▲ Station wagons now made up a separate series. This Country Sedan came with either six- or eight-passenger seating, priced at $2156 and $2287 respectively. Two-door Ranch Wagons were offered in base and Custom trim, and the Country Squire continued with its simulated wood paneling.

◄ Sun lovers often liked their Sunliners fully decked out. This one sports a continental kit, skirts, and dual exhausts, adding a few dollars to the $2224 base price. All '55s were slightly longer and lower, but still rode 115.5-inch wheelbase.

1955 Engine Availability

Engines	bore × stroke	bhp	availability
I-6, 223.0	3.62 × 3.60	120	S-all
V-8, 272.0	3.62 × 3.30	162	O-all
V-8, 272.0	3.62 × 3.30	182	O-all
Thunderbird			
V-8, 292.0	3.75 × 3.30	193	S-stickshift
V-8, 292.0	3.75 × 3.30	198	S-automatic

▲ Close to 50,000 Ford fans preferred their '55 roofs to fold down. This season's restyle put hooded headlamps above a full-width concave mesh grille, adding "speedlines" around wheel openings and a mere hint of fin. Cutting dogleg A-pillars into the bodyshell created the wraparound windshield.

▼ Three chrome-edged circles low in the center of the instrument panel held controls for an extra-cost MagicAire heater, radio, and clock.

◄ Interiors were just about as colorful as Ford bodies. On the "Astra-Dial" instrument panel, a semicircular speedometer sat up high, with a window "for daylight illumination."

▲ Ford's 272-cid V-8 developed 162 bhp (182 with dual exhausts and four-barrel carb). A 205-bhp Interceptor 292 V-8 aimed at police.

◄ Police and taxi fleets turned to Fords with enthusiasm. Some cabs shown have heavy-duty bumper guards and non-original grilles.

145

▲ Revised mainly in its vee'd twin-bar grille, the F-100 "Money Maker" pickup sold for $1460 and ranked as top seller, with 124,841 built.

▲ Rear vents on this Fairlane Town Sedan reveal the presence of factory air, available at mid-year for $435. Only 22,575 units were installed.

▲ Meteor Rideau, with a strange spear adorning its bodyside, was the Canadian version of the '55 Ford. Base and Niagara models also were sold.

Model Breakdown Chart

Mainline—wb 115.5		Wght	Price	Prod
70A	sdn 2d	3,119	1,707	76,698
70D	bus cpe	3,081	1,606	8,809
73A	sdn 4d	3,161	1,753	41,794
Customline—wb 115.5				
70B	sdn 2d	3,139	1,801	236,575
73B	sdn 4d	3,181	1,845	235,417
Fairlane—wb 115.5				
60B	Victoria htp cpe	3,251	2,095	113,372
64A	Crown Victoria htp cpe	3,313	2,202	33,165
64B	Crown Vic htp cpe, glass top	3,321	2,272	1,999
70C	club sdn 2d	3,155	1,914	173,311
73C	Town Sedan	3,201	1,960	254,437
76B	Sunliner conv cpe	3,315	2,224	49,966
Station Wagon—wb 115.5				
59A	Ranch 2d, 6P	3,376	2,043	40,493
59B	Custom Ranch 2d, 6P	3,394	2,109	43,671
79B	Country Sedan 4d, 8P	3,536	2,287	53,209
79C	Country Squire 4d, 8P	3,538	2,392	19,011
79D	Country Sedan 4d, 6P	3,460	2,156	53,075
Thunderbird—wb 102.0				
40A	conv 2S	2,980	2,944	16,155

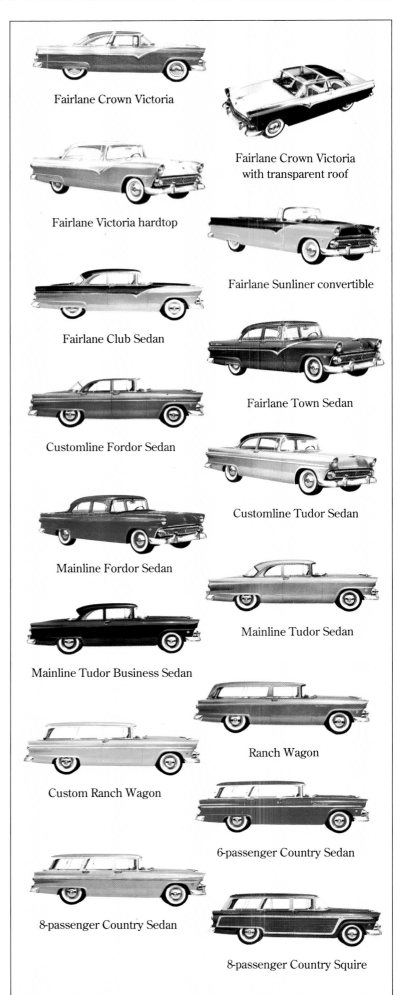

Fairlane Crown Victoria

Fairlane Crown Victoria with transparent roof

Fairlane Victoria hardtop

Fairlane Sunliner convertible

Fairlane Club Sedan

Fairlane Town Sedan

Customline Fordor Sedan

Customline Tudor Sedan

Mainline Fordor Sedan

Mainline Tudor Sedan

Mainline Tudor Business Sedan

Ranch Wagon

Custom Ranch Wagon

6-passenger Country Sedan

8-passenger Country Sedan

8-passenger Country Squire

1956

Ford stock goes on sale, starting with 10.2 million shares from Ford Foundation

Four-door hardtop debuts

Ford builds 1.4 million 1956 cars, but trails Chevrolet's 1.56 million

Most trucks adopt wraparound windshields

***Motor Trend* names entire line "Car of the Year"**

Ford joins Automobile Manufacturers Association; Henry II elected president

▶ "Lifeguard Design" made safety a selling point, including deep-dish steering wheel, extra-cost seatbelts, padded dash, and visors.

▼ Fords came in budget-price Mainline, mid-range Customline, and posh Fairlane trim—plus a separate station wagon series.

THE WORLD'S LARGEST SELLING V-8
...and Lifeguard Design is another reason why!

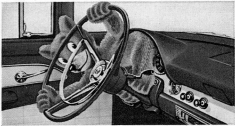

This Lifeguard steering wheel has a new deep-center construction to reduce the possibility of driver being thrown hard against the steering post in case of an accident. Our Ford engineers have mounted the rim of the wheel high above the recessed steering post to help "cushion" your chest against severe injuries from impact.

Optional Lifeguard padding protects you against accident injuries by providing a "crash cushion" on both the instrument panel and sun visors. It is five times more shock absorbent than foam rubber. New Lifeguard double-swivel rearview mirror that "gives" on impact and resists shattering is standard on all '56 Ford models.

You're twice as safe if you stay inside the car in an accident. Statistics prove it conclusively. So our Ford engineers have designed these new Lifeguard door latches with a *double grip* to reduce the possibility of doors springing open in a collision.

Look at this Ford seat belt! One-third stronger than required for airlines, it is securely anchored to reinforced, all-steel floor structure. Optional Ford seat belts can be adjusted or released with one hand ... are available in colors to harmonize with interiors.

THE NEW FORDOR VICTORIA

"And you'll drive safer ever after!"

FORD V·8
Sells More because it's Worth More !

Fairlane Sunliner convertible

Fairlane Crown Victoria Skyliner

Fairlane Crown Victoria

Fairlane Club Sedan

Fairlane Town Sedan

Fairlane Fordor Victoria

Customline Tudor Sedan

Customline Fordor Sedan

Country Squire wagon

8-passenger Country Sedan

Parklane station wagon

6-passenger Country Sedan

Custom Ranch Wagon

Ranch Wagon

Mainline Fordor Sedan

Mainline Tudor Business Sedan

▶ In addition to a modest facelift, T-Birds added a "continental" tire out back. Far more buyers took their extra-cost hardtop with new porthole windows than plain. Flip-open vents on front fenders helped cool the cockpit.

▲ Base T-Bird mill was the 292-cid V-8. A 312 V-8 yielded 215 bhp (225 with Fordomatic); or a whopping 245 bhp with dual four-barrels.

▲ T-Bird dash included tach and high-mount speedometer. Steering was slower than in '55, rear springs softer—just what buyers wanted.

▲ Exhaust outlets moved to edges of T-Bird's bumper. The outside tire improved trunk space and weight distribution. Price: $3151.

▼ Glamour sold cars in the '50s, and Ford's Sunliner had plenty. Pastel colors helped, too. Production rose to 58,147.

▲ For the first time, Victoria hardtop fans could get four doors to enter, for $55 more than a coupe.

▲ All that glitters is not gold, it's chrome—and many Crown Victorias were loaded with shiny add-ons. Volume sank to 9812 in final season.

▲ Ford couldn't let GM market a four-door hardtop alone. The Town Victoria arrived at mid-year, yet an impressive 32,111 found buyers.

▲ The plush Parklane was essentially a Ranch Wagon with Fairlane side trim and interior. Nearly twice as many were sold as Chevy's rival Nomad.

▲ Even more shoppers liked the pseudo-wood look of the Country Squire. A modest facelift included a wide-grate grille and oval parking lights.

▼ Even the mid-range Customline series got into the Victoria hardtop act, responding to Chevy's Two-Ten Sport Coupe. Sales lagged far behind the fancier Fairlane. All hardtops got the longer, more graceful Crown Vic roofline.

1956 Engine Availability

Engines	bore × stroke	bhp	availability
I-6, 223.0	3.62 × 3.60	137	S-all
V-8, 272.0	3.62 × 3.30	173	O-Mainline, Customline
V-8, 292.0	3.75 × 3.30	200	O-Fairlane wgn, (202 bhp w/auto)
V-8, 312.0	3.80 × 3.44	215	O-all (225 bhp w/auto)
Thunderbird			
V-8, 292.0	3.75 × 3.30	202	S-3-speed trans
V-8, 312.0	3.80 × 3.44	215	S-overdrive
V-8, 312.0	3.80 × 3.44	225	S-automatic
V-8, 312.0	3.80 × 3.44	245	O-all

▲ Bodyside trim was less ornate on this Customline Tudor than on Fairlanes. Engines tightened compression and added power. The base six ran 137 bhp, and the 272-cid V-8 rated 173. A four-barrel 292 was available, as were 215/225 bhp "Thunderbird Special" 312 V-8s.

▲ Produced by Ford Motor Co. of Canada, the Meteor came in three series, with Rideau the most luxurious of the lot—equivalent to the Fairlane. Rideaus were identified by a huge vee-bar at the grille, and a different form of bodyside sweepspear than U.S. models.

▲ With a few options installed, a Customline sedan added dash to suburban driveway. Headlamp brows and taillights grew in size. Only one in five Fords had seatbelts, partly due to a shortage. Workmanship remained so-so, with hood/fender shake added to the complaints.

Model Breakdown Chart

Mainline—wb 115.5		Wght	Price	Prod
70A	sdn 2d	3,143	1,850	106,974
70D	bus sdn 2d	3,088	1,748	8,020
73A	sdn 4d	3,183	1,895	49,448
Customline—wb 115.5				
64D	Victoria htp cpe	3,202	1,985	33,130
70B	sdn 2d	3,163	1,939	164,828
73B	sdn 4d	3,203	1,985	170,695
Fairlane—wb 115.5				
57A	Victoria htp sdn	3,369	2,249	32,111
64A	Crown Victoria htp cpe	3,289	2,337	9,209
64B	Crown Vic htp cpe, glass top	3,299	2,407	603
64C	Victoria htp cpe	3,274	2,194	177,735
70C	club sdn 2d	3,179	2,047	142,629
73C	Town Sedan	3,219	2,093	224,872
76B	Sunliner conv cpe	3,384	2,359	58,147
Station Wagon—wb 115.5				
59A	Ranch 2d, 6P	3,402	2,185	48,348
59B	Custom Ranch 2d, 6P	3,417	2,249	42,317
59C	Parklane 2d	3,432	2,428	15,186
79B	Country Sedan 4d, 8P	3,555	2,428	85,374
79C	Country Squire 4d, 8P	3,566	2,533	23,221
Thunderbird—wb 102.0				
40A	conv 2S	3,038	3,151	15,631

▲ A new wraparound windshield and revised grille were the foremost changes for this F-100 pickup, which started at $1577 with a 6½-foot box. Buyers could order a Custom Cab (with the first chrome grille face in the postwar era), wraparound rear window, and sidemounted spare. A record 289 truck models were offered, powered by a 133-bhp "Cost Cutter" six or a selection of V-8s, ranging up to 332-cid in "Big Job" models.

1957

"Big" '57 sports massive restyle—most extensive overhaul in a generation

Full-size Fords ride two different wheelbases

Ford outsells Chevrolet for model year, with record 1.67 million cars built

"Classic" Thunderbird earns handsome facelift in final two-seat season

Skyliner retractable hardtop debuts; so does Ranchero car-pickup

Supercharged 312-cid V-8 thunders out 300 horsepower

Ford takes 31.3 percent of truck market

25-millionth Ford V-8 built

William Ford named vice president for product planning and styling

Proving ground opens at Romeo, Michigan

▶ Wouldn't it have been great if this 1955 prototype had evolved into reality? Lincoln's Continental would have a four-door convertible in the early 1960s, but alas, such a body style never took the Ford nameplate. Styling for the '57s was well underway by this time. Several variants of this dip-down side molding would be used, depending on the series.

▲ Several features from this mid-1955 sketch by William Boyer wound up in the '57 T-Bird, including the deep wraparound windshield and broad exhaust outlets at bumper ends.

▲ T-Bird prototype exhibits canted fins that went into production. Abandoned were the wide eggcrate grille, slanted rear quarter windows, and louvered sculpture aft of front wheels.

▲ Janus-like full-size models let stylists and execs compare the virtues of two different themes. In this case, the right-hand rear end design won when the real '57 T-Birds debuted.

▲ Prototype of a hardtop coupe comes close to its final form in massive '57 restyling. This would be Ford's first use of sculptured panels, with sharp edges, creases, and curves.

▲ Front-end styling isn't far off the final mark, but the rear half of this prototype for a Parklane wagon never made the cut. Sharply angled tailgate suggests Chevy's Nomad.

▲ Elegant simplicity is one way to describe the final facelift of the two-seat Thunderbird. Widened to boost cooling, the grille got a square-mesh pattern. Note integral parking lights in the bold bumper.

▲ Hardly any car could avoid tailfins in '57, but at least the T-Bird's were subdued. Taillights grew larger, and the rear deck squarer. New bumpers lacked separate guards. Rear springs lost one leaf this year.

▲ Moving the spare tire back into the Thunderbird's trunk demanded a longer rear deck, but overall size shrunk. A rear-mounted tire remained optional, with few takers. Stylists wisely resisted tacking on doodads or tampering with the basic shape. A total of 21,380 were built in a longer model year.

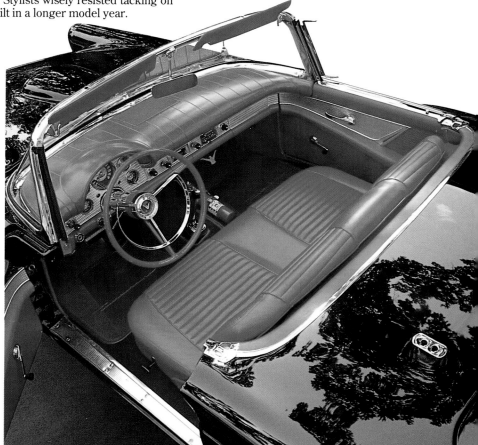

▲ Four versions of the 312-cid V-8 went under T-Bird hoods, including 208 with a supercharger. Costing $500 extra, the 300-bhp edition blasted to 60 mph in under seven seconds.

▶ Engine-turned appliqués added glitter to the T-Bird cockpit, with its hooded instrument cluster and telescoping steering column. Most styling touches echoed those in the restyled big Fords. Door panels repeated the car's logo.

▲ Fairlane and upper-notch Fairlane 500 rode a 118-inch wheelbase, versus 116 inches for Custom and Custom 300 models. This Fairlane two-door hardtop shows the new full-width rectangular grille, square front fenders, flatter hood, and sharply wrapped windshield with angled-back dogleg.

▲ No less alluring in its enlarged form, the Sunliner convertible sold for $2505, but options could add another thousand. Side trim in the Fairlane 500 series contained a golden anodized insert in its forward segment. Note the assertively hooded headlights and stand-up hood ornament.

▲ Supercharging wasn't limited to T-Birds. This Fairlane 500 two-door Club Sedan carries the rare, blown 312-cid V-8, throbbing with 300 horsepower. Standard engine was the 144-bhp six, and most 500s had one of the less muscular 272, 292, or 312 V-8 engines, with 190 to 245 bhp.

▲ Least costly model in the Fairlane and Fairlane 500 series was the Club Sedan. Full-length bodyside trim marks this as a 500, which outsold its Fairlane mate. Roof pillars were far thinner than in most sedans. All Fords were longer, wider, and lower—partly due to switch to 14-inch tires.

▲ For a two-door sedan, the Fairlane 500 exhibited a lot of flash for its $2281 price. "Ordinary" Fairlanes had less ambitious trim. Enlarged round taillights for '57 went beneath modest, canted blade-style fins. Rounding out the four-series line (plus wagons), Custom and Custom 300 models replaced the former Mainline and Customline series. All V-8s got higher-lift cams and low-profile carbs.

▲ In its second season, the airy Victoria hardtop sedan came in Fairlane or Fairlane 500 trim, with a $47 price difference. Top seller by more than five to one was the Fairlane 500, seen here.

▲ Ford earned an "A" for innovation with the Skyliner retractable hardtop, which cost $437 more than a convertible. A 272 V-8 was standard.

▲ A 10-inch flap at the front of the Skyliner's top folded when lowering, to squeeze under the rear-hinged deck. Rear fenders were elongated.

▲ Cargo space grew considerably with a wagon's back seat folded down. Interiors held a new instrument panel with curved ribbon speedometer.

▲ Top-selling wagon was the Country Sedan, offered with six- or nine-passenger seating. All wagons rode the shorter 116-inch wheelbase.

▲ Sales rose for the Country Squire in its bigger 1957 form, again with simulated wood trim. Total wagon volume grew by over 106,000 units.

▲ Borrowing a prewar idea, Ford debuted the Ranchero coupe-pickup, a concept destined to last 22 years. Based on the Ranch Wagon, with a double-wall cargo box, it cost $1920 in base trim, $2149 as a Custom.

▲ Wearing flashier brightwork, the Custom Ranchero outsold its standard mate, with 15,277 built (versus 6428 base models). This example has "Style-Tone" paint. A 144-bhp six was standard; 272 or 292 V-8 optional.

▲ Substituting for the '56 Mainline, the Custom series displayed a different style of bodyside trim than upper-level Fords. In addition to the $1991 two-door, Customs came in business sedan and four-door bodies.

▲ In this record production year, the lowest-priced Custom Fords sold slower than step-up Custom 300s. Ford's "Mileage Maker" six grew to 144 bhp, but shoppers liked the selection of V-8s, with 190 horses or more.

▲ Safety continued as a sales stimulus, though many dealers preferred to focus on performance. The '57 models had a Safety-Curve instrument panel with recessed controls (padding optional), smaller Lifeguard steering wheel, safety-swivel mirror, and double-grip door locks—plus available seatbelts.

▲ Canadian Meteors wore more complex bodyside trim than U.S. Fords, and a bold vee'd grille. Two series were sold: Niagara and Rideau.

▲ Bullet-like side trim, at rear bodysides only, identifies this Fairlane Town Sedan. Sales lagged behind the fancier Fairlane 500.

▲ A total of 44,127 Fairlane Victoria hardtops came off the line for '57, versus 183,202 Fairlane 500s, which sold for $46 more.

▲ In addition to a basic Ranch Wagon, Ford offered a Del Rio—essentially the same two-door with flashier trim, *à la* Country Sedan.

▲ Custom 300s were the top-selling Ford sedans for '57. Ball-joint suspension was simplified, with fewer parts and softer ride.

▲ Side trim on Custom 300 sedans was similar to that used on the Fairlane 500, but lower on the body. Door pillars were thicker, too.

Model Breakdown Chart

Custom—wb 116.0		Wght	Price	Prod
70A	sdn 2d	3,211	1,991	116,963
70D	bus sdn 2d	3,202	1,879	6,888
73A	sdn 4d	3,254	2,042	68,924
Custom 300—wb 116.0				
70B	sdn 2d	3,224	2,105	160,360
73B	sdn 4d	3,269	2,157	194,877
Fairlane—wb 118.0				
57B	Victoria htp sdn	3,411	2,357	12,695
58A	Town Sedan 4d	3,376	2,286	52,060
63B	Victoria htp cpe	3,366	2,293	44,127
64A	club sdn 2d	3,331	2,235	39,843
Fairlane 500—wb 118.0				
51A	Skyliner retrac conv cpe	3,916	2,942	20,766
57A	Victoria htp sdn	3,426	2,404	68,550
58B	Town Sedan 4d	3,384	2,286	193,162
63A	Victoria htp cpe	3,381	2,339	183,202
64B	club sdn 2d	3,346	2,281	93,756
76B	Sunliner conv cpe	3,536	2,505	77,726
Station Wagon—wb 116.0				
59A	Ranch 2d, 6P	3,455	2,301	60,486
59B	Del Rio 2d, 6P	3,462	2,397	46,105
79C	Country Sedan 4d, 9P	3,614	2,556	49,638
79D	Country Squire 4d, 6P	3,525	2,451	137,251
79E	Country Squire 4d, 9P	3,628	2,684	27,690
Thunderbird—wb 102.0				
40	conv 2S	3,145	3,408	21,380

1957 Engine Availability

Engines	bore × stroke	bhp	availability
I-6, 223.0	3.62 × 3.60	144	S-all exc 51A
V-8, 272.0	3.62 × 3.30	190	S-51A; O-others
V-8, 292.0	3.75 × 3.30	212	O-Fairlane, Fairlane 500, wgns
V-8, 312.0	3.80 × 3.44	245	O-all
Thunderbird			
V-8, 292.0	3.75 × 3.30	212	S-3-speed trans
V-8, 312.0	3.80 × 3.44	245	S-overdrive, automatic
V-8, 312.0	3.80 × 3.44	270/285	O-all (3-speed briefly)
V-8, 312.0	3.80 × 3.44	300	O-auto; few od/3sp (superchgd)

▲ All-new this year was the C-Series Tilt Cab truck, with a glass-laden, nearly cubical cab that tilted forward for drivetrain access. This Big Job C-900 was rated 30,000 pounds GVW. Features included a heavy-duty 332-cid V-8, double-channel frame, and 9000-pound front axle. Trucks in general had fewer engine choices, but more power. Pickup trucks now came in two

▼ With volume up by over 260,000, Ford needed plenty of haulers to send its cars to dealers. This year's styling evolved from the Mystere show car—especially the rear-quarter treatment and Fairlane 500 side molding. The '57s stuck to the road nicely and performed well. A Fairlane sedan with stick and 245-bhp Thunderbird Special V-8 could hit 60 in 9.5 seconds.

1958

America suffers worst recession in postwar era—car sales drop sharply

Thunderbird reintroduced as four-seater: pioneers personal-luxury concept

***Motor Trend* names unibody T-Bird "Car of the Year"**

Passenger cars get heavy facelift, big-block V-8s

Four-door Ranch Wagon debuts

Only 987,945 Fords built, to Chevy's 1.14 million

▲ Robert S. McNamara, one of Henry Ford II's postwar "Whiz Kids" who'd risen to Ford Division general manager in 1955, leans on a heavily restyled '58 Fairlane. By 1958, McNamara headed the corporation's Car & Truck Group, while a young Lee Iacocca was Ford Division's car marketing manager. McNamara would later serve a brief stint in the top spot, before becoming President Kennedy's Secretary of Defense. This was destined to be a volatile season for Ford, with the debut of the ill-fated Edsel amid a recession-wracked economy, but the compact Falcon soon would save the day.

▶ Thunderbird's styling cues were shared with regular Fords, including the grille, fins, and taillights. Later nicknamed "Squarebird," the four-seater gained 700-800 pounds and rode an 11-inch longer wheelbase (113 inches), transforming it into a posh "personal-luxury" cruiser that spawned many an imitator.

Brilliant new version of Ford's great American classic...the 4-passenger

THUNDERBIRD

Another first from Ford — a jewel of a car that's pure Thunderbird in design, spirit and performance...with full fine-car room, comfort and luxury for *four*

In the 1958 Thunderbird, Ford has created a wholly new size and type of fine car. It gives you Thunderbird compactness, Thunderbird handling and traditional Thunderbird performance—yet, miraculously, it now gives you full fine-car room and comfort for *four* people! It brings you interior appointments that are unbelievably imaginative and luxurious. Now, happily, you can share your Thunderbird thrills with deserving friends. Now it's *twice* the fun to own the car that became an American classic the very day it was introduced. For details about America's most excitingly different car,

turn the page, please

▲ This proposed sedan wears a full-width horizontal-bar grille, with parking lights built into the bumper. Tailfins already were formed at this stage, as were hooded quad headlamps.

▲ Details make a difference as models and mock-ups evolve into reality. This prototype's rear end looks closer to production, except for the extended roofline and back-window curve.

▲ Yet another grille treatment appeared on this prototype, with parking lights above the bumper. Rear sculpturing is more complex than the simple curve employed in final Fords.

Model Breakdown Chart

Custom—wb 116.0		Wght	Price	Prod
70A	sdn 2d	3,250	2,055	36,272
70D	bus sdn	3,227	1,967	4,062
73A	sdn 4d	3,278	2,109	27,811
Custom 300—wb 116.0				
70B	sdn 2d	3,300	2,305	137,169
73B	sdn 4d	3,328	2,159	135,557
Fairlane—wb 118.0				
57B	Victoria htp sdn	3,450	2,419	5,868
58A	Town Sedan 4d	3,427	2,275	57,490
63B	Victoria htp cpe	3,373	2,354	16,416
64A	club sdn 2d	3,375	2,221	38,366
Fairlane 500—wb 118.0				
51A	Skyliner retrac conv cpe	4,069	3,163	14,713
57A	Victoria htp sdn	3,488	2,499	36,509
58B	sdn 4d	3,452	2,428	105,698
63A	Victoria htp cpe	3,390	2,435	80,439
64B	club sdn 2d	3,380	2,374	34,041
76B	Sunliner conv	3,556	2,650	35,029
Station Wagon—wb 116.0				
59A	Ranch 2d, 6P	3,552	2,397	34,578
59B	Del Rio 2d, 6P	3,734	2,503	12,687
79A	Ranch 4d, 6P	3,608	2,451	32,854
79C	Country Sedan 4d, 9P	3,682	2,664	20,702
79D	Country Squire 4d, 6P	3,614	2,557	68,772
79E	Country Squire 4d, 9P	3,718	2,794	15,020
Thunderbird—wb 113.0				
63A	htp cpe	3,876	3,631	35,758
76A	conv cpe	3,944	3,929	2,134

1958 Engine Availability

Engines	bore × stroke	bhp	availability
I-6, 223.0	3.62 × 3.60	145	S-all exc 51A
V-8, 292.0	3.75 × 3.30	205	S-51A; O-others
V-8, 332.0	4.00 × 3.30	240	O-wgns (265 bhp w/auto)
V-8, 332.0	4.00 × 3.30	265	O-all
V-8, 352.0	4.00 × 3.50	300	O-all
Thunderbird			
V-8, 352.0	4.00 × 3.50	300	S-all
V-8, 430.0	4.30 × 3.70	350	O-prod questionable

▲ Realizing that the glamorous two-seater wasn't likely to turn a profit, McNamara wanted the next T-Bird to be a real moneymaker. That meant seating for four. His choice proved correct, with 37,892 built in a short model year (more than 1956-57 combined). Sales grew by half despite the recession.

▶ Skyliner retractables may be better remembered today, but far more Sunliner convertibles were sold in 1958. A total of 35,029 ragtops came off the line, with a $2650 sticker price—$513 less than a retrac'.

▲ A Skyliner in action was quite a sight. Though complex, the system was surprisingly reliable. First, the decklid lifted. Then, as the top began to rise, its front section tucked under. With the top down, the Skyliner displayed a clean decklid. Topping two tons, it got the 292 V-8 as standard and was the only regular Ford costing more than $3000.

▲ Four-door hardtops had their fans, but this Fairlane 500 Town Victoria sold fewer than half as many copies as its two-door counterpart. Fender skirts added a bit more dash. Quad headlamps and a mouthy bumper/grille were the main styling changes, while new grooves added strength to the roof panels.

▲ All Fairlane 500s, including the Victoria hardtop coupe, wore new side trim with a larger anodized insert. That didn't help sales, as volume slipped by more than 100,000. Not everyone voted aye on this year's Thunderbird-based facelift, but the ad slogan proved long-lived: "Have you driven a Ford lately?"

▲ Rather straightforward in tone for the late 1950s, the standard Ford dashboard centered on a hooded, wide-arc speedometer ahead of the driver. The new "FE-Series" big-block V-8 came in 332- or 352-cid size, with 240 to 300 bhp. Dual-range Cruise-O-Matic was new, complete with a hillholder.

159

▲ Most of the passenger-car styling changes also appeared on the Ranchero car-pickup, but it kept the round '57 taillights. A deluxe Custom 300 cost $2236, and Ranchero output slipped to 9950. Both 292- and 352-cid V-8s were optional, the latter cranking out 300 bhp.

▲ Popularity leader of the Fairlane 500 series was the four-door sedan, with 105,698 built. Optional air suspension found few takers.

▲ Low-end Fords, including this Custom 300, rode a shorter (116-inch) wheelbase. Ride was softer than '57, mechanical quality improved.

▲ Ranch Wagons wore Custom-series side trim and a moderate price tag, starting at $2397. Four-door Country Sedans sold better.

▲ The least-popular (and cheapest) Ford for '58 was the two-door Custom business sedan. Only 4062 were built, out of 68,145 Customs.

▲ Pickup-truck fans could enjoy smooth-fender design with the $1913 Styleside F-100, Ford's mass-market reply to Chevy's Cameo Carrier.

1958 Selected Colors

 Desert Beige
 Palomino Tan
Colonial White
Silvertone Green Metallic
Sun Gold
Gun Metal Gray Metallic #3

 Bali Bronze Metallic
Azure Blue
Gulfstream Blue
Seaspray Green
Torch Red
Silvertone Blue Metallic

1959

Galaxie luxury series debuts at mid-year, takes 27 percent of volume

Skyliner retractable enters its final season

First steps taken toward extended service intervals

Ford and Chevy race neck-and-neck in production, topping 1.4 million cars

Compact race begins as Studebaker launches Lark

Imported cars hit record calendar-year sales

Ford establishes credit/finance subsidiary

▼ Billed as "the world's most beautifully proportioned cars," the '59 line consisted of 23 models. Contrary to the radically finned Chevrolet and Plymouth, Ford's squared-up design echoed that of the restyled Thunderbird.

Main Street or Wall Street, Ford's Sunliner says "solid investment"

Safe place to put your money...

Right from the starting price, the 59 Fords save your money. Ford prices start at the very lowest of the most popular three. And you'll find surprising facts like these in your new Ford Owners Manual: "Regular gasoline is recommended for standard engines, Six and Thunderbird V-8 . . . go 4000 miles without changing oil . . . your Ford muffler is aluminized to normally last twice as long." This same economy manual is yours in any one of Ford's 23 best-selling models. Savings? Ford wrote the book.

EXTRA DIVIDENDS FROM FORD: HULA-HOOP-WIDE DOORS . . . AND HEAD ROOM APLENTY

Get extra savings now during Ford Dealer's DIVIDEND DAYS
Share in special saving dividends plus Ford's built-for-people dividends · Full 6-passenger space · Room to wear your hat · Deep springing and cushioning in every seat · Wider door openings that give you easier in-and-out traffic

59 FORDS

WORLD'S MOST BEAUTIFULLY PROPORTIONED CARS

▲ With the recession not yet over, Ford took a conservative path, promoting economy and value.

▲ Recession or not, the Sunliner convertible found plenty of takers as output leaped by 10,000 units. Turquoise/white was a popular two-tone mix, adding a dash of daring to the conservative stance. Hooded quad headlamps sat above a full-width grille with four rows of floating "stars." Windshields curved upward as well as sideways. All rode a 118-inch wheelbase; sedans grew six inches longer.

▲ As usual, Ford went through a succession of mock-ups before settling on the final design. This bizarre rendition with formal roofline bore little kinship to production four-doors.

▲ Horizontal fins in this proposed Ford suggest the '60 model, but massive taillamp enclosures didn't make the grade. Cars in background appear closer to 1959 design.

▲ Two-faced mock-ups were useful, displaying alternate themes for consideration. Note the different door-window treatments, deeply creased decklid, and full-length sculpturing.

▲ Like the Continental that would arrive for '61, this four-door wagon-style prototype was designed as a pillarless hardtop with rear-hinged back doors. Sharply canted fins were more prominent than those used in production.

▲ Styling approaches '59 reality in this two-door Fairlane 500 prototype. Even the bodyside trim looks near completion. Taillamps were close to production, but final hardtops adopted different rear-glass curvatures.

▲ Bodyside adornments seen on this Fairlane 500 prototype wouldn't be quite as extensive in the production version, but the roofline and overall profile were just about established for the final 1959 design.

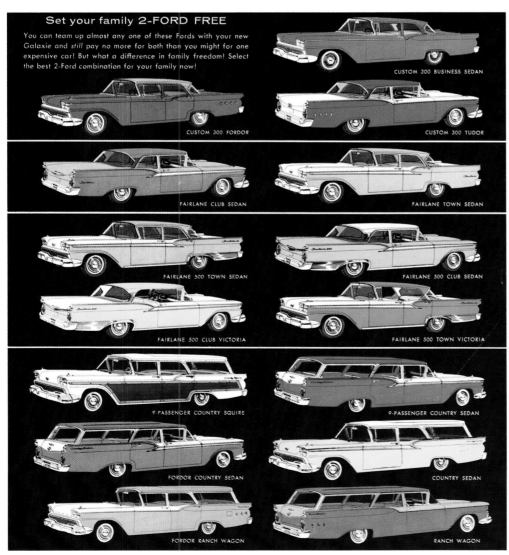

Set your family 2-FORD FREE

You can team up almost any one of these Fords with your new Galaxie and *still* pay no more for both than you might for one expensive car! But what a difference in family freedom! Select the best 2-Ford combination for your family now!

CUSTOM 300 BUSINESS SEDAN

CUSTOM 300 FORDOR

CUSTOM 300 TUDOR

FAIRLANE CLUB SEDAN

FAIRLANE TOWN SEDAN

FAIRLANE 500 TOWN SEDAN

FAIRLANE 500 CLUB SEDAN

FAIRLANE 500 CLUB VICTORIA

FAIRLANE 500 TOWN VICTORIA

9-PASSENGER COUNTRY SQUIRE

9-PASSENGER COUNTRY SEDAN

FORDOR COUNTRY SEDAN

COUNTRY SEDAN

FORDOR RANCH WAGON

RANCH WAGON

▲ Once again, the Skyliner had a longer, rear-hinged deck-lid to hold the retractable roof.

▲ Long fin-like cylinders with chromed ridges topped the rear quarters of '59 models, ending in backup lights. Round taillights were huge.

◄ Like ads from a few years earlier, this promotion pushed the idea of *twin* Fords for the family. Economic recovery during '59 helped Ford run nearly neck-and-neck with Chevrolet.

163

▲ Thunderbird production nearly doubled in this full model year, to 67,456. As part of the minor facelift, pointed chrome moldings on lower-bodyside "bullets" replaced the former five hashmarks. A reworked rear suspension switched from coil to leaf springs.

▲ A total of 10,261 lucky customers could choose a Thunderbird ragtop in 1959, for $283 more than the hardtop. Horizontal grille bars were matched at the taillights. With a new optional Lincoln 350-bhp, 430-cid V-8 on tap, this year's Bird could dash to 60 mph in a snappy nine seconds or so.

Model Breakdown Chart

Custom 300—wb 118.0		Wght	Price	Prod
58E	sdn 4d	3,436	2,273	249,553
64F	sdn 2d	3,360	2,219	228,576
64G	bus sdn	3,334	2,132	4,084
Fairlane—wb 118.0				
58A	Town Sedan 4d	3,466	2,411	64,663
64A	club sdn 2d	3,382	2,357	35,126
Fairlane 500—wb 118.0				
57A	Victoria htp sdn	3,502	2,602	9,308
58B	sdn 4d	3,468	2,530	35,670
63A	Victoria htp cpe	3,416	2,537	23,892
64B	club sdn 2d	3,388	2,476	10,141
Galaxie—wb 118.0				
51A	Skyliner retrac htp cpe	4,064	3,346	12,915

		Wght	Price	Prod
54A	sdn 4d	3,456	2,582	183,108
64H	club sdn 2d	3,388	2,528	52,848
65A	Victoria htp cpe	3,428	2,589	121,869
75A	Victoria htp sdn	3,544	2,654	47,728
76B	Sunliner conv cpe	3,578	2,839	45,868
Station Wagon—wb 118.0				
59C	Ranch 2d, 6P	3,640	2,567	45,588
59D	Del Rio 2d, 6P	3,664	2,678	8,663
71E	Country Sedan 4d, 9P	3,818	2,829	28,811
71F	Country Sedan 4d, 6P	3,768	2,745	94,601
71G	Country Squire 4d, 9P	3,808	2,958	24,336
71H	Ranch 4d, 6P	3,736	2,634	67,339
Thunderbird—wb 113.0				
63A	htp cpe	3,813	3,696	57,195
76A	conv cpe	3,903	3,979	10,261

1959 Engine Availability

Engines	bore × stroke	bhp	availability
I-6, 223.0	3.62 × 3.60	145	S-all exc 51A
V-8, 292.0	3.75 × 3.30	200	S-51A; O-others
V-8, 332.0	4.00 × 3.30	225	O-all
V-8, 352.0	4.00 × 3.50	300	O-all
Thunderbird			
V-8, 352.0	4.00 × 3.50	300	S-all
V-8, 430.0	4.30 × 3.70	350	O-all

▲ This Galaxie prototype, nearing final stage, made it clear that the T-Bird's boxy roof would sit well on the squared-off '59 lower body.

▲ At mid-year, the Fairlane 500 with its narrow C-pillars was augmented by the Galaxie, which borrowed T-Bird's wide-quarter roof.

▲ Only a nine-seat version of the woody-look Country Squire was listed, accounting for a small portion of the 269,338 wagons built.

▲ Taillights on this Ranchero prototype are close to finished style, but sharp fins would disappear. Note the two different cab designs.

▲ Production Rancheros had backup lights like passenger cars and offered an "economy" V-8 option. Model-year sales rose to 14,169.

▲ A horizontal speedometer sat in a large square instrument cluster, but the new white-on-silver gauges weren't so easy to read.

1960

Compact Falcon debuts, along with Chevrolet Corvair, Plymouth Valiant, and Mercury Comet

Falcon scores big sales—435,676 built in first year

Sliding metal sunroof offered on Thunderbird

Lee Iacocca becomes Ford Division general manager

Robert S. McNamara succeeds Henry Ford II as president, leaves after one month to be Secretary of Defense

▼ Success of the Falcon didn't lure everyone away from "full-size" Fords. This ad features the popular new semi-fastback Starliner hardtop.

See "FORD STARTIME" in living color Tuesdays on NBC   Ford Falcon: easiest car in the world to own

Introducing a wonderful new world of savings in the new-size 1960 Ford *Falcon*

Look at the price tag for big news! For all its big-car comfort, styling and power, the Falcon delivers *for less* than many imported economy cars.

Honest-to-goodness six-passenger comfort. Plenty of room for six . . . *and all their luggage!*

New 6-cylinder engine . . . up front for greater safety and stability. A brand-new power plant specifically designed to power the Falcon over America's hills and highways with "big car" performance and safety.

World's most experienced new car. The Falcon was proven over every mile of numbered Federal Highway in Experience Run, U.S.A., a grueling demonstration climaxing Ford's 3 years and 3 million miles of testing and development.

Up to 30 miles a gallon on regular gas. Experience Run, U.S.A. proved the Falcon's exceptional gas mileage and oil economy.

Made in U.S.A. . . . serviced everywhere. The Falcon is a product of Dearborn, Michigan, automotive capital of the world. Every part of the Falcon has been designed for maximum durability and dependable performance. Falcon service is available at over 7,000 Ford Dealers across the country.

FORD DIVISION *Ford Motor Company,*

FORD BUILDS THE WORLD'S MOST BEAUTIFULLY PROPORTIONED CARS

FORD—The Finest Fords of a Lifetime   FALCON—The New-Size Ford   THUNDERBIRD—The World's Most Wanted Car

▲ The "new-size" Falcon, on a 109.5-inch wheelbase and 32.5 inches shorter than other Fords, was roomy even for six. After the 1958 recession, Americans were clamoring for smaller cars.

Easier to get in and out! No projecting dog-legs! Windshield posts sweep forward out of the way for easy entry and exit.

NEW SLOPING HOOD GIVES YOU UP TO 40 SQ. FT. OF INCREASED VISIBILITY FORWARD

Full-range visibility means safer, more comfortable driving. There's 31% more windshield area and a gracefully sloping hood to give the most commanding view of the road. There's a wider angle of vision through the rear window, too. Ford's greater glass area all around means greater, safer visibility . . . it's not overhead where it causes passenger discomfort from sun glare and heat.

Full-width comfort! Greater shoulder, hip and leg room. Ford's built-for-people design brings you *full* room for six in the finest limousine tradition. Chair-high seats are posture-perfect, specially shaped and beautifully, lastingly upholstered. And even the man-in-the-middle, front seat or rear, has plenty of stretch-out room.

Roomy, low-level trunk for easy loading. Ford's big trunk is extra easy to load and unload. Its low-lift opening is only 27" from the ground (just over "knee-high").

A wonderful new world of elegance ...and built-for-people comfort

Beautiful from any *Point of View* . . . Worth more from every *Point of Value* . . .

The 1960 Fords bring you a new Viewpoint in Styling. Here is a refined, restrained new kind of styling elegance that is so very reminiscent of the fabulous Thunderbird. Classic, sculptured lines are united into a flowing harmony in steel.

Gracefully sloping hood, sweeping side contours, Thunderbird roofline, airy picture windows . . . every beautiful proportion proclaims the new spirit in advanced automotive design.

Ford, for 1960, presents a new Viewpoint on Comfort. The rich new Ford interiors give the driver and his passengers the kind of room that is the mark of the true luxury car. Here's shoulder room, leg room, headroom, hip room and hat room to spare. And Ford's greatly increased glass area is placed where it adds wonderful new visibility . . . not overhead where it would let in the sun's glare and heat.

THESE ARE THE FINEST FORDS OF A LIFETIME

And leave it to the world's most experienced builder of V-8's to blaze the way in power. Ford's new Thunderbird V-8's open up an exciting new world of smooth, quiet, economical action. They're built by Ford engine specialists, the world's master builders of modern, short-stroke, deep-block V-8's. Both standard Ford engines—Thunderbird 292 V-8 and Mileage Maker Six—perform beautifully on regular gasoline.

Economy is one of Ford's biggest value points. You *start* saving with the low Ford price. New truck-size brakes last longer. Fords go 4000 miles without oil changes, have standard, double-life aluminized mufflers, and a finish that needs no waxing. Let your Ford dealer introduce you to the beautifully proportioned, beautifully economical 1960 Fords today.

FORD DIVISION *Ford Motor Company,*

The new 9-passenger Country Sedan is one of 5 all-new, wider, roomier, altogether wonderful 1960 station wagons from Ford, America's station wagon specialists.

The new Ford Starliner, with its racy roofline and optional Thunderbird 352 Special V-8, is one of the most distinctive, liveliest cars on the American Road. And it gives you luxurious 6-passenger comfort!

See "FORD STARTIME" in living color Tuesdays on NBC

'60 FORDS

The new 1960 Ford Sunliner is the exciting new concept in sport-loving, lively living cars . . . combining sizzling performance with rakish style lines for a new world of sunshine elegance.

FORD—The Finest Fords of a Lifetime   FALCON—The New-Size Ford   THUNDERBIRD—The World's Most Wanted Car

▲ Meteor Montcalm was the Canadian version of the top-ranked full-size Ford. Like other Meteors, this convertible displays a different grille pattern than American '60s, with vertical bars. Rideau and Rideau 500 were the "lesser" levels. Top engine choice was the 352-cid V-8, rated 300 bhp.

▼ Horizontal fins on the Canadian Montcalm were identical to those installed on the Fairlane/Galaxie series, but six round lights replaced the American-style single half-moon taillamps. The back panel was bright finished, and lower-bodyside trim moldings were longer for Canadian consumption.

▲ Total restyling of the big Fords added an inch to wheelbase and 5.7 inches to length. Width reached a whopping 81.5 inches. Headlamps moved down into the wide U-shaped grille, below a broader hood. Straight A-pillars replaced the old dogleg posts, embracing a taller compound-curve windshield. Body-sides adopted mild contouring. Output of the Galaxie Victoria hardtop sedan fell by more than 8500 units.

▲ Robert S. McNamara, to the left of Henry Ford II, became Ford president on November 9, 1960.

▲ Ford took the name of its new Starliner from '53 Studebaker. Its gently curved roofline boosted aerodynamics, and helped attract 68,461 customers.

▲ Popularity champ of the big Ford line was the Fairlane 500 Town Sedan, followed by the cheaper four-door Fairlane and posh Galaxie Town Sedan.

▲ Two-door sedans found fewer customers than four-doors, but both the Fairlane two-door and Fairlane 500 Club Sedan topped 90,000-unit volume.

▲ Production of the fake-wood Country Squire wagon slipped just a bit, whereas the Country Sedans dropped to only 78,579 for the year.

▲ Only one two-door station wagon remained, the $2586 Ranch Wagon, but its production was halved for '60. A total of 171,824 wagons were built.

167

▲ Falcon sedans came first, followed by two- and four-door station wagons in mid-1960. These were Ford's first wagons without a separate liftgate, and 74,310 were built (versus 361,366 sedans). Unlike Chevy's Corvair, the unibodied Falcon was fully conventional, with a new 144-cid front engine.

▲ Planning for the '60 compacts began in 1957, as the recession weakened the U.S. economy and imports were stealing sales. Falcon styling was as simple as its engineering, with roly-poly rounded edges, creased bodysides, and big round taillamps. This four-door wears the $66 DeLuxe trim.

▲ In the final year of its initial four-seat form, Thunderbird set a record with 90,873 built, 11,860 of them ragtops. Changes were modest, limited to nine hashmarks on rear fenders, cleaner side trim, a horizontal grille bar with three dividers (ahead of square mesh), and triple-taillight clusters.

▲ About 3900 examples of "the world's most wanted car" came with the 430-cid Lincoln engine, while 2536 had a $212 sliding metal sunroof.

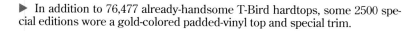

▶ In addition to 76,477 already-handsome T-Bird hardtops, some 2500 special editions wore a gold-colored padded-vinyl top and special trim.

Model Breakdown Chart

Falcon—wb 109.5

		Wght	Price	Prod
58A	sdn 4d	2,288	1,974	167,896
59A	wgn 2d	2,540	2,225	27,552
64A	sdn 2d	2,259	1,912	193,470
71A	wgn 4d	2,575	2,287	46,758

Custom 300—wb 119.0

		Wght	Price	Prod
58F	sdn 4d	3,576	2,284	572
64H	sdn 2d	3,465	2,230	302

Fairlane—wb 119.0

		Wght	Price	Prod
58E	sdn 4d	3,656	2,311	109,801
64F	sdn 2d	3,582	2,257	93,256
64G	bus sdn	3,555	2,170	1,733

Fairlane 500—wb 119.0

		Wght	Price	Prod
58A	Town Sedan 4d	3,663	2,388	153,234
64A	club sdn 2d	3,586	2,334	91,041

Galaxie—wb 119.0

		Wght	Price	Prod
54A	Town sdn 4d	3,684	2,603	104,784
62A	club sdn 2d	3,603	2,549	31,866
63A	Starliner htp cpe	3,617	2,610	68,461
75A	Victoria htp sdn	3,692	2,675	39,215
76B	Sunliner conv cpe	3,791	2,860	44,762

Station Wagon—wb 119.0

		Wght	Price	Prod
59C	Ranch 2d, 6P	3,881	2,586	27,136
71E	Country Sedan 4d, 9P	4,058	2,837	19,277
71F	Country Sedan 4d, 6P	4,012	2,752	59,302
71G	Country Squire 4d, 9P	4,072	2,967	22,237
71H	Ranch 4d, 6P	3,998	2,656	43,872

Thunderbird—wb 113.0

		Wght	Price	Prod
63A	htp cpe	3,799	3,755	76,477
63B	htp cpe, gold top	3,799	3,900*	2,536
76A	conv cpe	3,897	4,222	11,860

*Estimated

1960 Engine Availability

Engines	bore × stroke	bhp	availability
I-6, 144.3	3.50 × 2.50	90	S-Falcon only
I-6, 223.0	3.62 × 3.60	145	S-all exc Falcon
V-8, 292.0	3.75 × 3.30	185	O-all exc Falcon
V-8, 352.0	4.00 × 3.50	235	O-all exc Falcon
V-8, 352.0	4.00 × 3.50	300/360	O-all exc Falcon
Thunderbird			
V-8, 352.0	4.00 × 3.50	300	S-all
V-8, 430.0	4.30 × 3.70	350	O-all

▲ Transforming the new Falcon station wagon into a Courier sedan delivery, deleting the rear side windows, wasn't a tough job. Not many shoppers bought the notion, however, as only 2374 were built in a short model year.

▲ Disappointing sales of the 1957-59 Ranchero led Ford to move it onto the compact Falcon platform. Priced at $1875, the shrunken car-pickup was strictly Falcon: simple, reliable, cheap. Output spurted to 21,027 units.

▼ This would be the final season for the traditional panel delivery truck, to be replaced for 1961 by the Falcon-based Econoline series, like the pickup shown here. A total of 488 truck models was offered (up by 118). Ford marketed 14,893 Econoline pickups in 1961.

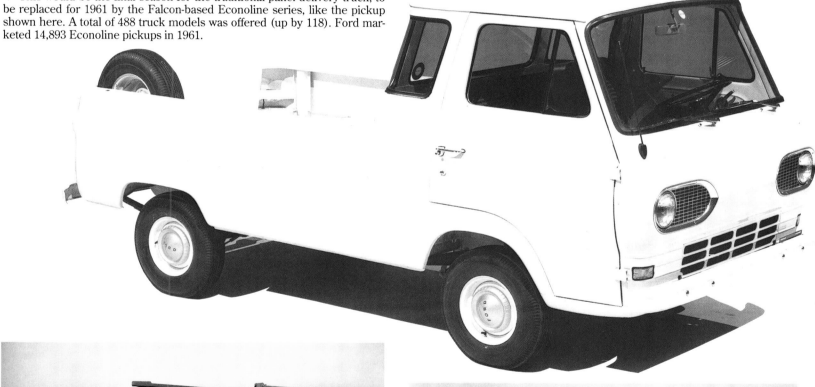

▲ Light-duty trucks adopted a fresh front-end with full-width "dumbbell" holding the headlights, and wide eggcrate latticework between rectangular parking lights. The F-600 could be optioned to 21,000-pound maximum.

▲ Stake and platform bodies were added to the four-wheel-drive F-100/250 series. This F-250 4×4 boasted stronger standard springs for 1960. Truck production reached 337,468 units, but still trailed Chevrolet's total.

1961

Ford tops Chevrolet in model-year production race, 1,338,790 to 1,318,014

Falcon-based Econoline van debuts, as does Corvair van

Third-generation Thunderbird launched

Big 390-cid V-8 debuts, with up to 401 horsepower

Falcon Futura arrives in mid-year

Fords get pre-lubed 30,000-mile chassis fittings and 6000-mile oil changes

Thunderbird gains Swing-Away steering wheel

October UAW strike threat averted

Look what's new since you last looked at Falcon

new Falcon Futura by Ford

COMPACT COUSIN OF THE THUNDERBIRD

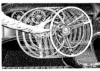

Here's a brand-new version of America's favorite compact . . . the new Falcon Futura. Notice the two front seats are separate—and both are custom-contoured. Futura colorings and trim schemes are exquisite originals, too. Deep-pile carpeting extends wall to wall. Arm rests for everyone add to the enchantment. And look! In Futura, personal effects ride right at your finger tips—elegantly concealed in a sleek console *between* the front seats. Only the men who designed the Thunderbird could have created this masterpiece! There are two lively engines to choose from: for extra power there's Falcon's zesty new 170 Special.

Handy personal console between seats

For *proven* economy—the famous Falcon 144. *With this engine and standard transmission a Falcon averaged 32.68 miles per gallon in this year's Mobilgas Economy Run . . . the highest mileage ever obtained by a 6- or 8-cylinder car in the 25-year history of the Run!* You get all these features in Futura—for a price that's *way below** other luxury compacts! The new Falcon Futura is at your Ford Dealer's. This is your personal car: see it now!   FORD DIVISION *Ford Motor Company.*   *Based on a comparison of manufacturers' suggested retail delivered prices.

UNMISTAKABLY NEW . . . UNMISTAKABLY THUNDERBIRD

The new adventure in Elegance

HERE, for 1961, is the most dramatically beautiful new line since Thunderbird last started a trend. Even at rest it looks like adventure—but when it begins to move, it is elegance come alive—a sports car in spirit, a luxury car in action.

The distinction of this unique 4-passenger automobile is based on a number of remarkable engineering advances. The new optional

Swing-Away Steering Wheel glides out of your way for easier, more graceful entrances and exits—yet locks safely in place before you can drive. Doors are wider, windshield

projections have been eliminated.

All horizons come closer with the new high-performance Thunderbird 390 Special V-8. And three power assists—all standard equipment—double your pleasure in getting there. New Cruise-O-Matic Drive introduces you to the silken-silk smoothness of vacuum-controlled shifting. New Power Steering reduces steering effort by 65%. New Power Brakes are larger, more positive—and adjust themselves automatically. And, with the Thunderbird's familiar trim dimensions on an even wider tread, you corner flatter, maintain a sports-car grip on the most wildly twisting roads.

Add durability features like three-phase rust-prevention treatment of the body and triple-life aluminized mufflers, and you realize why Thunderbird has the finest resale record of any luxury car. The 1961 Thunderbird should be almost a bankable item.

We think you'll agree the temptation to Thunderbird is now more irresistible than ever.   FORD DIVISION *Ford Motor Company.*

'61 THUNDERBIRD
UNIQUE IN ALL THE WORLD

Mention the National Geographic—It identifies you

▲ Responding to Chevy's Corvair Monza, Ford launched the Falcon Futura at mid-year, billed as "compact cousin of the Thunderbird." Sporty touches included contoured bucket seats alongside a mini-console and plusher deep-pile carpet. A floorshift for the manual transmission was optional. A total of 44,470 Futura coupes were built in a short season.

◄ *National Geographic* was the venue for this T-Bird ad, describing the restyled '61 edition as "a sports car in spirit, a luxury car in action . . . . Even at rest, it looks like an adventure." The optional Swing-Away steering wheel permitted graceful entrances and exits, while wider tread allowed flatter cornering. Sole engine: the 300-bhp, 390 Special V-8.

▲ In this 50th anniversary year of the Indianapolis Speedway, a slick new Thunderbird convertible paced the Memorial Day race. The four-seater's freshly tapered fuselage looked especially clean in ragtop dress.

▲ Dimensions changed little in the next-generation "Squarebird," which shared its cowl structure with the new Continental. Out back was a mere suggestion of fins, while the roofline had a more rounded appearance.

▲ When stowed, the "Squarebird" convertible top was fully hidden. Of the 73,051 T-Birds built this year, 10,516 were convertibles.

▲ Only two of the round rear housings shown in this clay model would last into production, and scalloped wheel openings would fade away. Final Thunderbird fins were more moderate.

▲ William Boyer penned the "projectile look" that wound up as '61 T-Bird. Elwood Engel's more formal mock-up became the Continental. Early clay used the giant turbine concept.

▲ Less Thunderbird "feel" is evident in this early clay model with its small round taillights and grille-like rectangular rear panel. Note the wraparound semi-bumpers.

▲ Sharp edges and a vast deck overhang gave this Thunderbird clay an off-balance appearance. Even the early renderings had abandoned the dogleg A-pillar of 1958-60.

▲ Tailfins were on the way out (or at least toned down), so this T-Bird's tall central fin disappeared in favor of twin narrow units, topped by a molding running from nose to tail.

▲ Curved glass would be part of the new Thunderbird's package, for a smoother appearance, but the wraparound back window on this prototype has almost a "bubbletop" look.

171

▲ Extensive facelifting gave full-size Fords a more squared-up stance, as they became slightly lighter and shorter. A horizontal bar split the concave grille's "pin-dot" pattern, flanked by outboard quad headlights. Large round taillights below subtle canted-blade fins harked back to 1957-59 styling. Galaxie Sunliner output nearly matched the 1960 total.

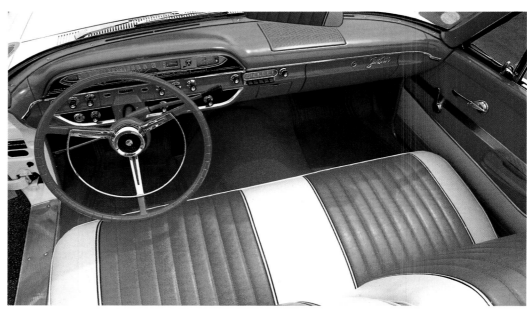

▶ Gauges for the full-size Ford sat in a hooded, recessed panel. At mid-year, the 300- and 375-bhp versions of the new 390 V-8 were augmented by a powerhouse with triple two-barrel carbs, cranking out 401 bhp. By late 1961, a four-speed gearbox was optional.

▲ Only one regular Ford topped the $3000 mark: the nine-passenger version of the Country Squire wagon. Choosing six seats saved $70. A total of 14,657 were built, out of 136,619 wagons in all. Price leader was the two-door Ranch Wagon, but it was the slowest seller of the half-dozen wagons.

▲ Top-selling big Ford was the Galaxie four-door sedan, shown here in styling mock-up form. The clean-looking '61 had a shorter deck and deeper trunk. Two-door sedans weren't moving well, but the Victoria hardtop coupe and sedan—priced just a little above sedans—found quite a few customers.

▲ The Starliner's long, semi-fastback roofline looked particularly good atop the latest Ford's lower body, but that didn't help sales. Production slid below 30,000, and the briefly popular hardtop wouldn't return for '62.

▲ A bigger (170 cid and 101 bhp) six-cylinder engine was available for Falcons, which earned a mild facelift with handsome convex grille. A 144-cid Falcon with manual shift averaged 32.68 mpg in the Mobilgas Economy Run.

▲ Like other full-size Fords, the Starliner could get the new "Thunderbird Special" 390 V-8, with 300 horsepower, in 375-bhp "Super" form or, later, 401 bhp. These choices gave Ford a hot rival to the new Chevy 409.

▲ Falcon production rose even higher than its impressive opening-season total, hitting 474,241 units. Wagons did better yet, climbing near 120,000. Also available: a downsized Courier, called Falcon Sedan Delivery.

▲ "The automotive sensation of 1961," as one writer put it, was the new Ford Econoline. Based on the Falcon, it came as a forward-control, 90-inch-wheelbase van, Station Bus, or pickup. Prices started at a modest $1880.

Model Breakdown Chart

Falcon—wb 109.5		Wght	Price	Prod
58A	sdn 4d	2,289	1,976	159,761
59A	wgn 2d	2,525	2,227	32,045
62A	Futura cpe	2,322	2,162	44,470
64A	sdn 2d (inc 50	2,254	1,914	150,032
	Economy sdns)			
71A	wgn 4d	2,558	2,270	87,933
Custom 300—wb 119.0				
58F	sdn 4d	3,516	—	303
64H	sdn 2d	3,405	—	49
Fairlane—wb 119.0				
58E	sdn 4d	3,634	2,317	96,602
64F	sdn 2d	3,536	2,263	66,875
Fairlane 500—wb 119.0				
58A	sdn 4d	3,642	2,432	98,917
64A	sdn 2d	3,551	2,378	42,468

Galaxie—wb 119.0		Wght	Price	Prod
54A	sdn 4d	3,619	2,592	141,823
62A	sdn 2d	3,537	2,538	27,780
63A	Starliner htp cpe	3,566	2,599	29,669
65A	Victoria htp cpe	3,594	2,599	75,437
75A	Victoria htp sdn	3,637	2,664	30,342
76B	Sunliner conv cpe	3,743	2,849	44,614
Station Wagon—wb 119.0				
59C	Ranch 2d, 6P	3,865	2,588	12,042
71E	Country Sedan 4d, 9P	4,011	2,858	16,356
71F	Country Sedan 4d, 6P	3,983	2,754	46,311
71G	Country Squire 4d, 9P	4,015	3,013	14,657
71H	Ranch 4d, 6P	3,960	2,658	30,292
71J	Country Squire 4d, 6P	3,969	2,943	16,961
Thunderbird—wb 113.0				
63A	htp cpe	3,958	4,172	62,535
76A	conv cpe	4,130	4,639	10,516

1961 Engine Availability

Engines	bore × stroke	bhp	availability
I-6, 144.3	3.50 × 2.50	85	S-Falcon
I-6 170.0	3.50 × 2.94	101	O-Falcon
I-6, 223.0	3.62 × 3.30	135	S-all exc Falcon
V-8, 292.0	3.75 × 3.30	175	S-all exc Falcon
V-8, 352.0	4.00 × 3.50	220	O-all exc Falcon
V-8, 390.0	4.05 × 3.78	300	O-all exc Falcon
V-8, 390.0	4.05 × 3.78	375/401	O-all exc Falcon
Thunderbird			
V-8, 390.0	4.05 × 3.78	300	S-all

1962

Fairlane becomes Ford's first mid-size model, starting new market niche

Thunderbird adds a two-seat Sports Roadster

406-cid V-8 available in big Fords

Three models debut at mid-year: Galaxie 500/XL, Falcon Sports Futura, and Fairlane Sports Coupe

Script-in-oval Ford logo returns

30-millionth Ford V-8 built on July 2

Chevrolet regains Number One in model-year output, beating Ford's 1,476,031 by over half a million

Shelby-American starts production of Cobra sports car with Ford V-8 power

2-for-1 Ford stock split announced in May

Ford exhibits Cougar 406 sport model with power gullwing doors

Just right – for just about everybody!

There's no new car anything like it! A foot shorter than the big ones, the new Ford Fairlane 500 fits in your garage as prettily as it sits on a beach. Its bigness is *inside*—where it's as roomy as some of the biggest Fords ever built. Although priced under many compacts, the new Fairlane 500 is a fine car from dual headlights to oversize trunk. The all-new Challenger V-8 engine (optional) is the world's first Economy Eight—and is as quick to save a dollar as it is to save time. Service has been reduced to a minimum—30,000 miles on many items, no more than twice a year or 6,000 miles on the rest . . . A dream car? It was until this year. Now you can see it and drive it at your Ford Dealer's.

'62 FORD
FAIRLANE 500
ONLY THE NAME'S THE SAME!

▲ "A foot shorter than the big ones" was Ford's way of describing the reworked Fairlane 500, adding that "its bigness is *inside*." New 221-cid and (at mid-year) 260 Challenger V-8 engines became optional, billed as the "world's first Economy Eight." Service intervals were lengthened on a number of components.

▲ The fancier Fairlane 500 four-door sedan sold for $2304 ($88 more than a base Fairlane sedan), and outsold the other four models in the series by a mile. Prices ranged from $2154 for a base two-door to $2403 for the 500 Sports Coupe. Fairlanes were six inches longer than Falcons in wheelbase, some 500 pounds heavier, with similar unit construction.

▲ Ford president Lee Iacocca shows off the new Fairlane, which was needed to fill the growing gap between the compact Falcon and full-size Fords, in both price and size. Ford stepped into that market before GM or Chrysler. With a 115.5-inch wheelbase and 197.6-inch length, Fairlane ranked as mid-size, but would have been full-size six years earlier.

▲ Anyone hankering for the old two-seat Thunderbirds had a new choice: the Sports Roadster, with a tapered fiberglass tonneau (headrests included) hiding rear seats. Kelsey-Hayes wire wheels were part of hefty $5439 tag.

▲ Sticker-priced at $4788 this year, a standard T-Bird convertible was no bargain-basement beauty—and no lightweight at a portly 4370 pounds. The Sports Roadster was both heavier and costlier.

▲ A thorough revamp of the basic 1960 bodyshell gave full-size Fords a bulkier look, with more rounded sheeetmetal. A flat, rather ornate grille helped provide a fresh face. The sporty new Galaxie 500/XL came as a Victoria hardtop or Sunliner convertible, with standard 292 V-8 engine.

▲ Full-size models had a selection of V-8s, all the way up to Ford's biggest ever: 406 cid, with 385 or 405 bhp. The latter, shown here, cost $380.

▲ Bucket seats and a floor gearshift helped give the Galaxie 500/XL its sporty flair. Other big Fords had bench seating and column lever.

▲ Two hardtops were offered for '62, with the Galaxie 500 Victoria the top seller of the pair—priced $594 under the sportier 500/XL. Galaxie was now the base series, 500 the step-up model, and 500/XL the all-out performance choice, with 41,595 XLs produced.

◄ Out back, fins were gone completely from the full-size Ford lineup, creating a straight-through fenderline. Round taillights now dipped into the bumper, connected by a broad "grille" that emphasized the car's width. Vinyl roofs were a common accessory on hardtops.

◄ Ford's 390-cid V-8, available on full-size models, came in an expansive selection of ratings, from moderate 300 to hot 401 bhp.

► With a 406 underhood, Ford had a rival to the latest big mills. The top-dog 405-bhp V-8 could shoot a heavy Ford to 60 in seven seconds.

▲ Best-seller in the big station wagon lineup was the plain-sided Country Sedan—three times as popular with six-passenger capacity than with seating for nine. The two-door Ranch Wagon was gone after 1961, but its four-door companion continued to attract customers.

▲ As usual, the simulated-wood Country Squire was a worthy member of the station-wagon crew. Only 31,780 were produced for 1962, almost evenly split between six- and nine-passenger seating, as opposed to 64,197 Country Sedans and 33,674 Ranch Wagons.

▲ Fairlanes and 500/XLs may have grabbed all the attention in 1962, but the best-seller at year's end was the Galaxie 500 four-door sedan. Galaxie production nearly doubled that of the mid-size Fairlane. Two-door sedans were more popular in base Galaxie series than the 500.

▲ Leadfoots liked the big 390 and 406 V-8s, but the 352-cid engine satisfied plenty of folks, developing its 220 bhp on regular fuel.

▲ Most popular V-8 for full-size Galaxies was the 292-cid version, which used a two-barrel carburetor to whip up its 170 horsepower.

▲ Standard in T-Birds, with either 300 or 340 horsepower (triple two-barrel carbs), the 390-cid V-8 also went under full-size hoods.

▲ Taking the place of the departed Starliner and its speed-shaped roofline was this Starlift accessory hardtop, which turned an ordinary Sunliner convertible into a wind-cheater of sorts.

▲ No Starlifts were listed in the selection of Ford models available for 1962 because the top was an extra-cost non-standard item, mounted atop a conventional full-size convertible.

▲ Only a handful of Starlift accessory tops were built. Fords needed a shape of this sort to remain competitive on stock-car tracks, but the add-on top was banned by NASCAR as "not production."

Model Breakdown Chart

Falcon—wb 109.5

		Wght	Price	Prod
58A	sdn 4d	2,279	2,047	126,041
58B	Deluxe sdn 4d	2,285	2,133	
59A	wgn 2d	2,539	2,298	20,025
59B	Deluxe wgn 2d	2,545	2,384	
62C	Futura cpe	2,343	2,273	17,011
64A	sdn 2d	2,243	1,985	143,650
64B	Deluxe sdn 2d	2,249	2,071	
71A	wgn 4d	2,575	2,341	66,819
71B	Deluxe wgn 4d	2,581	2,427	
71C	Squire wgn 4d	2,591	2,603	22,583

Fairlane—wb 115.5

54A	sdn 4d	2,848	2,216	45,342
62A	sdn 2d	2,815	2,154	34,264
54B	500 sdn 4d	2,865	2,304	129,258
62B	500 sdn 2d	2,832	2,242	68,624
62C	500 spt cpe	2,928	2,403	19,628

Galaxie—wb 119.0

54B	sdn 4d	3,636	2,507	115,594
62B	sdn 2d	3,554	2,453	54,930

Galaxie 500—wb 119.0

		Wght	Price	Prod
54A	sdn 4d	3,650	2,667	174,195
62A	sdn 2d	3,568	2,613	27,824
65A	Victoria htp cpe	3,568	2,674	87,562
65B	XL Victoria htp cpe	3,672	3,268	28,412
75A	Victoria htp sdn	3,640	2,739	30,778
76A	Sunliner conv cpe	3,730	2,924	42,646
76B	XL Sunliner conv cpe	3,831	3,518	13,183

Station Wagon—wb 119.0

71A	Country Squire 4d, 9P	4,022	3,088	15,666
71B	Country Sedan 4d, 6P	3,992	2,829	47,635
71C	Country Sedan 4d, 9P	4,010	2,933	16,562
71D	Ranch 4d, 6P	3,968	2,733	33,674
71E	Country Squire 4d, 6P	4,006	3,018	16,114

Thunderbird—wb 113.0

63A	htp cpe	4,132	4,321	69,554*
63B	Landau htp cpe	4,144	4,398	
76A	conv cpe	4,370	4,788	7,030*
76B	Sports Roadster conv cpe	4,471	5,439	1,427*

*Some sources list total of 68,127 hardtops/Landaus and 9,884 convertibles.

1962 Engine Availability

Engines	bore × stroke	bhp	availability
I-6, 144.3	3.50 × 2.50	85	S-Falcon
I-6, 170.0	3.50 × 2.94	101	O-Falcon
I-6, 223.0	3.62 × 3.60	138	S-all exc Falcon
V-8, 221.0	3.50 × 2.87	145	O-Fairlane
V-8, 260.0	3.80 × 2.87	164	O-Fairlane
V-8, 292.0	3.75 × 3.30	170	S-76B; O-all exc Falc, Fair
V-8, 352.0	4.00 × 3.50	220	O-all exc Falcon, Fairlane
V-8, 390.0	4.05 × 3.78	300/400	O-all exc Falcon, Fairlane
V-8, 390.0	4.05 × 3.78	375/401	O-all exc Falcon, Fairlane
V-8, 406.0	4.13 × 3.78	385/405	O-all exc Falcon, Fairlane

Thunderbird

V-8, 390.0	4.05 × 3.78	300	S-all
V-8, 390.0	4.05 × 3.78	340	O-all

▲ President Iacocca liked mid-year models, to take advantage of the busy spring selling season. Thus, the Falcon Futura, which had opened the model year, was replaced by an updated Futura at mid-year.

▲ One of three sporty 1962½ models marketed as "The Lively Ones" was the Falcon Futura, with a squared-off Thunderbird-style roof. With bucket seats and special hubcaps, it cost $202 more than a Deluxe two-door sedan.

▲ Not much time was needed for Ford to hit the million mark with the compact Falcon. Production dropped only a little in its third season, to a total of 396,129 (including 17,011 Futuras).

▲ This '62 F-850 Ford truck is labeled Super Duty. A 10-wheeler, it has been fitted out with a cement mixer to serve the construction trade, though this chassis was adaptable for many other uses as well. Note the solid front axle and the leaf-spring suspension. This truck is equipped with the more deluxe "Custom Cab" option.

▲ Commercial users who didn't need flash still had the Falcon Sedan Delivery—and Ranchero.

▲ Windowed all around, this $2287 Econoline was called the Falcon DeLuxe Club Wagon.

▲ Falcon's 170-cid six and left-side cargo doors were new options for Econolines.

▲ Light-duty trucks, including this F-250 4×4, wore revised grilles with a wide stylized star.

▲ Ford's H-Series tractor was the choice for long hauls, shown here as an HD-900 diesel.

▲ T-Series tandems, like this 950 diesel, often had a 266-bhp, 534-cid V-8.

1963

Performance-aimed "Lively Ones" debut at mid-year

"Total Performance" theme sets tone for season

Massive V-8s available, up to 427 cid

Falcon and Fairlane get new body styles

Car production passes 1.5 million, but trails Chevy's 2.1 million

Ford celebrates centennial of Henry I's birth and 60th Anniversary of company

"Whiz Kid" Arjay Miller named corporate president

Ford truck volume reaches postwar high

America's first fully synchronized three-speed gearbox installed

Mid-engine Ford V-8 finishes second at Indy 500

Ford tries—and fails—to buy Ferrari company

All 1963 engines add a PCV valve—first of the emissions controls

REPORT FROM MONACO

Ford premieres the Liveliest of the Lively Ones—new Command Performance Cars for 1963½

A new Royal Family of Fords has just made its bow before the car-wise audience that assembles each year for Europe's most famous road rally. The verdict: Vive la Ford! That regal roofline in the foreground looks like a convertible but isn't: it crowns the new Super Torque Ford Sports Hardtop. At left background: new Fairlane Sports Coupe offers a choice of two V-8s. At right: the hot, new Falcon Hardtop that introduces scatback styling to the compact field. American premiere at your Ford Dealer's!

America's liveliest, most care-free cars

FORD
FALCON · FAIRLANE · FORD · THUNDERBIRD

◀ Ford dangled a tempting array of new models at mid-year in 1963. The "new Royal Family of Fords" included a "Super Torque" Galaxie 500 Sports Hardtop with "regal roofline," a Fairlane Sports Coupe, and a Falcon Futura hardtop with "scatback styling." Falcon's sporty Sprint models also arrived late.

Tool kit for a Ford-built car

Another reason why Ford Motor Company cars are quality built. A whisk broom for occasional clean-ups may be the most important tool you will need all year. Standard on many Ford-built cars are self-adjusting brakes, 6,000 mile intervals between oil changes and minor lubrications, 30,000 miles between major lubrications, and life-of-the-car transmission fluid. These are just a few of the self-servicing features pioneered by Ford Motor Company in our determination to free you from car cares. They add up to the fact that our cars are quality built to last longer, need less care, and retain their value.

FORD: Falcon, Fairlane, Galaxie, THUNDERBIRD
MERCURY: Comet, Monterey, LINCOLN CONTINENTAL

PRODUCTS OF *Ford* MOTOR COMPANY

▼ Thunderbirds are "a most elusive species," this ad insisted, "with a rare talent for disappearing from the view of lesser cars." Ford promoted the two-passenger Sports Roadster as well as T-Bird's contoured bucket seats and Swing-Away steering wheel. A Limited Edition debuted in Monaco, with Grace Kelly on hand.

▲ Quality and reduced need for maintenance were major selling points in 1963, just as they would be three decades later. Ford ads promoted the self-adjusting brakes that were becoming available, longer intervals between oil changes and lube jobs, and "life-of-the-car" transmission fluid.

How to catch a Thunderbird

Find one that's standing still. In full flight this is a most elusive species—with a rare talent for disappearing from the view of lesser cars. It is powered by a Thunderbird 390 V-8 and equipped with features that make it remarkably easy to handle, exceptionally pleasant to ride in.

Although it may remind you of a sports car, particularly in the Sports Roadster version shown here, it still ranks among the world's foremost luxury cars. Interiors have contoured bucket seats, a personal console, deep-foam cushioning, glove-soft upholsteries and special

Thunderbird conveniences like the Swing-Away Steering Wheel.

A tradition of superb engineering has resulted in a program of refinement (a list of changes between '62 and '63 alone would make a small book.) As you might expect, Thunderbird—with its exceptionally high resale value—continues to be one of the finest investments in automotive history. May we suggest that you see your neighborhood Ford Dealer? He may have one in his showroom that's standing still.

Thunderbird
unique in all the world

179

▲ To get an early fix on public reaction to a sporty car for general consumption, Ford developed this mid-engine Mustang I in 1962. The two-seater drew plenty of favorable comment. Note the built-in exhaust tips.

▶ One of the earliest ideas for a sporty personal Ford was the Mustang I, a styling study first seen in 1962. A two-seater, it featured all-independent suspension, adjustable springs and shocks, tubular frame, and a built-in roll bar.

▲ Following the typical sequence of events, the Mustang I led to a running Mustang II prototype, shown nationwide in 1963.

▲ Observers of the Mustang II's rear saw a preview of the production ponycar, though the six vertical taillights wouldn't last.

▲ Round gauges in the Mustang II were destined to disappear, replaced by a Falcon-based instrument panel in the on-sale Mustang.

▲ This Fairlane show car toured the 1963 auto-show circuit. Note the "sedanca" half-roof and rounded rear wheel arches. No Fairlane 500s with unroofed front seats ever made production, but Ford was always experimenting with fresh ideas. Other cars on tour were the Allegro, Cougar II, and Mustang II.

◀ In this final year of T-Bird's third generation, not much was changed except for new flat-top wheel openings. Horizontal fender creaselines ran back to slanted hashmarks on doors. Convertibles were losing favor and volume dipped close to half its 1961 level.

▲ Only 455 Sports Roadster variants of the '63 Thunderbird were produced, with an eye-popping $5563 sticker price. Only 37 had the more potent 340-bhp engine rather than the standard 300 bhp. The soft top folded beneath the rear-hinged decklid, using a system similar to the 1957-59 retractable. Four models were offered, with only 5913 convertibles built.

▲ Not exactly the flashiest of the lot, the base hardtop coupe ranked as top-selling T-Bird by far, with 42,806 built this year. Price was $4445, while another $103 bought a Landau version. Total production of 14,139 Landaus included 2000 Limited Editions with white paint, matching leather, Rose Beige vinyl top, and knock-off wire wheel covers.

▲ Sculptured bodysides and squared-up roofs were prominent on the '63 Falcons, including the four-door sedan, offered in base and Futura form. Only half as many Futuras were produced, with a $114 price difference between the two.

▲ Falcons doffed their tops in '63 as both standard Futura and Sprint convertibles rolled off the line, the latter costing $130 more. Of the 35,794 Falcon ragtops, only 4602 were Sprints, making them prized by today's fans.

▲ At mid-year, a bucket-seat Futura Sprint joined the Falcon line, in ragtop and hardtop dress. Also new: a sharp semi-fastback hardtop, and the option of a 260-cid V-8 engine. A Sprint hardtop could run 0-60 in under 12 seconds.

181

▲ Sharpest of the nine models under the year-old mid-size nameplate was this 1963½ Fairlane 500 Sports Coupe, with bucket seats and a $2504 price tag. Long trim moldings led to slight fins. Fender emblems revealed a 260 V-8 engine.

▲ Most popular of the '63 Fairlanes—by far— was the Fairlane 500 four-door sedan, which showed flashier trim than its lower-cost mate.

▲ The Fairlane line included a trio of wagons: two Ranch Wagons and the top-dollar Country Squire, with 7983 built out of 61,601 in all.

▲ Budget-conscious Ford fans could elect the Fairlane two-door sedan at $2154. Its Fairlane 500 companion sold better, for $88 more.

▶ The slick "slantback" Galaxie XL hardtop coupe was a mid-year addition at $3268, yet found 33,870 customers by year's end.

▲ Ford bored its 406 V-8 to 427 cid, to create the top powerhouse: 410 bhp with one carb, 425 with twin four-barrels. Four-speed shift was mandatory.

▲ Top-flight stock-car drivers like Tiny Lund helped Ford beat Plymouth 23-19 on the NASCAR high-speed ovals in 1963.

▲ Twin Galaxie 500 convertibles targeted the sunshine set: a "plain" Sunliner and the bucket-seat XL
edition. Rakish "slantback" Sports Hardtops, not ragtops, ranked as the most popular 500 models.

▲ Somewhat subdued beneath the more glamorous Galaxie 500 was the
regular Galaxie series. This two-door sedan attracted 30,335 shoppers.
Galaxies got a major reskin with concave grille and bolder round taillights.

▲ Topping the full-size lineup was a quartet of Galaxie 500/XL models, including the $3333 Town Victoria four-door, which saw 12,596 copies. The
two-door Club Victoria borrowed T-Bird's squared-off roofline.

▲ Both six- and nine-passenger editions of the full-size Country Squire wagons were offered this year, priced at $3018 and $3088, along with a comparable pair of plain-bodied Country Sedans that cost less.

▲ Not all full-size Fords were flashy. Two new 300 sedans were priced
below Galaxie, aimed at fleet buyers. At mid-year, a 195-bhp 289 replaced
the 260 as base Galaxie V-8, but a 223-cid six was still standard.

▲ Continental introduced its four-door convertible for '61, but this "Galaxie" mock-up from early that
year never made the Ford roster. All of this ragtop's doors were front-hinged, unlike Lincoln's.

Model Breakdown Chart

Series 0 Falcon—wb 109.5		Wght	Price	Prod
54A	sdn 4d	2,337	2,047	62,365
62A	sdn 2d	2,300	1,985	70,630
Series 10 Falcon Futura—wb 109.5				
54B	sdn 4d	2,345	2,161	31,736
62B	sdn 2d	2,308	2,116	27,018
63B	htp cpe	2,438	2,198	28,496
63C	Sprint htp cpe	2,438	2,320	10,479
76A	conv cpe	2,645	2,470	31,192
76B	Sprint conv cpe	2,645	2,600	4,602
Series 20 Falcon Wagon—wb 109.5				
59A	wgn 2d	2,580	2,298	7,322
59B	Deluxe wgn 2d	2,586	2,384	4,269
71A	wgn 4d	2,617	2,341	18,484
71B	Deluxe wgn 4d	2,623	2,427	23,477
71C	Squire wgn 4d	2,639	2,603	8,269
Series 30 Fairlane—wb 115.5				
54A	sdn 4d	2,930	2,216	44,454
62A	sdn 2d	2,890	2,154	28,984
71B	Cus Ranch Wagon 4d	3,298	2,613	29,612
71D	Ranch Wagon 4d	3,281	2,525	24,006
71E	Squire Wagon 4d	3,295	2,781	7,893
Series 40 Fairlane 500—wb 115.5				
54B	sdn 4d	2,945	2,304	104,175
62B	sdn 2d	2,905	2,242	34,764
65A	htp cpe	2,923	2,324	41,641
65B	htp cpe, bkt sts	2,923	2,504	28,268

Series 50 300—wb 119.0		Wght	Price	Prod
54E	sdn 4d	3,627	2,378	44,142
62E	sdn 2d	3,547	2,324	26,010
Series 50 Galaxie—wb 119.0				
54B	sdn 4d	3,647	2,507	82,419
62B	sdn 2d	3,567	2,453	30,335
Series 60 Galaxie 500—wb 119.0				
54A	sdn 4d	3,667	2,667	205,722
62A	sdn 2d	3,587	2,613	21,137
63B	XL htp cpe, fstbk	3,772	2,674	100,500
65A	htp cpe	3,599	2,674	49,733
75A	htp sdn	3,679	2,739	26,558
76A	Sunliner conv cpe	3,757	2,924	36,876
65B	XL htp cpe	3,670	3,268	29,713
63C	XL spt htp cpe, fstbk	3,670	3,268	33,870
75C	XL htp sdn	3,750	3,333	12,956
76B	XL conv cpe	3,820	3,518	18,551
Series 70 Station Wagon—wb 119.0				
71A	Country Squire 4d, 9P	4,003	3,088	19,567
71B	Country Sedan 4d, 6P	3,977	2,829	64,954
71C	Country Sedan 4d, 9P	3,989	2,933	22,250
71E	Country Squire 4d, 6P	3,991	3,018	20,359
Series 80 Thunderbird—wb 113.0				
63A	htp cpe	4,195	4,445	42,806*
63B	Landau htp cpe	4,203	4,548	14,139*
76A	conv cpe	4,322	4,912	5,913*
76B	Sports Roadster conv cpe	4,396	5,563	455*

*Some sources list total of 59,000 hardtops/Landaus and 5,457 convertibles. Model 63B includes 2,000 Limited Edition Landaus with special trim; model 76B includes 37 units with 340-bhp engine.

1963 Engine Availability

Engines	bore × stroke	bhp	availability
I-6, 144.3	3.50 × 2.50	85	S-Falcon
I-6, 170.0	3.50 × 2.94	101	O-Falcon
I-6, 200.0	3.68 × 3.13	116	S-Fairlane
I-6, 223.0	3.62 × 3.60	138	S-all exc Falcon, Fairlane
V-8, 221.0	3.50 × 2.87	145	O-Fairlane
V-8, 260.0	3.80 × 2.87	164	S-Falcon Sprint; O-others
V-8, 289.0	4.00 × 2.87	271	O-Fairlane
V-8, 352.0	4.00 × 3.50	220	O-all exc Falcon, Fairlane
V-8, 390.0	4.05 × 3.78	300/330	O-all exc Falcon, Fairlane
V-8, 406.0	4.13 × 3.78	385/405	O-all exc Falcon, Fairlane
V-8, 427.0	4.23 × 3.78	410/425	O-all exc Falcon, Fairlane
Thunderbird			
V-8, 390.0	4.05 × 3.78	300	S-all
V-8, 390.0	4.05 × 3.78	340	O-all

▲ Either a fendered Flareside or smooth-flanked Styleside F-100 pickup could be bought.

▲ The ¾-ton F-250 pickup came as a 2WD or 4WD. Only 1835 4×4 Stylesides were built.

▲ This medium-duty F-600 carried a 12-foot stake-bed chassis and Custom Cab.

▶ Businesses on a budget liked the $2111 price of the Falcon sedan delivery almost as much as its seven-foot-long cargo bay. This year's Falcons displayed slightly more pointed front fenders and a convex grille. Both six-cylinder engines adopted hydraulic lifters. On another level, three modified Falcon Sprint hardtops ran in the Monte Carlo Rally.

▲ For $1890, Econoline pickup buyers got an upgraded interior and five-leaf rear springs, but little other change from '62 models.

▲ A total of 48,620 Econoline vans were built in 1963, including this $2069 version. That contrasts with 11,394 Econoline pickups.

▲ Only $1898 bought this Falcon-based Ranchero, but more than one-third of them had a DeLuxe Trim Package for $100 more.

1964

Mustang debuts at mid-year, sets pace for long-hood/short-deck "ponycar"

Thunderbird restyled, gets flow-through ventilation; big Fords fully revamped

Falcon and Fairlane earn a facelift— Thunderbolt attracts drag racers

Production hits 1,594,053, behind Chevy's 2.3 million

***Motor Trend* awards "Car of the Year" to entire line**

Front seatbelts installed on all '64 automobiles

Ford, GM, and American Motors adopt 2-year/24,000-mile warranties

Electrocoat primer process used on T-Birds

Basic oxygen steelmaking plant completed at Rouge

Ford exhibits truck-tractor with gas turbine

▲ Evolution of the amazingly successful Mustang "ponycar" is evident in this group shot. Front to rear: the Mustang I two-seat styling study that started it all; Mustang II running prototype, first seen at Watkins Glen in 1963; a 1965 production hardtop coupe; and the hot modified Shelby GT-350 fastback.

▶ In line with Lee Iacocca's taste for mid-year introductions, Mustang made its splashy debut on April 17, 1964. Ford considered it a '65 model, but there were subtle differences between the 1964½ and those built after summer. The stylish crest, its pony galloping across a red, white, and blue background, would become a familiar sight on American roads.

▲ The notion of a Mustang convertible also was mocked up as a Falcon-like coupe in 1962, with round taillamps and different roofline.

▲ This Allegro-based clay had oddly pointed front fenders and an eggcrate grille. An Allegro show car was displayed in 1963.

▲ Ford's Allegro theme allowed countless variations. This one shows a protruding hood and fenders, plus triangular quarter windows.

▲ Ultimate Mustang proportions were evident in early mock-ups, such as this 1962 version with narrow quarter windows and thick C-pillars.

▲ This racy fastback with long rear-quarter windows was another of the styling studies done under the "Allegro" project code.

▲ Finished in 1963, this clay is directly related to the final Joe Oros design, though it wears "Torino" script and a "Cougar" emblem.

▶ Mere weeks after its launch at the New York World's Fair, a Mustang arrived in Indiana to pace the Memorial Day "500" race. Ford wanted to create a youth-oriented car with four seats, floor shift, weighing 2500 pounds, priced under $2500, and using Falcon mechanical components. Of the seven final designs, one from a group headed by Joe Oros was selected.

▲ Riding a compact 108-inch wheelbase, Mustangs pioneered the "pony-car" concept with their long-hood/short-deck silhouette, bucket-seat interiors, and mild-to-wild options list. Initially priced at $2368 for a hardtop, $2614 for the convertible, they sent shoppers into a frenzy. In just four months, the entire 100,000-car allotment planned for the year was sold.

▲ A floor-mounted gearshift, long (extra-cost) console, and bucket seats were Mustang trademarks, while a racing-style steering wheel added an extra taste of gusto. The Falcon-derived instrument panel belied the car's sporty image, but a $70.80 Rally-Pac with column-mounted tachometer and clock played drivers a different tune.

▲ As depicted on the grille and rear of each early Mustang, the spirited pony seemed to symbolize the freedom of America's wide-open spaces—including, of course, the open road.

▲ Of the 680,989 Mustangs built between April 1964 and August 1965, just 121,538 were 1964½ models, including 28,833 convertibles. Engine choices added to its appeal, starting with a 170-cid six and 260-cid V-8. Options included three flavors of 289 V-8, whipping up as much as 271 horsepower.

◄ Plenty of T-Bird fans still liked to lower the top, as production rose to 9198 units, despite $4953 sticker price.

▲ No more Sports Roadsters were built, but as many as 50 open '64 Thunderbirds were fitted by dealers with its streamlined tonneau.

▲ Sharp sculpturing replaced the smooth-sided look of the prior T-Bird generation, while finless rear fenders held wide rectangular taillights.

◄ In this 1961 mock-up, we see a suggestion of what Thunderbird might have become in its next generation. Sculptured bodysides would indeed be part of the 1964 restyle, but not as complex as shown here. Ultra-wide C-pillars give the four-seater a formal appearance, and aren't much different from the production version. At this juncture, Ford wanted to blend the best of the two prior generations.

187

▲ Ford's compacts were tougher than some might have thought—a Falcon won the GT class at the prestigious Monte Carlo Rally.

▲ Falcon's lower reskin, with full-length sculpturing, gave a bulkier look. Sprints returned with a standard V-8 and bucket seats.

▲ Falcon fenders were pointier, rear end squarer. Three six-cylinder engines were available, as well as the Fairlane 289 V-8.

▲ Hottest Fairlane was the 500 Sports Coupe with bucket seats, but twice as many regular 500 hardtops were sold, at $161 less.

▲ About 54 slimmed-down, detrimmed Fairlane Thunderbolts went to drag racers for $3900, ready for battle with a "High Riser" 427 V-8.

▲ In its third season, Fairlane got a modest touch-up including new side trim and rounded, finless fenders. The four-door 500 sold best.

▲ Best-selling big Ford was the Galaxie 500 hardtop coupe, again available in standard or sporty 500/XL trim. Sheetmetal was more rounded for '64, and the deck longer, with seriously sculptured bodysides.

▲ Topping the full-size price list at $3495 was the Galaxie 500/XL convertible, but that didn't keep 15,169 from finding customers. Regular 500 ragtops sold even better. Many considered this year's XL the best ever.

▶ Theoretically "full-size," the Galaxie 500/XL's bucket-seat interior was fit for four (maybe five). Base engine was Ford's 289 V-8, but most XLs had the 300-bhp 390. This year's hardtop sedan adopted the semi-fastback look.

▲ Once again, the 427 V-8 was Ford's "Total Performance" star, blasting 410 or 425 bhp. A heavy 500/XL with 427 V-8 could hit 60 in 7.4 seconds.

Model Breakdown Chart

Series 0 Falcon—wb 109.5		Wght	Price	Prod
01	sdn 2d	2,365	1,996	36,441
01	Deluxe sdn 2d	2,380	2,096	28,411
02	sdn 4d	2,400	2,058	27,722
02	Deluxe sdn 4d	2,420	2,158	26,532
Series 10 Falcon Futura—wb 109.5				
11	htp cpe, bkt seats	2,545	2,325	8,607
12	conv cpe, bkt seats	2,735	2,597	2,980
13	Sprint htp cpe	2,813	2,436	13,830
14	Sprint conv htp cpe	3,008	2,671	4,278
15	conv cpe	2,710	2,481	13,220
16	sdn 4d	2,410	2,176	38,032
17	htp cpe	2,515	2,209	32,608
19	sdn 2d	2,375	2,127	16,833
Series 20 Falcon Wagon—wb 109.5				
21	wgn 2d	2,660	2,326	6,034
22	wgn 4d	2,695	2,360	17,779
24	Deluxe wgn 4d	2,715	2,446	20,697
26	Squire wgn 4d	2,720	2,622	6,766
Series 30 Fairlane—wb 115.5				
31	sdn 2d	2,855	2,194	20,421
32	sdn 4d	2,895	2,235	36,693
38	Ranch wgn 4d	3,290	2,531	20,980
Series 40 Fairlane 500—wb 115.5				
41	sdn 2d	2,863	2,276	23,447
42	sdn 4d	2,910	2,317	86,919
43	htp cpe	2,925	2,341	42,733
47	htp cpe, bkt sts	2,945	2,502	21,431
48	Ranch Cus wgn 4d	3,310	2,612	24,962
Series 50 Custom—wb 119.0				
51	500 sdn 2d	3,559	2,464	20,619
52	500 sdn 4d	3,659	2,518	68,828
53	sdn 2d	3,529	2,361	41,359
54	sdn 4d	3,619	2,415	57,964
Series 60 Galaxie 500—wb 119.0				
60	XL htp sdn	3,722	3,298	14,661
61	sdn 2d	3,574	2,624	13,041
62	sdn 4d	3,674	2,678	198,805
64	htp sdn	3,689	2,750	49,242
66	htp cpe	3,584	2,685	206,998
65	Sunliner conv cpe	3,759	2,947	37,311
68	XL htp cpe	3,622	3,233	58,306
69	XL conv cpe	3,687	3,495	15,169
Series 70 Station Wagon—wb 119.0				
72	Country Sedan 4d, 6P	3,973	2,840	68,578
74	Country Sedan 4d, 9P	3,983	2,944	25,661
76	Country Squire 4d, 6P	3,988	3,029	23,570
78	Country Squire 4d, 9P	3,998	3,099	23,120
Series 80 Thunderbird—wb 113.2				
83	htp cpe	4,431	4,486	60,552
85	conv cpe	4,586	4,953	9,198
87	Landau htp cpe	4,441	4,589	22,715

▼ Full-size Ford grilles wore three prominent vertical "vees" for an aggressive stance. New bodyside sculpturing gave an illusion of length.

▲ Thin-shell bucket seats held occupants a bit more securely in the '64 Galaxie 500/XL. Four-speed floor shift was mandatory with the 427 V-8.

1964 Engine Availability

Engines	bore × stroke	bhp	availability
I-6, 144.3	3.50 × 2.50	85	S-Flcn exc conv, Sprnt, Del wgns
I-6, 170.0	3.50 × 2.94	101	S-Flcn conv, Sprnt, Del wgn; O-other Flcn
I-6, 200.0	3.68 × 3.13	116	S-Fairlane; O-Falcon
I-6, 223.0	3.62 × 3.60	138	S-all exc Fairlane, Falcon
V-8, 260.0	3.80 × 2.87	164	S-Flcn Sprnt, Fairlane; O-Flcn
V-8, 289.0	4.00 × 2.87	195/271	S-60, 68, 69; O-all exc Flcn
V-8, 352.0	4.00 × 3.50	250	O-all exc Falcon, Fairlane
V-8, 390.0	4.05 × 3.78	300/330	O-all exc Falcon, Fairlane
V-8, 427.0	4.23 × 3.78	410/425	O-all exc Falcon, Fairlane
Thunderbird			
V-8, 390.0	4.05 × 3.78	300	S-all

189

1965

LTD debuts at luxury end of Ford's Galaxie series

Mustang completes its first full model year, with an astounding 680,989 sold

Shelby GT-350 launched

Ford car production hits 2,170,795, lags Chevrolet by 200,000

Industry sets all-time production record at 9,335,277 cars, nearly 1.4 million above 1955 total

Senate Subcommittee begins hearings on auto safety

Record 1.5 million trucks sold—more than one-third of them Fords

Lee Iacocca becomes vice president of corporate Car and Truck Group

Divorced Henry Ford II marries young jetsetter

U.S. and Canada agree to eliminate tariffs on new vehicles and components

▲ At start up time, a Mustang hardtop cost $2368 with six-cylinder power. A vinyl top added $75.80. Most buyers made multiple checks on the lengthy options list, which included a V-8, air conditioning, radio, Cruise-O-Matic, four-speed gearbox, and Rally Pac (with tachometer). A scale model cost a buck.

▲ As the 1965 model year began, the initial 260-cid Mustang V-8 was dropped, making a 200-bhp 289 the first option above the Falcon 170-cid six. Also available: 225- and 271-bhp hop-ups of the 289. Standard hubcaps are shown here, but styled wheels and wire wheel covers were popular "ponycar" extras.

▶ Ranking with the most popular soft tops of all time, the Mustang convertible drew 101,945 customers in its first long season (including "1964½" models). Most buyers chose a V-8, which could include a handling package.

190

▲ A semi-fastback 2+2 coupe joined the Mustang lineup in fall 1964, wearing jaunty air extractors instead of quarter windows. Space in back was tight, but the seatback folded. Fastbacks cost nearly as much as a convertible.

▶ A Mustang, Ford claimed, "has the look, the fire, the flavor of the great European road cars." Ford promoted the Gold Medal Tiffany Award it won for Excellence in American Design. Front disc brakes became available during 1965.

▲ Falcon grilles were simplified for 1965, but sheetmetal otherwise changed little from the '64 restyling. Hardtops were offered only in the flashier Futura series, though base sedans easily outsold their Futura counterparts. Collectors have taken a slight shine to final Futura Sprint hardtops and convertibles, largely due to their role as last-of-the-line. After 1965, the Falcon would become little more than a shortened Fairlane.

▲ Nearing the end of its styling cycle, the Falcon soon would abandon hardtop and convertible body styles, now that the sportier Mustangs were garnering so much attention. Only 3106 Sprints (including just 300 convertibles) were built for '65, plus 6315 regular Futura ragtops and 25,754 Futura hardtops. The convertible shown has the newly available 289-cid V-8, whose 200 horsepower delivered passable performance, if few thrills.

191

▲ Thunderbirds earned only a few trim changes this year, including chrome "C-spears" on front fenders. A Landau hardtop cost just $103 more than its unadorned mate. Later came the Limited Edition Special Landau, with "Ember-Glo" metallic paint and a parchment vinyl top. Only 4500 were built.

▲ Visible changes in the T-Bird line following its 1964 revamp included little more than a new mesh grille with six vertical bars and restyled wheel covers. On the nose, a 'Bird emblem replaced block lettering.

▲ Thunderbird's front bucket seats had a thin-shell appearance, in an otherwise posh cockpit. Note the full-width hooded instrument panel and long console with center armrest. Front disc brakes now were standard.

▲ No lightweight, the '65 Thunderbird convertible tipped the scales at 4588 pounds and measured 205.4 inches long overall. A Galaxie 500 ragtop, in contrast, weighed half a ton less. Sticker price for all this plushness neared the $5000 mark. Tri-section sequential taillights were new this year, originally planned for '64. Wheelbase was unchanged at 113.2 inches.

▲ Extensive bodyside sculpturing was evident on the Thunderbird, its creasework extending right through the fender skirts. A 300-bhp 390 V-8 remained the sole powerplant. A tonneau cover, as used on the abandoned Sports Roadster, remained available but found few takers. T-Bird production defied the industry's record sales, dipping below the 75,000 mark.

▲ Differing sharply from the angular styling that would be used on full-size Fords for 1965, this late-1962 "Galaxie" sedan mock-up displays horizontal quad headlamps, pointy fenders, and subtle bodyside trim lines.

▲ By the time of this early-1963 prototype, the squared-off look destined for big '65 Fords was more evident, though horizontal quad headlamps within a "dumbbell" shaped grille looked closer to what Dodge would offer.

▲ One of many Ford proposals that never happened in the real world, this fastback Galaxie mock-up from early 1963 did display a lower-body profile similar to the full-size version that would enter production for '65.

▲ Differing between the left and right side, like many actual-size Ford clay models and mock-ups, this view proposed an alternate treatment for the side windows, as well as longer triangular quarter windows.

▲ Production of the much-modified Galaxie 500/XL convertible slid by 35 percent, not unlike that of the similarly sporty hardtop, even in this boom year for the industry. Buyers, it seemed, were shunning sport for luxury.

▶ That brawny four-speed's gearshift lever looks ready to grab, inside this Galaxie 500/XL convertible. Bucket front seats contributed to the car's sporty demeanor, while a choice of half a dozen V-8s with as much as 425 horsepower could add stunning performance to the image. Billed as "all new," full-size Fords changed more for 1965 than in any year since 1949, adopting an angular, more stately stance with coil springs all around.

▲ Ford got a lot of advertising mileage out of its comparison test through Manhattan streets, which pitted an LTD against a $17,000 Rolls-Royce. Three Rolls chauffeurs claimed the Ford was quieter.

▲ Limousine conversions of the Ford LTD grew popular among cost-conscious VIPs. Lehmann-Peterson of Chicago was one of the top coachbuilders, known especially for Executive Limousine variants of the Lincoln Continental.

1965 Engine Availability

Engines	bore × stroke	bhp	availability
I-6, 170.0	3.50 × 2.94	101	S-Flcn exc Futura, Squire until 9/25/64
I-6, 200.0	3.68 × 3.13	120	S-Futura/Squire, Fairlane: O-Flcn
I-6, 240.0	4.00 × 3.18	150	S-all exc Flcn, Fairlane, LTD, XL
V-8, 289.0	4.00 × 2.87	200-271	S-LTD, XL; O-others
V-8, 352.0	4.00 × 3.50	250	O-all exc Falcon, Fairlane
V-8, 390.0	4.05 × 3.78	300/330	O-all exc Falcon, Fairlane
V-8, 427.0	4.23 × 3.78	425	O-all exc Falcon, Fairlane
Mustang			
I-6, 170.0	3.50 × 2.94	101	S-all through 9/24/64
I-6, 200.0	3.68 × 3.13	120	S-all after 9/25/64
V-8, 260.0	3.80 × 2.87	164	O-all through 9/25/64
V-8, 289.0	4.00 × 2.87	200	O-all after 9/25/64
V-8, 289.0	4.00 × 2.87	225/271	O-all
Thunderbird			
V-8, 390.0	4.00 × 3.78	300	S-all

▲ Clean, fresh, less aggressive styling marked the '65 Fords, including this Galaxie 500/XL hardtop, which nevertheless saw volume drop by more than half. On lesser models, a 240-cid "Big Six" replaced the base 223.

▲ Henry Ford II tried—but failed—to purchase Ferrari in the early Sixties. Undaunted and determined he pushed the "Total Performance" program to be a winner in every form of motorsport. In 1965, Jim Clark won the famed Indy 500 race in a 255-cid Lotus-Ford at an average speed of 160.729 mph.

▲ Ford's Fairlane suffered what some viewed as a poorly conceived reskinning, with awkward side trim. Production sunk to a record low. New this year was the Fairlane 500 Sports Coupe with bucket seats, of which 15,141 were built. Three 289 V-8s were optional, yielding up to 271 bhp.

▲ Differing in detail and bold striping from a tame Mustang fastback on the outside, Carroll Shelby's GT-350 enjoyed plenty of attention under the skin. Each began as a white fastback with 271-bhp 289 V-8 and Borg-Warner four-speed gearbox, but ended with 306 bhp and startling mobility.

▲ Failing in his attempt to purchase Ferrari, Henry Ford II focused on a more direct route to racing leadership. Development of the GT40 began at Ford of England, but by 1965 moved to Shelby American in California.

▲ Racing GT40s had 289 V-8s that developed up to 390 bhp. Mark III road-going versions used a 306-bhp V-8 and softer suspension. A total of 111 GT40s with the 289 V-8 would eventually be built, plus a dozen with a 427.

▲ Although GT40 production began at Slough, England, bodies and engines came from the U.S. Its name derived from the fact that the mid-engine coupe stood about 40 inches tall. Later work involved Kar Kraft in Detroit.

▲ Ford's first and second tries at Le Mans proved futile, after setting a new lap record, but that would change in 1966. Early GT40 design came from Eric Broadley of the Lola firm and John Wyer, formerly with Aston Martin.

Model Breakdown Chart

Series 0 Falcon—wb 109.5		Wght	Price	Prod
01	sdn 4d	2,366	2,020	35,858
01	Deluxe sdn 2d	2,381	2,120	13,824
02	sdn 4d	2,406	2,082	30,186
02	Deluxe sdn 4d	2,426	2,182	13,850
Series 10 Falcon Futura—wb 109.5				
13	Sprint htp cpe	2,749	2,337	2,806
14	Sprint conv cpe	2,971	2,671	300
15	conv cpe	2,673	2,481	6,315
16	sdn 4d	2,413	2,192	33,985
17	htp cpe	2,491	2,226	25,754
19	sdn 2d	2,373	2,144	11,670
Series 20 Falcon Wagon—wb 109.5				
21	wgn 2d	2,611	2,333	4,891
22	wgn 4d	2,651	2,367	14,911
24	Deluxe wgn 4d (Futura)	2,667	2,506	12,548
26	Squire wgn 4d	2,669	2,665	6,703
Series 30 Fairlane—wb 115.5				
31	sdn 2d	2,902	2,230	13,685

		Wght	Price	Prod
32	sdn 4d	2,954	2,271	25,378
38	wgn 4d	3,279	2,567	13,911
Series 40 Fairlane 500—wb 115.5				
41	sdn 2d	2,901	2,312	16,092
42	sdn 4d	2,959	2,353	77,836
43	htp cpe	2,973	2,377	41,405
47	htp cpe, bkt sts	2,984	2,538	15,141
48	wgn 4d	3,316	2,648	20,506
Series 50 Custom—wb 119.0				
51	sdn 2d	3,336	2,464	49,034
52	sdn 4d	3,408	2,518	96,393
53	500 sdn 2d	3,306	2,361	19,603
54	500 sdn 4d	3,378	2,415	71,727
Series 60 Galaxie 500—wb 119.0				
60	LTD htp sdn	3,578	3,313	68,038
62	sdn 4d	3,440	2,678	181,183
64	htp sdn	3,480	2,765	49,982
65	conv cpe	3,592	2,950	31,930
66	htp cpe	3,380	2,685	157,284

		Wght	Price	Prod
67	LTD htp cpe	3,486	3,233	37,691
68	XL htp cpe	3,497	3,233	28,141
69	XL conv cpe	3,665	3,498	9,849
Series 70 Station Wagon—wb 119.0				
71	Ranch 4d, 6P	3,869	2,763	30,817
72	Country Sedan 4d, 6P	3,879	2,855	59,693
74	Country Sedan 4d, 9P	3,893	2,959	32,344
76	Country Squire 4d, 6P	3,925	3,104	24,308
78	Country Squire 4d, 9P	3,937	3,174	30,502
Mustang*—wb 108.0				
07	htp cpe	2,583	2,372	501,965
08	conv cpe	2,789	2,614	101,945
09	fstbk cpe	2,633	2,589	77,079
Series 80 Thunderbird—wb 113.2				
83	htp cpe	4,470	4,486	42,652
85	conv cpe	4,588	4,953	6,846
87	Laundau htp cpe	4,478	4,589	20,974
87	Limited Ed Special Landau	4,500	4,639	4,500

*Note: 1965 Mustang production totals include 121,538 early (1964½) models.

1966

Four-wheel-drive Bronco sport/utility debuts—battles Jeep and Scout

Second-generation Fairlane accepts big-block V-8s, joins muscle-car brigade

Sporty Fairlane 500/XL and GT join lineup

All Ford wagons adopt dual tailgate that opens either up or sideways

Blue signature oval revived in ads, which declare that "Ford has a better idea"

Millionth Mustang built in March

Ford wins Sebring 12-hour Grand Prix

New W-Series of heavy trucks launched

Production edges past Chevrolet, at just over 2.2 million cars

Rear seatbelts become standard on all U.S. cars

▲ After four successful years, Ford's mid-size Fairlane was redone. The sportiest, most costly model was the 500/XL GT convertible at $3068, powered by a muscular 335-bhp 390 V-8. With only 4327 built, it was also the rarest. Most GT buyers chose a four-speed, or a GT/A with "Sport Shift" Cruise-O-Matic.

▲ Fairlane favorite was the 500 hardtop at $2378, which also came in GT trim. Formerly rather dowdy, the freshened Fairlane wore a clean, contemporary look. Hardtops adopted a semi-fastback roofline. Styling touches included vertical stacked headlamps and a single-bar grille with center emblem.

▲ Plopping the biggest available engine into a lightweight body always produces surprises. About 70 Fairlane two-doors were built with a 427 V-8 under the hood—normally installed only in big Fords—as a reaction to the Hemi-powered Dodge/Plymouth mid-sizes. These Fairlanes looked the part, too, with fiberglass hoods that contained a functional airscoop. They were intended solely for drag racing, not street driving. Tamer Fairlanes sold far above their 1965 level, with GTs beating out the XLs.

▲ Little more than detail changes greeted '66 Mustang shoppers, including a thin-bar grille backdrop and different standard hubcaps. Windsplits adorned the fake bodyside scoops (except on GTs).

▲ Shelby toned down the super-performance GT-350 in its second season, omitting the original side-exit exhausts and making the noisy Detroit Locker rear end optional. A total of 2380 GT-350s were built in '66.

▲ Hard to believe today, but renters from Hertz in the mid-1960s could get a raucous GT-350H Shelby fastback. This year's version had Plexiglas quarter windows in place of the Mustang's vents, and came in more colors.

▲ While Mustang production remained strong, convertibles sagged in popularity. Note the lower-body striping on this GT ragtop.

▲ The most popular Mustang power choice was the 200-bhp 289 V-8, also offered with 225 or 271 bhp. Hardtops outsold ragtops and fastbacks by far.

▲ Five-dial GT instrumentation replaced Mustang's Falcon-style dash. This one has Rally-Pac gauges and factory air conditioning, but no console.

1966 Engine Availability

Engines	bore × stroke	bhp	availability
I-6, 170.0	3.50 × 2.94	105	S-Falcon
I-6, 200.0	3.68 × 3.13	120	S-Flcn Futura/wgn, Fair exc GT, GTA; O-Flcn
I-6, 240.0	4.00 × 3.18	150	S-all exc Flcn, Fair; O-Flcn wgns
V-8, 289.0	4.00 × 2.87	200/225	S-XL, LTD; O-Flcn, Fair exc GT, GTA; 50, 60, 70 exc 7L
V-8, 352.0	4.00 × 3.50	250	O-all exc 7L, Fairlane, Falcon
V-8, 390.0	4.05 × 3.78	265	O-all exc 7L, Fair GT/GTA, Flcn
V-8, 390.0	4.05 × 3.78	315	O-all exc 7L, Fairlane, Falcon
V-8, 390.0	4.05 × 3.78	335	S-Fair GT/GTA; O-other Fair
V-8, 427.0	4.23 × 3.78	410/425	O-all exc 7L, 70, Fairlane, Flcn
V-8, 428.0	4.13 × 3.98	345	S-7L; O-others exc Fairlane, Flcn
Mustang			
I-6, 200.0	3.68 × 3.13	120	S-all
V-8, 289.0	4.00 × 2.87	200	O-all
V-8, 289.0	4.00 × 2.87	225/271	O-all
Thunderbird			
V-8, 390.0	4.00 × 3.78	315	S-all
V-8, 428.0	4.13 × 3.98	345	O-all

▲ Suggesting the tri-spinner front end of the early '50s, this was one of several full-size proposals with grilles akin to Mustang's.

▲ Details got attention on full-size Fords. The grille and hood pushed forward a bit, taillights were squared, rear arches enlarged.

▲ Big Fords proved their mettle in drag racing—especially with the single-overhead-cam 427 V-8 developed from Ford's NASCAR engine.

▼ Out of 19 full-size Fords, three were convertibles, including this 500/XL that sold for $3480. With a 428-cid V-8 it was known as the 7-Litre and cost $392 more. A mere $2934 bought an ordinary Galaxie 500 ragtop.

▲ A world leader could ride almost economically in this Galaxie 500 LTD Limousine. Commoners might prefer a plain four-door hardtop, for $3278.

▲ Thunderbirds earned a mild facelift for 1966. New Town Hardtop and Town Landau models wore ultra-wide C-pillars with no quarter windows.

◄ Two-seaters were still pondered regularly by Ford stylists and executives, even after that notion was nixed for the Mustang. This proposed sports car went under two names during the 1960s: Cobra and Cougar. Early in the Mustang's development period, a version of the two-seat Mustang I had been considered for production, powered by a mid-mounted German Ford V-4. A back seat was deemed essential, however, if the car was to appeal to young marrieds.

▲ Now essentially a shrunken Fairlane, the reworked Falcon came in base and Futura trim, with 182,669 built. Most interesting of the lot was this Futura pillared Sports Coupe with bucket seats.

▲ Ford aimed its compact 4×4 Bronco at the rival Jeep CJ and International Scout. Power came from a Falcon 170-cid six, with 289 V-8 optional later. Roadster, Sports Utility, and $2625 Wagon editions were sold.

▲ This would be the final season for the F-350 pickup with its nine-foot cargo box. A two-tier grille insert was the major change for F-100 to -600. A Monobeam front suspension was installed on the F-100 4WD pickup.

Model Breakdown Chart

		Wght	Price	Prod
Series 0 Falcon—wb 110.9, wgn 113.0				
01	club cpe	2,519	2,060	41,432
02	sdn 4d	2,559	2,114	34,685
06	wgn 4d	3,037	2,442	16,653
Series 10 Falcon Futura—wb 110.9, wgn 113.0				
11	club cpe	2,527	2,183	21,997
12	sdn 4d	2,567	2,237	34,039
13	spt cpe	2,597	2,328	20,289
16	wgn 4d	3,045	2,553	13,574
Series 30 Fairlane—wb 116.0, wgn 113.0				
31	club cpe	2,832	2,240	13,498
32	sdn 4d	2,877	2,280	26,170
38	wgn 4d	3,267	2,589	12,379
Series 40 Fairlane 500—wb 116.0, wgn 113.0				
40	SL GT htp cpe, V-8	3,493	2,843	33,015
41	club cpe	2,839	3,317	14,118
42	sdn 4d	2,884	2,357	68,635
43	htp cpe	2,941	2,378	75,947
44	XL GT conv cpe	3,070	3,068	4,327
45	conv cpe	3,169	2,603	9,229
46	XL conv cpe	3,184	2,768	4,560
47	XL htp cpe	2,969	2,533	23,942
48	Deluxe wgn 4d	3,277	2,665	19,826
49	Squire wgn 4d	3,285	2,796	11,558
Series 50 Custom—wb 119.0				
51	500 sdn 2d	3,397	2,481	28,789
52	500 sdn 4d	3,466	2,533	109,449
53	sdn 2d	3,355	2,380	32,292

		Wght	Price	Prod
54	sdn 4d	3,455	2,432	72,245
Series 60 Galaxie 500—wb 119.0				
60	LTD htp sdn	3,649	3,278	69,400
61	7 Litre htp cpe	3,914	3,621	8,705
62	sdn 4d	3,478	2,677	171,886
63	7 Litre conv cpe, V-8	4,059	3,872	2,368
64	htp sdn	3,548	2,762	54,884
65	conv cpe	3,655	2,934	27,454
66	htp cpe	3,459	2,685	198,532
67	LTD htp cpe	3,601	3,201	31,696
68	XL htp cpe	3,616	3,231	25,715
69	XL conv cpe	3,761	3,480	6,360
Series 70 Station Wagon—wb 119.0				
71	Ranch 4d	3,941	2,793	33,306
72	Country Sedan 4d, 6P	3,956	2,882	55,616
74	Country Sedan 4d, 9P	3,997	2,999	36,633
76	Country Squire 4d, 6P	4,026	3,182	27,645
78	Country Squire 4d, 9P	4,040	3,265	41,953
Mustang—wb 108.0				
01	htp cpe	2,488	2,416	499,751
02	fstbk cpe	2,519	2,607	35,698
03	conv cpe	2,650	2,653	72,119
Series 80 Thunderbird—wb 113.2				
81	Town Hardtop cpe	4,359	4,483	15,633
83	htp cpe	4,386	4,426	13,389
85	conv cpe	4,496	4,879	5,049
87	Laundau htp cpe	4,367	4,584	35,105

▲ Full size Fords could get an optional 427-cid V-8, rated 410 or 425 horsepower. The Galaxie 500 "7 Liter" hardtop and convertible took a 428-cid engine instead, with a 345 bhp-rating, like that offered in Thunderbirds.

1967

All-new Thunderbird debuts—including a sedan

Mustangs and big Fords restyled; GT-500 debuts

F-Series trucks restyled

Ford output falls by half a million—weaker demand for mid/full-size cars cited

Fords get dual-braking, four-way flashers, energy-absorbing steering wheel

Ford unveils prototype Comuta electric car

Henry Ford I elected to Automotive Hall of Fame

Ford of Europe formed

▶ Sportiness was becoming a big part of Ford's mid-size lineup. This ad promoted Fairlane's victory in a test of acceleration, braking, and economy. Other ads invited readers to "Join the Fairlaners . . . people who have more fun in the car that has more to offer."

SHOW YOUR STRIPES!

There's a lot of GT in every Fairlane.

A lot of GT spirit, luxury, and especially performance. Proof: In Union/Pure Oil Performance Trials, Fairlane took first in its class in a combined test of acceleration, braking, and gas economy. A specially prepared Fairlane won the Daytona 500. Pick your Fairlane—hardtop, convertible, sedan or wagon—and show your stripes! **FAIRLANE**

▲ Top-dollar choice among the 13 Fairlane models was this $3064 GT convertible. Note the dual exhausts and the "A" decklid badge, which reveals the presence of an automatic transmission, making this a "GT/A." Only 2117 GT ragtops were built. This one is rarer yet since it boasts the seldom-sold 427-cid V-8, which yielded a screaming 410 or 425 bhp.

▲ Modest restyling of the Fairlane's year-old "Coke-bottle" shape, on a 116-inch wheelbase, gave it a look similar to big Fords. Badges and taillamps got a reshuffling, bodyside moldings were widened, and a reworked single grille contained a chrome horizontal divider split by three vertical bars. Three trim levels were offered: base, 500, and upper-rung 500/XL.

200

▲ Fairlane customers could choose from the mid-size's hottest engines ever, including 270- or 320-bhp 390 V-8s. Even so, sales fell almost 25 percent. Hardtop coupes came in Fairlane 500, 500/XL, and GT dress.

▲ This year's Fairlane grille added a trio of vertical bars. The badge in the center of this hardtop's grille identifies it as a 500/XL, which sold 14,871 copies (well below the 70,135 Fairlane 500 hardtops and 18,670 GTs). Mimicking big Fords, the mid-size sported vertically stacked headlamps. Bright lower-body moldings gave the GT look to "lesser" Fairlanes.

▶ Close to 200 hefty 427-cid V-8 engines went into relatively lightweight Fairlane bodies for '67, borrowing the idea set forth in '64 with the Thunderbolt. Instead of amounting to a rapid-but-stark race car, however, the 427 could now be installed in any regular body, complete with conveniences. Available with one or two four-barrel carburetors, the solid-lifter mill could suck air through a broad hood scoop. A fiberglass hood was optional.

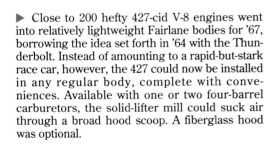

▲ Pseudo-wood decorated the bodysides of this Fairlane Squire wagon, just as it did every year on the bigger Country Squire. Only 8348 Fairlane Squires were produced for '67, with a base price of $2902. Front disc brakes were available on all Fairlane models, and the standard drum brakes were enlarged. All automatic transmissions could be shifted manually. Wagons couldn't get the wide-oval tires available on other Fairlanes.

▲ Nearly twice as many plain-sided Deluxe wagons as Fairlane Squires came off the line, selling for $184 less. Also available: a lower-priced Ranch Wagon, which found 10,881 customers. Base Fairlane engine was a 200-cid six, developing 120 horsepower, but wagon buyers could choose from a selection of hot V-8s, all the way to the 427 and 428. White-letter tires and striping could change a wagon's image from sedate carrier to sizzler.

▲ Restyled at front and rear, the GT-350 Shelby-Mustang gained a big-block GT-500 companion that outsold it two to one. Advertised at 355 bhp, its 428-cid V-8 actually produced closer to 400.

▲ Mustang GTs with automatic transmissions were easy to spot with their "GT/A" badges. A base hardtop sold for $2461, but all the extra equipment on this example added $1000 or so. The GT Equipment Group alone cost $205.

▲ Lower-body reskinning gave Mustangs a brawny, more aggressive stance. Length, width, and front track grew. A folding glass convertible backlight was available. The 2+2 coupe turned into a true fastback this year.

▲ A more imposing Mustang "twin-cowl" dash held two big circular dials and three small ones above. Note the big T-bar shift lever on a long console. A Competition Handling Package was offered with Mustang's GT Equipment Group, but few were ordered. Hottest of the 13 powertrains was the new Thunderbird 390 with 320 horses on tap, able to hit 60 mph in seven seconds.

1967 Engine Availability

Engines	bore × stroke	bhp	availability
I-6, 170.0	3.50 × 2.94	105	S-Falcon, exc Futura, wagons
I-6, 200.0	3.68 × 3.13	120	S-Flcn Futura wgns, Fair exc GTs
I-6, 240.0	4.00 × 3.18	150	S-all exc Falcon, Fairlane
V-8, 289.0	4.00 × 2.87	200	S-Fair GT, 500XL, LTD; O-others
V-8, 289.0	4.00 × 2.87	225	O-Falcon
V-8, 390.0	4.05 × 3.78	270	O-Fairlane
V-8, 390.0	4.05 × 3.78	315	O-Cus, Gal, LTD, Station Wgn
V-8, 390.0	4.05 × 3.78	320	O-Fairlane
V-8, 427.0	4.23 × 3.78	410/425	O-all exc Falcon
V-8, 428.0	4.13 × 3.98	345	O-all exc Falcon, Fairlane
Mustang			
I-6, 200.0	3.68 × 3.13	120	S-all
V-8, 289.0	4.00 × 2.87	200	O-all
V-8, 289.0	4.00 × 2.87	225/271	O-all
V-8, 390.0	4.05 × 3.78	320	O-all
Thunderbird			
V-8, 390.0	4.00 × 3.78	315	S-all
V-8, 428.0	4.13 × 3.98	345	O-all

▲ Handsome and potentially powerful, the Galaxie convertible came in base and scarcer XL form. Reworking gave big Fords a flowing, less straight-edged look with elliptical wheel openings and a two-element grille.

▶ Ford's auto-show exhibits in 1967 included this experimental "Magic Cruiser" fastback coupe, with an extra-long hatch that rose to transform it into a station wagon. Like most concept cars, it never entered production.

▲ On May 3, 1967, Ford built its 70-millionth car (a Galaxie) at the plant in Norfolk, Virginia. The 427 V-8 engine still was available.

▲ Full-size hardtop coupes adopted a "faster" roofline. Both Galaxie 500 and XL hardtops had larger triangular rear side windows and slimmer pillars, while the luxury LTD wore wide pillars. The former 7-Litre was now a $515.86 XL option package. XL sales hit a new low, but LTDs sold strongly.

▲ Ford Advanced Vehicles, formed as a subsidiary of Ford of Britain, developed the GT40 sports-racers, which had taken the top three spots at Le Mans in 1966. Roadgoing versions had softer suspensions than the race cars, as well as adjustable seats and a toned-down 289-cid engine with 306 or 335 horsepower. They were also better trimmed, but had no luggage space.

▲ Of the 100-plus GT40s produced, no more than 31 were considered road-going machines, including seven Mark IIIs. Built by Ford Advanced Vehicles and JW Automotive Engineering, GT40s through the Mark III used a steel semi-monocoque body/chassis with fiberglass panels. Shelby American and Kar Kraft, in the U.S., helped develop later J-Car/Mark IV racers.

▲ Finishing out the series of Ford's GT40-based sports-racers, the prototype "J-Car" evolved into the Mark IV, which took top honors at the 24 Hours of Le Mans in 1967. Their bigger, swoopier bodies consisted of aluminum honeycomb sections rather than steel, bonded and riveted together, beneath unstressed fiberglass panels. Only eight Mark IVs were built.

▲ The succession of GT40 sports-racers helped to satisfy Henry Ford II's wide-ranging interest in motorsport. A.J. Foyt and Dan Gurney gave Ford a second straight win at Le Mans, averaging 135.48 mph in the Mark IV, which carried a 500-bhp, 427-cid V-8. After the 1967 Le Mans race, Ford withdrew from competition, but a team from JW Automotive took victories in 1968-69.

▲ Minor touch-ups to the Falcon, all-new a year earlier, included a "cross-hair" grille. Sportiest of the seven models was this Futura Sports Coupe with bucket seats. Futura back panels added a brushed-metal appliqué. One new engine was offered: a 225-bhp 289 V-8. Ads asked buyers to "Go pert, peppy, and proud," but volume shrunk to a record low, down 65 percent.

▲ Purists may have been horrified, but the all-new T-Bird lineup included a Landau four-door sedan on a longer (117.2-inch) wheelbase, as well as twin hardtops with 114.7 inches between their wheels. Larger, heavier, and plusher, this fifth-generation would set the personal-luxury Ford's shape and character for the coming decade, leaving sportiness to Mustang and Fairlane. L. David Ash was responsible for front-end styling, while Bill Boyer's group did the roof, backlight, and rear half.

◄ Now wearing Fairlane front sheetmetal and trim instead of Falcon components, the Ranchero achieved a mid-size image, akin to Chevy's rival El Camino. Base, 500, and XL versions were offered, the latter including vinyl bucket seats and a console for its $2768 price. Power front disc brakes and 390-cid V-8 engines were new options; 17,243 '67 Rancheros were built.

Model Breakdown Chart

Falcon—wb 110.9, wgn 113.0		Wght	Price	Prod
10	sdn 2d	2,520	2,118	16,082
11	sdn 4d	2,551	2,167	13,554
12	wgn 4d	3,030	2,497	5,553
Falcon Futura—wb 110.9, wgn 113.0				
20	club cpe	2,528	2,280	6,287
21	sdn 4d	2,559	2,322	11,254
22	spt cpe	3,062	2,437	7,053
23	Squire wgn 4d	2,556	2,609	4,552
Fairlane—wb 116.0, wgn 113.0				
30	sdn 2d	2,832	2,297	10,628
31	sdn 4d	2,867	2,339	19,740
32	Ranch wgn 4d	3,283	2,643	10,881
33	500 club cpe	2,840	2,377	8,473
34	500 sdn 4d	2,887	2,417	51,522
35	500 htp cpe	2,927	2,439	70,135
36	500 conv cpe	3,244	2,664	5,428
37	Deluxe wgn 4d	3,291	2,718	15,902
38	Country Squire wgn 4d	3,302	2,902	8,348

Fairlane 500XL—wb 116.0		Wght	Price	Prod
40	htp cpe	2,955	2,724	14,871
41	conv cpe	3,272	2,950	1,943
42	GT htp cpe	3,301	2,839	18,670
43	GT conv cpe	3,607	3,064	2,117
Series 50 Custom—wb 119.0				
50	sdn 2d	3,430	2,441	18,107
51	sdn 4d	3,488	2,496	41,417
52	500 sdn 2d	3,482	2,553	18,146
53	500 sdn 4d	3,490	2,595	83,260
Galaxie 500—wb 119.0				
54	sdn 4d	3,500	2,732	130,063
55	htp cpe	3,503	2,755	197,388
56	htp sdn	3,571	2,808	57,087
57	conv cpe	3,682	3,003	19,068
58	XL htp sdn	3,594	3,243	18,174
59	XL conv cpe	3,794	3,493	5,161
LTD—wb 119.0				
62	htp cpe	3,626	3,362	46,036

		Wght	Price	Prod
64	sdn 4d	3,795	3,298	12,491
66	htp sdn	3,676	3,363	51,978
Station Wagon—wb 119.0				
70	Ranch 4d, 6P	3,930	2,836	23,932
71	Country Sedan 4d, 6P	3,943	2,935	50,818
72	Country Sedan 4d, 9P	4,023	3,061	34,377
73	Country Squire 4d, 6P	3,990	3,234	25,600
74	Country Squire 4d, 9P	4,030	3,359	44,024
Mustang—wb 108.0				
01	htp cpe	2,568	2,461	356,271
02	fstbk cpe	2,605	2,592	71,042
03	conv cpe	2,738	2,698	44,808
Series 80 Thunderbird—wb 114.7, 4d 117.2				
81	htp cpe	4,248	4,603	15,567
82	Landau htp cpe	4,256	4,704	37,422
84	Landau sdn 4d	4,348	4,825	24,967

1968

Ford, GM, and Chrysler mid-sizes revamped

New slogan appears: "Ford has a better idea"

Torino line debuts— includes rakish fastback

Ford output rises slightly, to just over 1.75 million cars, despite long strike

Ford trails Chevrolet in car output, races neck-and-neck in trucks

Shelby convertibles with rollbar appear

Exhaust-emissions laws now apply nationwide

"Passive" safety devices required on '68 models

Semon E. "Bunkie" Knudsen moves from GM to Ford presidency

Ford unveils high-mileage "clean air" experimental auto and rakish hatchback Mach 1 show car

Edsel Ford elected to Automotive Hall of Fame

GT40 earns sports-car championship for Ford

▲ Engineering vice president Harold C. MacDonald stands behind the experimental Techna two-door hardtop, claimed to contain more than 50 new ideas. Stylists included flush bumpers and omitted windshield posts, but the car was created as a test bed, allowing engineers to evaluate innovations.

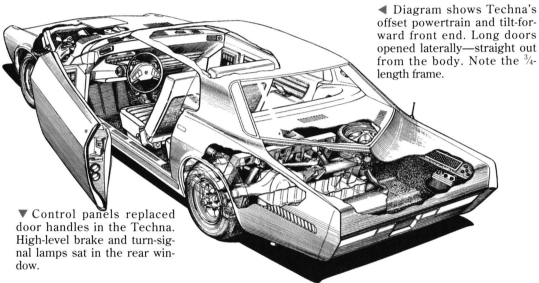

◀ Diagram shows Techna's offset powertrain and tilt-forward front end. Long doors opened laterally—straight out from the body. Note the ¾-length frame.

▼ Control panels replaced door handles in the Techna. High-level brake and turn-signal lamps sat in the rear window.

▶ Mechanics would have loved the Techna's tilt-up front end, which exposed the engine completely. The hood also contained an inspection hatch.

◄ Formerly offered only as a fastback coupe, the much-modified Shelby-Mustang now came as a convertible with built-in roll-over hoop. This year's facelift included a full-width hood scoop and louvers, and square running lights. Out back were sequential turn signals. The GT-350 switched to Ford's 250-bhp, 302-cid V-8. Few Paxton superchargers were installed.

▲ Both the GT-350 and GT-500 Shelby-Mustangs came in coupe and convertible form. The GT-500 again outsold its mate, two to one. Initially, it had the 428 engine (cut to 360 bhp); but some examples got 390 V-8s instead.

▲ Sequential taillamps were featured on Shelbys, with C-pillar vents replacing quarter windows. At mid-year came a GT-500KR ("King of the Road") with a more potent Cobra Jet 428 V-8. A total of 4450 Shelbys were built.

▲ Other than a revised grille and trim touch-ups, the Thunderbird carried on with little change. Early models carried either a 315-bhp 390 V-8 or optional "Thunderjet" 360-bhp 429, but the big one soon became standard.

▲ Sportiest of the big Fords was the 500/XL fastback hardtop coupe, on a 119-inch wheelbase. XL demand shot to its highest level since 1964, but the concept was changing. A 240-cid six was now standard, with three-speed manual shift; and the expected bucket seats and console became optional.

▲ Henry Ford II, "Bunkie" Knudsen, and Arjay Miller are seen here hovering over a 1968 Torino GT, the hot, new (and renamed) mid-size car that helped Dearborn win 20 NASCAR races that year.

207

▲ Mustang convertibles started at just $2814 in '68, but that didn't keep sales from sliding by 43 percent. A new Sports Trim Group included two-tone hood paint. Grilles were more deeply inset, without crossbars, allowing the galloping horse to "float." Top engine was a 390-bhp 427, priced at $755.

▲ Borrowing styling cues from the performance-packed Shelby, Ford offered a limited-production California Special hardtop, wearing a ducktail spoiler above wide taillamps and mid-bodyside tape stripes. Only fog lights occupied the plain grille cavity, which lacked the usual Mustang symbol.

▲ Mustang fastback sales fell by a depressing 40 percent this year. The GT equipment group on this example included dual exhausts with chromed quad outlets, a pop-open gas cap, and heavy-duty suspension, adding $147 to the $2712 sticker price. Optional "C-stripes" gave GTs a look of motion.

▲ Competition remained part of the ponycar's appeal, helped by the Cobra Jet engine package that arrived at mid-year. The setup included a vacuum-actuated ram-air induction system, complete with a brawny hood scoop.

▲ During 1968, a 335-horsepower Cobra Jet 428 engine replaced the big-block 427 as top Mustang choice. A few Mustangs got a hopped-up 302 with high-compression heads and wilder cam, aimed at Trans Am racing.

▲ William Clay Ford took the wheel of a Torino GT to pace the 52nd Annual Indianapolis 500 Race. Torino engine choices included a new 302 V-8.

1968 Engine Availability

Engines	bore × stroke	bhp	availability
I-6, 170.0	3.50 × 2.94	100	S-base Falcon cpes, sdns
I-6, 200.0	3.68 × 3.13	115	S-Fair, Tor, Flcn Fut wgn; O-Flcn
I-6, 240.0	4.00 × 3.18	150	S-all exc Futura, Tor GT, LTD
V-8, 289.0	4.00 × 2.87	195	O-Falcon
V-8, 302.0	4.00 × 3.00	210	S-LTD, Tor GT; O-all
V-8, 302.0	4.00 × 3.00	230	O-Falcon, Fairlane, Torino
V-8, 390.0	4.05 × 3.78	265	O-all exc Falcon
V-8, 390.0	4.05 × 3.78	315	O-all exc Falcon, Fairlane
V-8, 390.0	4.05 × 3.78	335	O-Fairlane
V-8, 427.0	4.23 × 3.78	390	O-Fairlane/Torino htps
V-8, 428.0	4.13 × 3.98	340	O-all exc Falcon, Fairlane
Mustang			
I-6, 200.0	3.68 × 3.13	115	S-all
I-6, 250.0	3.68 × 3.91	155	O-all (late)
V-8, 289.0	4.00 × 2.87	195	O-all
V-8, 302.0	4.00 × 3.00	220	O-all
V-8, 390.0	4.05 × 3.78	335	O-all
V-8, 427.0	4.23 × 3.78	390	O-all
V-8, 428.0	4.13 × 3.98	335	O-all (late)
Thunderbird			
V-8, 390.0	4.00 × 3.78	315	S-all
V-8, 429.0	4.36 × 3.59	360	O-all

▲ Revamping its mid-size lineup, Ford renamed the top series Torino. This GT hardtop coupe has a formal roofline, but fastbacks proved more popular.

▲ Costliest Falcon was this Futura wagon. Though little changed for '68 except for a new grille and square taillights, Falcon sales more than doubled.

▲ Early in 1968, the second-generation Econoline debuted as a '69 model, mid-sized rather than compact. This is a 12-seat Chateau Club Wagon.

▲ This F-100 Styleside pickup wore a simplified double-deck grille and had new "Flex-O-Matic" rear springs. A total of 285,015 were built, at $2237.

Model Breakdown Chart

Falcon—wb 110.9, wgn 113.0		Wght	Price	Prod
10	sdn 2d	2,680	2,252	29,166
11	sdn 4d	2,714	2,301	36,443
12	wgn 4d	3,123	2,617	15,576
Falcon Futura—wb 110.9, wgn 113.0				
20	sdn 2d	2,685	2,415	10,633
21	sdn 4d	2,719	2,456	18,733
22	spt cpe	2,713	2,541	10,077
23	wgn 4d	3,123	2,728	10,761
Fairlane—wb 116.0, wgn 113.0				
30	htp cpe	3,028	2,456	44,683
31	sdn 4d	2,986	2,464	18,146
32	wgn 4d	3,333	2,770	14,800
33	500 htp cpe	3,066	2,591	33,282
34	500 sdn 4d	3,024	2,543	42,930
35	500 fstbk htp cpe	3,080	2,566	32,452
36	500 conv cpe	3,226	2,822	3,761
37	500 wgn 4d	3,377	2,880	10,190
Torino—wb 116.0, wgn 113.0				
38	Squire wgn 4d	3,425	3,032	14,773
40	htp cpe	3,098	2,710	35,964

		Wght	Price	Prod
41	sdn 4d	3,062	2,688	17,962
42	GT fstbk htp cpe	3,208	2,747	74,135
43	GT conv cpe	3,352	3,001	5,310
44	GT htp cpe	3,194	2,772	23,939
Custom—wb 119.0				
50	sdn 2d	3,471	3,584	18,485
51	sdn 4d	3,498	2,642	45,980
52	500 sdn 2d	3,460	2,699	8,983
53	500 sdn 4d	3,511	2,741	49,398
Galaxie 500—wb 119.0				
54	sdn 4d	3,516	2,864	117,877
55	fstbk htp cpe	3,534	2,881	69,760
56	htp sdn	3,562	2,936	55,461
57	conv cpe	3,679	3,108	11,832
58	htp cpe	3,540	2,916	84,332
60	XL fstbk htp cpe	3,588	2,985	50,048
61	XL conv cpe	3,745	3,214	6,066
LTD—wb 119.0				
62	htp cpe	3,679	3,153	54,163
64	sdn 4d	3,596	3,135	22,834

		Wght	Price	Prod
66	htp sdn	3,642	3,206	61,755
Station Wagon—wb 119.0				
70	Ranch 4d, 6P	3,925	3,000	18,237
71	Ranch 500 4d, 6P	3,935	3,063	18,181
72	Ranch 500 4d, 9P	3,981	3,176	13,421
73	Country Sedan 4d, 6P	3,944	3,184	39,335
74	Country Sedan 4d, 9P	4,001	3,295	29,374
75	Country Squire 4d, 6P	4,013	3,539	33,994
76	Country Squire 4d, 9P	4,059	3,619	57,776
Mustang—wb 108.0				
01	htp cpe	2,635	2,602	249,447
02	fstbk cpe	2,659	2,712	42,581
03	conv cpe	2,745	2,814	25,376
Series 80 Thunderbird—wb 114.7, 4d 117.2				
83	htp cpe	4,366	4,716	9,977
84	Landau htp cpe	4,372	4,845	33,029
87	Landau sdn 4d	4,458	4,924	21,925

1969

New-generation Mustangs launched, including Mach 1 and pair of Bosses

Bigger (351-cid) "Windsor" small-block V-8 debuts

Hot mid-size models arrive: Cobra and Talladega

Full-size Fords restyled

Trucks get new engines

Ford's slogan for the season: "The Going Thing"

Production passes 1.8 million, yet trails Chevy's 2.1 million cars

Big-Ford sales top one million

302 V-8 offered in Bronco

NHTSA proposes mandatory "passive restraints"

"Bunkie" Knudsen leaves presidency in corporate shake-up

GT40 wins again at Le Mans

▲ Tamer than before, and more "busy" looking than stock Mustangs, the restyled Shelbys wore a three-inch-longer hood, reshaped front fenders, and a new nose with big loop bumper/grille (all in fiberglass). Out back, the clipped tail held a lip spoiler. Scoops seemed to be everywhere, with five NACA-style ducts on the hood alone. Full-length striping finished off the look. This GT-500 fastback started at $4709.

▲ Only 335 Shelby-Mustang GT-500 roll-bar ragtops were built this year, priced at $5027, as total production slid to 3150. Smaller-engined GT-350 convertibles powered by 290-bhp 351-cid V-8s sold even fewer copies, with only 194 rolling off the line in Michigan. The GT-500 kept its 428 Cobra Jet engine, but in less potent guise. Carroll Shelby himself dropped out of the production-car business in October 1969, and Lee Iacocca soon abandoned the Shelby-Mustang program.

▼ Long snout scanning the pavement, this Mustang Boss 302 in Trans Am trim appears eager to compete. Only 1934 were built, largely to qualify for SCCA racing. Power came from a high-output 302 V-8 officially rated 290 bhp, but actually snorting out closer to 400. In the Trans Am series, Ford lost to Chevrolet's Camaro—but created one more memorable Mustang.

▲ Bigger and heavier, the reworked Mustang kept its 108-inch wheelbase. Quad headlights (two in the grille) were new. This plush Grandé came with a vinyl roof, wire wheel covers, bright moldings, and teak-look interior.

▲ One of three hot new Mustangs, the Mach 1 featured simulated scoops, a decklid spoiler, and flat-black hood with "Shaker" scoop. Underneath lay a new 351 V-8 rated 250 horsepower, or even a 335-bhp 428 Cobra Jet mill.

▲ Created mainly to qualify the big "semi-hemi" 429-cid V-8 in NASCAR competition, the tough Boss 429 showed big hood and C-pillar scoops. Extensive modification by Kar Kraft was needed to stuff in the engine.

▲ Larry Shinoda styled the deep, angled front spoiler and adjustable rear airfoil of the Boss 302, sold in limited numbers at mid-year. Fastback production more than tripled in '69, though Mustang lost sales overall.

▲ Priced at $4964, the Landau coupe was the top Thunderbird seller. This year's roofline had a more formal look, with super-wide pillars replacing the vestigial rear quarter windows. An electric sunroof joined the options list.

▲ Thunderbird sedan popularity was dwindling, as output slid to 15,695. Annual touch-ups included a new grille, trim, and taillamps. Sole V-8 was the 360-bhp 429. Total T-Bird production hit its lowest point since 1958.

1969 Engine Availability

Engines	bore × stroke	bhp	availability
I-6, 170.0	3.50 × 2.94	100	S-Falcon exc Futura
I-6, 200.0	3.68 × 3.13	115	S-Futura
I-6, 240.0	4.00 × 3.18	150	S-all exc Flcn, Fair, Tor GT, LTD
I-6, 250.0	3.68 × 3.91	155	S-Fairlane, Tor exc GT, Cobra
V-8, 302.0	4.00 × 3.00	220	S-LTD, Tor GT; O-others
V-8, 351.0	4.00 × 3.50	250	O-Fairlane, Tor exc Cobra
V-8, 351.0	4.00 × 3.50	290	O-Fairlane, Tor exc Cobra
V-8, 390.0	4.05 × 3.78	265	O-full-size
V-8, 390.0	4.05 × 3.78	320	O-Fairlane, Tor exc Cobra
V-8, 428.0	4.13 × 3.98	335*	S-Tor Cobra; O-Fairlane
V-8, 429.0	4.36 × 3.59	320/360	O-full-size
Mustang			
I-6, 200.0	3.68 × 3.13	115	S-all exc Mach I, Boss
I-6, 250.0	3.68 × 3.91	155	O-all exc Mach I, Boss
V-8, 302.0	4.00 × 3.00	220	O-all exc Mach I, Boss
V-8, 302.0	4.00 × 3.00	290	S-Boss 302
V-8, 351.0	4.00 × 3.50	250	S-Mach I; O-others exc Boss
V-8, 351.0	4.00 × 3.50	290	O-all
V-8, 390.0	4.05 × 3.78	320	O-all
V-8, 428.0	4.13 × 3.98	335*	O-Mach I
V-8, 429.0	4.36 × 3.59	360/375	S-Boss 429
Thunderbird			
V-8, 429.0	4.36 × 3.59	360	S-all

*Available in standard and Ram Air versions.

▲ The big 429-cid V-8 engine was a tight squeeze under a Mustang's hood, but its major role lay on NASCAR tracks. The hot mill whipped out 360 bhp (375 for racing) and featured crescent-shaped combustion chambers.

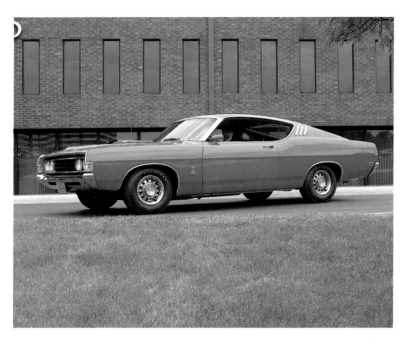

▲ Hottest member of the Fairlane/Torino lineup was the Cobra, a no-frills muscle car offered as a formal hardtop or in this SportsRoof fastback form. Prices under $3200 attracted muscle-buyers on a budget.

▲ Standard in the Torino Cobra, the 335-bhp Cobra Jet 428 V-8 was developed under Tom Feaheney and could have Ram Air induction.

▼ Nothing flashy about the sizzling Cobra's taxi-plain interior. Under its tie-down hood lurked a 335-bhp, 428-cid V-8, capable of acceleration to 60 mph in six seconds.

▲ No unnecessary doodads were evident on this Super Cobra with its detrimmed front end, shapely fastback profile, and rear-window slats. That tall hood scoop could gulp air into a 429-cid Super Cobra Jet engine.

▲ Aerodynamics were key to the design of the Talladega, named for the new Alabama speedway. Differences from ordinary Torinos included a longer nose with flush Cobra grille. Only 754 were built.

▲ Little was new in the seven-model Falcon series, including base and Futura four-doors, offering "Big car benefits at a compact car price." Specialty model was the vinyl-topped, slow-selling Futura Sports Coupe.

▲ Like all full-size Fords, the posh LTD enjoyed a full restyling on a longer 121-inch wheelbase. LTDs sold strongly, with 417,677 going to dealers, including 111,565 hardtop coupes. Note the wide C-pillars.

▲ Ford called its reworked LTD hardtop sedan, with a lower and wider stance, a "classic automobile" with its concealed headlamps in an ornate protruding grille. Custom and Galaxie 500 models wore simpler fronts.

▲ Full-size fastback hardtop coupes like this Galaxie XL were renamed SportsRoof and got tunnel-roof styling, with a nearly vertical backlight and sloping outrigger sail panels. No-vent side glass was new, too.

Model Breakdown Chart

Falcon—wb 110.9, wgn 113.0		Wght	Price	Prod
10	sdn 2d	2,700	2,283	29,262
11	sdn 4d	2,735	2,333	22,719
12	wgn 4d	3,100	2,660	11,568
Falcon Futura—wb 110.9, wgn 113.0				
20	sdn 2d	2,715	2,461	6,482
21	sdn 4d	2,748	2,498	11,850
22	spt cpe	2,738	2,598	5,931
23	wgn 4d	3,120	2,771	7,203
Fairlane—wb 116.0, wgn 113.0				
30	htp cpe	3,079	2,499	85,630
31	sdn 4d	3,065	2,488	27,296
32	wgn 4d	3,441	2,841	10,882
33	500 htp cpe	3,090	2,626	28,179
34	500 sdn 4d	3,082	2,568	40,888
35	500 fstbk htp cpe	3,137	2,601	29,849
36	500 conv cpe	3,278	2,851	2,264
37	500 wgn 4d	3,469	2,951	12,869
Torino—wb 116.0, wgn 113.0				
38	Squire wgn 4d	3,503	3,107	14,472
40	htp cpe	3,143	2,754	20,789
41	sdn 4d	3,128	2,733	11,971

		Wght	Price	Prod
42	GT fstbk htp cpe	3,220	2,840	61,319
43	GT conv cpe	3,356	3,090	2,552
44	GT htp cpe	3,173	2,865	17,951
45	Cobra htp cpe	3,490	3,164	—
46	Cobra fstbk htp cpe	3,537	3,189	—
Custom—wb 121.0				
50	sdn 2d	3,605	2,649	15,439
51	sdn 4d	3,628	2,691	45,653
52	500 sdn 2d	3,590	2,748	7,585
53	500 sdn 4d	3,640	2,790	45,761
70	Ranch wgn 4d	4,089	3,091	17,489
71	500 wgn 4d, 6P	4,102	3,155	16,432
72	500 wgn 4d, 9P	4,152	3,268	11,563
Galaxie 500—wb 121.0				
54	sdn 4d	3,690	2,914	104,606
55	fstbk htp cpe	3,700	2,930	63,921
56	htp sdn	3,725	2,983	64,031
57	conv cpe	3,860	3,159	6,910
58	htp cpe	3,655	2,982	71,920
73	Country Sedan wgn 4d, 6P	4,087	3,274	36,387
74	Country Sedan wgn 4d, 9P	4,112	3,390	27,517

XL—wb 121.0		Wght	Price	Prod
60	fstbk htp cpe	3,805	3,069	54,557
61	conv cpe	3,955	3,297	7,402
LTD—wb 121.0				
62	htp cpe	3,745	3,251	111,565
64	sdn 4d	3,745	3,209	63,709
66	htp sdn	3,840	3,278	113,168
75	Country Squire 4d, 6P	4,202	3,661	46,445
76	Country Squire 4d, 9P	4,227	3,738	82,790
Mustang—wb 108.0				
01	htp cpe	2,798	2,635	128,458
02	fstbk cpe	2,822	2,635	60,046
02	Boss 302 fstbk cpe, V-8	3,210	3,588	1,934
02	Boss 429 fstbk cpe, V-8	—	4,798	852
03	conv cpe	2,908	2,849	14,746
04	Grande htp cpe	2,873	2,866	22,182
05	Mach I fstbk cpe	3,175	3,139	72,458
Series 80 Thunderbird—wb 114.7, 4d 117.2				
83	htp cpe	4,348	4,824	5,913
84	Landau htp cpe	4,360	4,964	27,664
87	Landau sdn 4d	4,460	5,043	15,695

1970

Lee Iacocca named corporate president

Maverick compact debuts; Falcon enters final year

Mid-size Fords restyled on longer wheelbases; plush Torino Brougham added

Ponycar battle escalates with restyled Camaro and Firebird, new Challenger, and reworked Barracuda; Mustang volume skids badly

Ford builds nearly 2.1 million cars to Chevy's 1.8

Italian coachbuilders Ghia and Vignale bought by DeTomaso, which becomes Ford subsidiary

Ranchero Squire debuts

New long- and short-cab heavy trucks arrive, named "Louisville Line"

◄ Radical restyling gave the Thunderbird a new frontal look. Influenced by the now-departed Shinoda and Knudsen team, it featured an elongated hood and prominent vee'd nose—curiously similar to the '69 Pontiac Grand Prix. Headlamps were exposed for the first time since '66, separated from the grille.

► "Longer, lower, wider." That's what customers were presumed to want, and Ford complied with the T-Bird. In this overhead publicity shot, the hood looks a mile long above the pointy vee'd grille. Below lurked a 360-bhp "Thunderjet" 429-cid V-8 with Cruise-O-Matic, which could be shifted manually.

▲ Thunderbird's new protruding beak came to be known as the "Knudsen nose." Sticker price of this Landau sedan was $5182, but sales were sluggish with only 8401 built. Interiors held bench or bucket seats.

▲ Once again, a power sunroof was available on the Thunderbird hardtop coupe, sold in both base and landau-bar trim. The Landau coupe was by far the top T-Bird seller, as total model-year volume edged slightly upward.

214

▲ Just 636 leftover Shelby-Mustangs were marketed as 1970 models, after Lee Iacocca declared the program expired. Each one, including this GT-500 with 428-cid V-8, had a Boss 302 front spoiler and black hood.

▲ Even though the Shelby concept was extinct, after a stimulating run through the late '60s, some of its styling touches would reappear on 1971 Mustangs. Sequential taillamps stemmed from the 1965 Thunderbird.

▲ Ford exhibited this sleek Milano two-seat coupe early in 1970, to serve as a preview of the Mustang SportsRoof theme for '71. Note the split grille, hidden headlamps, ducted hood, and deeply vee'd quarter windows.

▲ Space looks ample beneath the powered hatch of the Milano show car. Luggage and seats were purple leather, while the body was "Ultra Violet." Taillights changed from red to amber to green, responding to driver action.

▲ Mustang hardtops accounted for half of total production, which slipped below 191,000. The slower-selling Grandé wore a landau vinyl top.

▲ Convertibles were dying, even in Mustang form, as Americans sought air conditioning. Ragtop output dropped 48 percent this season.

◀ Mustang's Boss 302 carried on for another season as a high-winding Trans Am Special, with a total of 6319 built. This time, the car regained the Trans Am championship for Ford. Front ends of all Mustangs reverted to single headlights as part of a tasteful facelift.

215

▲ Ford reprised the Mach 1 Mustang for another season, with a standard 250-bhp 351 V-8. This one had the 335-bhp Cobra Jet 428. Even the hot ones suffered in the sales race, as Mach 1 production dropped by 43 percent.

▲ The Cobra Jet 428 engine with Ram-Air added $376 to the $3271 sticker price of a Mach 1 fastback coupe. This popular Mustang model had a special grille with driving lamps, rear stabilizer bar, and GT Equipment Group.

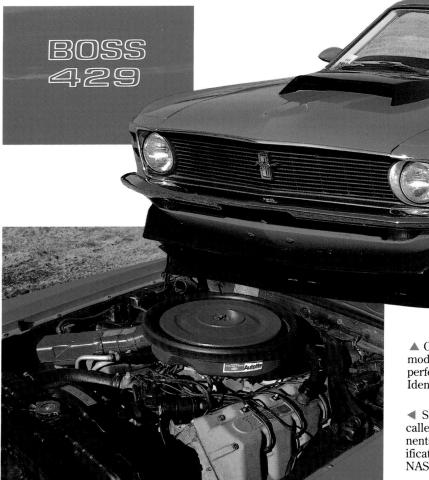

BOSS 429

▲ Only about 500 Boss 429s were produced by Kar Kraft for the 1970 model year, joining the 852 from 1969 to make this one of the rarest high-performance Mustangs. Note the big hood airscoop and rear wing spoiler. Identification was more subtle than on Boss 302 or Mach 1 Mustangs.

◀ Shoehorning the big 429-cid V-8 into a Mustang engine compartment called for special fabrication of suspension and inner fenderwell components by Kar Kraft, a Brighton, Michigan, subcontractor. Among other modifications, the battery moved into the trunk. The big-block V-8, built for NASCAR homologation, was installed in Mustangs instead of bigger Fords.

▲ Ribbed lower body trim and a special logo mark this Mustang coupe as a Mach 1. Bright wheel moldings weren't part of the $3271 base price.

▲ "SportsRoof" fastbacks weren't as popular as notchback Mustangs, but hinted at the Mach 1 look. Window slats added to the tough image.

▲ Mid-size Fords displayed new styling "shaped by the wind," with knife-edge front fenders and hidden wipers. Wheelbase grew an inch, width by two. "Sports slat" louvers were optional on Torino GT and Cobra hardtops.

▲ Fun-in-the-sun was still part of the mid-size picture, with this Torino GT convertible listing for $3212. Only 3939 found customers, however. Note the hidden headlamps, "Laser" striping, and styled steel wheels.

▶ Flexing its muscle again was the low-budget Cobra, with a 360-bhp 429 V-8 and black accents. Only the SportsRoof fastback was sold.

▲ With an extended snout reaching past the recessed headlamps, this Cobra looks ready for action—and could have a 429 Super Cobra Jet.

▲ Joining the Fairlane/Torino-based Ranchero series for '70 was this Squire edition, with simulated-wood appliqués like the Torino Squire.

Model Breakdown Chart

Maverick—wb 103.0		Wght	Price	Prod
91	sdn 2d	2,411	1,995	578,914
Falcon—wb 110.9, wgn 113.0				
10	sdn 2d	2,708	2,390	4,373
11	sdn 4d	2,753	2,438	5,301
12	wgn 4d	3,155	2,767	1,624
Falcon Futura—wb 110.9, wgn 113.0				
20	sdn 2d	2,727	2,542	1,129
21	sdn 4d	2,764	2,579	2,262
23	wgn 4d	3,191	2,878	1,005
"1970½" Falcon—wb 117.0, wgn 114.0				
26	sdn 2d	3,100	2,460	26,071
27	sdn 4d	3,116	2,500	30,443
40	wgn 4d	3,483	2,801	10,539
Fairlane 500—wb 117.0, wgn 114.0				
28	sdn 4d	3,166	2,627	25,780
29	htp cpe	3,178	2,660	70,636
41	wgn 4d	3,558	2,957	13,613
Torino—wb 117.0, wgn 114.0				
30	htp cpe	3,223	2,722	49,826
31	sdn 4d	3,208	2,689	30,117
32	htp sdn	3,239	2,795	14,312

		Wght	Price	Prod
33	Brougham htp cpe	3,293	3,006	16,911
34	fstbk htp cpe	3,261	2,899	12,490
35	GT htp cpe	3,366	3,105	56,819
36	Brougham htp sdn	3,309	3,078	14,543
37	GT conv cpe	3,490	3,212	3,939
38	Cobra fstbk htp cpe	3,774	3,270	7,675
42	wgn 4d	3,603	3,164	10,613
43	Squire wgn 4d	3,673	3,379	13,166
Custom—wb 121.0				
51	sdn 4d	3,545	2,850	42,849
52	500 htp cpe	3,510	2,918	2,677
53	500 sdn 4d	3,585	2,872	41,261
70	Ranch wgn 4d	4,079	3,305	15,086
71	500 wgn 4d, 6P	4,049	3,368	15,304
72	500 wgn 4d, 9P	4,137	3,481	9,943
Galaxie 500—wb 121.0				
54	sdn 4d	3,601	3,026	101,784
55	fstbk htp cpe	3,610	3,043	50,825
56	htp sdn	3,672	3,096	53,817
58	htp cpe	3,611	3,094	57,059
73	Country Sedan wgn 4d, 6P	4,089	3,488	32,209
74	Country Sedan wgn 4d, 9P	4,112	3,600	22,645

XL—wb 121.0		Wght	Price	Prod
60	fstbk htp cpe	3,750	3,293	27,251
61	conv cpe	3,983	3,501	6,348
LTD—wb 121.0				
62	htp cpe	3,727	3,356	96,324
62	Brougham htp cpe	3,855	3,537	
64	sdn 4d	3,701	3,307	78,306
64	Brougham sdn	3,829	3,502	
66	htp sdn	3,771	3,385	90,390
66	Brougham htp sdn	4,029	3,579	
75	Country Squire 4d, 6P	4,139	3,832	39,837
76	Country Squire 4d, 9P	4,185	3,909	69,077
Mustang—wb 108.0				
01	htp cpe	2,822	2,721	82,569
02	fstbk cpe	2,846	2,771	39,316
02	Boss 302 fstbk cpe, V-8	3,227	3,720	6,319
02	Boss 429 fstbk cpe, V-8	—	4,798	498
03	conv cpe	2,932	3,025	7,673
04	Grandé htp cpe	2,907	2,926	13,581
05	Mach I cpe	3,240	3,271	40,970
Series 80 Thunderbird—wb 114.7, 4d 117.2				
83	htp cpe	4,354	4,961	5,116
84	Landau htp cpe	4,630	5,104	36,847
87	Landau sdn 4d	4,464	5,182	8,401

▲ Freshening of full-size Fords included revised grille inserts and new back bumpers with horizontal taillamps. This was the last stand for the sporty XL, like this tunnel-roof hardtop. A bulged hood and grille center marked the LTD, XL, and Country Squire wagon.

▶ Only one convertible was included in the full-size lineup: this XL, with tall front seatbacks and a $3501 price tag. Production dropped by more than a thousand from 1969, with only 6348 going to dealers. More than four times as many XL hardtops were built. A 250-bhp, 351-cid V-8 was now standard on XLs.

▲ Ford needed an alternative to the sales-stealing imports, and found it in the compact Maverick, introduced on April 17, 1969—precisely five years after the Mustang. A whopping 578,914 found buyers in the long season.

▲ Billed as the "first car of the '70s at 1960s prices," Mavericks were nothing special in engineering, but the $1995 price let Ford push the two-door sedan as roomier, more powerful, and less troublesome than an import.

▲ Don't look for this Maverick Estate Coupe with "landaulet" half-roof on used-car lots; it was an idea car, to remind viewers of the classic era.

▲ "Bustleback" luggage carrier on the prototype Maverick Estate Coupe really looked like a trunk. Note the lack of an upper windshield frame.

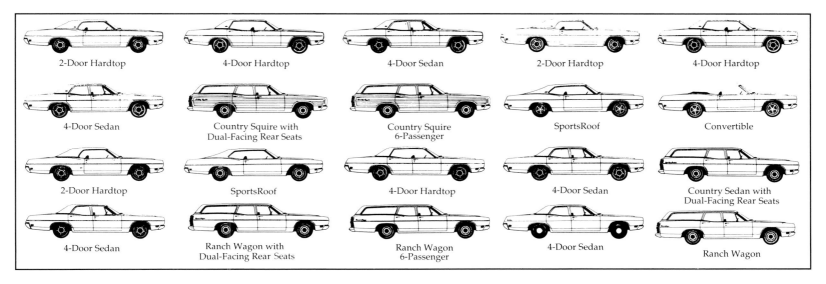

2-Door Hardtop	4-Door Hardtop	4-Door Sedan	2-Door Hardtop	4-Door Hardtop
4-Door Sedan	Country Squire with Dual-Facing Rear Seats	Country Squire 6-Passenger	SportsRoof	Convertible
2-Door Hardtop	SportsRoof	4-Door Hardtop	4-Door Sedan	Country Sedan with Dual-Facing Rear Seats
4-Door Sedan	Ranch Wagon with Dual-Facing Rear Seats	Ranch Wagon 6-Passenger	4-Door Sedan	Ranch Wagon

▲ Full-size models continued to sell well, accounting for 40 percent of car sales. Popularity leader was the posh LTD, including this new Brougham hardtop sedan, topping two tons. A 429 V-8 helped move all that bulk.

▲ "Built for quiet inside and out," the luxurious LTD Brougham also came in hardtop coupe, hardtop sedan, and four-door sedan form. All full-size Fords had new rear and side ornamentation, and more formal grilles. With the addition of the Broughams, big-Ford model choices ballooned to 21.

▲ Falcons continued into the 1970 model year with little change, given a brief respite because of a sales hike. After their demise, the Falcon name reemerged briefly on this "1970½" stripped version of the Fairlane.

▲ Because the carryover Falcons lasted only part way into the model year, only 15,694 were built, including 1005 of these Futura station wagons that offered 85.2 cubic feet of cargo space. Base engine was a 200-cid six, with 302 V-8 optional. Falcons aimed at reliable, low-budget transportation.

1970 Engine Availability

Engines	bore × stroke	bhp	availability
I-6, 170.0	3.50 × 2.94	105	S-Maverick
I-6, 200.0	3.68 × 3.13	120	S-Falcon; O-Maverick
I-6, 240.0	4.00 × 3.18	150	S-full size exc XL, LTD
I-6, 250.0	3.68 × 3.91	155	S-Tor exc GT, Brghm, Squire, Cobra
V-8, 302.0	4.00 × 3.00	220	S-Tor GT/Brghm/Squire, Cobra; O-others
V-8, 351.0	4.00 × 3.50	250	S-XL, LTD, big wgns; O-all exc Flcn, Cobra
V-8, 351.0	4.00 × 3.50	300	O-Torino exc Cobra
V-8, 390.0	4.05 × 3.78	265	O-all full-size
V-8, 429.0	4.36 × 3.59	320	O-all full-size
V-8, 429.0	4.36 × 3.59	360	S-Tor Cobra; O-Ford, Torino
V-8, 429.0	4.36 × 3.59	370	O-Tor exc wgns
V-8, 429.0	4.36 × 3.59	375*	O-Torino, Cobra

Mustang

I-6, 200.0	3.68 × 3.13	115	S-all exc Mach I, Boss 302
I-6, 250.0	3.68 × 3.91	155	O-all exc Mach I, Boss 302
V-8, 302.0	4.00 × 3.00	220	O-all exc Mach I, Boss 302
V-8, 302.0	4.00 × 3.00	290	S-Boss 302

Engines	bore × stroke	bhp	availability
V-8, 351.0	4.00 × 3.50	250	S-Mach I; O-others exc Boss 302
V-8, 351.0	4.00 × 3.50	300	O-all
V-8, 428.0	4.13 × 3.98	335*	O-Mach I
V-8, 429.0	4.36 × 3.59	375	O-Mach I, Boss

Thunderbird

V-8, 429.0	4.36 × 3.59	360	S-all

*Available in standard and Ram Air versions.

1970½ Engine Availability

Engines	bore × stroke	bhp	availability
I-6, 250.0	3.68 × 3.91	155	S-Falcon
V-8, 302.0	4.00 × 3.00	220	O-Falcon
V-8, 351.0	4.00 × 3.50	250/300	O-Falcon
V-8, 429.0	4.36 × 3.59	360	O-Falcon
V-8, 429.0	4.36 × 3.59	370	O-Falcon (w/o Ram Air)

1971

Subcompact Pinto debuts, along with Chevy's Vega

Mustangs bigger than ever; full-size Fords restyled

Car production again edges past Chevy, at 2,054,351

Ford signs UAW pact, staves off strike prospect

GM lowers compression ratios; others wait for '72

Ford sells Autolite firm, adopts Motorcraft name

DeTomaso Pantera debuts; sold by Lincoln-Mercury

▲ Ford president Lee Iacocca stands alongside the subcompact Pinto, equipped with optional vinyl roof. Chunky styling on a 94.2-inch wheelbase was sporty in a curious way. The "frisky new little car" came with a 75-bhp 1.6-liter four or optional two-liter. A three-door Runabout joined the sedan later.

▲ Planning for the next-generation Mustang II was well underway when this Mach 1 mock-up was created in mid-1969, but nothing this radical ever made production. Note the nearly horizontal fastback profile and vast glass.

▲ This "302" proposal for the 1974 Mustang displayed a front end similar to the Mach 1 fastback design, but featured a dual set of quarter windows. Early mock-ups were based on the existing Mustang's 108-inch wheelbase.

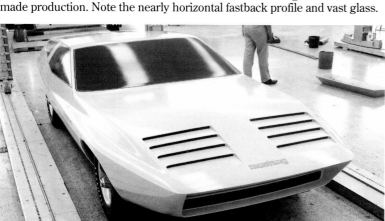

▲ Front view of the Mustang 302 mock-up from mid-1969 shows wide louvers across the hood, a sharp creaseline around the front of the body, and a rectangular grille opening below. No headlights are evident.

▲ Startling as the front and side views of the Mustang mock-ups may have been, this monstrous back panel was the real eye-popper. Hard to imagine this ponycar on the road—especially with those enclosed rear wheels.

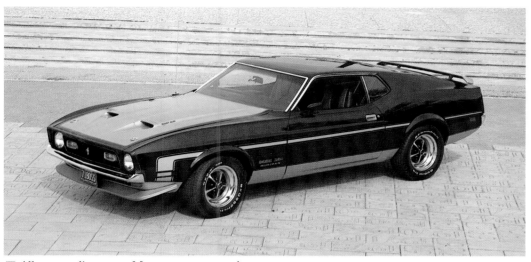

◄ In this final season for Boss Mustangs, the Boss 351 featured Ram-Air induction with its 330-bhp "Cleveland" 351 V-8 engine, operating on 11.0:1 compression. Styling was similar to the Mach 1 except for special mid-flank striping and front spoiler, and flat-black hood paint. Note the twin hood scoops. About 1800 were built, capable of hitting 60 in 5.8 seconds.

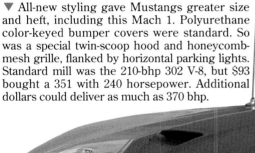

▼ All-new styling gave Mustangs greater size and heft, including this Mach 1. Polyurethane color-keyed bumper covers were standard. So was a special twin-scoop hood and honeycomb-mesh grille, flanked by horizontal parking lights. Standard mill was the 210-bhp 302 V-8, but $93 bought a 351 with 240 horsepower. Additional dollars could deliver as much as 370 bhp.

▲ Bigger than ever, the dramatically restyled Mustang still couldn't capture a good crop of customers as volume dropped by 41,000. Convertibles fared little better, with only 6121 going to market. Styling mimicked Ford's Le Mans racers and reflected the tastes of the Shinoda/Knudsen team. The clipped back panel was inspired by the departed Shelby-Mustang.

▲ With the base 145-bhp, 250-cid six-cylinder engine, a Mustang coupe cost just $2911. Stuff in a big V-8 with Ram Induction and sporty wheels, and the price shot up by $500 or more. Most popular model was the hardtop coupe. Top engine choices: the new four-barrel 429 Cobra Jet, yielding 370 horsepower, or even the seldom-seen Super Cobra Jet with 375 bhp.

▲ Prices for this year's Ranchero began at $2851, but this GT ran $3273. A mid-year 500 model served as a lower-cost alternative to the GT. Car-pickups could even get a 429-cid V-8.

▲ Ford's compact 4×4 sport-utility had a new heavy-duty front axle, said to have been proven in racing. A 302-cid V-8 was optional. A total of 19,784 Bronco wagons and pickups were built.

▲ Topping the Econoline parade was the Chateau Club Wagon, which cost $3827 with deluxe upholstery and plenty of brightwork. Seating was available for five, eight, or 12.

▼ Restyling gave full-size Fords a massive bumper/grille, with deeply inset quad head-lamps alongside an eggcrate center. The hardtop coupe came in Galaxie 500, LTD, and LTD Brougham trim. A new 400-cid V-8 was one of the options.

▲ After a brief rebirth of quarter windows, two-door Thunderbirds reverted to huge, blind sail panels. More conservative front-end styling focused on a new beaked horizontal-bar grille. As before, the Landau coupe sold best.

▲ Subtle grille and trim refinements were the only evident changes in the "award-winning" Torino design. Luxury leader was the Brougham, offered as a four-door or two-door hardtop. Volume totaled just 13,001 units.

▲ Simulated wood decorated the bodysides of the Torino Squire wagon, which wore concealed headlights in a restyled grille. Standard engine was a 302-cid V-8 developing 210 horsepower. The hefty mid-size wagon could hold either six or eight passengers. The Fairlane name was gone.

▲ Continuing its appeal to the "sports-oriented youth market," the rakish mid-size fastback hardtop came in both Torino GT and Cobra form, with long rear quarter windows and a two-section grille. Cobras were down-graded to a 351 V-8 with 285 bhp, but a 370-bhp 429 remained available.

◀ To spark Maverick sales, Ford added a sporty Grabber two-door with Charblack grille and two-tone hood, plus a four-door sedan on stretched wheelbase.

▲ Power brakes were standard on this F-250 pickup truck, which could have an AM/FM radio. Ford promised that light-duty pickups, which wore new two-tiered grilles, delivered "tasteful styling and comfortable ride." Price of an F-250 pickup was $3145, with either the Styleside or Flareside body.

▲ This example of Ford's "big ones" out of the new Louisville plant had a dual airbrake sytem and tilting front end. Over 1100 models were sold.

Model Breakdown Chart

Pinto—wb 94.2		Wght	Price	Prod
10	fstbk sdn 2d	1,949	1,919	288,606
11	Runabout htchbk sdn 3d	1,993	2,062	63,796
Maverick—wb 103.0, 4d 109.9				
91	fstbk sdn 2d	2,546	2,175	159,726
92	sdn 4d	2,641	2,234	73,208
93	Grabber fstbk sdn 2d	2,601	2,354	38,963
Torino—wb 117.0, wgn 114.0				
25	formal htp cpe	3,168	2,706	37,518
27	sdn 4d	3,163	2,672	29,501
40	wgn 5d	3,514	3,023	21,570
30	500 formal htp cpe	3,170	2,887	89,966
31	500 sdn 4d	3,160	2,855	35,650
32	500 htp sdn	3,196	2,959	12,724
34	500 fstbk htp cpe	3,179	2,943	11,150
42	500 wgn 5d	3,514	3,170	23,270
33	Brougham formal htp cpe, V-8	3,209	3,175	8,593
36	Brougham formal htp sdn, V-8	3,256	3,248	4,408
43	Squire wgn 5d, V-8	3,583	3,560	15,805

		Wght	Price	Prod
35	GT fstbk htp cpe, V-8	3,287	3,150	31,641
37	GT conv, V-8	3,428	3,408	1,613
38	Cobra fstbk htp cpe	3,525	3,295	3,054
Ford—wb 121.0				
51	Custom sdn, 4d	3,700	3,288	41,062
70	Custom Ranch Wagon 4d, V-8	4,222	3,890	16,696
53	Custom 500 sdn, 4d	3,705	3,426	33,765
72	Custom 500 Ranch Wgn 5d, 2S, V-8	4,231	3,982	25,957
72	Custom 500 Ranch Wgn 5d, 3S, V-8	4,281	4,097	
54	Galaxie 500 sdn, 4d	3,782	3,594	98,130
56	Galaxie 500 htp sdn	3,838	3,665	46,595
58	Galaxie 500 htp sdn	3,783	3,628	117,139
74	G500 Ctry Sdn wgn 5d, 2S, V-8	4,246	4,074	60,487
74	G500 Ctry Sdn wgn 5d, 3S, V-8	4,296	4,188	
61	LTD conv, V-8	4,053	4,094	5,750
62	LTD htp cpe, V-8	3,919	3,923	103,896
63	LTD sdn 4d, V-8	3,981	3,931	92,260
64	LTD htp sdn, V-8	3,976	3,969	48,166

		Wght	Price	Prod
76	Country Squire wgn 5d, 2S, V-8	4,306	4,380	130,644
76	Country Squire wgn 5d, 3S, V-8	4,356	4,496	
66	LTD Brougham sdn 4d, V-8	4,111	4,094	26,186
67	LTD Brougham htp sdn, V-8	4,016	4,140	27,820
68	LTD Brougham htp cpe, V-8	3,945	4,097	43,303
Mustang—wb 109.0				
01	htp cpe	2,982	2,911	65,696
02	fstbk cpe	2,950	2,973	23,956
02	Boss 351 fstbk cpe, V-8	3,281	4,124	
03	conv	3,102	3,227	6,121
04	Grandé htp cpe	3,006	3,117	17,406
05	Mach I fstbk cpe, V-8	3,220	3,268	36,499
Series 80 Thunderbird—wb 114.7, 4d 117.2				
83	htp cpe	4,389	5,295	9,146
84	Landau htp cpe	4,360	5,438	20,356
87	Landau sdn 4d	4,496	5,516	6,553

1971 Engine Availability

Engines	bore × stroke	bhp	availability
I-4, 98.6	3.19 × 3.06	75	S-Pinto
I-4, 122.0	3.58 × 3.03	100	O-Pinto
I-6, 170.0	3.50 × 2.94	100	S-Maverick
I-6, 200.0	3.68 × 3.13	115	O-Maverick
I-6, 240.0	4.00 × 3.18	140	S-Ford
I-6, 250.0	3.68 × 3.91	145	S-Tor exc Cobra; O-Mav
V-8, 302.0	4.00 × 3.00	210	S-Mav, Ford Cus, Tor exc Cobra
V-8, 351.0	4.00 × 3.50	240	S-Ford exc Cus
V-8, 351.0	4.00 × 3.50	285	S-Tor Cobra; O-Torino
V-8, 400.0	4.00 × 4.00	260	O-Ford
V-8, 429.0	4.36 × 3.59	320/360	O-Ford
V-8, 429.0	4.36 × 3.59	370	O-Torino

Mustang	bore × stroke	bhp	availability
I-6, 250.0	3.68 × 3.91	145	S-all exc Mach 1, Boss 351
V-8, 302.0	4.00 × 3.00	210	S-Mach 1; O-all exc Boss 351
V-8, 351.0	4.00 × 3.50	240	O-all exc Boss 351
V-8, 351.0	4.00 × 3.50	285	O-all exc Boss 351
V-8, 351.0	4.00 × 3.50	330	S-Boss 351; O-others
V-8, 429.0	4.36 × 3.59	370/375	O-all
Thunderbird			
V-8, 429.0	4.36 × 3.59	360	S-all

1972

All-new Torino debuts, abandons unit construction

Thunderbird earns full revamping, akin to new Continental Mark IV

"Sure Track" anti-skid device on rear wheels becomes T-Bird option

Econolines add sliding right cargo door

Ford car production nears 2.25 million, trails Chevrolet by 174,000

Ford's corporate net income hits record level

Ford joins rivals in quoting SAE net horsepower and torque ratings

U.S./Canadian Ford truck output hits 987,394 units

▲ Notchback coupes came in Gran Torino and Sport form. Standard engines were the 250-cid six and 302 V-8, with options up to 429-cid.

▲ Torino four-door sedans, called "pillared hardtops," measured 207.3 inches. Front disc brakes were standard. Gran and Squire models had a "mouth" grille between quad headlamps.

▲ Topping the restyled mid-size line was the Gran Torino Sport, sold as a notchback or SportsRoof hardtop coupe. Ford claimed the new separate chassis with rear coil springs helped improve handling, but a softer ride was the main goal. Two-doors rode a 114-inch wheelbase; four-doors had four extra inches. Note the massive hood and simulated scoop. Sports could get a Rallye Equipment Group for $443.

224

◀ Simpler grilles on full-size Fords, suggesting the new T-Bird, were bisected by a new front-bumper crosspiece. Rear bumpers extended up to the trunk sill. This Galaxie 500 four-door hardtop wore new rocker panel and wheel lip moldings, but sold slower than its two-door mate—or the four-door sedan. Two-doors could have an electric sliding sunroof.

▲ One of seven full-size wagons, the woody-look LTD Country Squire was billed as "best-selling in the industry," with over 96 cubic feet of cargo space, six- or eight-passenger capacity, and standard 351-cid V-8. An optional lockable storage compartment went on the left quarter panel. An impressive 121,419 found customers. Big Fords rode a 121-inch wheelbase.

▲ Among the 19 models that made up the full-size Ford lineup, only fleet and taxi variants kept the "Big Six" and 302 V-8 as standard equipment. Others turned to a 351-cid V-8 as the base engine. Options included 400-cid and 429-cid V-8s, the latter developing 208 horsepower. This would be the final appearance of a full-size Ford convertible, with just 4234 built.

▲ Popularity leader of this year's Mustang clan was the base hardtop coupe, with 57,350 built and a $2729 sticker price with six-cylinder power. Total ponycar production, however, sank 16 percent, to 125,000. Note the tunnel-roof rear end with "flying buttress" sail panels that extended to the back panel. Plain hubcaps were standard, with full wheel covers optional. Engine choices shrank to five, as the big-block 429 bit the dust.

▲ As was customary, the luxury-appointed Mustang Grandé sold only one-third as many copies as the base hardtop, though its list price was only $186 higher. A vinyl roof and unique body stripes were standard. Changes were slight this year, after the major restyling for 1971. All engines were detuned to meet tighter emissions regulations. Top powerplant this time was the 351-cid V-8, yielding as much as 275 horsepower.

▲ A hot body color plus black striping and hood accenting could turn even a mild-mannered soft-topped Mustang into a dazzling sight. Convertible production edged upward slightly, to 6401 for the model year.

▼ With Mustang sales drooping, Ford had to take steps. At mid-year, they launched a red/white/blue "Sprint" Decor Option for hardtops and Sports-Roof fastbacks. All were painted white with red accent striping, broad blue hood stripes and rocker panels, and stars-and-stripes shields.

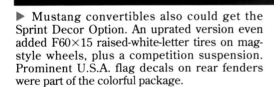

▲ Mustang drivers faced a down-to-business dashboard made up of recessed round gauges. Convertible buyers needed only to use a finger to raise and lower the top, which was power-operated. Hottest Mustang of the lot was still the Mach 1 fastback, with its standard 302-cid V-8.

▶ Mustang convertibles also could get the Sprint Decor Option. An uprated version even added F60×15 raised-white-letter tires on mag-style wheels, plus a competition suspension. Prominent U.S.A. flag decals on rear fenders were part of the colorful package.

▼ Mustangs with the Sprint Decor Option displayed complimentary blue/white colors inside.

1972 Engine Availability

Engines	bore × stroke	bhp	availability
I-4, 98.6	3.19 × 3.06	54	S-Pinto exc wgn
I-4, 122.0	3.58 × 3.03	86	S-Pinto wgn; O-Pinto
I-6, 170.0	3.50 × 2.94	82	S-Maverick
I-6, 200.0	3.68 × 3.13	91	O-Maverick
I-6, 240.0	4.00 × 3.18	103	S-Ford
I-6, 250.0	3.68 × 3.91	95	S-Torino
I-6, 250.0	3.68 × 3.91	98	O-Maverick
V-8, 302.0	4.00 × 3.00	140	S-Torino, Ford Cus V-8
V-8, 302.0	4.00 × 3.00	143	O-Maverick
V-8, 351.0	4.00 × 3.50	153	S-Ford wgn; O-Ford
V-8, 351.0	4.00 × 3.50	161	O-Torino
V-8, 351.0	4.00 × 3.50	248	O-Torino
V-8, 400.0	4.00 × 4.00	168	O-Torino
V-8, 400.0	4.00 × 4.00	172	O-Ford
V-8, 429.0	4.36 × 3.59	205	O-Torino
V-8, 429.0	4.36 × 3.59	208	O-Ford
Mustang			
I-6, 250.0	3.68 × 3.91	99	S-all exc Mach I
V-8, 302.0	4.00 × 3.00	141	S-Mach 1; O-others
V-8, 351.0	4.00 × 3.50	177/ 266/275	O-all
Thunderbird			
V-8, 429.0	4.36 × 3.59	212	S-all
V-8, 460.0	4.36 × 3.85	224	O-all

▲ A revamped, bigger Thunderbird shared its structure with the Continental. Only one coupe model remained, with optional landau bars and a 429- or 460-cid V-8. Sales rose 60 percent.

▲ Sales of two-door Pintos fell by 37 percent; those of the versatile hatchback tripled. A station wagon added at mid-year sold well, with either plain or woody-look Squire bodysides.

▲ Little was new in the Maverick series except for availability of an optional 302 V-8. At mid-year, a Luxury Decor Option arrived with copper-color vinyl top and bodyside moldings.

▲ F-Series pickups could be ordered with a tempting selection of extras. A 300-cid six replaced the 240 as base F-250/300 engine. Stylesides started at $2703, for an F-100.

▲ The four-wheel-drive craze wouldn't emerge for years, but 4WD pickups had their fans—even if few left the road. F-Series trucks wore a split grille; 4×4s could have power brakes.

▲ Aiming at developing nations, Ford created this compact Fiera truck with a British "Kent" engine, built in the Philippines. The utility vehicle was engineered for easy assembly.

◄ Broncos gained standard bucket seats with vinyl upholstery for '72, and could get 6.50×16 tires. At mid-year, a deluxe Ranger option became available on the wagon, including special paint with white accents and a swing-away outside spare tire. This Bronco's emblem reveals the 302-cid V-8 beneath its hood.

Model Breakdown Chart

Pinto—wb 94.2		Wght	Price	Prod
10	fstbk sdn 2d	2,061	1,960	181,002
11	Runabout htchbk sdn 3d	2,099	2,078	197,290
12	wgn 3d	2,283	2,265	101,483
Maverick—wb 103.0, 4d 109.9				
91	fstbk sdn 2d	2,654	2,140	145,931
92	sdn 4d	2,751	2,195	73,686
93	Grabber fstbk sdn 2d	2,708	2,309	35,347
Torino—wb 114.0, 4d 118.0				
25	formal htp cpe	3,374	2,673	33,530
27	sdn 4d	3,442	2,641	33,486
40	wgn 5d	3,840	2,955	22,204
30	Gran Torino Formal htp cpe	3,410	2,878	132,284
31	Gran Torino sdn 4d	3,484	2,856	102,300
42	Gran Torino wgn 5d	3,874	3,096	45,212
35	GT Sport fstbk htp cpe, V-8	3,470	3,094	60,794
38	Gran Torino form htp cpe, V-8	3,466	3,094	31,239

		Wght	Price	Prod
43	Squire wgn 5d, V-8	3,938	3,486	35,595
Ford—wb 121.0				
51	Custom sdn 4d	3,742	3,246	33,014
70	Custom Ranch wgn 5d, V-8	4,304	3,852	13,064
53	Custom 500 sdn 4d	3,808	3,377	24,870
72	C 500 Ranch Wagon 5d, 2S, V-8	4,314	3,941	16,834
72	C 500 Ranch Wagon 5d, 3S, V-8	4,364	4,051	
54	Galaxie 500 sdn 4d	3,848	3,537	104,167
56	Galaxie 500 htp sdn	3,910	3,604	28,939
58	Galaxie 500 htp cpe	3,852	3,572	80,855
74	G500 Ctry Sdn wgn 5d, 2S, V-8	4,349	4,028	55,238
74	G500 Ctry Sdn wgn 5d, 3S, V-8	4,399	4,136	
62	LTD htp cpe, V-8	3,999	3,882	101,048
63	LTD sdn 4d, V-8	4,065	3,890	104,167
64	LTD htp sdn, V-8	4,060	3,925	33,742
61	LTD conv, V-8	4,165	4,057	4,234

		Wght	Price	Prod
76	LTD Ctry Squire wgn 5d, 2S, V-8	4,393	4,318	121,419
76	LTD Ctry Squire wgn 5d, 3S, V-8	4,443	4,430	
66	LTD Brougham sdn 4d, V-8	4,095	4,031	36,909
67	LTD Brougham htp sdn, V-8	4,090	4,074	23,364
68	LTD B'ham formal htp cpe, V-8	4,031	4,034	50,409
Mustang—wb 109.0				
01	htp cpe	2,983	2,729	57,350
02	fstbk cpe	2,952	2,786	15,622
03	conv	3,099	3,015	6,401
04	Grandé htp cpe	3,008	2,915	18,045
05	Mach 1 fstbk cpe, V-8	3,046	3,053	27,675
Series 80 Thunderbird—wb 120.4				
87	htp cpe	4,373	5,293	57,814

1973

Ford and Chevrolet both gain in car production; Ford Number Two again

Five-mph front "crash bumpers" mandatory

Engines detuned in response to emissions standards

Full-size Ford sales rise past 850,000 units

F-Series trucks redesigned

Ford truck production tops million mark in 1973 year

▲ Both an automatic transmission and power steering became available on the '73 four-wheel-drive Bronco. Ford advised that the sport-utility was "a popular choice for the outdoor-minded." A 200-cid six replaced the 170 as base engine, developing 84 (net) horsepower. The pickup model was dropped, leaving only the $3636 full-top wagon, with upgraded trim. A total of 21,894 Broncos were built this year.

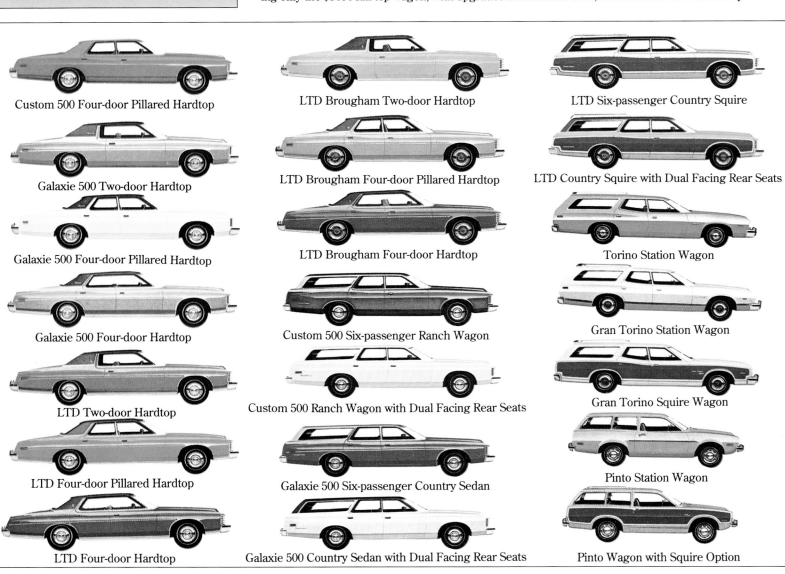

Custom 500 Four-door Pillared Hardtop

Galaxie 500 Two-door Hardtop

Galaxie 500 Four-door Pillared Hardtop

Galaxie 500 Four-door Hardtop

LTD Two-door Hardtop

LTD Four-door Pillared Hardtop

LTD Four-door Hardtop

LTD Brougham Two-door Hardtop

LTD Brougham Four-door Pillared Hardtop

LTD Brougham Four-door Hardtop

Custom 500 Six-passenger Ranch Wagon

Custom 500 Ranch Wagon with Dual Facing Rear Seats

Galaxie 500 Six-passenger Country Sedan

Galaxie 500 Country Sedan with Dual Facing Rear Seats

LTD Six-passenger Country Squire

LTD Country Squire with Dual Facing Rear Seats

Torino Station Wagon

Gran Torino Station Wagon

Gran Torino Squire Wagon

Pinto Station Wagon

Pinto Wagon with Squire Option

▲ Despite a whopping $1144 price hike, Thunderbird popularity grew by nearly 30,000 customers with this year's facelift. Small parallelogram "opera" windows were a new $80 option with vinyl-topped T-Birds.

▲ Torinos got shallower grilles and reshaped fenders to fit the bulky front bumpers—not the most handsome of add-ons. A new Brougham hardtop and sedan topped the Gran Torino series, wearing a wide-rectangle grille.

▲ A Luxury Decor Option (LDO) added elegance to the Maverick sedan, with reclining front seats and a vinyl roof. Sales rose 14 percent.

▲ Full-size Fords, like this LTD Brougham, were reskinned below the beltline and gained a flatter nose—plus "federal" front bumpers.

▲ Galaxie 500 "pillared hardtops" wore full-width crosshatch grilles that differed from the posher LTDs. A 351-cid V-8 was standard.

Torino Two-door Hardtop

Gran Torino Brougham Two-door Hardtop

Mustang Mach 1

Torino Four-door Pillared Hardtop

Gran Torino Brougham Four-door Pillared Hardtop

Maverick Two-door Sedan

Gran Torino Sport Two-door Hardtop

Mustang Hardtop Coupe

Maverick Four-door Sedan

Gran Torino Sport SportsRoof

Mustang SportsRoof Coupe

Maverick Grabber

Gran Torino Two-door Hardtop

Mustang Convertible

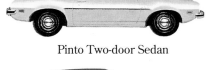
Pinto Two-door Sedan

Gran Torino Four-door Pillared Hardtop

Mustang Grandé

Pinto Three-door Runabout

▲ A 302-cid V-8, rated 136 bhp net, remained standard in the Mach 1 Mustang, which sold for $3088 with a competition suspension and choice of two hood designs. Many shoppers chose one of the 351 V-8s instead.

▼ Only minor changes were evident in the final "fat" Mustangs, including five-mph front bumpers. Mustang sales rose by almost 10,000, but convertibles almost doubled after Ford announced this would be the last.

▲ Mustang buyers still studied the options list carefully. This year's included two types of vinyl top, forged aluminum wheels, and "dual ram induction." A color-keyed cover improved the look of "federal" bumpers.

1973 Engine Availability

Engines	bore × stroke	bhp	availability
I-4, 98.6	3.19 × 3.06	54	S-Pinto exc wgn
I-4, 122.0	3.58 × 3.03	83	S-Pinto wgn; O-Pinto
I-6, 200.0	3.68 × 3.13	84	S-Maverick
I-6, 250.0	3.68 × 3.91	88	O-Maverick
I-6, 250.0	3.68 × 3.91	92	S-Torino exc 35 & wagons
V-8, 302.0	4.00 × 3.00	137/138	S-Torino 35 & wgns; O-other Torino, Mav.
V-8, 351.0	4.00 × 3.50	158/159	S-Ford; O-Torino
V-8, 351.0	4.00 × 3.50	246	O-Torino cpe
V-8, 400.0	4.00 × 4.00	168	O-Torino, Ford
V-8, 429.0	4.36 × 3.59	201	O-Torino, Ford
V-8, 460.0	4.36 × 3.85	202	O-Ford
Mustang			
I-6, 250.0	3.68 × 3.91	95	S-all exc Mach 1
V-8, 302.0	4.00 × 3.00	136	S-Mach 1; O-others
V-8, 351.0	4.00 × 3.50	154/156	O-all
Thunderbird			
V-8, 429.0	4.36 × 3.59	208	S-all
V-8, 460.0	4.36 × 3.85	219	O-all

▲ Not for a decade would Ford offer another convertible. This one sports the optional "tutone" hood for extra pizzazz. Radial tires were optional.

▲ Mustang was the last Ford convertible, as the LTD dropped out. This ragtop shows plenty of options, including upgraded wheels and tires.

▲ The muscle car era had faded, but this Gran Torino Sport SportsRoof still looked the part with its raised-white-letter tires and racing mirrors.

▲ Rancheros gained the same modifications as Torino, with a new frontal look and low-back bench seats. Brakes grew larger; wider tires optional.

▲ Squire woodlike trim gave the little Pinto wagon a richer appearance, for an extra $237.

▲ Pinto Runabouts ran second to wagons in sales. Note the toughened front bumper.

▲ Pinto volume again ran close to half a million. Forged aluminum wheels were available.

Model Breakdown Chart

Pinto—wb 94.2	Wght	Price	Prod
10	fstbk sdn 2d	2,115	2,021	116,146
11	Runabout htchbk sdn 3d	2,145	2,144	150,603
12	wgn 3d	2,386	2,343	217,763

Maverick—wb 103.0, 4d 109.9	Wght	Price	Prod
91	fstbk sdn 2d	2,730	2,248	148,943
92	sdn 4d	2,844	2,305	110,382
93	Grabber fstbk sdn 2d	2,770	2,427	32,350

Torino—wb 114.0, 4d 118.0	Wght	Price	Prod
25	htp cpe	3,548	2,732	28,005
27	sdn 4d	3,620	2,701	37,524
40	wgn 5d V-8	4,063	3,198	23,982
30	Gran Torino htp cpe	3,591	2,921	}138,962
30	Gran Torino B'ham htp cpe	3,598	3,071	
31	Gran Torino sdn 4d	3,675	2,890	}98,404
31	Gran Torino B'ham sdn 4d	3,690	3,051	

		Wght	Price	Prod
42	Gran Torino wgn 5d, V-8	4,097	3,344	60,738
43	Gran Torino Squire wgn 5d, V-8	4,129	3,559	40,023
35	Gran Torino Sport fstbk htp cpe, V-8	3,664	3,154	51,853
38	Gran Torino formal htp cpe, V-8	3,650	3,154	17,090

Ford—wb 121.0		Wght	Price	Prod
53	Custom 500 sdn 4d	4,059	3,606	42,549
72	C 500 Ranch Wagon 5d, 2S	4,529	4,050	}22,432
72	C 500 Ranch Wagon 5d, 3S	4,579	4,164	
54	Galaxie 500 sdn 4d	4,086	3,771	85,654
56	Galaxie 500 htp sdn	4,102	3,833	25,802
58	Galaxie 500 htp cpe	4,034	3,778	70,808
74	G500 Country Sdn Wgn 5d, 2S	4,555	4,146	}51,290
74	G500 Country Sdn Wgn 5d, 3S	4,605	4,260	

		Wght	Price	Prod
62	LTD htp cpe	4,059	3,950	120,864
63	LTD sdn 4d	4,107	3,958	122,851
64	LTD htp sdn	4,123	4,001	28,606
76	LTD Country Squire wgn 5d, 2S	4,579	4,401	}142,983
76	LTD Country Squire wgn 5d, 3S	4,629	4,515	
66	LTD Brougham sdn 4d	4,130	4,113	49,553
67	LTD Brougham htp sdn	4,148	4,157	22,268
68	LTD Brougham htp cpe	4,077	4,107	68,901

Mustang—wb 109.0		Wght	Price	Prod
01	htp cpe	3,040	2,760	51,480
02	fstbk cpe	3,053	2,820	10,820
03	conv	3,171	3,102	11,853
04	Grandé htp cpe	3,059	2,946	25,274
05	Mach 1 fstbk cpe, V-8	3,115	3,088	35,440

Series 80 Thunderbird—wb 120.4		Wght	Price	Prod
87	htp cpe	4,505	6,437	87,269

1974

Smaller Mustang II debuts, with first U.S. engine using metric measurements—redefines ponycar concept

Motor Trend names Mustang II "Car of the Year"

"Energy crisis" triggers gasoline shortages and rising fuel prices—soon affects car sales

Ford car output dips below 2.2 million

Ford remains Number Two in car production, but leads in 1974 truck sales

Ford's corporate earnings slide by 58 percent

All 1974 cars required to have short-lived seatbelt interlock, plus five-mph bumpers at both ends

Ford president Lee Iacocca proposes moratorium on new federal regulations—government disagrees

▲ Henry Ford II shows Anna Muccioli the slimmed-down Mustang II, which happened to appear at the height of the Energy Crisis. Mrs. Muccioli had complained about the prior ponycar's chubbiness. Ford's goal: a shorter wheelbase, four-speed gearbox, small engines, and luxurious appointments.

▲ Lee Iacocca served as driving force behind the mini-ponycar, reprising his role with the original Mustang. He realized sportiness was now the secret, and was proved right as sales approached 376,000.

▶ Mustang's familiar symbol seemed to have slowed from a gallop to a trot, suggesting the smaller engines and less-muscular action.

◀ Ideas for the trim Mustang II came from several Ford design groups, and the recently acquired Ghia coachbuilding firm. A fastback styled by Lincoln-Mercury under Al Mueller was chosen, but deluxe versions wore Ghia badges.

▲ By 1971, all Mustang mock-ups turned to smaller dimensions. This "Anaheim" notchback by Don DeLaRossa almost failed to survive.

▲ Four of the five final clay models reviewed in November 1971 were fastbacks, but the less-rakish notchback body wasn't destined to die.

▲ Sleek hatchbacks drew attention, but most Mustang buyers still chose a notchback body. Ford briefly considered a two-seat fastback.

▲ Lines of this fastback mock-up from September 1971 are close to production models, but vent wings and fake scoops wouldn't last.

▲ Taillights and other details on this mock-up from early 1972 would be modified, but the new Mustang's basic look was clearly established.

▲ A Mercury Capri based on the Mustang II was considered, but dismissed because the original Capri still sold well.

◀ Mustang II notchbacks came in plain and (shown here) upmarket Ghia form, with sunroof optional. Wheelbase was 96.2 inches, versus 108 for the original, and the new version was 20 inches shorter and four inches narrower than a '73 Mustang—and far lighter in weight. Interiors were styled mainly by L. David Ash, who tried to combine "restrained elegance" with a "get-up-and-go" feel. Bucket seats and full instruments (with tachometer) were standard.

▲ Though toned-down, the Mach 1 designation reappeared on the sportiest variant of the Mustang II. A German-built 2.8-liter (170-cid) V-6 with dual exhausts was standard, while others used an overhead-cam 2.3-liter four as base engine. White-letter tires and black rocker panels marked the Mach 1.

▲ Fastback 2+2s gained a European-style lift-up hatch. Mustang IIs shared a number of components with the little Pinto. Both were unibodied, with similar suspensions and rack-and-pinion steering. Mustang versions were modified for better handling, however, and had front disc brakes. Shorter wheelbases made the back seats tight, but plush upholstery came in pleated cloth, vinyl, or optional leather. No V-8 engine was considered initially.

233

▲ Except for the addition of vertical grille bars and parking lights, little changed in the mid-size Torino. This Gran Torino Brougham also had new bumpers, hood ornament, and taillights. Two-doors could get Thunderbird-style opera windows, as well as fender skirts. Torino sales declined but remained strong, with 428,625 going to dealerships (including the new Elite).

◄ Poshest member of the Torino line, with plenty of simulated wood adorning its interior, was the new Elite, added at mid-year. The "Thunderbird-inspired" pillared coupe rode a Mercury Cougar XR-7 chassis, now that Cougars no longer were related to Mustang. Elite quickly became Ford's most popular mid-size by far, with a standard 351-cid V-8 engine.

▲ Newly required bumpers and other safety equipment in 1973 and '74 accounted for a large part of the weight increase in the Gran Torino wagon, which gained 335 pounds since 1972. Prices also rose dramatically, but the three Torino wagons—base, Gran, and Squire—attracted 68,096 customers.

▲ A more aggressive eggcrate grille, single headlamps in square nacelles, and a central hood bulge identified the plush Gran Torino Elite coupe, rival to Chevrolet's Monte Carlo. Note the twin slim opera windows (called "Twindows"), whereas other Torino two-doors made do with single panes.

▲ Lincoln's 460-cid V-8, optional since 1972, became standard this year, rated 220 bhp. That extra oomph was needed, since T-Birds had been gaining a lot of weight—and rising sharply in price. Output slipped to 58,443.

▲ Segmented taillights contained a large central back-up light with stylized logo, but little other change was evident in Thunderbirds. Fresh options included "Autolamp" headlight operation and an electric moonroof.

▲ Like many '74 models trying to comply with federal standards, Mavericks suffered from a deep rear bumper that looked too heavy for the car.

▲ An 84-bhp, 200-cid six remained standard in Mavericks, with 250 six and 140-bhp, 302 V-8 optional. Production rose a bit, to 301,048.

▲ Pintos earned several engineering upgrades, a result of having some of their parts installed on the new Mustang. A two-liter four was now standard.

1974 Engine Availability

Engines	bore × stroke	bhp	availability
I-4, 122.0	3.58 × 3.03	80	S-Pinto
I-4, 140.0	3.78 × 3.13	82	O-Pinto
I-6, 200.0	3.68 × 3.13	84	S-Maverick
I-6, 250.0	3.68 × 3.91	91	O-Maverick, Torino
V-8, 302.0	4.00 × 3.00	140	S-Torino; O-Maverick
V-8, 351.0	4.00 × 3.50	162	S-Ford exc 76; O-Tor
V-8, 400.0	4.00 × 4.00	170	S-Ford 76; O-Tor, Ford

	bore × stroke	bhp	availability
V-8, 460.0	4.36 × 3.85	220	O-Torino, Ford
Mustang			
I-4, 140.0	3.78 × 3.13	88	S-all exc Mach 1
V-6, 170.8	3.66 × 2.70	105	S-Mach 1; O-others
Thunderbird			
V-8, 460.0	4.36 × 3.85	220	S-all

◄ Here, a full-size Ford receives final attention before rolling off the assembly line. Big Fords were essentially carryovers for '74, except that the 429-cid V-8 no longer was offered. All optional V-8s, including the huge 460, gained solid-state ignition that helped reduce emissions and also lengthened the interval between tune-ups. Full-size models weren't drawing customers in the wake of the Energy Crisis, as output sank by 46 percent.

▲ A new fine-checked grille and stand-up hood ornament were the only changes evident on this LTD Brougham "pillared hardtop" sedan.

▲ Steel-belted radials went on LTD Broughams, which accounted for 17 percent of full-size Fords. This was the last year for pillarless hardtops.

◄ Full-size wagons still tempted plenty of customers at dealerships. This year's roster included Custom 500 Ranch Wagons and Galaxie 500 Country Sedans. Sales leaders, however, were the costlier Country Squires, which could be ordered with or without woodgrain trim. A 351-cid V-8 was standard on all except the Country Squire, which had a 400-cid engine.

Custom 500 Four-door Pillared Hardtop

Galaxie 500 Two-door Hardtop

LTD Four-door Pillared Hardtop

LTD Brougham Four-door Hardtop

LTD Country Squire "Wagonmaster" Wagon

◄ Bronco sport-utilities continued to sell well despite competition from Chevrolet/GMC and Dodge/Plymouth. Only a few details changed for '74, including a new lighted quadrant for the optional Cruise-O-Matic transmission. Price was $4182 with the 84-horsepower, 200-cid six-cylinder engine, but a 302 V-8 was available. Ranchero car-pickups adopted the new Torino front end and could get its 460-cid V-8 engine as well as a fancy Brougham Decor Group.

Model Breakdown Chart

Pinto—wb 94.2		Wght	Price	Prod
10	fstbk sdn 2d	2,372	2,527	132,061
11	Runabout htchbk sdn 3d	2,406	2,676	174,754
12	wgn 3d	2,576	2,771	237,394
Maverick—wb 103.0, 4d 109.9				
91	fstbk sdn 2d	2,739	2,790	139,818
92	sdn 4d	2,932	2,824	137,728
93	Grabber fstbk sdn 2d	2,868	2,923	23,502
Torino—wb 114.0, 4d 118.0				
25	htp cpe	3,709	3,236	22,738
27	sdn 4d	3,793	3,239	31,161
40	wgn 5d	4,175	3,818	15,393
30	Gran Torino htp cpe	3,742	3,411	76,290
31	Gran Torino sdn 4d	3,847	3,454	72,728
42	Gran Torino wgn 5d	4,209	4,017	29,866
32	Gran Torino Brougham htp cpe	3,794	3,975	26,402
33	Gran Torino Brougham sdn 4d	3,887	3,966	11,464
43	Gran Torino Squire wgn 5d	4,250	4,300	22,837
38	Gran Torino Sport htp cpe	3,771	3,824	23,142
21	Gran Torino Elite htp cpe	NA	4,437	96,604
Ford—wb 121.0				
53	Custom 500 sdn 4d	4,180	3,982	28,941
72	C 500 Ranch Wagon 5d, 2S	4,654	4,488	12,104
72	C 500 Ranch Wagon 5d, 3S	4,687	4,608	
54	Galaxie 500 sdn 4d	4,196	4,164	49,661
56	Galaxie 500 htp sdn	4,212	4,237	11,526
58	Galaxie 500 htp cpe 5d	4,157	4,211	34,214
74	G500 Country Sdn wgn 5d, 2S	4,690	4,584	22,400
74	G500 Country Sdn wgn 5d, 3S	4,722	4,704	
62	LTD htp cpe	4,215	4,389	73,296
63	LTD sdn 4d	4,262	4,370	72,251
64	LTD htp sdn	4,277	4,438	12,375
76	LTD Cntry Squire wgn 5d, 2S*	4,752	4,898	64,047
76	LTD Cntry Squire wgn 5d, 3S*	4,785	5,018	
66	LTD Brougham sdn 4d	4,292	4,647	30,203
67	LTD Brougham htp sdn	4,310	4,717	11,371
68	LTD Brougham htp cpe	4,247	4,669	39,084
Mustang II—wb 96.2				
02	cpe 2d	2,654	3,134	177,671
03	htchbk cpe 3d	2,734	3,328	74,799
04	Ghia cpe 2d	2,820	3,480	89,477
05	Mach 1 htchbk cpe 3d, V-6	2,778	3,674	44,046
Series 80 Thunderbird—wb 120.5				
87	htp cpe	4,825	7,330	58,443

*Prices with optional woodgrain bodyside trim. Non-woodgrain version $136 less.

◄ Only one Bronco four-wheel-drive model, the Wagon, was offered by '74. A total of 18,786 were produced, down from 21,894 in 1973. Broncos could be upgraded with an optional Ranger package that included a white power dome and spare-tire carrier. Styleside pickup trucks were now available with longer-wheelbase "SuperCab" styling for extra seating capacity.

1975

Granada "deluxe compact" launched, billed as "designed for the times"

Ford promotes Granada's virtues against "New Generation" Mercedes-Benz

Maverick intended for oblivion, but hangs on

Third-generation Econoline series debuts to rival Chevrolet's G-series vans

Auto sales remain sluggish after 1973-74 oil crisis

Ford car production drops by 610,000 units—second again to Chevrolet

Ford's car market share falls below 18 percent

Mustang II adds V-8 option, sales slump by half in their second year

Rebates employed to spark new-car sales

▲ Ford president Lee Iacocca stands behind another car that enjoyed his influence: the new Granada, originally intended to replace the Maverick. Granada sedans came in two- and four-door form, and base or upscale Ghia guise. Wheelbase was the same 109.9 inches as a Maverick four-door and suspensions were similar, but Granadas measured 10 inches longer. Kinship with Maverick wasn't easy to spot.

▲ Granada four-doors wore the boxy formal body more handsomely than two-doors. Styling was directed by Eugene Bordinat. Softer springs and shocks than a Maverick's promised "big car" ride, while front discs handled the stopping chore. Granadas sold well, with 302,658 rolling off the line this year.

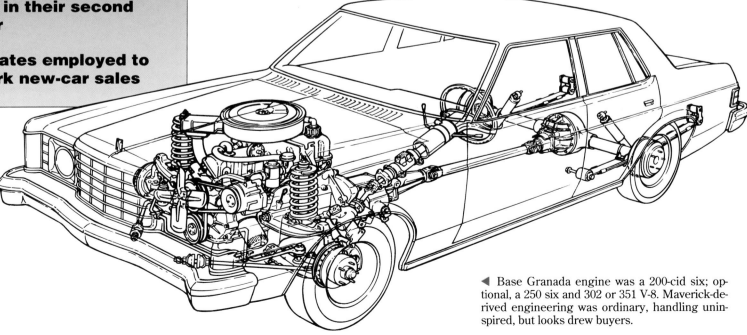

◀ Base Granada engine was a 200-cid six; optional, a 250 six and 302 or 351 V-8. Maverick-derived engineering was ordinary, handling uninspired, but looks drew buyers.

▲ Ford made no secret of the Granada's resemblance to Mercedes-Benz sedans, especially in the formal grille and stand-up hood ornament. Styling blended Ford cues with European ideas. Note the trendy opera windows.

▲ Plush Granada interiors could be mistaken for Lincoln's, with lots of simulated wood but few instruments. Ghias got separate reclining front seats. A floorshift was offered for manual or automatic transmission.

▲ Fender badges reveal a new 302 V-8 within this Mustang Ghia, sold only with automatic. Note slim opera windows. A power moonroof was optional.

▲ Not destined for production, the Targa-topped Sportiva II was displayed at shows and racetracks to promote the debut of the trimmer Mustang II.

Mustang II Hardtop

Mustang II Ghia

Mustang II Three-door Hatchback

Mustang II Mach 1 Hatchback

▲ Gran Torino Broughams weren't a hot item in 1974, as production shrank to 10,778 units. Ford boasted that even base Torinos had power brakes/steering, V-8 power, and automatic.

▲ Ford's poshest mid-size, the Elite hardtop coupe, ranked as one of the most expensive Torino models—and definitely the most popular. Output rose nearly 28 percent, to 123,372. Little changed in the Torino line except for addition of catalytic converters to engines.

◄ While Elite coupes gained popularity, sales of other Torinos declined by more than 150,000. Far more Gran Torinos found customers than did the base models, despite the Gran's higher price tags. Four-doors rode a 118-inch wheelbase, four inches longer than two-doors.

▲ Ford elected to keep the Maverick around after Granada's debut, but sales fell 46 percent. Grabbers could get a stiff suspension.

▲ More power went under Pinto hoods, in the form of a standard 2.3-liter four. An MPG model with catalytic converter came at mid-year.

▲ A Copper or Silver Luxury Group could add color to a T-Bird. All-disc brakes, optional since '72, offered Sure-Track anti-locking.

▲ Modest restyling of full-size Fords included a flatter, more rectangular grille and a raised rear deck. Two-door coupes wore slim vertical windows in their B-pillars, ahead of the triangular quarter glass. LTD Landaus now topped the lineup, followed by the LTD Brougham, LTD, and Custom 500.

1975 Engine Availability

Engines	bore × stroke	bhp	availability
I-4, 140.0	3.78 × 3.13	83	S-Pinto
V-6, 170.8	3.66 × 2.70	97	O-Pinto #11,12
I-6, 200.0	3.68 × 3.13	75	S-Mav, Granada exc Ghia
I-6, 250.0	3.68 × 3.91	72	S-Granada Ghia; O-Mav, Grnda
V-8, 302.0	4.00 × 3.00	122	O-Maverick, Granada
V-8, 351.0	4.00 × 3.50	143	O-Granada
V-8, 351.0	4.00 × 3.50	148-150	S-Torino
V-8, 400.0	4.00 × 4.00	144/158	S-Ford 74, 76; O-Torino, other Ford
V-8, 460.0	4.36 × 3.85	216	O-Torino, Ford
Mustang			
I-4, 140.0	3.78 × 3.13	83	S-all exc Mach 1
V-6, 170.8	3.66 × 2.70	97	S-Mach 1; O-others
V-8, 302.0	4.00 × 3.00	122	O-all
Thunderbird			
V-8, 460.0	4.36 × 3.85	194	S-all

▲ Concealed headlamps identified the top-of-the-line LTD Landau four-door "pillared hardtop," which also sported wraparound taillights with integral side marker lights. Inside were split bench seats and a burled walnut dash. Country Squire wagons now displayed Landau trim. The Galaxie name was gone.

▲ In their third generation, with body-on-frame construction, Econolines weren't all light-duty. This Cutaway Chassis was rated 8750-11,000 pounds GVW. Wheelbases grew to 124, 138, and 158 inches. Note the longer hood.

▲ Roomier than before, the Custom Club Wagon could seat eight on a short-wheelbase chassis or a dozen on long-wheelbase. "Captain's chairs" were optional. A 351 V-8 was standard on Econolines, with options up to 460-cid.

Model Breakdown Chart

Pinto—wb 94.4, wgn 94.7		Wght	Price	Prod
10	fstbk sdn 2d	2,495	2,769	64,081
11	Runabout htchbk sdn 3d	2,528	2,984	68,919
12	wgn 3d	2,692	3,153	90,763
Maverick—wb 103.0, 4d 109.9				
91	fstbk sdn 2d	2,896	3,025	90,695
92	sdn 4d	3,018	3,061	63,404
93	Grabber fstbk sdn 2d	2,903	3,282	8,473
Granada—wb 109.9				
81	sdn 4d	3,279	3,756	118,168
82	sdn 2d	3,230	3,698	100,810
83	Ghia sdn 4d	3,392	4,283	43,652
84	Ghia sdn 2d	3,342	4,225	40,028
Torino—wb 114.0, 4d 118.0				
25	htp cpe	3,981	3,954	13,394
27	sdn 4d	4,053	3,957	22,928
40	wgn 4d	4,406	4,336	13,291

		Wght	Price	Prod
30	Gran Torino htp cpe	3,992	4,314	35,324
31	Gran Torino sdn 4d	4,084	4,338	53,161
42	Gran Torino wgn 5d	4,450	4,673	23,951
43	Gran Torino Squire wgn 5d	4,490	4,952	
32	Gran Torino Brougham htp cpe	4,081	4,805	4,849
33	Gran Torino Brougham sdn 4d	4,157	4,837	5,929
38	Gran Torino Sport htp cpe	4,038	4,790	5,126
21	Elite htp cpe	4,154	4,767	123,372
Ford—wb 121.0				
53	Custom 500 sdn 4d	4,377	4,477	31,043
72	Custom 500 Ranch Wagon 5d	4,787	5,067	6,930
62	LTD htp cpe	4,359	4,753	47,432
63	LTD sdn 4d	4,408	4,712	82,382

		Wght	Price	Prod
74	LTD wgn 5d, 2S	4,803	5,158	22,936
74	LTD wgn 5d, 3S	4,836	5,283	
66	LTD Brougham sdn 4d	4,419	5,099	32,327
68	LTD Brougham sdn 2d	4,391	5,133	24,005
76	LTD Country Squire wgn 5d, 2S	4,845	5,440	41,550
76	LTD Country Squire wgn 5d, 3S	4,878	5,565	
64	LTD Landau sdn 4d	4,446	5,453	32,506
65	LTD Landau sdn 2d	4,419	5,484	26,919
Mustang II—wb 96.2				
02	cpe 2d	2,718	3,529	85,155
03	htchbk cpe 3d	2,754	3,818	30,038
04	Ghia cpe 2d	2,762	3,938	52,320
05	Mach 1 htchbk cpe 3d, V-6	2,879	4,188	21,062
Series 80 Thunderbird—wb 120.4				
87	htp cpe	4,893	7,701	42,685

1976

America celebrates Bicentennial, and auto industry rebounds

Ford sinks in market share

Mustang II third in sales among domestic subcompacts, barely behind new Chevette; Pinto leads that race

Granada hits Number One ranking among compacts, tops Nova and Volaré

Chevrolet beats Ford in truck sales, partly due to Econoline shortage

Cobra II package offered on Mustang II— tries to revive image of Shelby-Mustangs

Ford considers production of compact van, but soon abandons project

Lincoln-Mercury launches upgraded Capri II

Henry Ford II hospitalized for angina attack—tones down his flamboyant style

▲ Eye-appealing Stallion paint/stripe options were offered on the Mustang II, Pinto, and Maverick for '76, priced from $72 to $329. Dark rocker panels, hoods, and rear panels (and Maverick/Mustang roof) accented the silver bodies. Huge fender decals depicted fiery steeds, so no one could miss a Stallion. Also included were raised-white-letter tires, racing mirrors, and stiffened suspensions.

▲ Hidden headlamps again differentiated the LTD Landau sedans from lesser full-size Fords, none of which changed much for '76. All-disc brakes joined the options list, along with a half-vinyl two-door roof. Biggies sold rather well. Production rose by more than 54,000 after slipping badly in 1975. Base engine was a 351-cid V-8 (400 on wagons), with 460 optional. A Landau Luxury Group cost up to $708.

Gran Torino Brougham Four-door Pillared Hardtop

Gran Torino Two-door Hardtop

Torino Four-door Wagon

Torino Two-door Hardtop

Gran Torino Four-door Pillared Hardtop

Grand Torino Four-door Wagon

Torino Four-door Pillared Hardtop

Gran Torino Brougham Two-door Hardtop

Gran Torino Squire Wagon

▲ Base coupes were the top Mustang sellers, accounting for 42 percent of the 187,567 mini-ponycars built. This coupe wears the $169 exterior accent group. A moonroof was optional on any Mustang, silver or brown tinted.

▲ Stripes, louvers, and spoilers on the Mustang Cobra II option triggered memories of the muscle-car era—and an optional 134-bhp, 302 V-8 brought a tiny taste of its "feel." Cobras came only in white with blue striping.

▲ This T-topped mutant of the Mustang toured 1976 auto shows, reminiscent of the earlier Sportiva II. Removable roof panels wouldn't become a production option until '77, and no Mustang II convertible was built.

▲ Differences from 1974-75 were slight, though Mustang IIs could be customized with a variety of options. Base fastback popularity doubled, but Mach 1 sales declined sharply. Total production was close to the '76 level.

▲ Concept-car stylists created the four-in-one Prima, which appeared to be a two-seat compact pickup with tailgate. Adding and removing clip-on panels transformed the Prima into a two-seat coupe, a wagon, or a hatchback.

1976 Engine Availability

Engines	bore × stroke	bhp	availability
I-4, 140.0	3.78 × 3.13	92	S-Pinto
V-6, 170.8	3.66 × 2.70	103	O-Pinto
I-6, 200.0	3.68 × 3.13	81	S-Mav, Gran exc Ghia
I-6, 250.0	3.68 × 3.91	90	S-Gran Ghia; O-Mav, Gran
V-8, 302.0	4.00 × 3.00	134/138	O-Granada, Maverick
V-8, 351.0	4.00 × 3.50	152/154	S-Tor, Elite, Ford exc wgns; O-Granada
V-8, 400.0	4.00 × 4.00	180	S-Ford wgns; O-Tor, Ford Elite
V-8, 460.0	4.36 × 3.85	202	O-Torino, Elite, Ford
Mustang			
I-4, 140.0	3.78 × 3.13	92	S-all exc Mach 1
V-6, 170.8	3.66 × 2.70	103	S-Mach 1; O-others
V-8, 302.0	4.00 × 3.00	134	O-all
Thunderbird			
V-8, 460.0	4.36 × 3.85	202	S-all

▲ Rather than remaining part of the Torino series, the Elite hardtop coupe went its own way for '76, and output jumped to 146,475. "Twindows" were standard; moonroof extra. New options included bucket seats and floorshift. For '77, a cheaper T-Bird would take its place.

▲ Thunderbird sales recovered, as 52,935 went to customers at the close of the luxury coupe's seventh generation. Options included a power lumbar seat and quadrasonic eight-track.

▲ Borrowing a cue from wagons, Pinto Runabouts could get simulated-wood Squire trim this year, for an extra $305. Interiors held new low-back seats with plaid surfaces.

▲ A new fine-mesh grille with square parking lights decorated '76 Pintos. New this year: a stripped Pony, priced $130 below the MPG sedan. A half-vinyl roof was optional on sedans.

▲ Except for trim shuffling, Granadas showed little change. Ford pushed its kinship to both Mercedes-Benz and Cadillac Seville. Ghia four-doors could get a Luxury Decor group for $642.

▲ For $482, a Sports Sedan package gave the "precision-size" Granada two-door special paint, pinstripes, floor shift, and leather-rim steering wheel. All-disc brakes were optional.

▲ Front disc brakes finally became standard on Mavericks, which wore a new split grille; but that didn't keep sales from slipping. The Grabber was gone, but an LDO package cost $508.

▲ Compact Mavericks remained in the lineup alongside the Granada, largely becuse of uncertainty about oil supplies. Of the 139,687 built, 43 percent were two-door fastbacks.

▲ New options were the only notable changes for Gran Torino two-doors, including bucket seats, automatic parking-brake release, power trunk release, and a space-saver spare tire.

244

▲ Gas mileage got a boost in Ford mid-sizes, including the Gran Torino Brougham four-door pillared hardtop. Just 7656 Broughams were built, and the Gran Torino Sport departed.

▲ Simulated wood decorated the sides of the Ranchero Squire, which wore a Gran Torino front end and new steel-belted radials. The 16,072 Rancheros built included base and 500 models.

▲ In addition to the Styleside shown here, facelifted F-Series pickups came with Flareside bodies and short (6½ foot) cargo boxes, after several years out of the lineup. Ranger or XLT trim tarted up any pickup.

▲ Front disc brakes were standard in all F-Series 4×4s, including this F-250 Styleside pickup, which contained a tough Spicer front axle for rough off-road treks. New this year: a youth-oriented Econoline Cruising Van.

Model Breakdown Chart

Pinto—wb 94.4, wgn 94.7		Wght	Price	Prod
10	Pony MPG fstbk sdn 2d, I-4	2,450	2,895	92,264
10	MPG fstbk sdn 2d, I-4	2,452	3,025	
10	sdn 2d, V-6	2,590	3,472	
11	MPG htchbk sdn 3d, I-4	2,482	3,200	92,540
11	Squire MPG htchbk sdn 3d, I-4	2,518	3,505	
11	Runabout htchbk sdn 3d, V-6	2,620	3,647	
11	Squire htchbk sdn 3d, V-6	2,656	3,952	
12	MPG wgn 3d, I-4	2,635	3,365	105,328
12	Squire MPG wgn 3d, I-4	2,672	3,671	
12	wgn 3d, V-6	2,773	3,865	
12	Squire wgn 3d, V-6	2,810	4,171	
Maverick—wb 103.0, 4d 109.9				
91	fstbk sdn 2d	2,846	3,117	60,611
92	sdn 4d	2,956	3,189	79,076
Granada—wb 109.9				
81	sdn 4d	3,222	3,798	187,923
82	sdn 2d	3,172	3,707	161,618

		Wght	Price	Prod
83	Ghia sdn 4d	3,392	4,355	52,457
84	Ghia sdn 2d	3,334	4,265	46,786
Torino—wb 114.0, 4d 118.0				
25	htp cpe	3,976	4,172	34,518
27	sdn 4d	4,061	4,206	17,394
30	Gran Torino htp cpe	3,999	4,461	23,939
31	Gran Torino sdn 4d	4,081	4,495	40,568
32	Gran Torino Brougham htp cpe	4,063	4,883	3,183
33	Gran Torino Brougham sdn 4d	4,144	4,915	4,473
40	wgn 5d	4,409	4,521	17,281
42	Gran Torino wgn 5d	4,428	4,769	30,596
43	Gran Torino Squire wgn 5d	4,454	5,083	21,144
Elite—wb 114.0				
21	htp cpe	4,169	4,879	146,475
Ford—wb 121.0				
52	Custom 500 sdn 2d	—	—	7,037
53	Custom 500 sdn 4d	4,298	4,493	23,447
72	Custom 500 Ranch Wagon 5d	4,737	4,918	4,633

		Wght	Price	Prod
62	LTD sdn 2d	4,257	4,780	62,844
63	LTD sdn 4d	4,303	4,752	108,168
74	LTD wgn 5d, 2S	4,752	5,207	30,237
74	LTD wgn 5d, 3S	4,780	5,333	
66	LTD Brougham sdn 4d	4,332	5,245	32,917
68	LTD Brougham sdn 2d	4,299	5,299	20,863
76	LTD Country Squire wgn 5d, 2S	4,809	5,523	47,379
76	LTD Country Squire wgn 5d, 3S	4,837	5,649	
64	LTD Landau sdn 4d	4,394	5,560	35,663
65	LTD Landau sdn 2d	4,346	5,613	29,673
Mustang II—wb 96.2				
02	cpe 2d	2,717	3,525	78,508
03	htchbk cpe 3d	2,745	3,781	62,312
04	Ghia cpe 2d	2,768	3,859	37,515
05	Mach 1 htchbk cpe 3d, V-6	2,822	4,209	9,232
Series 80 Thunderbird—wb 120.4				
87	htp cpe	4,808	7,790	52,935*

*includes 30 commemorative editions.

1977

"When America needs a better idea," slogan says, "Ford puts it on wheels"

GM downsizes full-size car fleet; Ford shuffles nameplates on existing designs

LTD II replaces Torino as mid-size Ford

Thunderbird shrinks in size and price, usurps Elite's role as "premium" mid-size

60th Anniversary of Ford truck production

Ford truck sales hit record high, at 1,214,622

F-Series pickup remains top-selling U.S. vehicle

▲ Abandoning the Elite hardtop coupe, Ford used its platform to create a much different—and far cheaper—Thunderbird. Styling touches included concealed headlamps, plus a "basket handle" roof with wrapover chrome bands and tiny opera windows, ahead of large rear quarter glass. A 302-cid V-8 was standard, 351 and 400 V-8s optional. SelectShift Cruise-O-Matic was the sole transmission.

▲ Ads promoted the T-Bird's Elite-based "new look . . . new size [and] new price," which dropped by more than $2700 to just $5063. Wheelbase shrunk by 6.4 inches, weight by 900 pounds. Only one model was offered initially; then the Town Landau was revived, with more equipment and a whopping $7990 sticker.

▲ In the course of seven generations, Thunderbirds had turned into overweight guzzlers, prompting Ford to downsize its luxury coupe. The need grew greater, with Corporate Average Fuel Economy rules due to take effect in 1978. Production shot upward to a new record, with 318,140 built—far beyond the old Elite or the new LTD II series. Lighter weight and steering refinements made T-Bird driving more fun.

246

▲ Both the aggressive-look Cobra II package and new optional T-bar roof—with lift-out glass panels—are evident on this '77 Mustang II hatchback. Notchbacks could get a tilt-up/removable sunroof. Even so, sales skidded.

▲ This modification of Mustang's Stallion package—dubbed Stallion II—didn't make it into production. Instead, Ford offered a Rallye Appearance Package with black paint and gold accents, plus a performance option.

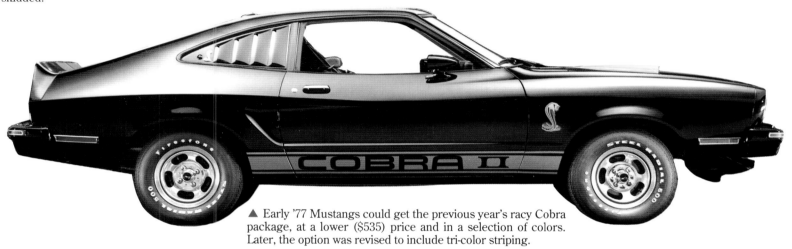

▲ Early '77 Mustangs could get the previous year's racy Cobra package, at a lower ($535) price and in a selection of colors. Later, the option was revised to include tri-color striping.

▲ Reacting to GM's downsized big cars, Ford advertised its LTD—including this Landau four-door pillared hardtop—as "the full-size car that kept its size," touting its "wider stance [and] road-hugging weight."

▲ Little changed for '77, full-size "Wagonmaster" wagons came in plain or woody-look Country Squire form. LTD engines ranged from 351 to 460 cid (biggest in the industry), but wagons used a 400 V-8 as base powerplant.

▲ Landaus ranked as top-dollar full-size Fords, as the Brougham line departed. Retaining its 121-inch wheelbase, LTD sales rose in 1977; but then, big cars in general sold well. Illuminated entry was a new option.

1977 Engine Availability

Engines	bore × stroke	bhp	availability
I-4, 140.0	3.78 × 3.13	89	S-Pinto
V-6, 170.8	3.66 × 2.70	93	O-Pinto, exc Pony
I-6, 200.0	3.68 × 3.13	96	S-Maverick, Granada
I-6, 250.0	3.68 × 3.91	98	S-Gran Ghia; O-Mav, Gran
V-8, 302.0	4.00 × 3.00	122	O-Granada
V-8, 302.0	4.00 × 3.00	130	S-LTD II exc wgns
V-8, 302.0	4.00 × 3.00	137	O-Maverick
V-8, 351.0	4.00 × 3.50	135	O-Granada
V-8, 351.0	4.00 × 3.50	149	S-LTD II wgns; O-LTD II
V-8, 351.0	4.00 × 3.50	161	S-LTD exc wgns; O-LTD II wgns
V-8, 400.0	4.00 × 4.00	173	S-LTD wgns; O-LTD II, LTD
V-8, 460.0	4.36 × 3.85	197	O-LTD
Mustang			
I-4, 140.0	3.78 × 3.13	89	S-all exc Mach 1
V-6, 170.8	3.66 × 2.70	93	S-Mach 1; O-others
V-8, 302.0	4.00 × 3.00	139	O-all
Thunderbird			
V-8, 302.0	4.00 × 3.00	130	S-all
V-8, 351.0	4.00 × 3.50	135	S-in Calif.; O-all
V-8, 400.0	4.00 × 4.00	173	O-all

▲ Promoted as the first "new-generation" car, the Granada showed little change and output edged downward. This one wears the Sports Coupe package with gold accents.

▲ Except for fresh colors and a handful of new options, the compact Maverick entered its final season unchanged. Output slipped below 99,000, but Ford had other irons in its fire now.

▲ Taking over Torino's spot, the LTD II wore an Elite-style nose with pointed grille and stacked headlamps. Ads pushed this "sporty new trim-size line in the LTD tradition."

▼ With only a mild facelift, the old Torino turned into a "new" LTD II, keeping its parent's nine-model lineup. Customers bought the transition, as output rose 20 percent.

▲ Borrowing an idea from the Econoline Cruising Van to lure young shoppers, Ford debuted a Pinto Cruising Wagon with a similar small porthole on its blanked side panels.

▲ This variant of Pinto's Cruising Wagon displayed bolder, more vivid striping than its standard mate. The package included a spoiler, carpeted walls, and Sports Rallye extras.

▲ Power came to Pinto in the form of an optional 2.8-liter V-6, yet output fell by nearly 88,000 cars. Pintos wore a new "soft" nose and could get assorted sporty options.

▲ Based on the Econoline E-150 with its Chateau-level trim, the youth-oriented Cruising Van featured a porthole and choice of striping patterns: L-shaped or wraparound "rainbow."

▲ A new 200-bhp diesel engine was available in the C-8000 tilt cab tractor. Also optional: an 18,500-pound single-speed rear axle, and an Allison automatic transmission.

▲ A Ranger package added brightwork and a fancy interior to the basic F-150 Styleside pickup, which could have two-tone paint. F-150s came with two- or four-wheel drive.

248

▲ Model designations on "Louisville Line" and other medium/heavy trucks were simplified for 1977. This LN-600 chassis-cab increased its GVW rating to 16,500 pounds at mid-year.

▲ W-Series long-haul diesel rigs entered their final year of production, including this WT-9000 tandem with sleeper cab. By year's end, Ford regained the Number One spot in truck sales.

▲ As part of this year's model shake-up, the F-500 series merged with F-600 and the F-700 with F-800. Mid-range Fords, including this F-600 Crew-cab chassis, could get a sliding window.

▲ Long-haul operators were drawn to models like this LT-9000. Flashy paint marked big haulers with Owner-Operator packages.

▲ Rancheros got a new look with LTD II front styling. A 302 V-8 was standard. Top seller was this $4984 striped GT, with 12,462 built.

▲ This Special Decor Group for Bronco 4×4s included a black-out grille, tape stripes, and bright window trim. Base price was $5260.

Model Breakdown Chart

Pinto—wb 94.4, wgn 94.7		Wght	Price	Prod
10	Pony sdn 2d, L-4	2,313	3,099	48,863*
10	sdn 2d	2,376	3,237	
11	Runabout htchbk sdn 3d	2,412	3,353	74,237*
12	wgn 3d	2,576	3,548	79,449*
12	Squire wgn 3d	2,614	3,891	
Maverick—wb 103.0, 4d 109.9				
91	fstbk sdn 2d	2,864	3,322	40,086
92	sdn 4d	2,970	3,395	58,420
Granada—wb 109.9				
81	sdn 4d	3,222	4,118	163,071
82	sdn 2d	3,172	4,022	157,612
83	Ghia sdn 4d	3,276	4,548	35,730
84	Ghia sdn 2d	3,222	4,452	34,166
LTD II—wb 114.0, 4d 118.0				
25	S htp cpe	3,789	4,528	9,531
27	S sdn 4d	3,894	4,579	18,775

		Wght	Price	Prod
30	htp cpe	3,789	4,785	57,449
31	sdn 4d	3,904	4,870	56,704
32	Brougham htp cpe	3,898	5,121	20,979
33	Brougham sdn 4d	3,930	5,206	18,851
40	S wgn 5d, 2S	4,393	4,806	9,636
40	S wgn 5d, 3S	4,410	4,906	
42	wgn 5d, 2S	4,404	5,064	23,237
42	wgn 5d, 3S	4,421	5,164	
43	Squire wgn 5d, 3S	4,430	5,335	17,162
43	Squire wgn 5d, 3S	4,447	5,435	
LTD—wb 121.0				
52	Custom 500 sdn 2d	—	—	4,139
53	Custom 500 sdn 4d	—	—	5,582
62	LTD sdn 2d	4,190	5,128	73,637
63	LTD sdn 4d	4,240	5,152	160,255
64	LTD Landau sdn 4d	4,319	5,742	65,030
65	LTD Landau sdn 2d	4,270	5,717	44,396
72	Custom 500 Ranch Wagon 5d	—	—	1,406

		Wght	Price	Prod
74	LTD wgn 5d, 2S	4,635	5,415	90,711
74	LTD wgn 5d, 3S	4,679	5,541	
74	Country Squire wgn 5d, 2S	4,674	5,866	
74	Country Squire wgn 5d, 3S	4,718	5,992	
Mustang II—wb 96.2				
02	cpe 2d	2,688	3,702	67,783
03	htchbk cpe 3d	2,734	3,901	49,161
04	Ghia cpe 2d	2,728	4,119	29,510
05	Mach 1 htchbk cpe 3d, V-6	2,785	4,332	6,719
Thunderbird—wb 114.0				
87	htp cpe	3,907	5,063	318,140
87	Town Landau cpe	4,104	7,990	

*Incl. some units produced as 1978 models but sold as 1977 models.

249

1978

Ford Motor Company celebrates 75th Anniversary

Diamond Jubilee Thunderbird and Lincoln Mark V arrive; T-Bird output sets record

Corporate Average Fuel Economy (CAFE) standard takes effect at 18 mpg

Fairmont compact debuts; subcompact Fiesta arrives from Europe

Enlarged Bronco emerges; Ford holds lead in trucks

Ford car production rises, Chevrolet's falls, but Ford remains Number Two

First half of year yields record company profit

Henry Ford II fires president Lee Iacocca in June—Iacocca assumes helm at Chrysler in November

▲ Ford of Europe's minicar, the front-drive Fiesta, entered the U.S. market as an early 1978 model. Paving the way for the '80s Escort, the frugal subcompact hatchback was designed at Dearborn and built in Germany, engineered for easy maintenance. Ghia and Sport option groups were offered.

▲ Sole Fiesta engine was a transverse 98-cid four, developing 66 horsepower. MacPherson struts were installed up front, a rigid axle with coil springs at rear. Price tag: $3680.

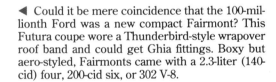

▲ First Ford to downsize was the Fairmont, built on a new "Fox" platform with 105.5-inch wheelbase. Fairmont compared to Audi and Volvo in size and design, weighing some 300 pounds less than the departed Maverick. A Futura coupe joined the initial four models at mid-year.

◄ Could it be mere coincidence that the 100-millionth Ford was a new compact Fairmont? This Futura coupe wore a Thunderbird-style wrapover roof band and could get Ghia fittings. Boxy but aero-styled, Fairmonts came with a 2.3-liter (140-cid) four, 200-cid six, or 302 V-8.

▲ Granadas earned a modest update in their fourth season, including single rectangular headlights. Base engine grew to a 250-cid six, and the 351 V-8 departed. Opera windows added a chrome rib, to become "Twindows."

▲ Ford's stab at a "European Sports Sedan" was the Granada ESS, with heavy-duty suspension, sport mirrors, and blackout trim. Granada output dropped sharply, doubtless hurt by the Fairmont's debut.

▲ Some models, like the mid-size, rather costly LTD II, never quite caught on. Fewer model and engine choices were offered, and the wagon was dropped.

▲ Obviously Mustang-based, this IMSA Cobra took full advantage of the 2+2's smooth lines. Never raced, it tempted auto show crowds.

▲ Couldn't get much wilder than a King Cobra, loaded with stripes, spoilers, black accents, and 302 V-8, for an added $1253 (T-top extra).

▲ Restrained Mustang fans might order a tasteful Ghia, with half-vinyl roof—and perhaps "Wilshire" seating and a willing V-8.

▲ A $207 Fashion Accessory Package for notchback Mustangs targeted women, reminiscent of similarly chauvinistic appeals in the 1950s.

▲ Revised during 1977, the Cobra II option continued into 1978 as a tamer, lower-cost alternative to the no-holds-barred King Cobra.

▲ Both base and Ghia Mustangs sold well, and total output stayed strong. Still, Mustang II never hooked enthusiasts like the original.

▼ Options like a T-roof or moonroof tempted plenty of T-Bird buyers. For those who really wanted to flaunt it, the truly opulent Diamond Jubilee Edition ran into five figures.

▲ Before long, rear-drive subcompacts would be old news. For now, Pinto showed little change beyond optional variable-ratio power steering.

▲ Small businesses could now order a small truck, in the form of a Pinto Panel Delivery. Most regular Pinto options were available.

▲ Based on the little Fiesta, the Ghia-styled Tuareg off-road concept vehicle appeared at the Geneva Salon. Replicas were sold in Europe.

▲ Like Chevrolet's Blazer, Bronco grew to pickup size, on an F-150 chassis. That added a foot to wheelbase. A 351-cid V-8 was standard.

▲ New colors and options helped keep the Ranchero GT, 500, and Squire alive. A few Shelby GTs were created, all in black.

▲ Compact pickups were catching on strong, and the Japanese-built Courier sold 70,546 copies despite minimal change. This one has XLT trim.

▲ F-Series pickups wore a brawny new face that echoed the big Louisville Line. This F-100 Styleside has the "B" Free Wheeling package.

▲ Conventional rigs like this one still had their fans, but Ford introduced a new CL-9000 cabover replacement for the W-Series.

▲ SuperCab Styleside pickups could be obtained with a seemingly endless array of add-ons. Twin exhaust stacks weren't a common sight.

Model Breakdown Chart

Pinto—wb 94.4, wgn 94.7*		Wght	Price	Prod
10	Pony sdn 2d	2,321	3,139	62,317
10	sdn 2d	2,400	3,629	
11	Runabout htchbk sdn 3d	2,444	3,744	74,313
12	wgn 3d	2,579	4,028	52,269
12	Squire wgn 3d	2,614	4,343	

Fairmont—wb 105.5				
91	sdn 2d	2,590	3,624	78,776
92	sdn 4d	2,632	3,710	136,849
93	Futura cpe	2,626	4,103	116,966
94	wgn 5d	2,740	4,063	128,390
94	Squire wgn 5d	2,748	4,428	

Granada—wb 109.9				
81	sdn 2d	3,132	4,300	110,481
81	Ghia sdn 2d	3,192	4,685	
81	ESS sdn 2d	3,190	4,872	
82	sdn 4d	3,167	4,390	139,305
82	Ghia sdn 4d	3,275	4,776	
82	ESS sdn 4d	3,225	4,962	

LTD II—wb 114.0, 4d 118.0				
25	S htp cpe	3,746	4,850	9,004
27	S sdn 4d	3,836	4,935	21,122
30	htp cpe	3,773	5,112	76,285
30	Brougham htp cpe	3,791	5,448	

		Wght	Price	Prod
31	sdn 4d	3,872	5,222	64,133
31	Brougham sdn 4d	3,901	5,558	

LTD—wb 121.0				
62	LTD htp cpe	3,972	5,398	57,466
63	LTD sdn 4d	4,032	5,483	112,392
64	LTD Landau htp cpe	4,029	5,970	27,305
65	LTD Landau sdn 4d	4,081	6,055	39,836
74	LTD wgn 5d, 2S	4,532	5,885	71,285
74	LTD wgn 5d, 3S	4,567	6,028	
74	Country Squire wgn 5d, 2S	4,576	6,304	
74	Country Squire wgn 5d, 3S	4,601	6,447	

Mustang II—wb 96.2				
02	cpe 2d	2,656	3,555	81,304
03	htchbk cpe 3d	2,702	3,798	68,408
04	Ghia cpe 2d	2,694	3,972	34,730
05	Mach 1 htchbk cpe 3d, V-6	2,733	4,253	7,968

Thunderbird—wb 114.0				
87	htp cpe	3,907	5,411	333,757
87	Town Landau cpe	4,104	8,420	
87	Diamond Jubilee cpe	4,200	10,106	18,994

Note: Fiesta not included (import).

1978 Engine Availability

Engines	bore × stroke	bhp	availability
I-4, 140.0	3.78 × 3.13	88	S-Pinto, Fairmont
V-6, 170.8	3.66 × 2.70	90	O-Pinto, exc Pony
I-6, 200.0	3.68 × 3.13	85	O-Fairmont
I-6, 250.0	3.68 × 3.91	97	S-Granada
V-8, 302.0	4.00 × 3.00	134	S-LTD II, LTD exc wgns
V-8, 302.0	4.00 × 3.00	139	S-Granada; O-Fairmont
V-8, 351.0	4.00 × 3.50	144/145	S-LTD wgns; O-LTD II, LTD
V-8, 351.0	4.00 × 3.50	152	O-LTD II
V-8, 400.0	4.00 × 4.00	166	O-LTD II, LTD
V-8, 460.0	4.36 × 3.85	202	O-LTD

Mustang			
I-4, 140.0	3.78 × 3.13	88	S-all exc Mach 1
V-6, 170.0	3.66 × 2.70	90	S-Mach 1; O-others
V-8, 302.0	4.00 × 3.00	139	O-all

Thunderbird			
V-8, 302.0	4.00 × 3.00	134	S-all
V-8, 351.0	4.00 × 3.50	152	O-all
V-8, 400.0	4.00 × 4.00	166	O-all

1979

Energy crisis II triggers worst recession since the '30s

Inflation sends gasoline prices soaring

Automobiles unaffected at first, as industry racks up near-record volume

Ford launches fifth-generation Mustang and downsized LTD

Ford's market share skids to record postwar low

Philip Caldwell serves as Ford president

Second-generation Capri debuts, akin to Mustang

Imports capture 22.7 percent market share

▲ Clean, crisp Mustang lines blended the best of European and U.S. themes. Though clearly sporty, its minimally adorned demeanor bespoke restrained elegance. Bigger inside and out, the next Mustang's 100.4-inch wheelbase was 4.2 inches longer than Mustang II, yet the car weighed a couple of hundred pounds less. A simple nose sweeping down from a taller cowl accentuated the racy profile.

▲ Both the hatchback Mustang (shown here) and the notchback coupe, which was designed first, were offered in upscale Ghia trim. Vertical slats behind quarter windows reminded observers of the Mercedes-Benz 450SLC. Engines were borrowed from the Mustang II. Extensive use of lightweight materials kept weight down. Interiors contained full instruments and twin steering-column stalks.

▲ Not long after the Mustang II's debut, styling of its successor was underway. This early wood mock-up borrowed overall shape from the II fastback. Basics were settled in 1976.

▲ Mustang for the '80s developed from a diverse series of sketches, clay models, and fiberglass mock-ups. Formal details and B-posts of 1975 proposal suggest the '80 Thunderbird.

▲ Various formal themes for the Mustang were proposed in 1975, focusing on Ford's evolving "Fox" platform. Nose appearance looks close to final form, despite screened headlights.

▲ Curves in this late-1975 mock-up would give way to a straight-edged look. Making the right styling choice was vital, as this design was destined to last more than a decade.

▲ The squared-off stance that marked the real-world Mustang was evident in this 1975 mock-up. Clay models were wind tunnel-tested, creating the most slippery shape ever done by Ford.

▲ This deeply wrapped-around backlight never made it to Mustang production. Even the Mustang symbol would be changed for '79, galloping again after slowing down on the Mustang II.

▲ A turbocharged version of the 2.3-liter four-cylinder engine, rated as high as 140 bhp, went into the Mustang Turbo. Cobra trim cost an extra $1173, including special suspension and TRX tires; snake was optional.

▲ A Mustang driven by Jackie Stewart paced the 63rd Indianapolis 500 Race. Ford issued about 11,000 replicas, which would inspire the next year's Cobra. Mustang ranked seventh in 1979 popularity, with 369,936 built.

▶ The "5.0" badge on this Mustang Ghia's front fender reveals the 302-cid, 140-bhp V-8 inside. Other choices: a 2.3-liter four, Turbo four, 170.8-cid V-6, and, later, a 200-cid inline six.

▲ This early 1976 Mustang mock-up displayed a close resemblance to the forthcoming Fairmont, which evolved from the same platform. The nose would change to an angled style, but midsection shape is comparable to the production design.

▶ Ford's design director Jack Telnack, a force behind the tiny Fiesta, stands beside a Mustang Cobra. Proposals came from three teams: corporate studios, Ghia, and Advanced Design. Telnack's team, including Fritz Mayhew, David Rees, and Gary Haas, submitted the "winning" model. Their goal: a more aerodynamic ponycar, on a shortened version of the "Fox" platform.

▲ Kinship to the Fairmont Futura coupe's stylish quarter-window treatment was evident in this 1976 Mustang proposal. When stylists were finished, the Fairmont tie wasn't easy to spot.

255

▲ Two years after GM downsized its full-size cars, Ford followed suit with the LTDs. Wheelbases shrunk by seven inches, yet big Fords gained space inside. Underneath was a new all-coil suspension. Customers evidently liked the boxy-but-clean bodies. Despite price hikes, production rose sharply.

▲ Landaus weren't as popular as base LTDs, but helped Ford amass 356,535 full-size models. Regular sedans replaced the "pillared hardtops."

▲ Standard LTDs had single headlamps, Landaus quads. Plain and Country Squire wagons rounded out the line, which retained separate frames.

1979 Selected Colors

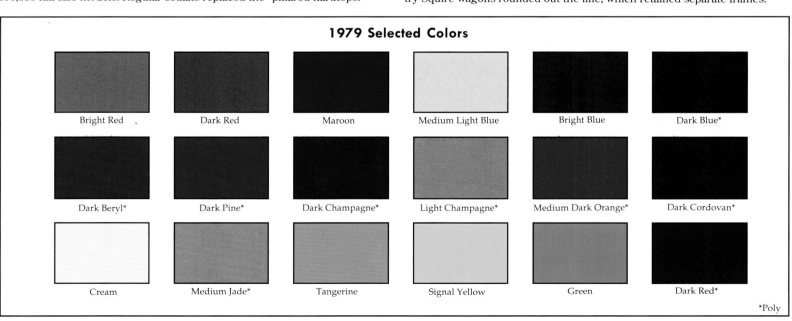

Bright Red	Dark Red	Maroon	Medium Light Blue	Bright Blue	Dark Blue*
Dark Beryl*	Dark Pine*	Dark Champagne*	Light Champagne*	Medium Dark Orange*	Dark Cordovan*
Cream	Medium Jade*	Tangerine	Signal Yellow	Green	Dark Red*

*Poly

◀ Fairmont sales fell as the nation's economy sagged, but the compact remained popular. Two-door sedans, as shown here, found the fewest customers—well behind the twin station wagons. Changes were few, apart from several new options. A four-speed gearbox was available with any engine, including the 302-cid V-8. An extra $329 bought the sporty ES package, with black-out trim and handling suspension.

▼ Judicious selections from the ample options list could turn an ordinary Fairmont four-door sedan into a handsome people-carrier. Choices included tilt steering and cruise control, as well as "performance" instruments. Whether stripped down or optioned-out, close to one-third of Fairmont sales were four-doors.

▲ Ford immodestly named its Granada "An American Classic," but output dropped considerably. Lack of interest deleted the all-disc brake option.

▲ A Ghia Luxury Group for the uniquely styled Futura coupe, with its wide tapered B-pillars, was announced at mid-year as "top-of-the-line" Fairmont.

1979 Engine Availability

Engines	bore × stroke	bhp	availability
I-4, 140.0	3.78 × 3.13	88	S-Pinto, Fairmont
V-6, 170.8	3.66 × 2.70	102	O-Pinto exc Pony
I-6, 200.0	3.68 × 3.13	85	S-Fairmont
I-6, 250.0	3.68 × 3.91	97	S-Granada
V-8, 302.0	4.00 × 3.00	129	S-LTD
V-8, 302.0	4.00 × 3.00	133	S-LTD II
V-8, 302.0	4.00 × 3.00	137	O-Granada
V-8, 302.0	4.00 × 3.00	140	O-Fairmont
V-8, 351.0	4.00 × 3.50	142	O-LTD
V-8, 351.0	4.00 × 3.50	151	O-LTD II, LTD

Mustang	bore × stroke	bhp	availability
I-4, 140.0	3.78 × 3.13	88	S-all
I-4T, 140.0	3.78 × 3.13	140	O-all
V-6, 170.8	3.66 × 2.70	109	O-all
I-6, 200.0	3.68 × 3.13	91	O-all (late)
V-8, 302.0	4.00 × 3.00	140	O-all
Thunderbird			
V-8, 302.0	4.00 × 3.00	133	S-all
V-8, 351.0	4.00 × 3.50	135/151	O-all

257

▶ A touched-up, bolder grille was the major change in Thunderbirds, related to LTD II for the last time. Taillights were now split by a back-up light. More vital for go-power, the 400-cid V-8 was gone, leaving only the base 302 and optional 351. This T-top cost $747 extra. A pricey Heritage replaced the Diamond Jubilee Edition, with the same blanked rear quarters.

▲ German-built Fiestas showed little change except for taller front seatbacks, but their base price rose to $4198. Testers praised the mini hatchback's pep and fuel mileage.

▲ One last facelift gave this Pinto Runabout a neater grille and rectangular headlights. An ESS appearance option was offered this year, the Rallye package later, with small spoiler.

▲ A colorful Cruising Package, with porthole, added $566 to the Pinto wagon's price and could also be ordered on Runabouts. Power front disc brakes were standard, V-6 power optional.

▲ Pintos suffered painful publicity after earlier models were charged with having unsafe fuel fillers. This Squire wagon, like other facelifted Pintos, sold fairly well regardless.

▲ Econolines sported a cleaner front end with rectangular headlamps. The Cruising Van could have hinged doors instead of a single sliding door. Portholes were available on Chateaus.

▲ A "Quad Captain's Chair Package" for Club Wagons, including this Chateau, contained four swiveling seats. Long-wheelbase versions with that option included a fold-up snack table.

▲ Econoline Super Wagons rode the same 138-inch wheelbase as a Club Wagon, but with a 20-inch extension tacked onto the rear. A 302 V-8 was now optional on all three Econoline series.

▲ This LTD II wears a Sports Touring Package, which included two-tone paint in an unusual pattern plus white-letter tires on Magnum 500 wheels. A half-vinyl roof cost $116 extra.

▲ Never a hot item, the mid-size LTD II skidded badly in sales in its final season. Only 18,300 hardtop coupes were built, including this Brougham. The 400 V-8 was gone.

▲ A minor mainstay since the late 1950s, the Ranchero ended its tenure with volume rising to 25,010. This GT cost $6289. Truck buyers were turning to sport-utilities and fancy pickups.

▲ F-Series pickups got rectangular headlamps. This F-100 Custom short-box Flareside with 300-cid six cost $5085. Striking stripes and black bumpers came with the Free Wheeling option.

▲ SuperCab pickups with passenger space behind the front seat came in F-100, F-150, F-250, and F-350 guise. A 4×4 edition was added to the F-350 line, with regular or SuperCab.

▲ Bright vinyl-insert moldings identified the Ranger XLT version of this Styleside F-Series pickup. Trucks could be fitted fancy or plain, with individual extras or option packages.

Model Breakdown Chart

Pinto—wb 94.4, wgn 94.7		Wght	Price	Prod
10	Pony fstbk sdn 2d	2,329	3,434	75,789
10	fstbk sdn 2d	2,396	3,939	
11	Runabout htchbk sdn 3d	2,442	4,055	69,383
12	Pony wgn 3d	NA	3,899	53,846
12	wgn 3d	2,571	4,338	
12	Squire wgn 3d	2,607	4,654	
Fairmont—wb 105.5				
91	sdn 2d	2,524	4,102	54,798
92	sdn 4d	2,578	4,220	133,813
93	Futura cpe	2,580	4,463	106,065
94	wgn 5d	2,708	4,497	100,691
94	Squire wgn 5d	NA	4,856	
Granada—wb 109.9				
81	sdn 2d	3,088	4,678	76,850
81	Ghia sdn 2d	3,124	5,051	
81	ESS sdn 2d	3,140	5,211	
82	sdn 4d	3,134	4,782	105,526
82	Ghia sdn 4d	3,168	5,157	
82	ESS sdn 4d	3,210	5,317	
LTD II—wb 114.0, 4d 118.0				
25	S htp cpe	3,781	5,561	834
27	S sdn 4d	3,844	5,661	9,649
30	htp cpe	3,797	5,799	18,300
30	Brougham htp cpe	3,815	6,135	
31	sdn 4d	3,860	5,924	19,781
31	Brougham sdn 4d	3,889	6,259	
LTD—wb 114.3				
62	LTD sdn 2d	3,421	6,184	54,005
63	LTD sdn 4d	3,463	6,284	117,730
64	LTD Landau sdn 2d	3,472	6,686	42,314
65	LTD Landau sdn 4d	3,527	6,811	74,599
74	LTD wgn 5d, 2S	3,678	6,550	37,955
74	LTD wgn 5d, 3S	—	6,699	
76	Country Squire wgn 5d, 2S	3,719	7,006	29,932
76	Country Squire wgn 5d, 3S	—	7,155	
Mustang—wb 100.4				
02	cpe 2d	2,471	4,071	156,666
03	htchbk cpe 3d	2,491	4,436	120,535
04	Ghia cpe 2d	2,579	4,642	56,351
05	Ghia htchbk cpe 3d	2,588	4,824	36,384
Thunderbird—wb 114.0				
87	cpe	3,893	5,877	284,141
87/607	Town Landau cpe	4,284	8,866	
87/603	Heritage cpe	4,178	10,687	

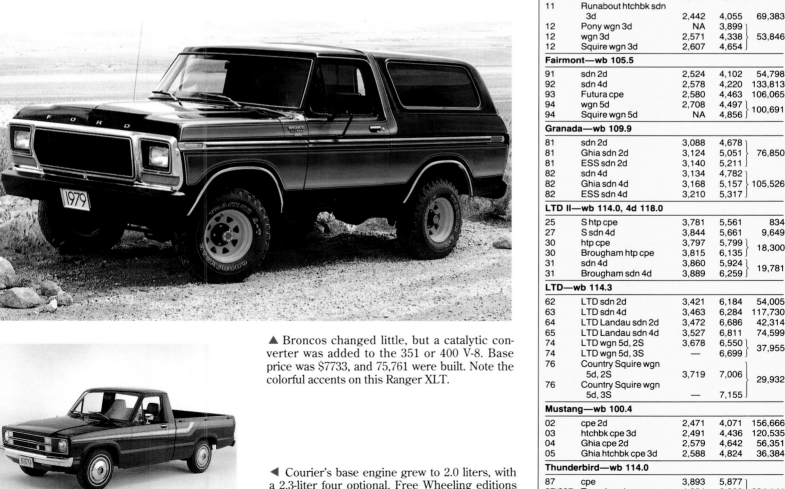

▲ Broncos changed little, but a catalytic converter was added to the 351 or 400 V-8. Base price was $7733, and 75,761 were built. Note the colorful accents on this Ranger XLT.

◄ Courier's base engine grew to 2.0 liters, with a 2.3-liter four optional. Free Wheeling editions showed new tri-tone striping. A total of 76,883 were sold, starting at $4861.

1980

"Stagflation" is latest catchword—mix of stagnant economy and inflation

Chevrolet builds nearly twice as many cars as Ford

All-new, Fairmont-based Thunderbird bows

Ford suffers financial crisis—$1.54 billion loss

Henry Ford II resigns as chairman, replaced by Philip Caldwell; Donald E. Petersen named president

For first time in the company's history no Ford has charge

Jack Telnack and Don Kopka take helm of Ford styling

Special Vehicle Operations (SVO) department formed

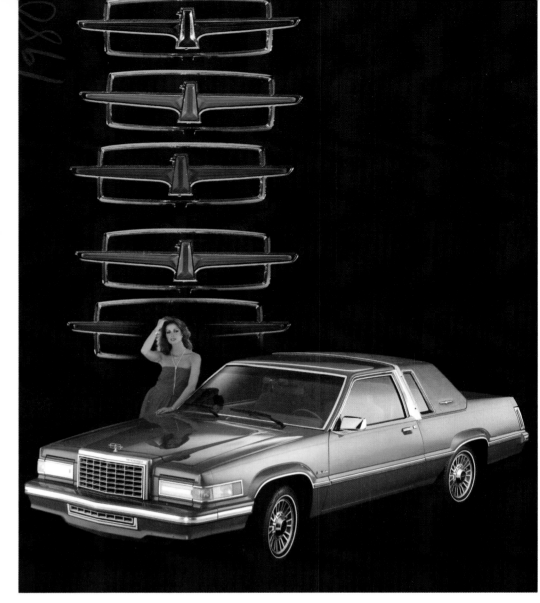

▲ Though 16 inches shorter than its predecessor, the ninth-generation Thunderbird kept many styling cues, including wrapped parking lights and prominent B-pillars. Engines shrank to 255- and 302-cid size.

▲ Designers Dennis Jameyfield and Kyu Kim discuss the final sketch of the new T-Bird, unibodied for the first time since 1966. Aerodynamics were a prime factor, though styling seemed blocky and ornate.

▲ Not everyone fell for the new T-Bird, as output dipped 45 percent. A Silver Anniversary edition joined the two basic models later.

▲ A squarish, formal stance marked the downsized T-Bird, which dropped to 19th in sales. Weight of the base model fell by 775 pounds, boosting mileage.

▶ This posh Town Landau coupe listed for $3604 more than a base Thunderbird and included a four-speed overdrive automatic transmission, among many other attractions.

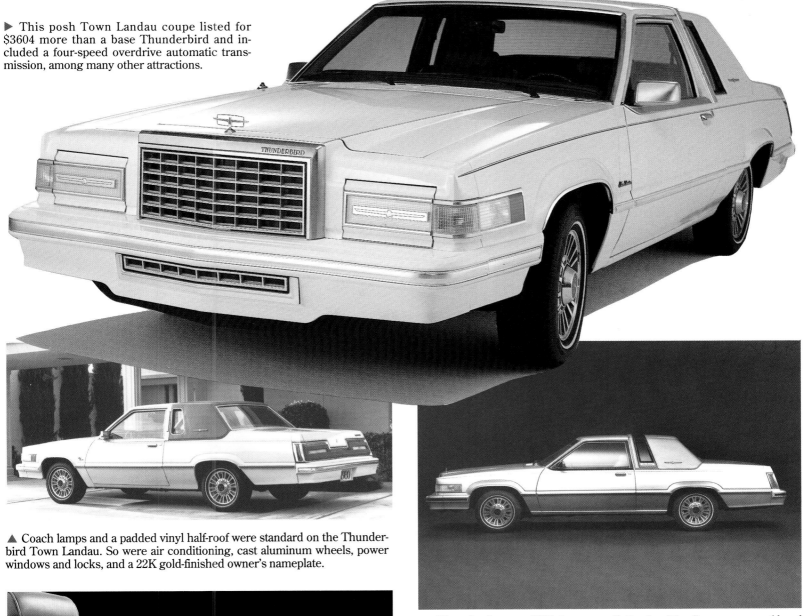

▲ Coach lamps and a padded vinyl half-roof were standard on the Thunderbird Town Landau. So were air conditioning, cast aluminum wheels, power windows and locks, and a 22K gold-finished owner's nameplate.

▲ Silver Anniversary T-Birds wore a distinctive "tiara" wrapover roof band with specially shaped quarter windows and nameplate, and carried a 131-bhp, 302 V-8. Six color combinations were used, all with Dove Gray interiors. Price of this special model was $11,679, nearly double that of the base coupe.

◀ A Town Landau's leather-lined interior was just one of the Thunderbird's available plush comforts. Base coupes came with a cloth/vinyl bench seat.

▲ Mustang Cobras changed more than ordinary models, earning a mild facelift inspired by the '79 Indy Pace Car. Front/rear spoilers were more prominent, the three-slat grille was modified, low fog lamps installed, and the hood wore a broad new scoop. Offered only on hatchbacks, the Cobra package went for $1482 including Turbo four, plus $88 for a hood decal.

► Convertibles still weren't part of the Mustang picture, but $644 bought a diamond-grain vinyl carriage roof. Under the hood, a 255-cid V-8 replaced the 302 as top engine, yielding 118 horsepower. Halogen headlamps and P-metric radials were new. Output fell by close to 100,000, yet Mustang wound up seventh in sales. Options were more numerous than ever.

▲ Only about one in 25 Mustangs had a 140-bhp Turbo four under its hood. Base engine was the 88-bhp four, with inline six or V-8 optional.

▲ Hatchbacks included Sport fittings at no extra cost, yet sold fewer copies than notchback Mustangs. Both bodies could be ordered in Ghia trim.

1980 Engine Availability

Engines	bore × stroke	bhp	availability
I-4, 140.0	3.78 × 3.13	88	S-Pinto, Fairmont
I-4, 140.0	3.78 × 3.13	140	O-Fairmont
I-6, 200.0	3.68 × 3.13	91	O-Fairmont
I-6, 250.0	3.68 × 3.91	90	S-Granada
V-8, 255.0	3.68 × 3.00	119	O-Fairmont, Granada
V-8, 302.0	4.00 × 3.00	130	S-LTD
V-8, 302.0	4.00 × 3.00	134	O-Granada
V-8, 351.0	4.00 × 3.50	140	O-LTD

Mustang	bore × stroke	bhp	availability
I-4, 140.0	3.78 × 3.13	88	S-all
I-4T, 140.0	3.78 × 3.13	140	O-all
I-6, 200.0	3.68 × 3.13	91	O-all
V-8, 255.0	2.68 × 3.00	118	O-all
Thunderbird			
V-8, 255.0	3.68 × 3.00	115	S-all
V-8, 302.0	4.00 × 3.00	131	S-Sil. Ann.; O-others

▲ One of the rarest Fairmonts has to be a Futura coupe with a Turbo four, listed at $481. Otherwise, a 255-cid V-8 was top choice, replacing the 302. Fairmont's economy attracted quite a few buyers.

▲ Even the little Fiesta had a Sport Option, including black window surrounds and taping, rear stabilizer, and tachometer. A flip-up sunroof and tinted glass could be added. Base price was $4493, with 68,595 sold.

▲ Fords continued their popularity among police fleets. This full-size LTD passed official tests for maneuverability and performance. With the new high-output 5.8-liter V-8 on tap, it was certified for high-speed pursuit.

▶ Top-selling big Ford (by far) was this LTD four-door sedan, available with a 302- or 351-cid V-8 and new four-speed automatic. Posh Crown Victorias wore wrap-over roof trim.

▼ With the demise of the LTD II, Granada hung on as Ford's sole mid-size, but production sank by more than half. Part of the loss could be attributed to the still-suffering U.S. economy. Standard engine was the 90-bhp, 250-cid six.

▲ Granada Ghias, like this four-door, wore accent striping and wide bodyside moldings. Sporty ESS Granadas had black trim outside, bucket seats inside. Two-tone paint cost $180. Both 255- and 302-cid V-8s were offered.

▲ Wildest Pinto of the lot, one more time, was the wagon's Cruising Package, which added $606 to the base price. Colorful striping and such doodads as portholes didn't help Pinto last any longer. Neither did ESS trim and Rallye Packs on other bodies. Still, the subcompact had enjoyed a long life, albeit one fraught with controversy after a series of horrid fires in early models. Now, Ford was readying its Escort "world car."

▲ A Squire station wagon was the top-dollar choice in Pinto's final season. Total volume dipped to 185,054, but more than 3.1 million Pintos had been built over its decade of life. No V-6 Pintos appeared this year.

▲ Billed as the "first new truck of the '80s," the restyled F-Series could have a bewildering variety of options, enhancing both its practicality and its beauty. Choices included extra- and super-duty cooling systems.

▲ Triple-striped Cruising Vans, complete with portholes, continued to lure youthful buyers. Econoline V-8 engine choices reached as high as 400 and 460 cid, depending on the model.

▲ Ford promoted the "I-want-to-work" look of medium-duty trucks, like this tractor/trailer. F-600/700/800 models wore a new fiberglass front end with swept-back fenders.

▲ New square headlamps flanked a Louisville-style eggcrate grille, of ABS plastic, in mid-range trucks. Ford's truck share came to 31.7 percent, but light-duty models fared better.

▲ Some things rarely change, including the F-Series pickup's ranking as top-selling vehicle in America. Ranger Stylesides could have 4WD, with first-ever independent front suspension.

▲ Fiberglass rear fenders on Flareside pickups achieved a muscular look, augmented by Free Wheeling packages. Ford touted the truck's "wind tunnel tested aerodynamic styling."

▲ Even the most utilitarian medium-duty cargo haulers displayed a handsome face, now made of fiberglass and ABS. Ford expressed pride in its trucks' ability to wear a variety of bodies.

1980 Selected Colors

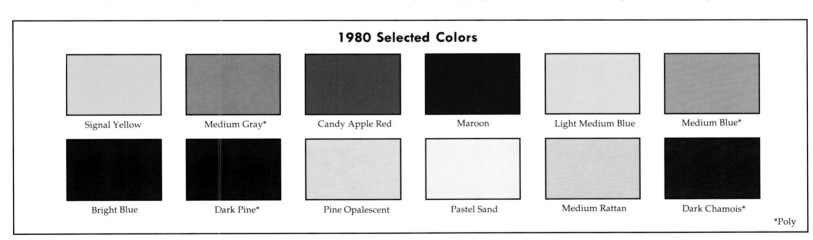

Signal Yellow | Medium Gray* | Candy Apple Red | Maroon | Light Medium Blue | Medium Blue*

Bright Blue | Dark Pine* | Pine Opalescent | Pastel Sand | Medium Rattan | Dark Chamois*

*Poly

Model Breakdown Chart

Pinto—wb 94.4, wgn 94.7		Wght	Price	Prod
10	Pony fstbk sdn 2d	2,377	4,117	84,053
10	fstbk sdn 2d	2,385	4,605	
11	Runabout htchbk sdn 3d	2,426	4,717	61,842
12	Pony wgn 2d	2,545	4,627	
12	wgn 3d	2,553	5,004	39,159
12/604	Squire wgn 3d	2,590	5,320	

Fairmont—wb 105.5		Wght	Price	Prod
91	sdn 2d	2,576	4,894	45,074
92	sdn 4d	2,610	5,011	137,812
92	Futura sdn 4d	—	5,390	5,306
93	Futura cpe	2,623	5,325	51,878
94	wgn 5d	2,735	5,215	77,035

Granada—wb 109.9		Wght	Price	Prod
81	sdn 2d	3,135	5,541	60,872
81/602	Ghia sdn 2d	3,168	5,942	
81/933	ESS sdn 2d	3,199	6,031	
82	sdn 4d	3,168	5,664	29,557
82/602	Ghia sdn 4d	3,209	6,065	
82/933	ESS sdn 4d	3,240	6,154	

LTD—wb 114.3		Wght	Price	Prod
	S sdn 2d	—	—	553
61	S sdn 4d	3,464	6,875	19,283
62	sdn 2d	3,447	7,003	15,333
63	sdn 4d	3,475	7,117	51,630
64	Crown Victoria sdn 2d	3,482	7,628	7,725
65	Crown Victoria sdn 4d	3,524	7,763	21,962
72	S wgn 5d, 2S	3,707	7,198	3,490
72	S wgn 5d, 3S	3,748	7,344	

		Wght	Price	Prod
74	wgn 5d, 2S	3,717	7,463	11,718
74	wgn 5d, 3S	3,758	7,609	
76	Crown Victoria wgn 5d, 2S	3,743	7,891	9,868
76	Crown Victoria wgn 5d, 3S	3,784	8,042	

Mustang—wb 100.4		Wght	Price	Prod
02	cpe 2d	2,514	4,884	128,893
03	htchbk cpe 3d	2,548	5,194	98,497
04	Ghia cpe 2d	2,582	5,369	23,647
05	Ghia htchbk cpe 3d	2,606	5,512	20,285

Thunderbird—wb 108.4		Wght	Price	Prod
87	cpe	3,118	6,432	156,803
87/607	Town Landau cpe	3,357	10,036	
87/603	Silver Anniversary cpe	3,225	11,679	

1981

Subcompact front-drive Escort "world car" debuts

Granada moves onto Fairmont-based chassis

Car production dips below a million—lowest since 1958

Output skids on all models except Escort and Granada

Oldsmobile nearly sends Ford into third in sales

Ford suffers another huge loss: $1.06 billion

Slogan asks: "Have you driven a Ford, lately?"

Pinto exonerated in court; controversy continues

Japanese agree to limit car exports to U.S.

▲ Developed at a cost of $3 billion, the Escort was built in five countries. This four-door GL liftgate (wagon) sold for $6178.

▲ Five Escort trim levels were offered, up to this luxury GLX and a sporty SS (later renamed GT). The tiny "bustle" deck cut drag and lift.

▲ Unlike Pintos, "international size" Escorts were front-drive. The 94.2-inch wheelbase was close to Pinto's, but hatchbacks were seven inches shorter overall (wagons 15 inches) and three inches narrower, yet roomier.

◄ Not all Escorts were plain. This GLX wagon wears $243 Squire trim. Ford's "Erika" small-car project began in 1972. Escort soon became second-best U.S. seller, with 128,173 liftbacks and 192,554 hatchbacks built.

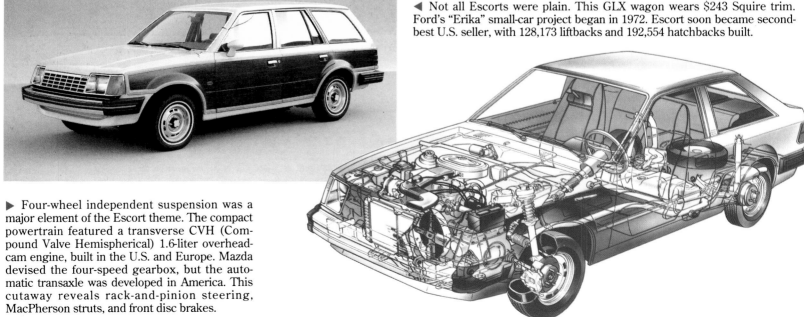

▶ Four-wheel independent suspension was a major element of the Escort theme. The compact powertrain featured a transverse CVH (Compound Valve Hemispherical) 1.6-liter overhead-cam engine, built in the U.S. and Europe. Mazda devised the four-speed gearbox, but the automatic transaxle was developed in America. This cutaway reveals rack-and-pinion steering, MacPherson struts, and front disc brakes.

▲ A 4.2-liter replaced the 5.0 as top Fairmont V-8, and a diagnostic display became optional. Four-doors like this $6361 Futura sold best.

▲ A Futura wagon joined the Fairmont coupe and sedan in mid-1980. This one shows the Squire option. Output slid 33 percent this year.

▲ Mustangers could order an $874 T-top and power windows. Only 5327 had the 255-cid V-8, rated 115 bhp, as volume skidded by one-third.

▲ Two-door Crown Victorias—poshest members of the LTD line—never sold nearly as well as four-doors. Note the wrap-over roof band.

▲ Only 9443 LTD Country Squires were built for 1981, priced at $8640, out of 22,462 full-size wagons in all. Big Fords in general were not selling well, and selection dropped to eight models. A 4.2-liter (255-cid) V-8 was now standard in LTDs; 302 and 351 V-8s optional.

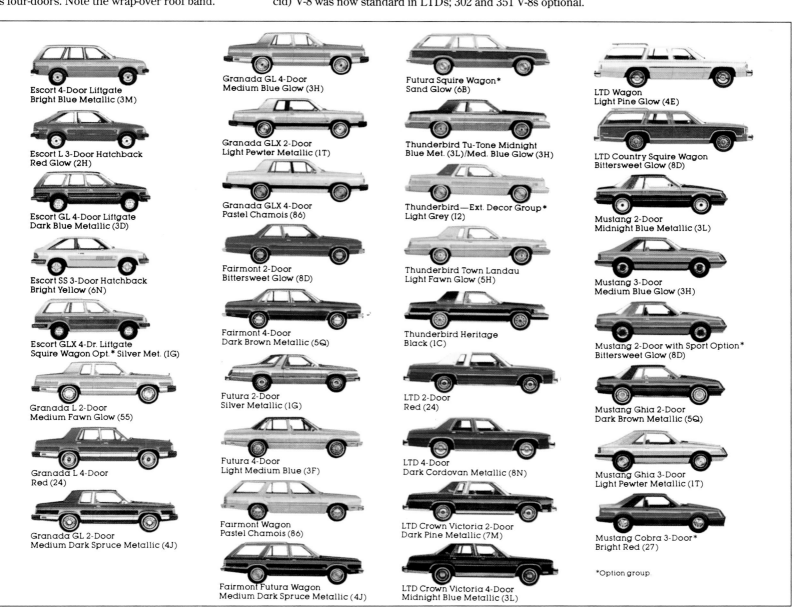

Escort 4-Door Liftgate
Bright Blue Metallic (3M)

Escort L 3-Door Hatchback
Red Glow (2H)

Escort GL 4-Door Liftgate
Dark Blue Metallic (3D)

Escort SS 3-Door Hatchback
Bright Yellow (6N)

Escort GLX 4-Dr. Liftgate
Squire Wagon Opt.* Silver Met. (1G)

Granada L 2-Door
Medium Fawn Glow (55)

Granada L 4-Door
Red (24)

Granada GL 2-Door
Medium Dark Spruce Metallic (4J)

Granada GL 4-Door
Medium Blue Glow (3H)

Granada GLX 2-Door
Light Pewter Metallic (1T)

Granada GLX 4-Door
Pastel Chamois (86)

Fairmont 2-Door
Bittersweet Glow (8D)

Fairmont 4-Door
Dark Brown Metallic (5Q)

Futura 2-Door
Silver Metallic (1G)

Futura 4-Door
Light Medium Blue (3F)

Fairmont Wagon
Pastel Chamois (86)

Fairmont Futura Wagon
Medium Dark Spruce Metallic (4J)

Futura Squire Wagon*
Sand Glow (6B)

Thunderbird Tu-Tone Midnight
Blue Met. (3L)/Med. Blue Glow (3H)

Thunderbird—Ext. Decor Group*
Light Grey (I2)

Thunderbird Town Landau
Light Fawn Glow (5H)

Thunderbird Heritage
Black (1C)

LTD 2-Door
Red (24)

LTD 4-Door
Dark Cordovan Metallic (8N)

LTD Crown Victoria 2-Door
Dark Pine Metallic (7M)

LTD Crown Victoria 4-Door
Midnight Blue Metallic (3L)

LTD Wagon
Light Pine Glow (4E)

LTD Country Squire Wagon
Bittersweet Glow (8D)

Mustang 2-Door
Midnight Blue Metallic (3L)

Mustang 3-Door
Medium Blue Glow (3H)

Mustang 2-Door with Sport Option*
Bittersweet Glow (8D)

Mustang Ghia 2-Door
Dark Brown Metallic (5Q)

Mustang Ghia 3-Door
Light Pewter Metallic (1T)

Mustang Cobra 3-Door*
Bright Red (27)

*Option group

267

▲ This year's Granada was actually a restyled Fairmont, adopting the compact's 105.5-inch wheelbase. A bit longer and heavier than Fairmont, it displayed more formal styling and a plusher interior. Chassis settings were softened for a cushy ride, but downsizing improved maneuverability.

▲ Shrinking of Granada's dimensions brought a notable surge in sales, as production rose by some 30,000 units. The aero restyle was claimed to deliver a 21-percent boost in gas mileage, yet add space inside. Three trim levels were sold, with four- and six-cylinder engines or a 4.2-liter V-8.

▲ Flareside pickups continued to attract fans. A basic F-100 half-tonner cost $6026; the heavier-duty F-150 started at $6300. A Ranger XLT package included contrasting-color "FORD" letters on the tailgate, among other extras. White-letter tires added to a Flareside's eye-appeal. For economy, a 255-cid (4.2-liter) V-8 was newly optional for F-100 models. Four-speed automatic was available on 4×2 F-100/150/250 trucks with a 302 V-8.

◄ Ford flaunted its $9085 Bronco as the only full-size 4×4 with independent front suspension. Optional automatic locking hubs promised that the driver wouldn't have to endure "muddy, frozen, or wet feet." Two Snow Plow Preparation Packages were available (as on F-Series trucks). Halogen headlamps and P-metric radial tires were standard; power windows and door locks optional. A total of 37,396 were built, three-fourths with V-8 power.

1981 Engine Availability

Engines	bore × stroke	bhp	availability
I-4, 97.6	3.15 × 3.13	65	S-Escort
I-4, 140.0	3.78 × 3.13	88	S-Fairmont, Granada
I-6, 200.0	3.68 × 3.13	88	O-Fairmont, Granada
V-8, 255.0	3.68 × 3.00	115/120	S-LTD; O-Fmont, Gran
V-8, 302.0	4.00 × 3.00	130	O-LTD
V-8, 351.0	4.00 × 3.50	145	O-LTD
Mustang			
I-4, 140.0	3.78 × 3.13	88	S-all
I-4T, 140.0	3.78 × 3.13	140	O-all
I-6, 200.0	3.68 × 3.13	88/94	O-all
V-8, 255.0	3.68 × 3.00	115	O-all
Thunderbird			
I-6, 200.0	3.68 × 3.13	88	S-all exc Heritage
V-8, 255.0	3.68 × 3.00	115	S-Heritage; O-others
V-8, 302.0	4.00 × 3.00	130	O-all

▲ Sales vice president Philip Benton (right) waves as he stands alongside the 250,000th Escort to roll off the line at Wayne, Michigan, on May 13, 1981. From Day One, Escort sold better than its Pinto predecessor.

▲ With this Omaha Standard stake platform or any other body, Ford's F-800 was one tough and versatile truck. Ford took 42.7 percent of truck production, versus Chevy's 34.5 percent.

▲ Topping the Club Wagon line was this King of Clubs option for the E-150, with swivel/recline captain's chairs up front and a host of luxury options including tinted rear "Privacy Glass."

▲ Mazda-built Courier compact pickups continued with little change. Note attractive turbine-style wheel covers. Trucks now had to meet an 18-mpg CAFE standard (4×4s, 15.5).

▲ Base Thunderbird price rose by $1119, but that wasn't so shocking in 1981. Stepping up from the basic, this Town Landau included a wrap-over band ahead of its vinyl rear roof.

▲ Thunderbird production dropped by half this year, even though all models got Exterior Luxury Group trim. A 3.3-liter six was now standard, with 4.2- or 5.0-liter V-8 optional.

▲ Replacing the 1980 Silver Anniversary model as top T-Bird was this $11,355 Heritage, with a standard 4.2-liter V-8. This roof also was used on Town Landaus, with small coach windows.

Model Breakdown Chart

Escort—wb 94.2		Wght	Price	Prod
05	htchbk sdn 3d	1,962	5,158	
05/60Q	L htchbk sdn 3d	1,964	5,494	
05/60Z	GL htchbk sdn 3d	1,987	5,838	192,554
05/602	GLX htchbk sdn 3d	2,029	6,476	
05/936	SS htchbk sdn 3d	2,004	6,139	
08	liftbk sdn 4d	2,074	5,731	
08/60Q	L liftbk sdn 4d	2,075	5,814	
08/60Z	GL liftbk sdn 4d	2,094	6,178	128,173
08/602	GLX liftbk sdn 4d	2,137	6,799	
08/936	SS liftbk sdn 4d	2,114	6,464	
Fairmont—wb 105.5				
20	S sdn 2d	NA	5,701	23,066
20	sdn 2d	2,590	6,032	
21	sdn 4d	2,640	6,151	104,883
21/605	Futura sdn 4d	2,674	6,361	
22	Futura cpe	2,645	6,347	24,197
23	wgn 5d	2,754	6,384	59,154
23/605	Futura wgn 5d	2,788	6,616	
Granada—wb 105.5				
26	L sdn 2d	2,752	6,474	
26/602	GL sdn 2d	2,773	6,875	35,057
26/933	GLX sdn 2d	2,777	6,988	
27	L sdn 4d	2,795	6,633	
27/602	GL sdn 4d	2,822	7,035	86,284
27/933	GLX sdn 4d	2,829	7,148	
LTD—wb 114.3				
31	S sdn 4d	3,490	7,527	17,490
32	sdn 2d	3,496	7,607	6,279
33	sdn 4d	3,538	7,718	35,932
34	Crown Victoria sdn 2d	3,496	8,251	11,061
35	Crown Victoria sdn 4d	3,538	8,384	39,139
37	S wgn 5d, 2S	3,717	7,942	2,465
38	wgn 5d, 2S	3,719	8,180	10,554
39	Country Squire wgn 5d, 2S	3,737	8,640	9,443
Mustang—wb 100.4				
10	cpe 2d	2,537	6,171	77,458
15	htchbk cpe 3d	2,557	6,408	77,399
12	Ghia cpe 2d	2,571	6,645	13,422
13	Ghia htchbk cpe 3d	2,606	6,729	14,273
Thunderbird—wb 108.4				
42	cpe	3,064	7,551	
42/60T	Town Landau cpe	3,127	8,689	86,693
42/607	Heritage cpe V-8	3,303	11,355	

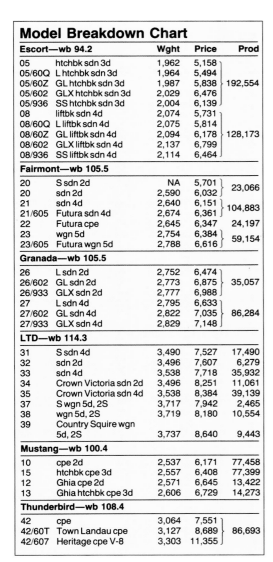

1982

Henry Ford II retires, but remains on Ford's board

Two-seat EXP coupe launched to lure young singles

302 V-8 returns to Mustang — but GM issues restyled Camaro and Firebird

3.8-liter V-6 debuts . . . propane engine announced

Recession finally bottoms: Industry suffers lowest sales in two decades

Escort shoots to Number One spot, ahead of Chevette

Blue oval emblems with "Ford" script return

Aerovan concept vehicle predicts mid-1980s Aerostar

▲ Heritage again served as top Thunderbird. A new "Essex" 112-bhp, 3.8-liter V-6 was now the step-up engine above the 3.3-liter six, with 4.2-liter the sole V-8. A newly optional "Tripminder" calculated trip/mileage data.

◀ The former Fairmont wagon moved to the up-scale Granada series, with standard 200-cid six. Options included the new 232 (3.8-liter) V-6 and automatic. An L wagon cost $7983. Wagons could have a $282 Squire woody package.

On sale in April 1981 as an early '82, the EXP ▲ coupe was Ford's first two-seater since the original T-Bird. Longer and lower than Escort, it rode that subcompact's 94.2-inch wheelbase.

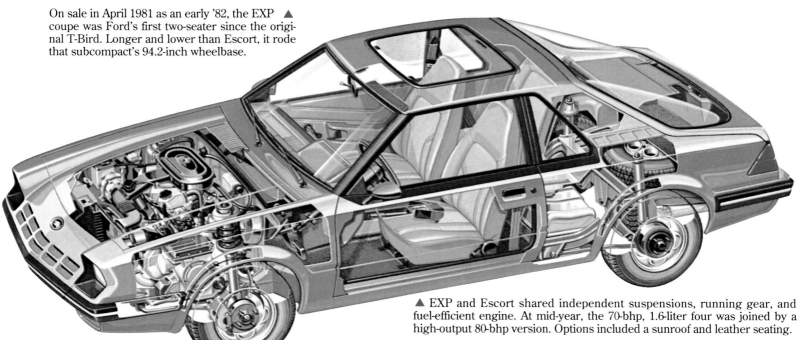

▲ EXP and Escort shared independent suspensions, running gear, and fuel-efficient engine. At mid-year, the 70-bhp, 1.6-liter four was joined by a high-output 80-bhp version. Options included a sunroof and leather seating.

270

▲ Escort's lineup expanded to three body styles with the addition of a five-door hatchback sedan. A total of 130,473 were built. Lackluster performance and controversial styling of EXP (at rear), especially its "frog-eye" headlights, hurt sales. Only 98,256 EXPs were built. EXPs had a notchback roof, while Mercury's equivalent LN7 was a "bubbleback."

◄ Five-door wagons in three trim levels accounted for 23 percent of the 385,132 Escorts built for 1982, helping turn Ford's subcompact into the top American seller. A Squire option could give wagons the "woody" look. Replacing the SS, this year's GT hatchback had a handling suspension, but the same engine choices as other models: a 70-bhp or (later) 80-bhp four.

1982 Engine Availability

Engines	bore × stroke	bhp	availability
I-4, 97.6	3.15 × 3.13	70	S-Escort, EXP
I-4, 97.6	3.15 × 3.13	80	O-late Escort, EXP
I-4, 140.0	3.78 × 3.13	86	S-Fairmont, Granada
I-6, 200.0	3.68 × 3.13	87	S-Gran wgn; O-Fmont, Gran
V-6, 232.0	3.80 × 3.40	112	O-Granada
V-8, 255.0	3.68 × 3.00	122	S-LTD; O-Fmont (police)
V-8, 302.0	4.00 × 3.00	132	S-LTD wgn; O-LTD
V-8, 351.0	4.00 × 3.50	165	S-LTD (police only)

Mustang	bore × stroke	bhp	availability
I-4, 140.0	3.78 × 3.13	88	S-all
I-6, 200.0	3.68 × 3.13	88	O-all
V-8, 255.0	3.68 × 3.00	120	O-all
V-8, 302.0	4.00 × 3.00	157	S-GT; O-all
Thunderbird			
I-6, 200.0	3.68 × 3.13	88	S-all exc Heritage
V-6, 232.0	3.80 × 3.40	112	O-all exc Heritage
V-8, 255.0	3.68 × 3.00	120	S-Heritage; O-others

▲ Ads proclaimed: "The Boss is Back!" That meant a high-output 157-bhp, 302-cid V-8 powered either the bold GT (shown) or, at extra cost, less-assertive Mustangs.

▼ With the toughened 302 (5.0-liter) V-8 on tap, a GT was the quickest Mustang offered in years, able to blast to 60 in less than eight seconds. Only manual shift was offered. Priced at a modest $8308, GTs drew 23,447 customers out of 130,418 Mustangs built. Appearance was similar to the earlier Cobra, *sans* snake, with integral fog lamps and a rear lip spoiler.

▲ Unveiled at the 1982 Chicago Auto Show, a Mustang convertible was promised for summer but didn't go on sale until the '83 model year.

▲ An optional two-way tailgate for the new Granada wagon contained a flip-up "hatch" window for loading/unloading of small items.

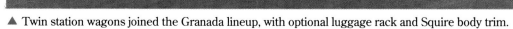

▲ Twin station wagons joined the Granada lineup, with optional luggage rack and Squire body trim.

272

▲ Sticker-priced at $7094, the F-150 Flareside pickup (foreground) had a 6½-foot box and available four-wheel drive. A 300-cid six was standard; three V-8s available. A 3.8-liter V-6 was standard in F-100 Flaresides.

▲ F-Series Stylesides could be trimmed with XL, XLS, or top-dog XLT Lariat packages, in four duty ratings. A new F-100 FS (Fuel Saver) had a city EPA rating of 22 mpg. Ford clung to a tight lead in light-truck volume.

◄ All Fairmonts were called Futura this year, and the 200-cid six was the most potent engine.

► SuperCab versions of the F-150 and F-250 pickup had space for optional seats in back.

Model Breakdown Chart

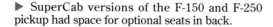

Escort—wb 94.2		Wght	Price	Prod
05	htchbk sdn 3d	1,920	5,462	
05	L htchbk sdn 3d	1,926	6,046	
05	GL htchbk sdn 3d	1,948	6,406	165,660
05	GLX htchbk sdn 3d	1,987	7,086	
05	GT htchbk sdn 3d	1,963	6,706	
06	htchbk sdn 5d	1,926	5,668	
06	L htckbk sdn 5d	2,003	6,263	
06	GL htchbk sdn 5d	2,025	6,622	130,473
06	GLX htchbk sdn 5d	2,064	7,302	
08	L wgn 5d	2,023	6,461	
08	GL wgn 5d	2,043	6,841	88,999
08	GLX wgn 5d	2,079	7,475	
EXP—wb 94.2				
01	htchbk cpe 3d	2,146	7,387	98,256
Fairmont Futura—wb 105.5				
20	sdn 2d	2,616	5,985	8,222
21	sdn 4d	2,664	6,419	101,666
22	spt cpe	2,640	6,517	17,851
Granada—wb 105.5				
26	L sdn 2d	2,732	7,126	
26	GL sdn 2d	2,758	7,543	12,802
26	GLX sdn 2d	2,776	7,666	
27	L sdn 4d	2,764	7,301	
27	GL sdn 4d	2,794	7,718	62,339
27	GLX sdn 4d	2,812	7,840	

		Wght	Price	Prod
28	L wgn 5d	2,965	7,983	45,182
28	GL wgn 5d	2,995	8,399	
LTD—wb 114.3				
31	S sdn 4d	3,522	8,312	22,182
32	sdn 2d	3,496	8,455	3,510
33	sdn 4d	3,526	8,574	29,776
34	Crown Victoria sdn 2d	3,523	9,149	9,287
35	Crown Victoria sdn 4d	3,567	9,294	41,405
37	S wgn 5d, 2S	3,725	8,783	2,973
38	wgn 5d, 2S	3,741	9,073	9,294
39	Country Squire wgn 5d, 2S	3,741	9,580	9,626
Mustang—wb 100.4				
10	L cpe 2d	2,568	6,345	45,316
10	GL cpe 2d	2,585	6,844	
16	GL htchbk cpe 3d	2,622	6,979	45,901
16	GT htchbk cpe 3d, V-8	2,597	8,308	23,447
12	GLX cpe 2d	2,600	6,980	5,828
13	GLX htchbk cpe 3d	2,636	7,101	9,926
Thunderbird—wb 108.4				
42	cpe, I-6/V-8	3,068	8,492	
42/60T	Town Landau cpe, I-6/V-8	3,131	9,703	45,142
42/607	Heritage cpe, I-6/V-8	3,303	12,742	

▲ Club Wagons in E-100/150/250 form started at $8501, with a selection of four V-8 engines.

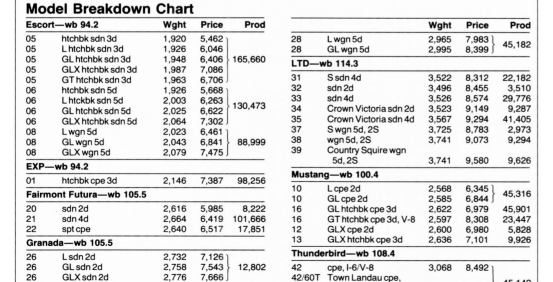

1983

Ford finishes fourth in U.S. production, behind Olds and Buick—first time out of top two since 1905

Ford hangs onto second spot in sales . . . Escort still leads subcompact field

Dramatic Thunderbird restyling sets aerodynamic tone for new products

Compact Ranger pickup debuts as early '83 model

Ford regains top rank in light truck production

Ad slogan promises "Quality is Job 1"

President Donald Petersen takes high-performance driving course—suggests new thinking at Ford

Henry Ford II elected to Automotive Hall of Fame

▲ For its 10th generation, Thunderbird stuck to the tested "Fox" platform but slimmed down to basics. At mid-year, serious drivers could pay $11,790 for the Turbo Coupe, with a multi-port-injected 142-bhp turbo four, five-speed gearbox, special handling package, and fog lamps in an under-bumper spoiler.

▲ Wheelbase shortened by 4.4 inches (to 104) and the T-Bird narrowed by three inches, with rear overhang trimmed, windshield raked back, contours rounded. "Conceived for today," the ads swooned, it had "an eye on tomorrow." Aerodynamics and aircraft-style doors were in; tack-ons like half-vinyl roofs out.

▲ Nitrogen-pressurized shocks boosted T-Bird handling. Base engine was a 3.8-liter V-6; optional, a revived, fuel-injected 302 (5.0-liter) V-8 with 130 bhp. The new look sold, as volume rose from a paltry 45,142 to 121,999.

An Alternative Fuel Option...PROPANE!

Ford Division is offering a Propane Option to fleet customers on its 1983 LTD 4-Door Sedans. These factory-produced, propane-fueled cars will be powered by Ford's 2.3L I-4 engine with a SelectShift automatic transmission.

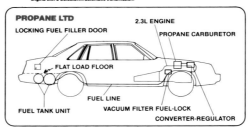

The Propane Powered Ford LTD

Propane is liquefied petroleum gas and is commonly referred to as LPG. The propane used in automobiles vaporizes at normal atmospheric temperature and pressure. For this reason it is stored under a normal pressure of 150 psi to remain in liquid state. It is in this liquid state that propane is dispensed into, and retained in, the fuel tank of the car. It is therefore sold by the litre or gallon as are conventional fuels. The operator fueling the vehicle simply screws the filler nozzle by hand on to the receptacle located behind the car's fuel filler door, turns on the valves and pumps the desired amount of fuel.

A casual observer would be hard-pressed to identify Ford's propane LTD from its comparable gasoline-fueled version. Except for the PROPANE FUELED nameplate, there is no visual difference outside or under the vehicle itself. Even the engine compartment requires a second look to detect the small converter and fuel-lock units. The unique and easily serviced propane carburetor is located under the air cleaner. The fuel tank is located under the trunk to provide a large flat load floor in the luggage compartment.

The real difference in the propane-powered car is in the driving! The starting and smooth flow of power when pulling away or passing other vehicles must be experienced. This performance results from Ford's 2.3L propane-powered engine.

Factory-Produced VERSUS Conversion

The factory-produced propane-fueled LTD provides important engineering advantages which should be kept in mind when comparing to cars converted to propane after having left the factory:

- The LTD propane car is engineered for optimum engine performance, i.e. increased compression ratio, revised timing, special piston rings, etc.
- Vehicle design changes have been made to ensure compatibility with the propane system, i.e.—higher capacity rear springs, increased diameter of front stabilizer bar, larger tires, wider wheel rims, increased stiffness in rear suspension arm bushings, unique rear shock absorbers, etc.
- Ford's propane engines and cars have been extensively tested on the dynamometer and "on the road"
- The propane-powered LTD is backed by Ford, with full vehicle warranty and a nationwide dealer network for parts and service.

The product advantages engineered into the car by Ford should be as important as the fueling change itself. In addition, the cost of Ford's propane option is less than a typical propane conversion after the car has left the factory. Add this to the payback potential in fuel cost and maintenance savings and the factory-produced car becomes especially well worth considering with high mileage fleet or taxi operators.

Ford's Propane Option...

...can provide an attractive alternative to Fleet Operators who are looking for ways to reduce operating costs. Propane is particularly well suited to high mileage accumulation and/or high idle time intra-city type applications. The Ford propane fuel system offers the following potential benefits.

1. Lower Fuel Costs...Propane prices vary widely depending upon location and tax structure. However, on average, the bulk price of propane is presently about two-thirds the price of gasoline. Propane contains less energy per gallon than does gasoline, so overall fuel consumption increases depending upon application. Preliminary Ford testing, based upon a modification of EPA test procedures, indicates that fuel economy values for the propane engine will approach that of the gasoline-powered vehicle. Even with slightly higher fuel consumption, the cost savings can be substantial due to the lower initial cost. As gasoline prices escalate to even higher levels, industry sources predict the price differential between gasoline and propane could be even greater, resulting in increased cost savings.

2. Longer Engine Life...Propane enters the engine as a dry gas and as such, does not wash lubricating oil from the upper cylinder wall area. A characteristic of propane is that in burning, it does not produce carbon and other wear causing deposits in the combustion chamber area. This adds up to the potential for increased bearing, piston and cylinder bore life. High mileage fleets should experience much longer intervals between engine rebuilds for instance. On the subject of maintenance, you should be aware of the relative simplicity of the propane gas carburetion system.

As previously noted, propane enters the combustion chamber as a gas. As such, it burns smoothly and completely, resulting in easy engine starting and smooth acceleration; — no annoying stumbles or hesitation. Also, the higher octane of propane provides you with a reduced tendency to knock on acceleration. Minimum adjustments or overhauls are required. Fleets will appreciate the reduced down-time potential.

3. Engineered by Ford Especially for Propane...The Ford Propane System installation provides many important engineering advantages which include:

- Increased compression ratio to take advantage of propane's higher octane.
- Distributor curve is recalibrated to obtain the optimum spark advance for propane.
- Design changes are made to the intake manifold gasket to obtain the lower manifold temperatures required with propane.
- Locking fuel filler door to discourage pilferage and vandalism.
- Unique piston rings, for improved wear-in.

The last item should be of particular importance to a potential owner. Unique piston rings are provided due to ring seating problems encountered with conventional rings in many aftermarket propane conversions. Installation of an after-market propane conversion on a new gas engine without ring replacement may result in failure of the rings to seat properly. The end result could be excessive oil consumption for the life of the engine. It is important to keep these advantages in mind when comparing with after-market conversions.

4. Ford Service and Warranty...Ford dealers will perform any necessary service and warranty repairs. Technicians at Ford dealers will be provided with specialized training in the principles of operation and repair techniques of the propane fuel system. All the unique propane fuel system parts are available directly from Ford Motor Company, through the normal parts distribution system.

After-market propane conversions are warranted by the manufacturer of the conversion kit. Installation of after-market propane conversion kits may affect the manufacturer's engine warranty. The Ford propane installation is covered by the same warranty provisions as gasoline-powered cars.

*Consult Warranty Facts booklet for specific warranty information.

5. Fuel Availability...Stationary engines, farm tractors and lift trucks have been operating on propane in North America for 20-30 years. However, use of propane as a road vehicle fuel in North America has been limited due to the availability and low cost of gasoline. This has not been the case in countries such as Italy, Japan, The Netherlands and Belgium, where up to 38% of all vehicles are fueled by propane. In North America, the recent rapid escalation of gasoline and diesel fuel prices has made propane more attractive.

At current production levels, about 60% of the propane produced is extracted from natural gas and 40% from refining crude oil. Approximately 90% of the propane used in the United States can be produced by domestic suppliers with non-OPEC countries supplying the remaining 10%. While future market conditions are difficult to predict, the price and availability of propane currently appears to be more stable than other petroleum products.

Many propane refilling stations exist across the United States, and it is anticipated that like unleaded gasoline and diesel fuel, there will be a rapid growth in the number of propane outlets as the propane-fueled vehicle population increases. A booklet containing a list of propane refilling stations is provided with each vehicle.

Ford's 2.3L propane-powered engine and larger fuel tank (25 U.S. gallons of propane versus 16.0 gallons of gasoline) greatly increase the cruising range of the propane car. Based on projected city/highway mileage ratings, the propane car has a range of about 400-500 miles between fill-ups, and almost 35% farther than the equivalent gasoline fueled car.

The benefits of propane will be greatest for commercial fleets with ten or more vehicles that return to a home base daily. Such fleets can set up their own fueling facility, thereby achieving convenience and increasing their fuel cost savings. Service and taxi vehicle fleets, especially, will find propane most attractive.

The following options are required on the Propane-Powered LTD

- 54 AH battery
- P195/75R14 tires
- Engine block heater
- Automatic SelectShift transmission

The following options are not available on the Propane-Powered LTD

- 45 AH battery
- Altitude emissions
- California emissions system
- Electronic instrument cluster
- Extended range fuel tank
- Fingertip speed control
- Floor-mounted shift
- Heavy-Duty Fleet Package
- Heavy-Duty Suspension Package
- Leather-wrapped steering wheel
- P185/75R14 tires
- Styled steel wheels
- Tripminder

▲ Installed in a handful of late Granadas, a propane-powered 2.3-liter engine was optional in LTDs aimed at fleet buyers. Ford promised reduced fuel costs and longer engine life.

▲ Replacing the deleted Granada, a new mid-size LTD was one more offshoot of the Fairmont, now wearing aero-look lower-body sheetmetal and a sloped rectangular grille. Four-door sedans had a slant-back six-window greenhouse with slightly lipped trunklid and 60-degree back window, and came in base and Brougham trim. Total LTD volume for the model year came to 155,758—well above the final Granadas.

▲ Passengers in the Thunderbird Turbo Coupe luxuriated in contoured Lear-Siegler bucket seats with open-mesh head restraints. They featured inflatable lumbar support, adjustable thigh support and side bolsters, and reclining backrests. Dashboards included a tachometer.

▲ A 200-cid (3.3-liter) six-cylinder engine was standard in the $8577 LTD wagon, while sedans had a 2.3-liter four. A 3.8-liter V-6 was optional in both. Squire trim added $282.

▲ For $388 more, LTD buyers could move up from a basic sedan to a Brougham, with an array of conveniences but no dramatic appearance change. All wagons had automatic shift.

▲ LTD technical features included rack-and-pinion steering, plus gas-pressurized struts and shocks. The 2.3-liter four used fast-burn technology. Aero styling kept air-drag low.

▲ Ford's experimental Probe series probed aerodynamic limits, paving the way for production cars. Front skirts on the Probe IV flexed during turns.

▲ With the emergence of the smaller LTD, all full-size Fords were renamed LTD Crown Victoria. Sole powertrain was a fuel-injected 5.0-liter V-8 with overdrive automatic.

▲ Both Country Squire and plain-bodied station wagons continued as part of the renamed full-size lineup. Output of 20,343 wagons included base and budget-priced "S" editions.

▲ A multi-port injected, 88-bhp version of Escort's 1.6-liter four went into the GT. Also new: a five-speed gearbox, body add-ons, and uprated suspension. The base Escort was gone.

▲ Three versions of the 1.6-liter four were available in this year's EXP, which added a five-speed transmission with upshift indicator. Output dropped sharply in EXP's second year.

▲ A four-barrel carb helped send the Mustang GT's 5.0 V-8 from 157 to 175 bhp. A 3.8 V-6 replaced the inline six option for other models—restyled this year with a rounded nose.

▲ After convertibles faded, aftermarket firms turned out a few open Mustangs. Now Ford issued a coupe modified by Cars & Concepts, with roll-down quarter windows, in GLX or GT trim.

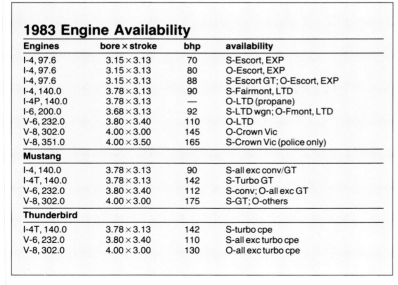

▲ Because CAFE standards applied to light trucks, aerodynamics were vital. Here, a Ranger visits the wind tunnel.

▲ Replacing the Mazda-built Courier was Ford's compact Ranger, made in the U.S. Scaled-down from the F-Series, they were offered with 4WD.

▲ Downsizing would bring a Bronco II mate for the big Bronco sport-utility, as an '84 model. Meanwhile, Broncos got a modified 302 V-8.

1983 Engine Availability

Engines	bore × stroke	bhp	availability
I-4, 97.6	3.15 × 3.13	70	S-Escort, EXP
I-4, 97.6	3.15 × 3.13	80	O-Escort, EXP
I-4, 97.6	3.15 × 3.13	88	S-Escort GT; O-Escort, EXP
I-4, 140.0	3.78 × 3.13	90	S-Fairmont, LTD
I-4P, 140.0	3.78 × 3.13	—	O-LTD (propane)
I-6, 200.0	3.68 × 3.13	92	S-LTD wgn; O-Fmont, LTD
V-6, 232.0	3.80 × 3.40	110	O-LTD
V-8, 302.0	4.00 × 3.00	145	O-Crown Vic
V-8, 351.0	4.00 × 3.50	165	S-Crown Vic (police only)
Mustang			
I-4, 140.0	3.78 × 3.13	90	S-all exc conv/GT
I-4T, 140.0	3.78 × 3.13	142	S-Turbo GT
V-6, 232.0	3.80 × 3.40	112	S-conv; O-all exc GT
V-8, 302.0	4.00 × 3.00	175	S-GT; O-others
Thunderbird			
I-4T, 140.0	3.78 × 3.13	142	S-turbo cpe
V-6, 232.0	3.80 × 3.40	110	S-all exc turbo cpe
V-8, 302.0	4.00 × 3.00	130	O-all exc turbo cpe

▲ A total of 80,883 Fairmonts were produced in its final half-year run, including 7882 Futura sport coupes and a pair of new price-leader "S" sedans. For '84, Fairmont would be replaced by the front-drive Tempo.

▲ Luxury wasn't ignored in the restyled Thunderbird. The top-dollar Heritage had unique quarter windows and coach lamps, electronic instruments, and velour upholstery.

▲ Harold A. Poling (left) and Ford Motor Company president Donald E. Petersen (right) show off the new Mustang convertible. Petersen and design head Jack Telnack earn credit for blazing the new path in Ford styling.

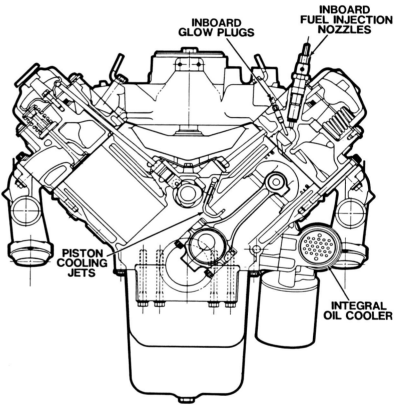

▲ Trucks got few changes, apart from new Caterpillar diesel engines for F-Series mediums. Most F-Series front axles grew heavier, for higher payloads. Note the Louisville eggcrate grille on this F-700 conventional.

▲ F-Series trucks and Econoline/Club Wagons on 250/350 chassis could get a 6.9-liter engine, billed as a "true-truck diesel." Ford claimed 160-162 bhp and 307-314 lbs/ft of torque. Ranger pickups also could have diesel power.

Model Breakdown Chart

Escort—wb 94.2		Wght	Price	Prod
04	L htchbk sdn 3d	2,016	5,639	
05	GL htchbk sdn 3d	1,959	6,384	151,386
06	GLX htchbk sdn 3d	1,993	6,771	
07	GT htchbk sdn 3d	2,020	7,339	
13	L htckbk sdn 5d	2,078	5,846	
14	GL htchbk sdn 5d	2,025	6,601	84,649
15	GLX htchbk sdn 5d	2,059	6,988	
09	L wgn 5d	2,117	6,052	
10	GL wgn 5d	2,052	6,779	79,335
11	GLX wgn 5d	2,083	7,150	
EXP—wb 94.2				
01	htchbk cpe 3d	2,156	6,426	
01/ 301B	HO htchbk cpe 3d	—	7,004	
01/ 302B	HO spt htchbk cpe 3d	—	7,794	19,697
01/ 303B	Luxury htchbk cpe 3d	—	8,225	
01/ 304B	GT htchbk cpe 3d	—	8,739	

Fairmont Futura—wb 105.5		Wght	Price	Prod
35	sdn 2d	2,890	6,444	3,664
35/41K	S sdn 2d	2,628	5,985	
36	sdn 4d	2,933	6,590	69,287
36/41K	S sdn 4d	2,672	6,125	
37	spt cpe	2,908	6,666	7,882
LTD—wb 105.5				
39	L sdn 4d	2,912	7,777	111,813
39/60H	Brougham sdn 4d	2,845	8,165	
40	wgn 5d L-6	3,092	8,577	43,945
LTD Crown Victoria—wb 114.3				
43	sdn 4d	3,748	10,094	81,859
43/41K	S sdn 4d	3,732	9,130	
42	sdn 2d	3,732	10,094	11,414
44	Country Squire wgn 5d, 2S	3,901	10,253	20,343
44/41E	wgn 5d, 2S	3,895	10,003	
44/41K	S wgn 5d, 2S	3,891	9,444	

Mustang—wb 100.4		Wght	Price	Prod
26	L cpe 2d	2,684	6,727	
26/60C	GL cpe 2d	2,743	7,264	33,201
26/602	GLX cpe 2d	2,760	7,398	
28/60C	GL htchbk cpe 3d	2,788	7,439	
28/602	GLX htchbk cpe 3d	2,801	7,557	
28/932	GT htchbk cpe 3d, V-8	2,969	9,328	64,234
28/932	Turbo GT htchbk cpe 3d	—	9,714	
27/602	GLX conv cpe, V-6	2,807	12,467	23,438
27/932	GT conv cpe, V-8	—	13,479	
Thunderbird—wb 104.0				
46	cpe, V-6/V-8	3,076	9,197	121,999
46/607	Heritage cpe, V-6/V-8	3,076	12,228	
46/934	Turbo cpe, L-4T	—	11,790	

1984

U.S. car sales top 10 million—first time since 1979

Ford produces 1.1 million cars in U.S., edges Buick out of third place

Ford company's market share rises to 19.26 percent

Ford earns record profit: $2.91 billion

Front-drive compact Tempo bows as early '84 model

Escort ranks Number Two in domestic car sales

Compact Bronco II sport-utility launched . . . Chevy offers rival Blazer

Ford leads in light-truck production

Ranger pickup production beats Chevrolet's S-10

Ford and GM fail to meet 27-mpg CAFE standard

▲ Sophisticated and European-oriented, the SVO Mustang was the first limited-edition from Ford's Special Vehicle Operations. Unique styling included a grille-less nose, single head-lamps, and "biplane" spoiler. An SVO cost $6018 more than the GT. Only 4508 were built.

▶ Air-to-air intercooled, the SVO's turbo four was electronically controlled to vary boost pressure up to 14 psi. Result: 175 bhp at 4500 rpm, and 210 lbs/ft of torque. A cockpit switch "tuned" engine electronics to the grade of fuel used. A five-speed gearbox with Hurst linkage sent all that oomph to the V-rated 16-inch tires, which rode cast aluminum wheels.

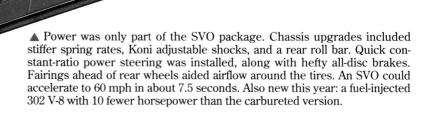

▲ Power was only part of the SVO package. Chassis upgrades included stiffer spring rates, Koni adjustable shocks, and a rear roll bar. Quick constant-ratio power steering was installed, along with hefty all-disc brakes. Fairings ahead of rear wheels aided airflow around the tires. An SVO could accelerate to 60 mph in about 7.5 seconds. Also new this year: a fuel-injected 302 V-8 with 10 fewer horsepower than the carbureted version.

▲ Attempting a Euro-style road car, Ford debuted an LX edition of the LTD at mid-year, with blackout trim and powered by a 165-bhp, 302 V-8. Only 3260 were built in 1984-85.

▲ A formal cloth "coach roof" with blind sail panels and "Frenched" backlight went on the LTD Brougham. The inline six was out, leaving only a four and V-6. LTD sales rose smartly.

▲ Four-door LTD Crown Victorias could have an optional Brougham roof, but little other change was evident. Big cars sold well as gas prices fell. Output jumped to 173,489.

▲ With the addition of a top-dollar Fila, the Thunderbird flock expanded to four. Named for an Italian sportswear maker, Filas had white/dark-charcoal paint and red/blue stripes.

▲ Thunderbird Turbo Coupes could have an automatic transmission this year, and the 140-bhp engine added a viscous fan. Note the low rectangular fog lamps and black body trim.

▲ A $12,661 elan replaced the Heritage as midrange Thunderbird. The base V-6 added port fuel injection for 120 bhp, but a 140-bhp V-8 was available. Parking lights were now amber.

1984 Engine Availability

Engines	bore × stroke	bhp	availability
I-4, 97.6	3.15 × 3.13	70	S-Escort
I-4, 97.6	3.15 × 3.13	80	S-EXP; O-Escort
I-4, 97.6	3.15 × 3.13	84	S-Escort LX, GT; O-Esc, EXP
I-4T, 97.6	3.15 × 3.13	120	S-Escort GT, EXP turbo
I-4D, 121.0	3.39 × 3.39	52	O-Escort, Tempo
I-4, 140.0	3.70 × 3.30	84	S-Tempo
I-4, 140.0	3.78 × 3.13	88	S-LTD
I-4P, 140.0	3.78 × 3.13	—	O-LTD (propane)
V-6, 232.0	3.80 × 3.40	120	S-LTD wgn; O-LTD
V-8, 302.0	4.00 × 3.00	140	S-Crown Vic
V-8, 302.0	4.00 × 3.00	155	S-Crown Vic wgn
V-8, 302.0	4.00 × 3.00	165	S-LTD LX
V-8, 351.0	4.00 × 3.50	180	S-Crown Vic (police only)
Mustang			
I-4, 140.0	3.78 × 3.13	88	S-all exc conv/GT
I-4T, 140.0	3.78 × 3.13	145	S-Turbo GT
I-4T, 140.0	3.78 × 3.13	175	S-SVO
V-6, 232.0	3.80 × 3.40	120	S-conv; O-all exc GT
V-8, 302.0	4.00 × 3.00	165	O-all
V-8, 302.0	4.00 × 3.00	175	S-GT
Thunderbird			
I-4T, 140.0	3.78 × 3.13	145	S-turbo cpe
V-6, 232.0	3.80 × 3.40	120	S-all exc turbo cpe
V-8, 302.0	4.00 × 3.00	140	O-all exc turbo cpe

▲ Marking Mustang's 20th year, Ford issued a "Shelby White" Anniversary edition with maroon GT-350 rocker stripes. On regular Mustangs, solid headrests replaced open-type. Later came integrated fog lamps and staggered rear shocks.

◄ Carroll Shelby protested Ford's decision to call its Anniversary Mustang GT-350, and brought a copyright infringement lawsuit. About 5260 were built: hatchbacks and convertibles.

▲ Ready to rival GM's X-cars and Chrysler's K-cars, the front-drive Tempo emerged with an all-new body, chassis, and engine. Aero touches, derided as "jellybean" styling by some, included a sloped nose and sloped windshield.

▲ Topping the Tempo line, a GLX four-door stickered at $7621. Base and L models were cheaper, and four-doors outsold two-doors by far, though the latter had a sportier look. Tempo volume hit 402,214 in a long model year.

▶ With a 99.9-inch wheelbase, a Tempo measured 20 inches shorter overall than the old Fairmont. Chassis features included MacPherson struts, rack-and-pinion steering, and independent "Quadrilink" rear suspension. The 2300 "High Swirl Combustion" 2.3-liter overhead-cam four developed 85 horsepower. A diesel engine also was offered.

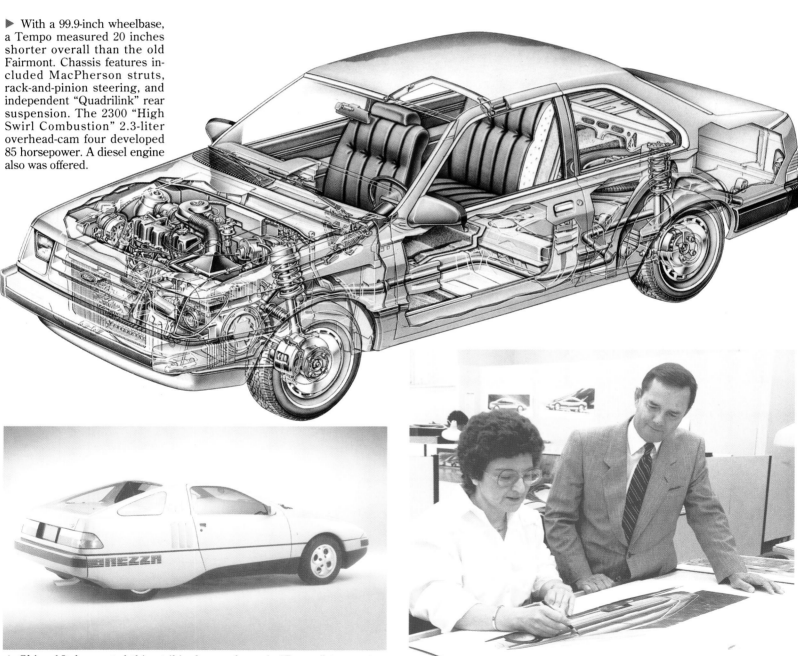

▲ Ghia of Italy created this strikingly aerodynamic "Brezza" two-seater, with a mid-mounted Escort powertrain, EXP parts, and enclosed wheels.

▶ Ford stylists were always at work creating new concept vehicles—many yielding ideas for production. Donald F. Kopka headed Ford design.

▲ EXPs borrowed a "bubbleback" hatch from the Mercury LN7. Turbo Coupes had 120 bhp.

▲ Basic full-size pickup was the F-150. This $7376 Styleside shows XL trim and dual tanks.

▲ A 115-bhp, 2.8-liter V-6 powered the compact Bronco II, which debuted in March 1983. Based on the Ranger, it was smaller and more agile than the big Bronco, on a 10.7-inch-shorter wheelbase and five inches lower.

▲ Bronco IIs had a fixed roof, unlike the removable roof on big Broncos, and a $9998 sticker. The sporty XLS package added tri-color tape striping, blackout trim, and wheelwell "spats." A luxury XLT also was offered.

Model Breakdown Chart

Escort—wb 94.2		Wght	Price	Prod
04	htchbk sdn 3d	2,016	5,629	
04	L htchbk sdn 3d	2,080	5,885	
05	GL htchbk sdn 3d	2,122	6,382	184,323
07	GT htchbk sdn 3d	2,170	7,593	
07/935	GT turbo htchbk sdn 3d	—	8,680	
13	htchbk sdn 5d	2,078	5,835	
13	L htckbk sdn 5d	2,146	6,099	99,444
14	GL htchbk sdn 5d	2,188	6,596	
15	LX htchbk sdn 5d	2,222	7,848	
09	L wgn 5d	2,176	6,313	
10	GL wgn 5d	2,216	6,773	88,756
11	LX wgn 5d	2,249	7,939	

EXP—wb 94.2				
01/A80	htchbk cpe 3d	2,212	6,653	
01/A81	Luxury cpe 3d	2,235	7,539	23,016
01/A82	Turbo cpe 3d	2,243	9,942	

Tempo—wb 99.9				
18	L sdn 2d	2,286	6,936	
19	GL sdn 2d	—	7,159	107,065
20	GLX sdn 2d	—	7,621	
21	L sdn 4d	2,348	6,936	
22	GL sdn 4d	—	7,159	295,149
23	GLX sdn 4d	—	7,621	

LTD—wb 105.6				
39	sdn 4d	2,830	8,605	154,173
39/60H	Brougham sdn 4d	—	9,980	
39/93B	LX sdn 4d, V-8	—	11,098	*
40	wgn 5d, I-6	3,123	9,102	59,569

LTD Crown Victoria—wb 114.3				
43	sdn 4d	3,730	10,954	130,164
43/41K	S sdn 4d	3,728	9,826	
42	sdn 2d	3,689	10,954	12,522
44	Country Squire wgn 5d, 2S	3,936	11,111	
44/41E	wgn 5d, 2S	3,931	10,861	30,803
44/41K	S wgn 5d, 2S	3,880	10,136	

Mustang—wb 100.5				
26	L cpe 2d	2,736	7,098	37,780
26/602	LX cpe 2d	2,757	7,290	
28	L htchbk cpe 3d	2,782	7,269	
28/602	LX htchbk cpe 3d	2,807	7,496	
28/932	GT htchbk cpe 3d, V-8	3,013	9,578	
28/932	Turbo GT htchbk cpe 3d	2,869	9,762	86,200
28/939	SVO turbo htchbk cpe 3d	2,992	15,596	
27/602	LX conv cpe, V-6	3,020	11,849	
27/932	GT conv cpe, V-8	3,124	13,051	17,600
27/932	Turbo GT conv cpe	3,004	13,245	

Thunderbird—wb 104.0				
46	cpe, V-6/V-8	3,155	9,633	
46/607	elan cpe, V-6/V-8	3,221	12,661	170,533
46/606	Fila cpe, V-6/V-8	3,326	14,471	
46/934	Turbo cpe, I-4T	3,073	12,330	

*3,260 LTD LX models built in 1984-85 model years combined.

1985

Happy days here again: automakers earning record-setting profits

Import sales pass 2.8 million—but include U.S.-built "transplants"

Ford and Mazda plan future products jointly

Ford's market share eases back to 18.8 percent

Donald Petersen replaces Philip Caldwell as Ford's chairman . . . Harold "Red" Poling named president

Chevrolet edges past Ford in truck sales

F-Series pickups remain top-selling U.S. vehicles

Tempos with airbags sold to government and insurers

New Taurus previewed early in 1985; on sale as '86

▲ At mid-year, a restyled Second Series Escort emerged, with aero-styled headlamps. The sporty GT, shown here, wore a narrow two-slat grille and a front air dam with fog lights, but abandoned the Turbo engine option. Bigger 1.9-liter engines replaced the original 1.6-liter fours, either carbureted with 86 bhp or fuel-injected with 108. Five-speed gearboxes got a revised shift pattern.

▲ More reliable water-cooled bearings went into the Thunderbird Turbo Coupe's engine, eliminating the need for a "coast-down" period before shutting the motor off. Turbo Coupes had a reworked instrument panel with analog gauges. Price was $13,365—up $1035. T-Bird output dropped to 151,851.

▲ Thunderbirds had come a long way in three decades, from stylish two-seater to the performance-packed Turbo Coupe of 1985. Among other changes in that time, V-8 engines had grown in power, then disappeared from the scene—and were now making a comeback. In this 30th anniversary year, Ford issued a few thousand lackluster special editions—essentially elans painted Medium Regatta Blue.

▲ Minor LTD restyling put a Ford oval into the center of an eggcrate grille, and revised sedan taillights. The base four rose to 88 bhp.

▲ A Brougham sedan cost $388 more than a base LTD. A total of 162,884 sedans were built, plus 42,642 wagons, which had a 232-cid V-6.

▲ Although the LTD LX Euro-sedan with 165-bhp V-8 returned for a second season, it would soon disappear. Note the body-color grille.

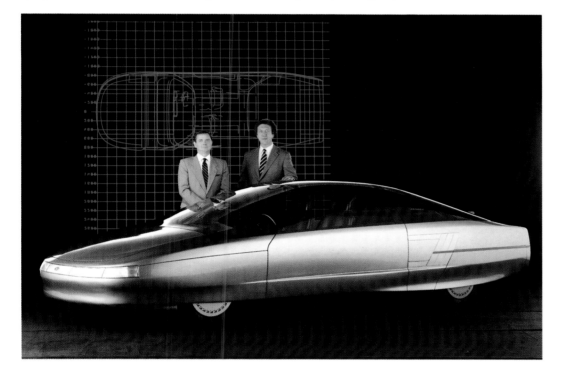

▲ A mid-engine was intended as powerplant for the Probe V, which had a drag coefficient lower than an F-15 fighter. Ford claimed it could maintain 50-mph speed using only five bhp.

◄ Aerodynamics and wind-tunnel testing were keys to Ford's success in the 1980s. As if prior Probe concept vehicles weren't slippery enough, Ford created the Probe V with skirted wheels, thermoplastic skin, and sliding doors.

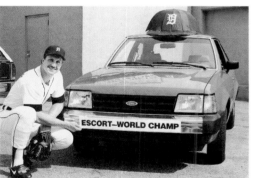

▲ Escorts certainly ranked as sales champs. Production rose by an impressive 34,600, after the mid-year debut of an aero Second Series.

▲ Minor changes to the LTD Crown Victoria included gas shocks and a diagnostic monitor. A self-leveling rear suspension was optional.

▲ Four-doors in base and fleet "S" form far outsold the equally priced LTD Crown Victoria two-door sedan. Flash-to-pass was new.

1985 Engine Availability

Engines	bore × stroke	bhp	availability
I-4, 97.6	3.15 × 3.13	70	S-Escort
I-4, 97.6	3.15 × 3.13	80	S-EXP; O-Escort
I-4, 97.6	3.15 × 3.13	84	S-Escort LX, GT; O-Escort
I-4T, 97.6	3.15 × 3.13	120	S-Escort, EXP turbo
I-4, 113.5	3.23 × 3.46	86	S-late Escort
I-4D, 121.0	3.39 × 3.39	52	O-Escort, Tempo
I-4, 140.0	3.70 × 3.30	86	S-Tempo
I-4, 140.0	3.70 × 3.30	100	O-Tempo
I-4, 140.0	3.78 × 3.13	88	S-LTD
I-4P, 140.0	3.78 × 3.13	—	O-LTD (propane)
V-6, 232.0	3.80 × 3.40	120	S-LTD wgn; O-LTD
V-8, 302.0	4.00 × 3.00	140	S-Crown Vic
V-8, 302.0	4.00 × 3.00	155	O-Crown Vic

Engines	bore × stroke	bhp	availability
V-8, 302.0	4.00 × 3.00	165	S-LTD LX
V-8, 351.0	4.00 × 3.50	180	S-Crown Vic (police only)
Mustang			
I-4, 140.0	3.78 × 3.13	88	S-all exc conv/GT
I-4T, 140.0	3.78 × 3.13	175	S-SVO
V-6, 232.0	3.80 × 3.40	120	S-conv; O-all exc GT
V-8, 302.0	4.00 × 3.00	180	O-all
V-8, 302.0	4.00 × 3.00	210	S-GT
Thunderbird			
I-4T, 140.0	3.78 × 3.13	155	S-turbo cpe
V-6, 232.0	3.80 × 3.40	120	S-all exc turbo cpe
V-8, 302.0	4.00 × 3.00	140	O-all exc turbo cpe

▲ Fuel injection gave Tempo's 2300 HSC engine 86 horsepower. A 100-bhp version was part of a $900 Sport GL package, including upgraded suspension. Tempos came in three trim levels.

▲ A Tempo GLX four-door sold for $1142 more than a GL, adding a tilt wheel, power steering, and power locks. Model-year output of 339,087 gave Tempo sixth spot in domestic sales.

▲ EXP Turbo Coupe drivers had 120 horsepower to play with, for $2412 more than a Luxury coupe. The basic 1.6-liter four yielded 80 bhp. EXP production soon halted for a while.

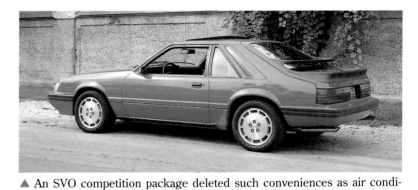

▲ An SVO competition package deleted such conveniences as air conditioning and stereo, knocking $1417 off the basic price. A Turbo GT also returned briefly. In addition, the L Mustang was dropped, while remaining models adopted a front end similar to the SVO, with a single air slot.

▲ In mid-1985, the Mustang SVO returned with flush aero "composite" headlamps and 50-series tires on 16-inch wheels. Internal tweaks to the 2.3-liter Turbo engine, including an air-to-air intercooler, boosted output by 30, to 205 bhp. Sales skidded to a mere 1954 this year.

▼ Ford's carbureted 302-cid (5.0-liter) V-8, standard on the Mustang GT, added roller tappets and a high-performance cam, raising horsepower by 35 (to 210). GTs got "Gatorback" tires from the SVO, plus gas-pressurized front shocks and a "quadra-shock" rear setup. Similar modifications boosted the fuel-injected 302 V-8's output to 180 bhp, but that was available only with automatic. Mustang prices were competitive against Japanese rivals.

▲ Roof lights on ponycars are hardly a common sight in most regions, but Mustangs occasionally went on duty tracking speeders and chasing criminals. Ads noted that a Special Pursuit 5.0L coupe with "total driving performance" was "the choice of police forces in 15 states." No surprise, perhaps, since *Motor Trend* noted of the civilian Mustang that its 210-bhp V-8 delivered "axle-creaking torque reminiscent of another time."

▲ Compact Ranger pickups often were loaded with options, including four-wheel drive, a V-6, and an XL package. A no-frills Ranger "S" pickup sold for only $5993, but the regular short-bed and long-bed editions, base-priced at $6675 and $6829, proved a lot more popular. The base Ranger four-cylinder engine switched to fuel injection. Meanwhile, more than 562,000 F-Series pickups found customers.

▲ Four-wheel-drive Bronco II prices rose about nine percent, starting at $10,889 with V-6 power and standard five-speed gearbox. This XLT version included pivoting vent windows. An Eddie Bauer edition added dark "privacy glass."

Model Breakdown Chart

Escort—wb 94.2		Wght	Price	Prod
04/41P	htchbk sdn 3d	1,990	5,620	
04	L htchbk sdn 3d	1,979	5,876	
05	GL htchbk sdn 3d	2,047	6,374	112,406*
07	GT htchbk sdn 3d	2,140	7,585	
07/935	GT turbo htchbk sdn 3d	2,172	8,680	
13	htchbk sdn 5d	2,078	5,835	
13/41P	L htckbk sdn 5d	2,055	5,827	62,709*
14	GL htchbk sdn 5d	2,114	6,588	
15	LX htchbk sdn 5d	2,175	7,840	
09	L wgn 5d	2,071	6,305	
10	GL wgn 5d	2,139	6,765	45,740*
11	LX wgn 5d	2,198	7,931	
Escort Second Series 1985½—wb 94.2				
31	sdn 3d	2,142	5,856	
31	L sdn 3d	—	6,127	100,554
32	GL sdn 3d	—	6,642	
36	L sdn 5d	2,195	6,341	48,676
37	GL sdn 5d	—	6,855	
34	L wgn 5d	2,223	6,622	36,998
35	GL wgn 5d	—	7,137	
EXP—wb 94.2				
01/A80	htchbk cpe 3d	2,098	6,697	
01/A81	Luxury cpe 3d	2,124	7,585	26,462
01/A82	Turbo cpe 3d	2,232	9,997	
Tempo—wb 99.9				
18	L sdn 2d	2,271	7,052	
19	GL sdn 2d	2,302	7,160	72,311
20	GLX sdn 2d	2,372	8,253	
21	L sdn 4d	2,328	7,052	
22	GL sdn 4d	2,358	7,160	266,776
23	GLX sdn 4d	2,428	8,302	
LTD—wb 105.6				
39	sdn 4d, I-4/V-6	2,852	8,874	
39/60H	Brougham sdn 4d, I-4/V-6	2,857	9,262	162,884
39/938	LX sdn 4d, V-8	2,904	11,421	
40	wgn 5d, V-6	2,990	9,384	42,642
LTD Crown Victoria—wb 114.3				
43	sdn 4d	3,588	11,627	154,612
43/41K	S sdn 4d	3,709	10,609	
42	sdn 2d	3,552	11,627	13,673
44	Country Squire wgn 5d, 2S	3,763	11,809	
44/41E	wgn 5d, 2S	3,758	11,559	30,825
44/41K	S wgn 5d, 2S	3,883	10,956	
Mustang—wb 100.5				
26/602	LX cpe 2d	2,657	6,885	56,781
28/602	LX htchbk cpe 3d	2,729	7,345	
28/932	GT htchbk cpe 3d, V-8	3,063	9,885	84,623
28/939	SVO turbo htchbk cpe 3d	2,991	14,521	
27/602	LX conv cpe, V-6	2,907	11,985	15,110
27/932	GT conv cpe, V-8	3,165	13,585	
Thunderbird—wb 104.0				
46	cpe, V-6/V-8	3,004	10,249	
46/607	elan cpe, V-6/V-8	3,041	11,916	151,851
46/606	Fila cpe, V-6/V-8	3,108	14,974	
46/934	Turbo cpe, I-4T	2,990	13,365	
*Estimated totals.				

285

1986

NINETEEN EIGHTY-SIX NINETEEN EIGHTY-SIX NINETEEN EIGHTY-SIX NINETEEN

Ford Taurus (and Mercury Sable) debut, clinching Ford's lead in aero styling

Motor Trend **names Taurus "Car of the Year"**

Aerostar van debuts as early '86, marketed with Rapid-Spec Package options

U.S. car sales hit highest level since 1973 . . . light-truck sales set record

Ford rises in auto production, slips in sales

Corporate profits top GM for first time since 1924

Tax reform cuts rates

Central high-mount stoplamps required

CAFE standard cut to 26 mpg: Ford and GM claim 27.5 mpg would kill big cars

▲ Starting with its debut at the Chicago Auto Show in February 1985, millions gazed upon the daringly styled Taurus—but it didn't go on sale until December. A hot item from the start, the front-drive aero mid-size hit number six in domestic sales. New from the ground up, at a cost of some $3 billion, Taurus replaced the rear-drive LTD. The 0.32 drag coefficient ranked with the world's best.

▲ North American executive vice president Louis R. Ross (left) appears pleased with the new Taurus. Also satisfied was Robert A. Lutz (right), then chairman of Ford of Europe, but soon to move to Chrysler. He's standing beside the Merkur Scorpio, honored as "European Car of the Year 1986."

▲ Topping the Taurus sedan line was the LX, priced at $13,351. Riding a 106-inch wheelbase, the front-drive Taurus lineup included sedans and wagons in four series: L, MT5, GL, and LX. Early models all had a 140-bhp, 3.0-liter V-6 with four-speed automatic. Later came a 2.5-liter four.

▲ Taurus wagons like this LX had a unique rear silhouette, and held 81 cubic feet of cargo. Most sheetmetal differed from the related Mercury Sable. Billed as a "world class touring car," the MT5 sedan came with a five-speed manual gearbox, tachometer, and 88-bhp four-cylinder engine.

▲ Updated for 1985½ with an aero-style front end and bigger 1.9-liter engine, Escorts continued with minimal change. Powered by a 108-bhp hop-up of that four-cylinder mill, this sporty GT wore an asymmetrical grille, lower body cladding, and front/rear spoilers. Price tag: $8112.

▲ Handling was part of Escort's GT package, including a toughened suspension with rear stabilizer. At the bottom of the scale, a no-frills Pony tackled the low-priced imports. Escort production rose, enhancing its Number Two sales status. The 1.9-liter engine was rated 86 or 108 bhp.

▲ Thunderbird output rose a tad to 163,965. Base and elan editions carried a V-6 or optional 5.0-liter V-8, which added multi-point fuel injection and roller tappets.

▲ Just three T-Birds emerged: base, elan, and the hot Turbo Coupe. Turbo output jumped to 155 bhp with a five-speed (145 with automatic). Ford billed the Turbo as "ultimate Thunderbird for the driving enthusiast." The trendy Fila departed, but a sliding power moonroof was available.

▲ Sequential fuel injection and roller tappets helped give the full-size Ford's 5.0-liter V-8 150 horsepower. LTD Crown Victoria prices ranged from $12,188 for the fleet-oriented "S" sedan to $13,817 for an LX Country Squire wagon. Production plunged near 124,000, partly due to price hikes.

▲ For $1120 extra, the buyer of a basic LX coupe could get a 200-bhp 5.0-liter V-8 (now with sequential fuel injection) and upgraded suspension, ordinarily found in the Mustang GT hatchback or convertible. Mustangs enjoyed a whopping 43 percent increase in volume for '86.

▶ Not exactly low-budget at $14,523, a Mustang GT convertible offered plenty of "go" with its 200-bhp V-8, which cranked out 285 pounds/feet of torque. Both V-6 and V-8 engines adopted viscous engine mounts. This was the final year for the turbo-four SVO, with only 3382 built.

▲ After leaving the lineup early in the previous model year, a reworked EXP arrived as a 1986½ model, now sporting an aero-look front end.

▲ Luxury and Sport Coupe editions of the new EXP were sold, the latter with a 108-bhp HO version of the 1.9-liter engine and a firmer suspension.

288

▲ Modest restyling gave the compact Tempo a twin-slot front end with aero halogen headlamps, as well as new full-width taillights. GL and LX editions were offered. A driver's airbag cost $815 extra.

▲ Though viewed as family cars, a Tempo GL took on another personality with the addition of a Sport option, which added $934 to the $7358 price. Bigger (14-inch) tires were installed this year, with 15-inchers available.

▲ Four-door Tempos outsold their two-door mates by roughly three to one. Production slipped by 18 percent this year, to 277,671, but Tempos hung onto fifth spot in domestic sales. This GL sedan listed for $7508.

▲ One of the concept vehicles touring the auto-show circuit was this Ghia Vignale wagon, on a Tempo platform. A raised rear roof section slid forward to convert the wagon into a pickup of sorts, or it carried seven people.

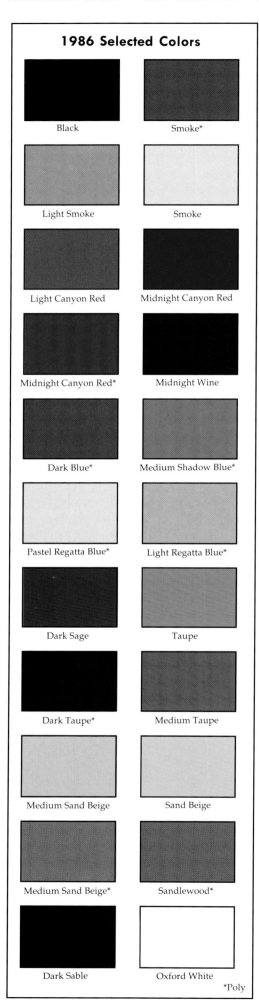

1986 Selected Colors

Black	Smoke*
Light Smoke	Smoke
Light Canyon Red	Midnight Canyon Red
Midnight Canyon Red*	Midnight Wine
Dark Blue*	Medium Shadow Blue*
Pastel Regatta Blue*	Light Regatta Blue*
Dark Sage	Taupe
Dark Taupe*	Medium Taupe
Medium Sand Beige	Sand Beige
Medium Sand Beige*	Sandlewood*
Dark Sable	Oxford White

*Poly

▲ Ford also exhibited a racy Cobra 230 ME at this year's auto shows, with a mid-mounted engine. Note the roof spoiler and single windshield wiper. Concept cars made a comeback in the 1980s, drawing crowds into manufacturers' display areas—people who just might stop at a Ford dealership afterward, for a quick spin in a production model. The Cobra tag no longer was used for Mustangs.

▲ Introduced in summer 1985, the unibody Aerostar amounted to a scaled-down traditional van with a slanted snout. Rear-drive like Chevy's Astro, it could tow more than front-drive Dodge/Plymouth mini-vans, rode a long 119-inch wheelbase, and weighed a hefty 3500 pounds. Passenger van prices began at $9064; a 115-bhp, 2.8-liter V-6 cost extra. At mid-year, that was replaced by a 3.0 V-6.

◄ Like their big F-Series brothers, Ranger pick-ups now came in SuperCab form on a 125-inch wheelbase, with a new fuel-injected 2.9-liter V-6. Ranger 4×4s could get "Touch Drive" for shifting into 4WD at the touch of a button.

▶ Little-changed full-size pickups came in F-150, F-250, and F-350 editions, starting at $8625. Customers could custom-tailor their trucks with a broad array of options. A two-wheel-drive Bronco II joined the truck lineup.

▲ Both Aerostars and Econolines came in cargo-hauling form. A Payload Package boosted the smaller van's capacity to 2000 pounds. Note the Aerostar's aero lines, against the squared Econoline—but not everyone took to the sloped front. Aerostars had all-coil suspension and four or V-6 power.

Model Breakdown Chart

Escort—wb 94.2

		Wght	Price	Prod
31/41P	Pony sdn 3d	2,159	6,052	
31	L sdn 3d	2,153	6,327	228,013
32	LX sdn 3d	2,238	7,234	
33	GT sdn 3d	2,364	8,112	
36	L sdn 5d	2,201	6,541	
37	LX sdn 5d	2,281	7,448	117,300
34	L wgn 5d	2,233	6,822	
35	LX wgn 5d	2,311	7,729	84,740

EXP—wb 94.2

		Wght	Price	Prod
01	cpe 3d	2,311	7,186	
01/931	Luxury cpe 3d	2,413	8,235	30,978

Tempo—wb 99.9

		Wght	Price	Prod
19	GL sdn 2d	2,339	7,358	
20	GLX sdn 2d	2,461	8,578	69,101
22	GL sdn 4d	2,398	7,508	
23	GLX sdn 4d	2,522	8,777	208,570

Taurus—wb 99.9

		Wght	Price	Prod
29	L sdn 4d, I-4/V-6	2,979	9,645	
29/934	MT5 sdn 4d, I-4	2,878	10,276	178,737
29/60D	GL sdn 4d, V-6	3,009	11,322	
29/60H	LX sdn 4d, V-6	3,109	13,351	
30	L wgn 5d, V-6	3,184	10,763	
30/934	MT5 wgn 5d, I-4	3,076	10,741	57,625
30/60D	GL wgn 5d, V-6	3,214	11,790	
30/60H	LX wgn 5d, V-6	3,306	13,860	

LTD—wb 105.6

		Wght	Price	Prod
39	sdn 4d, V-6	3,001	10,032	58,270
39/60H	Brougham sdn 4d, V-6	3,009	10,420	

		Wght	Price	Prod
40	wgn 5d, V-6	3,108	10,132	14,213

LTD Crown Victoria—wb 114.3

		Wght	Price	Prod
43	sdn 4d	3,748	12,562	
43/60H	LX sdn 4d	3,781	13,784	97,314
43/41K	S sdn 4d	3,715	12,188	
42	sdn 2d	3,708	13,022	
42/60H	LX sdn 2d	3,754	13,752	6,559
44	Country Squire wgn 5d, 2S	3,937	12,655	
44/60H	LX Country Squire wgn 5d, 2S	3,829	13,817	20,164
44/41E	wgn 5d, 2S	3,930	12,405	
44/41E	LX wgn 5d, 2S	3,821	13,567	
44/41K	S wgn 5d, 2S	3,921	12,468	

Mustang—wb 100.5

		Wght	Price	Prod
26	LX cpe 2d	2,795	7,189	
27	LX conv cpe, V-6	3,044	12,821	106,720
27	GT conv cpe, V-8	3,269	14,523	
28	LX htchbk cpe 3d	2,853	7,744	
28	GT htchbk cpe, V-8	3,139	10,691	117,690
28/937	SVO turbo htchbk cpe 3d	3,140	15,272	

Thunderbird—wb 104.0

		Wght	Price	Prod
46	cpe, V-6/V-8	3,182	11,020	
46	elan cpe, V-6/V-8	3,238	12,554	163,965
46	Turbo cpe, I-4T	3,172	14,143	

1986 Engine Availability

Engines	bore × stroke	bhp	availability
I-4, 113.5	3.23 × 3.46	86	S-Escort, EXP
I-4, 113.5	3.23 × 3.46	108	S-Escort GT; O-Escort
I-4D, 121.0	3.39 × 3.39	52	O-Escort, Tempo
I-4, 140.0	3.70 × 3.30	86	S-Tempo
I-4, 140.0	3.70 × 3.30	100	O-Tempo
I-4, 153.0	3.70 × 3.60	88	S-late Taurus
V-6, 182.0	3.50 × 3.15	140	S-Taurus LX, wgn; O-Taurus
V-6, 232.0	3.80 × 3.40	120	S-LTD
V-8, 302.0	4.00 × 3.00	150	S-Crown Vic
V-8, 351.0	4.00 × 3.50	180	S-Crown Vic (police only)
Mustang			
I-4, 140.0,	3.78 × 3.13	145/155	S-turbo cpe
I-4T, 140.0	3.78 × 3.13	200	S-SVO
V-6, 232.0	3.80 × 3.40	120	S-conv; O-all exc GT
V-8, 302.0	4.00 × 3.00	200	S-GT
Thunderbird			
I-4T, 140.0	3.78 × 3.13	88	S-all exc conv/GT
V-6, 232.0	3.80 × 3.40	120	S-all exc turbo cpe
V-8, 302.0	4.00 × 3.00	150	O-all exc turbo cpe

1987

Henry Ford II dies of pneumonia on September 29

Jack Telnack takes reins of Ford Design . . . "Fritz" Mayhew takes his spot

Ford profits hit record $4.63 billion—up 41 percent—to beat GM

Ford company's market share tops 20 percent

Performance is back, as gas prices stay low

Tempos get All-Wheel-Drive option

Thunderbird earns reskin; Mustang a major facelift

Anti-lock braking goes into Thunderbird Turbo Coupe

Motor Trend names T-Bird "Car of the Year," chairman Petersen "Man of the Year"

Don Petersen: top business leader in *Fortune* survey

Planned sixth-generation Mustang abandoned after protest—becomes '88 Probe instead

Passive restraints needed on 10 percent of cars

Taurus ranks as top-selling car—ahead of Escort

▲ Fully reskinned, though on the existing chassis, Thunderbirds looked even more aero-styled, wearing flush headlamps and side glass. Two front ends were created: a protruding grille-less nose between aero headlights on the $16,805 Turbo Coupe and a bright eggcrate grille on base and LX 'Birds.

▲ New luxury LX and Sport Thunderbirds took the place of the departed elan. Sport models mixed the 150-bhp, 5.0-liter V-8 with the Turbo Coupe's chassis, body, and interior. Turbo Coupes contained a pair of functional hood scoops, and added anti-lock all-disc brakes and Automatic Ride Control.

▲ Intercooling boosted the Thunderbird Turbo Coupe's engine to 190 bhp (150 with automatic). Unidirectional 16-inch tires were used.

▲ A base Thunderbird listed at only $12,972, while the sport coupe and the luxurious LX (shown here) edged past the $15,000 mark.

◀ Extensive facelifting gave Mustangs a fresh, smooth look, led by aero-style headlamps. Fans who didn't wish to flaunt the aggressive nature of their favorite ponycar could skip the mean-looking GT and elect a more restrained LX, with narrow twin-slot grille and Ford oval. Paying an extra $1885 above the LX's $8043 base price bought a 5.0-liter V-8 package, including the GT suspension. That meant 225-horsepower action and a brawny 300 pounds/feet of torque.

◀ A no-grille nose and a lower air dam with integrated fog lamps highlighted the reworked Mustang GT, looking tougher than ever. At the rear sat a deck spoiler and slotted "decorator" taillights. Tacked-on lower-body skirting contained fake ducts ahead of each wheel.

▼ All of the Mustang GT convertible's body trimmings sat low to the ground, imparting a squared-off look to the car's aero restyling. Aluminum wheels held fat 16-inch "Gatorback" rubber. Sticker-priced at $15,724, the GT ragtop cost $2884 more than an open LX, which came with a 90-bhp four or optional V-8. A V-8 ponycar could hit 60 mph in six seconds.

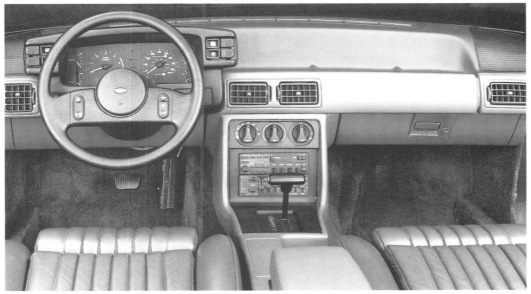

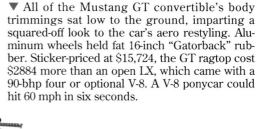

◀ All Mustangs gained a new instrument panel, which looked suspiciously similar to the one in the Mazda 626. No surprise, since Ford's tie with its Japanese cousin was tightening. A cutaway at the top created a parcel shelf and a feeling of spaciousness. An upright pod held rocker switches on each side, while temperature controls went on the drop-down console, with square vents across the upper rail. Mustang's four-cylinder engine finally turned to fuel injection, but the V-6 option disappeared.

293

▲ If a basic LTD Crown Victoria four-door seemed a trifle humdrum, a $665 Brougham Roof might add the requisite touch of class. Big Fords sold well, now with standard factory air.

▲ Biggest news for the compact Tempo was availability of an All-Wheel-Drive series. The part-time switch-on 4WD system was meant for use on slick pavement, not for off-road runs.

▲ Prices of the compact 4×4 Ranger pickup began at $10,124, but STX, XLT, or GT equipment and a Sport Appearance Group could add plenty to that total. A 2.9-liter V-6 was available.

▲ Topping the little-changed Taurus line were the LX sedan and wagon, which came with a 140-bhp, 3.0-liter V-6 and four-speed overdrive automatic. Taurus volume rose by 58 percent.

▲ A higher-output (94-bhp) version of the 2.3-liter four went into AWD Tempos, which rivaled 4WD imports. Base engines rated 86 bhp. Three-speed automatics were "fluidically linked."

▲ Rear anti-lock brakes became standard on the Bronco II sport-utility and Ranger pickups, which wore more galvanized body panels. Two-wheel drives added gas-pressurized shocks.

▲ Following its 1986½ revival as part of the Escort line, the two-seat EXP lured 5000 fewer buyers despite boosts in engine output.

▲ A high-output 115-bhp, 1.9-liter four went under the hood of the EXP Sport Coupe, while the Luxury Coupe made do with 90 horses.

▲ Ford's two-seater never quite captured the fancy of youthful customers. Both EXP engines were now fuel-injected: throttle-body on the base four, port injection on the Sport Coupe's 115-bhp high-output edition. The same powertrains were used in Escorts, which got motorized seatbelts.

1987 Engine Availability

Engines	bore × stroke	bhp	availability
I-4, 113.5	3.23 × 3.46	90	S-Escort, EXP
I-4, 113.5	3.23 × 3.46	115	S-Esc GT, EXP spt; O-Esc
I-4D, 121.0	3.39 × 3.39	58	O-Escort
I-4, 140.0	3.70 × 3.30	86	S-Tempo
I-4, 140.0	3.70 × 3.30	94	S-Tempo AWD; O-Tempo
I-4, 153.0	3.70 × 3.60	90	S-Taurus exc LX/wgn
V-6, 182.0	3.50 × 3.15	140	S-Taurus LX, wgn; O-Taurus
V-8, 302.0	4.00 × 3.00	150	S-Crown Vic
V-8, 351.0	4.00 × 3.50	180	S-Crown Vic (police only)

Mustang	bore × stroke	bhp	availability
I-4, 140.0	3.78 × 3.13	90	S-LX
V-8, 302.0	4.00 × 3.00	225	S-GT; O-LX
Thunderbird			
I-4T, 140.0	3.78 × 3.13	190	S-turbo cpe
I-4T, 140.0	3.78 × 3.13	150	S-turbo cpe (automatic)
V-6, 232.0	3.80 × 3.40	140	S-all exc turbo cpe
V-8, 302.0	4.00 × 3.00	150	O-all exc turbo cpe

▲ Passenger Aerostars now had a standard 3.0-liter V-6; cargo vans kept the four. Base price was $10,682. Optional seats turned into a bed.

▲ Aero styling was doing wonders for Ford cars, so full-size F-Series pickups got similar treatment, plus anti-lock rear brakes.

▲ Flush headlamps and rounded edges marked the restyled pickups. This F-150 SuperCab Styleside pickup wears XLT Lariat trim.

▲ Though a tad ungainly, extra doors made it easier to slide inside a full-size pickup. More than 550,000 F-Series trucks were sold.

▲ Three engines went into big Broncos: 4.9-liter six, 5.0 V-8, or 5.8 V-8. Aero-restyled, 4WD Broncos could have "Touch Drive."

▲ Tacking 20 inches onto an Econoline created this spacious E-250 Super Van. Vans didn't get the anti-lock rear brakes added to F-Series.

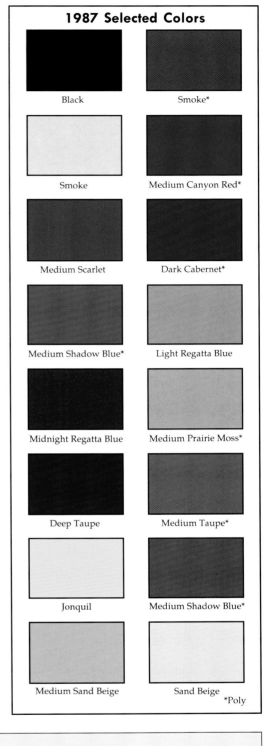

1987 Selected Colors

Black

Smoke*

Smoke

Medium Canyon Red*

Medium Scarlet

Dark Cabernet*

Medium Shadow Blue*

Light Regatta Blue

Midnight Regatta Blue

Medium Prairie Moss*

Deep Taupe

Medium Taupe*

Jonquil

Medium Shadow Blue*

Medium Sand Beige

Sand Beige

*Poly

Model Breakdown Chart

Escort—wb 94.2		Wght	Price	Prod
20	Pony sdn 3d	2,180	6,436	
21	GL sdn 3d	2,187	6,801	206,729
23	GT sdn 3d	2,516	8,724	
25	GL sdn 5d	2,222	7,022	102,187
28	GL wgn 5d	2,274	7,312	65,849

EXP—wb 94.2				
18	spt cpe 3d	2,388	8,831	25,888
17	Luxury cpe 3d	2,291	7,622	

Tempo—wb 99.9				
31	GL sdn 2d	2,462	8,043	
32	LX sdn 2d	2,562	9,238	
33	Spt GL sdn 2d	2,667	8,888	70,164
34	AWD (4WD) sdn 2d	2,667	9,984	
36	GL sdn 4d	2,515	8,198	
37	LX sdn 4d	2,617	9,444	
38	Spt GL sdn 4d	2,720	9,043	212,468
39	AWD (4WD) sdn 4d	2,720	10,138	

Taurus—wb 106.0		Wght	Price	Prod
50	L sdn 4d, I-4/V-6	2,982	10,491	
51	MT5 sdn 4d, I-4	2,886	11,966	278,562
52	GL sdn 4d, I-4/V-6	3,045	11,498	
53	LX sdn 4d, V-6	3,113	14,613	
55	L wgn 5d, V-6	3,186	11,722	
56	MT5 wgn 5d, I-4	3,083	12,534	
57	GL wgn 5d, V-6	3,242	12,688	96,201
58	LX wgn 5d, V-6	3,309	15,213	

LTD Crown Victoria—wb 114.3				
73	sdn 4d	3,741	14,355	
72	S sdn 4d	3,708	13,860	105,789
74	LX sdn 4d	3,788	15,454	
70	cpe 2d	3,724	14,727	
71	LX cpe 2d	3,735	15,421	5,527
78	Country Squire wgn 5d	3,920	14,507	
76	wgn 5d	3,920	14,235	*
75	S wgn 5d	3,894	14,228	

*See next column for total production figure for 78, 76, 75, 79, and 77.

		Wght	Price	Prod
79	LX Country Squire wgn 5d	4,000	15,723	17,562
77	LX wgn 5d	4,000	15,450	

Mustang—wb 100.5				
40	LX cpe 2d, I-4/V-8	2,862	8,043	
44	LX conv cpe, I-4/V-8	3,059	12,840	64,704*
45	GT conv cpe, V-8	3,214	15,724	
41	LX htchbk cpe 3d, I-4/V-8	2,920	8,474	94,441*
42	GT htchbk cpe, V-8	3,080	11,835	

Thunderbird—wb 104.2				
60	cpe, V-6/V-8	3,202	12,972	
61	spt cpe, V-8	3,346	15,079	128,135
62	LX cpe, V-6/V-8	3,245	15,383	
64	Turbo cpe, I-4T	3,380	16,805	

*Some industry sources state that 58,100 two-doors, 80,717 hatchbacks and 20,328 convertibles were built.

1988

100th Anniversary of the automobile celebrated

Edsel B. Ford II and William Clay Ford Jr. join board of directors

Ford's car share tops 21.5 percent—highest since 1979—to GM's 36 percent

Escort is top-selling car, Taurus third, Tempo fifth

Ford's $5.3 billion earnings top GM again

Ford buys 80 percent of Hertz Rent-a-Car

Ford leads in truck volume; grabs 30.7 percent of light-truck market

Passive restraints required on 25 percent of cars

▲ After reaching best-seller status in 1987, the mid-size Taurus returned with a more potent engine option. Formerly used only in rear-drive Fords, the 3.8-liter V-6 came only with four-speed automatic. Output was the same 140 horsepower as the 3.0 V-6, but the 3.8 yielded 55 more lbs/ft of torque. The MT5 wagon was dropped due to slow sales. Production rose to 387,577. This LX sedan sold for $15,295.

▲ Minor Mustang updating added little more than a stronger (540-amp) battery. A 5.0-liter V-8 package added $1885 to the LX hatchback's $9221 price, including upgraded suspension.

▲ With a V-8 under its hood, an LX Mustang could deliver performance comparable to a GT. This LX convertible has the 225-bhp, 5.0-liter V-8, but sold for $13,702 with a four.

▲ A four-cylinder Mustang LX coupe cost just $8726. A total of 211,225 ponycars were built.

▲ Subtle Euro-style facelift for 1988½ gave Escorts new front fenders, bodyside moldings, 14-inch wheels, and gas shocks. This $9093 GT wore an eggcrate grille below the bumper.

▲ Escort revisions were mainly at the back, with more rounded lines and new taillights. Bumpers were smoother and more integrated.

▲ An LX series replaced the prior GL Escort at mid-year, priced at $7127 for the three-door. The low-dollar Pony also returned, at $6747.

▲ In its second series, the Escort LX five-door wagon cost $8058. Only one model of the two-seat EXP remained for its final year.

▲ Reskinning gave compact Tempos more of a Taurus look. Both 2.3-liter engines added port fuel injection, now rated at 98 or 100 bhp.

▲ Introduced in May 1987 in the West, the Korean-built Festiva went national for '88. A carbureted 1.3-liter four developed 58 bhp.

▲ Tall and boxy, on a 90.2-inch wheelbase, the mini Festiva three-door was a Mazda design with Ford cues. Price: $5765 ($6868 in LX trim).

1988 Engine Availability

Engines	bore × stroke	bhp	availability
I-4, 113.5	3.23 × 3.46	90	S-Escort, EXP
I-4, 113.5	3.23 × 3.46	115	S-Escort GT
I-4, 140.0	3.70 × 3.30	98	S-Tempo
I-4, 140.0	3.70 × 3.30	100	S-Tempo AWD, GLS
I-4, 153.0	3.70 × 3.60	90	S-Taurus exc LX/wgn
V-6, 182.0	3.50 × 3.15	140	S-Taurus LX, wgn; O-Taurus
V-6, 232.0	3.80 × 3.40	140	O-Taurus
V-8, 302.0	4.00 × 3.00	150	S-Crown Vic
V-8, 351.0	4.00 × 3.50	180	S-Crown Vic (police only)

Mustang	bore × stroke	bhp	availability
I-4, 140.0	3.78 × 3.13	90	S-LX
V-8, 302.0	4.00 × 3.00	225	S-GT; O-LX
Thunderbird			
I-4T, 140.0	3.78 × 3.13	190	S-turbo cpe
I-4T, 140.0	3.78 × 3.13	150	S-turbo cpe (automatic)
V-6, 232.0	3.80 × 3.40	140	S-all exc turbo cpe
V-8, 302.0	4.00 × 3.00	155	S-Sport; O-all exc turbo cpe

▶ Multi-point fuel injection added 20 horse-power and 14 pounds/feet of torque to the Thunderbird V-6, and a balance shaft smoothed its running. The Sport V-8 got dual exhausts and a freshened interior, with analog gauges and articulated front seats. Optional on base and LX Birds, the V-8 was rated 155 bhp. Production rose by nearly 20,000, to 147,243.

▼ Woody-look Country Squire wagons continued to attract buyers. This $16,643 LX wears the LTD Crown Victoria's aero facelift, which included a new hood, grille, and bumpers in a rounded front end. Crown Vics added equipment, and options came in Rapid-Spec packages.

▲ Never a significant seller, the two-door sedan left the LTD Crown Victoria lineup. Big sedans got a new decklid and Oldsmobile-style taillights. This well-trimmed LX four-door with wrapover roof band sold for $16,134.

▲ An XLT package added at least $3437 to the $11,165 price of an Aerostar wagon. A $6233 Eddie Bauer option included a "convert-a-bed."

▲ Cruise control was part of the Bronco's $1409 XLT option. An Eddie Bauer edition added $3965. The base 4.9-liter six rated 150 bhp.

▲ New for the compact Bronco II sport-utility was an XL Sport package, which cost an extra $1213. A Mazda-built five-speed was standard.

▲ Trim and equipment were upgraded a bit in the F-150 XLT Lariat pickup, including interval wipers. Flareside bodies were out.

▲ Note the tandem wheels on this F-350 Lariat Crew Cab pickup, ready to haul 5270 pounds. Carburetors were gone from light trucks.

▲ A V-6 was standard in the Ranger STX 4×4 pickup. The Mazda-built five-speed manual had synchro reverse. Rangers started at $6793.

▲ Designed by Derek Millsap as part of a Ford-sponsored program for students, the five-seat Bronco DM-1 show car had a steel-reinforced fiberglass body with integral rollbar.

▲ Quite a few concept sport-utilities were created in the late 1980s, including this stylized Bronco DM-1. Virtually egg-shaped, the little 4×4 would have fit in at the beach or ski lodge, guided by a navigational system.

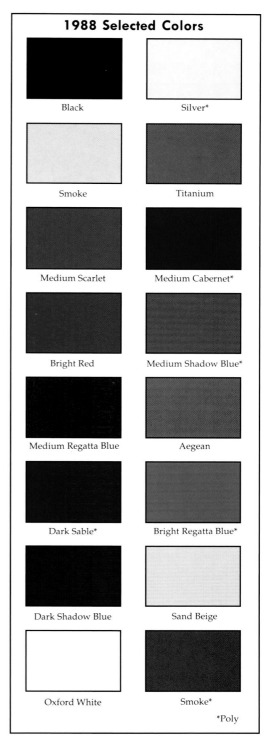

1988 Selected Colors

Black | Silver*
Smoke | Titanium
Medium Scarlet | Medium Cabernet*
Bright Red | Medium Shadow Blue*
Medium Regatta Blue | Aegean
Dark Sable* | Bright Regatta Blue*
Dark Shadow Blue | Sand Beige
Oxford White | Smoke*

*Poly

Model Breakdown Chart

	Escort—wb 94.2	Wght	Price	Prod
20	Pony sdn 3d	2,180	6,632	251,911*
21	GL sdn 3d	2,187	6,949	
23	GT sdn 3d	2,516	9,055	
25	GL sdn 5d	2,222	7,355	113,470**
28	GL wgn 5d	2,274	7,938	56,654**

	Escort Second Series 1988½—wb 94.2*	Wght	Price	Prod
90	Pony sdn 3d	—	6,747	—
91	LX sdn 3d	2,258	7,127	—
93	GT sdn 3d	—	9,093	—
95	LX sdn 5d	2,295	7,457	—
98	LX wgn 5d	2,307	8,058	—

	EXP—wb 94.2	Wght	Price	Prod
17	Luxury cpe 3d	2,291	8,037	—

	EXP Second Series 1988½—wb 94.2	Wght	Price	Prod
88	Luxury cpe 3d	2,359	8,201	—

	Tempo—wb 99.9	Wght	Price	Prod
31	GL sdn 2d	2,536	8,658	49,930
33	GLS sdn 2d	2,552	9,249	
36	GL sdn 4d	2,585	8,808	
37	LX sdn 4d	2,626	9,737	263,332
38	GLS sdn 4d	2,601	9,400	
39	AWD (4WD) sdn 4d	2,799	10,413	

	Taurus—wb 106.0	Wght	Price	Prod
50	L sdn 4d, I-4/V-6	3,005	11,699	
51	MT5 sdn 4d, I-4	2,882	12,835	
52	GL sdn 4d, I-4/V-6	3,049	12,200	294,576
53	LX sdn 4d, V-6	3,119	15,295	
55	L wgn 5d, V-6	3,182	12,884	
57	GL wgn 5d, V-6	3,215	13,380	93,001
58	LX wgn 5d, V-6	3,288	15,905	

	LTD Crown Victoria—wb 114.3	Wght	Price	Prod
73	sdn 4d	3,779	15,218	
72	S sdn 4d	3,742	14,653	110,249
74	LX sdn 4d	3,820	16,134	

		Wght	Price	Prod
78	Country Squire wgn 5d	3,998	15,613	
76	wgn 5d	3,991	15,180	
79	LX Country Squire wgn 5d	4,070	16,643	14,940
77	LX wgn 5d	3,972	16,210	

	Mustang—wb 100.5	Wght	Price	Prod
40	LX cpe 2d, I-4/V-8	2,894	8,726	71,890
44	LX conv cpe, I-4/V-8	3,081	13,702	33,344
45	GT conv cpe, V-8	3,341	16,610	
41	LX htchbk cpe 3d, I-4/V-8	2,961	9,221	74,331
42	GT htchbk cpe, V-8	3,193	12,745	

	Thunderbird—wb 104.2	Wght	Price	Prod
60	cpe, V-6/V-8	3,280	13,599	
61	Sport cpe, V-8	3,450	16,030	147,243
62	LX cpe, V-6/V-8	3,324	15,585	
64	Turbo cpe, I-4T	3,415	17,250	

*Incl. 1988½ and EXP   **Incl. 1988½

1989

All-new T-Bird named *Motor Trend* "Car of the Year"

Thunderbird SC and Taurus SHO push performance . . . front-drive Probe debuts

Total U.S. car sales dip below 9.9 million

William Clay Ford Sr. retires as vice-chairman—no Ford in top management

Edsel Ford II heads world corporate marketing

Ford buys Jaguar company

Ford profits skid 28 percent . . . car share edges up to 22.2 percent

Ford clings to Number One in truck sales

▲ After three seasons as a mid-size family hauler, the popular Taurus turned to performance. Beneath the hood of the new SHO sedan lurked a "Super High Output" 3.0-liter V-6 engine, developed and built by Yamaha, in Japan. A handful of ground-effects elements, and an air dam with fog lamps, warned that this was no tame Taurus, but one that could blast to 60 in eight seconds or less and hit 140 mph.

▲ Only a Mazda-built five-speed manual transaxle sent the Taurus SHO's 220 horses to the pavement; no automatics need apply. The SHO's $19,739 sticker was $4457 higher than a mid-level LX sedan, or $7961 above the base model. The stick shift-only MT5 was dropped.

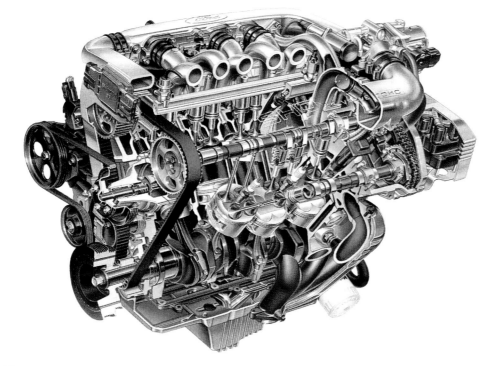

▲ Except for lettering molded into the back bumper and modest aero lower panels, the potent SHO didn't look much different from an ordinary Taurus. A handling suspension and all-disc brakes were installed. Inside were multi-adjustable front seats and analog guages.

◄ The twin-cam, 24-valve Taurus SHO engine developed 220 bhp at 6000 rpm, and 200 lbs/ft of torque. Six sequential injectors were used.

▲ Little change was evident in regular Taurus models except minor revisions to the grille, headlamps, taillamps, and door panels. Model-year production edged up a bit to 395,261. This LX wagon listed for $16,524.

▲ Ordinary Taurus sedans, like this $15,282 LX, outsold the hot SHO by far. The regular LX V-6 produced 140 bhp. Ford planned to build at least 20,000 SHOs in this first year, but only about 12,000 went to dealers.

▲ Redesigned atop the same rear-drive layout as before, the 11th-generation Thunderbird wore a smooth new body: 3.4 inches shorter and nearly an inch lower. Wheelbase was stretched 8.8 inches, to 113. "Thunderbird SC" molded into the bumper means this is the hot one, with a supercharged V-6.

▲ Independent rear suspension was new to Thunderbirds. Speed-sensitive power steering was standard. This mid-range LX sold for $16,817, while a base 'Bird stickered at $14,612. The 140-bhp V-6 came only with automatic. Turbo and V-8 engines were gone.

◄ The T-Bird Super Coupe's blown 3.8-liter V-6 cranked out 210 bhp and 315 lbs/ft of torque (100 lbs more than a regular V-6). Included in the $19,823 price: a handling suspension, anti-lock all-disc brakes, articulated sport seats, and variable shock damping. Despite increased weight, an SC could zip to 60 in 7.1 seconds with five-speed shift, or 7.8 with automatic.

301

▲ Performance fans had a little-changed Mustang GT to tempt them, its 5.0-liter V-8 whipping out 225 bhp and 300 lbs/ft of torque. For $13,272, the GT hatchback included a heavy-duty suspension, Traction-Lok axle, 225/60VR-15 tires, power windows and locks, and a handy driver's foot rest.

▲ Bold colors attracted more attention than some Mustangers wanted. Formerly standard, bodyside molding inserts were now a GT option.

▲ Ordering an LX 5.0L Sport Mustang coupe brought V-8 "go" without the GT's rather gaudy styling. Not too many took the 90-bhp four.

▲ "Nothing else delivers so much bang for so few bucks," declared CONSUMER GUIDE™ of the Mustang GT.

▼ Both LX and GT Mustang convertibles now had multi-adjustable, articulated sport seats. Standard fittings included a five-speed manual gearbox, power brakes and steering, tinted glass, remote mirrors, and full instrumentation including a tachometer. Production dropped slightly this year, to 209,769 Mustangs. Development of a sixth-generation Mustang already was confirmed, but was not destined to happen until the mid-1990s. Meanwhile, Ford had a new front-drive sporty Probe coupe on the market.

▲ Instead of a V-8 engine option, the "LX 5.0L Sport" Mustang was a series of three body styles, including this $17,001 convertible.

▲ Just $14,140 bought an open LX Mustang with a 2.3-liter four-cylinder engine—but it had a hard time pushing close to 3000 pounds.

▲ Prior to its May 1988 debut, Ford planned the swoopy front-drive Probe as a Mustang replacement—until rear-drive fans balked. Probe and related Mazda MX-6 were built at Flat Rock, Michigan, with similar drivetrains.

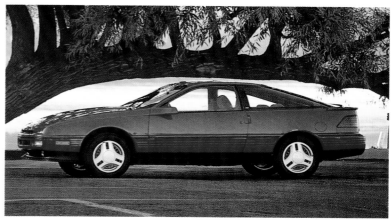

▲ Sporty Probe GTs wore an air slot above the front bumper, a spoiler out back, and lower-body cladding. Power came from an intercooled turbo 2.2-liter four, rated at 145 bhp. Driver-variable shock damping was standard.

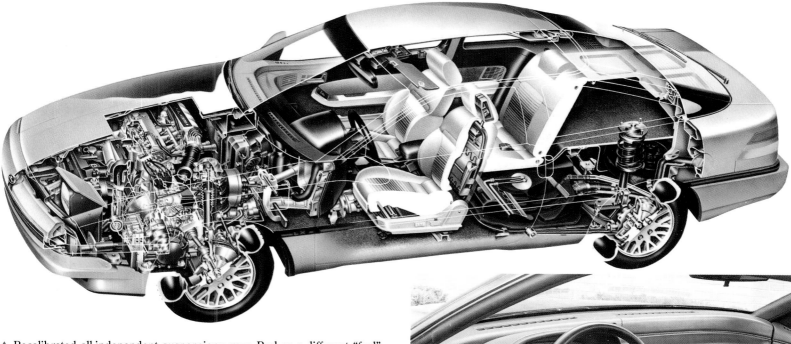

▲ Recalibrated all-independent suspensions gave Probes a different "feel" than their MX-6 kin. Base engine was a 110-bhp, 2.2-liter (12-valve) four.

▶ In the cozy 2+2 cockpit of a Probe LX and GT, the instrument pod moved in concert with the tilt wheel. A GT could accelerate to 60 mph in less than seven seconds. More than 211,000 Probes were sold by the end of 1989.

1989 Engine Availability

Engines	bore × stroke	bhp	availability
I-4, 113.5	3.23 × 3.46	90	S-Escort
I-4, 113.5	3.23 × 3.46	115	S-Escort GT
I-4, 133.0	3.39 × 3.70	110	S-Probe GL/LX
I-4T, 133.0	3.39 × 3.70	145	S-Probe GT
I-4, 140.0	3.70 × 3.30	98	S-Tempo
I-4, 140.0	3.70 × 3.30	100	S-Tempo AWD, GLS
I-4, 153.0	3.70 × 3.60	90	S-Taurus exc LX/wgn
V-6, 182.0	3.50 × 3.15	140	S-Taur LX sdn, wgn; O-Taur
V-6, 182.0	3.50 × 3.15	220	S-Taurus SHO
V-6, 232.0	3.80 × 3.40	140	S-Taurus LX wgn; O-Taurus
V-8, 302.0	4.00 × 3.00	150	S-Crown Vic
V-8, 351.0	4.00 × 3.50	180	S-Crown Vic (police only)

Mustang	bore × stroke	bhp	availability
I-4, 140.0	3.78 × 3.13	90	S-LX
V-8, 302.0	4.00 × 3.00	225	S-GT; O-LX
Thunderbird			
V-6, 232.0	3.80 × 3.40	140	S-Base/LX
V-6, 232.0	3.80 × 3.40	210	S-Super Cpe (superchgd)

▶ Full-size Fords, like this $16,767 LTD Crown Victoria LX sedan, saw little change beyond replacing the low-oil warning with a "check engine" indicator. Six Crown Vic models made the lineup. Model-year production rose to 134,103, all of them built in Canada. At the other end of the size spectrum, Korean-built Festivas could have an automatic transmission.

▲ F-Series pickups, including this Styleside 4×4, showed only detail trim revisions. Some models got an electronically controlled automatic.

▲ Ranger compact pickups were restyled to look more like this full-size F-150, with a larger 2.3-liter (100-bhp) base engine and GT or STX options.

▲ Revised front-end styling gave Bronco IIs an aero look—closer to the big Bronco. Changes included new fenders, hood, grille, front bumper, and integrated aero headlights/turn signals. Sales fell to just below 109,000.

▲ Borrowing an idea from the old "SuperWagon," Aerostars now came in regular or extended-body form, with 15.4 extra inches tacked onto the rear for added cargo space. All models wore a new grille and front bumper.

▼ The Econoline E-250 XL Super Van rode a 138-inch wheelbase and the rear of the van was stretched 20 inches (overall length 227).

▲ An Eddie Bauer package added $6503 to the Aerostar's $11,567 starting price, including such extras as two-tone paint, captain's chairs, tach, and swing-away spare tire. A new XL Sport Wagon wore lower-body cladding.

▲ Front captain's chairs were part of the XLT package available for Club Wagons, all on a 138-inch wheelbase. Electronic four-speed automatic was available for heavy-duty models, with an on-off button for overdrive.

Model Breakdown Chart

Escort—wb 94.2		Wght	Price	Prod
90	Pony sdn 3d	2,235	6,964	
91	LX sdn 3d	2,242	7,349	
93	GT sdn 3d	2,442	9,315	363,122
95	LX sdn 5d	2,313	7,679	
98	LX wgn 5d	2,312	8,280	
Probe—wb 99.0				
20	GL htchbk 3d	2,715	10,660	
21	LX htchbk 3d	2,715	11,644	133,650*
22	GT htchbk 3d	2,870	13,794	
Tempo—wb 99.9				
31	GL sdn 2d	2,529	9,057	
33	GLS sdn 2d	2,545	9,697	
36	GL sdn 4d	2,587	9,207	292,978
37	LX sdn 4d	2,628	10,156	
38	GLS sdn 4d	2,603	9,848	

		Wght	Price	Prod
39	AWD (4WD) sdn 4d	2,787	10,860	**
Taurus—wb 106.0				
50	L sdn 4d, I-4/V-6	3,001	11,778	
52	GL sdn 4d, I-4/V-6	3,046	12,202	
53	LX sdn 4d, V-6	3,076	15,282	
—	SHO sdn 4d, V-6	3,078	19,739	395,261
55	L wgn 5d, V-6	3,172	13,143	
57	GL wgn 5d, V-6	3,189	13,544	
58	LX wgn 5d, V-6	3,220	16,524	
LTD Crown Victoria—wb 114.3				
73	sdn 4d	3,730	15,851	
74	LX sdn 4d	3,770	16,767	
78	Country Squire wgn 5d	3,935	16,527	
76	wgn 5d	3,941	16,209	134,103
79	LX Country Squire wgn 5d	4,013	17,556	
77	LX wgn 5d	3,915	17,238	

Mustang—wb 100.5		Wght	Price	Prod
40	LX cpe 2d, I-4	2,754	9,050	
40	LX 5.0L spt cpe 2d, V-8	3,045	11,410	
44	LX conv cpe, I-4	2,966	14,140	
44	LX 5.0L conv cpe, V-8	3,257	17,001	
45	GT conv cpe, V-8	3,333	17,512	209,769
41	LX htchbk cpe 3d, I-4	2,819	9,556	
41	LX 5.0L spt htchbk 3d, V-8	3,110	12,265	
42	GT htchbk cpe, V-8	3,194	13,272	
Thunderbird—wb 113.0				
—	cpe, V-6	3,542	14,612	
—	LX cpe, V-6	3,554	16,817	114,868
—	Super Cpe, V-6	3,701	19,823	

*Calendar-year sales
**Production for 39 included in total for 31, 33, 36, 37, and 38 in previous column.
Note: Full-size (Crown Victoria) station wagons in the 1980s could have an optional dual-facing rear seat.

1990

Donald E. Petersen retires as chairman; replaced by Harold "Red" Poling

Philip E. Benton Jr. named company president; Allan Gilmour president of Ford Automotive Group

Ford company assets top $5.7 billion

Probe adds V-6 engine . . . anti-lock braking offered in Taurus and Probe

Taurus second in sales, Escort fourth

Ranger ranks Number One in small pickups

Bronco II and new Explorer lead sport-utility sales

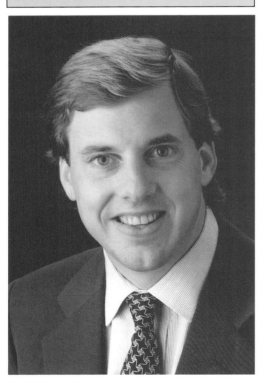

▲ William Clay Ford Jr. directed business strategy for the Ford Automotive Group. He and cousin Edsel—now executive head of corporate marketing—also served on Ford's board.

306

▲ Ford's Michigan-built, Japanese/American Probe GT again was powered by a turbocharged 145-bhp, 2.2-liter four, but now an automatic transaxle was available. Instead of the Mazda four, this year's mid-level Probe LX got a 140-bhp, 3.0-liter Taurus V-6 for added mid-range oomph, plus all-disc brakes.

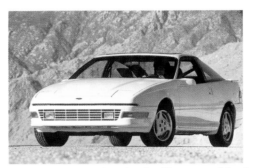

▲ All Probes had revised taillamps and body-color, below-the-bumper grilles: eggcrate style with fog lamps on the GT, fine mesh on others.

▲ An automatic-adjusting suspension helped enhance Probe GT performance, while lumbar adjustment kept the front passenger comfortable.

▲ All Probes could now get leather seat trim, while the LX had a "soft-feel" steering wheel. Sales slumped after an impressive debut.

▲ Anti-lock braking was optional on the $13,008 Probe LX. A Probe GL with 110-bhp four cost $11,470, while the GT listed at $14,726.

▲ A new Escort was expected later in the model year, so carryover models changed little except for the addition of rear shoulder belts. Base price of the LX three-door was $7806.

▲ All three Mustang body styles were available in the LX 5.0L Sport series, which included a 225-bhp V-8 engine. Base LX models kept the 88-bhp four. Mustangs added a driver's airbag and rear shoulder belts.

▲ Ordering an LX 5.0L Sport Mustang hatchback with V-8 power meant paying $3045 more than the price of a four-cylinder. Leather trim was available with the V-8, as were clearcoat paint and a Power Equipment Group.

▲ A Mustang GT convertible sold for $622 more than a 5.0 LX. The Silver Anniversary Mustang introduced at the Chicago Auto Show was just a V-8 LX convertible with emerald-green metallic paint and a white interior.

▲ Base-priced at $13,986, the Mustang GT hatchback relied on aero-look add-ons to give it a bolder look than the equivalent LX 5.0L Sport. All models added map pockets, but interiors no longer held a tilt wheel.

▲ Mini Festivas adopted a Taurus-like front end, with a new five-speed gearbox and 63-bhp engine. Power steering was now available.

▲ Bolder-looking than ever, this restyled Escort GT debuted in spring 1990 as an early '91 model, with a 127-horsepower engine.

▲ Until the arrival of all-new '91 models, Escorts carried on with minimal change and a 90-bhp engine. The LX wagon listed for $8737.

▲ Still attracting a sizable share of customers, the compact Tempo added footwell and trunk lights, floormats, and restyled wheels.

▲ All-new for '89, the Thunderbird coupe could get new Power Equipment and Luxury groups. An LX started at $17,283, with 140-bhp V-6.

▲ Super Coupes drew plenty of publicity for the rear-drive Thunderbird, though not every buyer needed its 210-bhp supercharged engine.

▲ Fender badges and special emblems marked the "Anniversary Thunderbird," which turned out to be less startling than some fans expected.

◄ To honor T-Bird's 35th anniversary, Ford issued 5000 commemorative editions, based on the Super Coupe. Each had black over "titanium" paint, blue striping, and black wheels.

▲ Safety led the Taurus changes, with a new driver's airbag in a tilt wheel, and an anti-lock braking option for sedans. This $16,180 LX could get speed-sensitive power steering.

▲ Taurus wagons came in L, GL, or LX trim, with 3.0- or 3.8-liter V-6 engines. A revised instrument panel contained cup and coin holders. Optional: a CD player and tachometer.

▲ Anti-lock braking, a handling suspension, and five-speed gearshift enhanced the Taurus SHO's highly praised road skills. The Yamaha 220-bhp dual-overhead-cam V-6 had dual exhausts.

1990 Engine Availability

Engines	bore × stroke	bhp	availability
I-4, 113.5	3.23 × 3.46	90	S-Escort
I-4, 113.5	3.23 × 3.46	115	S-Escort GT
I-4, 133.0	3.39 × 3.70	110	S-Probe GL
I-4T, 133.0	3.39 × 3.70	145	S-Probe GT
I-4, 140.0	3.78 × 3.13	88	S-Mustang LX
I-4, 140.0	3.70 × 3.30	98	S-Tempo
I-4, 140.0	3.70 × 3.30	100	S-Tempo AWD, GLS
I-4, 153.0	3.70 × 3.60	90	S-Taurus exc LX/wgn
V-6, 182.0	3.50 × 3.15	140	S-Probe LX; Taurus LX sdn, wgn; O-Taurus
V-6, 182.0	3.50 × 3.15	220	S-Taurus SHO
V-6, 232.0	3.80 × 3.40	140	S-Taurus LX wgn, TBird; O-Taurus
V-6, 232.0	3.80 × 3.40	210	S-TBird Super Cpe (supercharged)
V-8, 302.0	4.00 × 3.00	150	S-Crown Vic
V-8, 302.0	4.00 × 3.00	225	S-Mustang GT, LX 5.0L

► Ford displayed its new Service Bay Diagnostic System, intended to help the technician "fix a vehicle right the first time," at the dealers' convention in early 1990. Dealers would begin installing the system in '91.

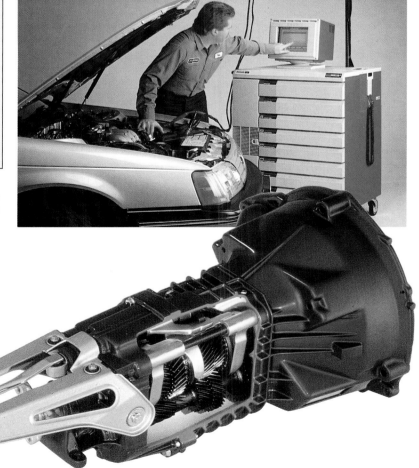

► Mustangs and Thunderbird Super Coupes offered this 5-speed overdrive manual transmission. The SHO was the only Taurus to offer a 5-speed; all others came with automatic. Meanwhile, the LTD Crown Victoria added a driver-side air bag.

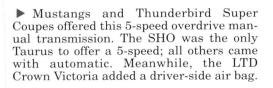

▲ A technician working on this F-150 pickup could use its modified engine electronics to get diagnostic data. Prices began at $10,249.

▲ Electronics shifted the optional automatic for the Bronco's 4.9-liter six and 5.8 V-8. An Eddie Bauer option added $3556 to the price.

▲ Ranger STX and XLT 4×4 pickups could have a larger 155-bhp, 4.0-liter V-6, ranking as the most powerful engine ever in a Ford compact.

▲ For its final season, the Bronco II sport-utility changed little. Price was $13,001 with a 2.9-liter V-6 ($14,704 for 4WD).

▲ Full-time four-wheel-drive became available in Aerostar vans and wagons, with a larger (4.0-liter) V-6 and anti-lock rear brakes.

▲ A bigger Explorer sport-utility debuted in spring 1990 as a '91 model. Unlike the Bronco II, it came with either two or four doors.

Model Breakdown Chart

	Escort—wb 94.2	Wght	Price	Prod
90	Pony sdn 3d	2,242	7,402	
91	LX sdn 3d	2,249	7,806	
93	GT sdn 3d	2,427	9,844	196,310
95	LX sdn 5d	2,310	8,136	
98	LX wgn 5d	2,313	8,737	

	Probe—wb 99.0			
20	GL htchbk 3d	2,730	11,470	
21	LX htchbk 3d	2,970	13,008	109,898
22	GT htchbk 3d turbo	3,000	14,726	

	Tempo—wb 99.9			
31	GL sdn 2d	2,529	9,483	
33	GLS sdn 2d	2,545	10,300	
36	GL sdn 4d	2,587	9,633	265,893
37	LX sdn 4d	2,628	10,605	
38	GLS sdn 4d	2,603	10,448	
39	AWD (4WD) sdn 4d	2,808	11,331	

	Taurus—wb 106.0			
50	L sdn 4d, I-4/V-6	2,956	12,640	
52	GL sdn 4d, I-4/V-6	2,979	13,113	
53	LX sdn 4d, V-6	3,125	16,180	
54	SHO sdn 4d, V-6	3,533	21,633	333,001
55	L wgn 5d, V-6	3,244	14,272	
57	GL wgn 5d, V-6	3,258	14,722	
58	LX wgn 5d, V-6	3,285	17,771	

	LTD Crown Victoria—wb 114.3			
73	sdn 4d	3,821	17,257	
74	LX sdn 4d	3,861	17,894	
76	wgn 5d	3,978	17,668	
77	LX wgn 5d	3,952	18,418	121,591
78	Country Squire wgn 5d	3,972	17,921	
79	LX Country Squire wgn 5d	4,050	18,671	

	Mustang—wb 100.5			
40	LX cpe 2d, I-4	2,759	9,456	
40	LX Sport cpe 2d, V-8	3,037	12,164	
41	LX htchbk cpe 3d, I-4	2,824	9,962	
41	LX Sport htchbk 3d, V-8	3,102	13,007	
44	LX conv cpe, I-4	2,960	15,141	128,189
44	LX Sport conv cpe, V-8	3,238	18,183	
42	GT htchbk cpe, V-8	3,191	13,986	
45	GT conv cpe, V-8	3,327	18,805	

	Thunderbird—wb 113.0			
60	Coupe 2d	3,581	14,980	
62	LX cpe 2d	3,618	17,283	113,957
64	Super cpe 2d	3,809	20,390	

1990 Selected Colors

Medium Bisque*   Bisque Frost*   Race Yellow   Pastel Alabaster

Alabaster Solid   Medium Woodrose*   Woodrose*   Currant Red Solid*

Midnight Currant Red*   Electric Currant Red*   Medium Cabernet Solid   Wild Strawberry*

Medium Sandalwood*   Sandalwood Frost*   Bright Currant Red*   Medium Red Solid

Vermillion Solid   Crystal Blue*   Light Crystal Blue*   Clear Crystal Blue Frost*

Medium Regatta Blue*   Spinnaker Blue Solid   Twilight Blue   Ultra Blue*

*Poly

1991

All-new Escort debuts as early '91 . . . Explorer takes over from Bronco II

Thunderbird V-8 revived

Ford Division leads in total sales—1,081,290 cars and 1,263,324 trucks—in weak year for industry

Half of top 10 models are Fords, yet company loses record $2.3 billion

Ford ranks first in trucks for sixth straight year . . . F-Series is top-selling vehicle for 10th year

Big Bronco gets Silver Anniversary Package

Service Bay Diagnostics available to dealers

▲ Supercharging again was the main feature of the Thunderbird Super Coupe, whose V-6 engine eked out 210 horsepower and 315 lbs/ft of torque. A five-speed manual transmission was standard; four-speed automatic $595 extra. Though hefty, an SC was agile and capable—and once again had a V-8 companion.

◄ After two years on the side-lines, a 5.0-liter V-8 option rejoined base and LX T-Birds. Tighter exhaust limited output to 200 bhp (25 less than in a Mustang) and 275 lbs/ft of torque. Though not quite neck-snapping, pickup with a V-8 Bird was swift enough—worth $1080 extra to quite a few buyers.

▲ Whether in base or LX trim, the '91 Thunderbird offered a solid "feel" and modern look. A sport instrument cluster on the $17,334 LX replaced the prior electronic setup (now optional). Seat trim was revised on all models. Automatic temperature control and a maintenance monitor were optional.

▲ Styled by Ford, the new Escort rode a Mazda platform with 98.4-inch wheelbase. The fuel-injected 1.9-liter four yielded 88 horsepower.

▲ An LX Escort wagon listed for $9680, with a five-speed gearbox; automatic optional. A low-profile dashboard held analog gauges.

▲ Mazda's 127-bhp, 1.8-liter twin-cam four, with port injection, powered the latest Escort GT, which could now have automatic. Bold GTs had an asymmetrical grille and hatch spoiler.

◀ "Transplant" Probes, built in Michigan but Mazda-based, came with the same three engines: 110-bhp four in the GL; 145-bhp, 3.0-liter V-6 in the LX; turbo four in the aggressive-look GT shown here. LX and GT coupes had all-disc brakes with optional ABS. Not the hottest sellers, Probes rated high in customer surveys.

▲ New 16-inch alloy wheels sent the Mustang GT's 225-horsepower muscle to the pavement. A new convertible top folded closer to the body.

▲ Note the roll-style headrests in the Mustang GT interior. LX 5.0L notchbacks now had articulated front seats like the hatchback.

▲ Subtler than a GT, the Mustang LX 5.0L had just as much go-power. Output for four-cylinder models jumped from 88 to 105 bhp.

1991 Engine Availability

Engines	bore × stroke	bhp	availability
I-4, 113.5	3.23 × 3.46	88	S-Escort
I-4, 109.0	3.27 × 3.35	127	S-Escort GT
I-4, 133.0	3.39 × 3.70	110	S-Probe GL
I-4T, 133.0	3.39 × 3.70	145	S-Probe GT
I-4, 140.0	3.78 × 3.13	105	S-Mustang LX
I-4, 140.0	3.70 × 3.30	98	S-Tempo
I-4, 140.0	3.70 × 3.30	100	S-Tempo AWD, GLS
I-4, 153.0	3.70 × 3.60	105	S-Taurus

Engines	bore × stroke	bhp	availability
V-6, 182.0	3.50 × 3.15	140/145	S-Probe LX; Taurus LX sdn, wgn; O-Taurus
V-6, 182.0	3.50 × 3.15	220	S-Taurus SHO
V-6, 232.0	3.80 × 3.40	140	S-Taurus LX wgn, TBird; O-Taurus
V-6, 232.0	3.80 × 3.40	210	S-TBird Super Cpe (supercharged)
V-8, 302.0	4.00 × 3.00	150	S-Crown Vic
V-8, 302.0	4.00 × 3.00	200	O-Thunderbird
V-8, 302.0	4.00 × 3.00	225	S-Mustang GT, LX 5.0L

▶ Far more refined than most muscle machines, the Taurus SHO, with its 220-bhp Yamaha V-6, wore new wheels and tires. A new four-speed automatic with electronically controlled shifting went into other Taurus models, sold in three trim levels with a 3.0- or 3.8-liter V-6. Sequential fuel injection boosted the L sedan's four to 105 bhp. Wagons could now get ABS.

▲ F-Series trucks could have an electronic four-speed transmission. Automatic locking hubs became standard on late 4WD F-250/350s. The in-box spare tire carrier was gone.

▲ The Explorer Sport included privacy glass, leather-wrapped steering wheel, and alloy wheels. Touch Drive was standard on 4×4s. Top-of-the-line: a $21,315 Eddie Bauer four-door.

▲ Ford's F-150 Nite "street machine" was dressed in black with subtle striping and deep-dish aluminum wheels. The 185-bhp, 5.0-liter or 210-bhp, 5.8-liter V-8 had "ample power."

▲ Smoother in style, more civilized than the Bronco II, the new Explorer had flush glass and came with two or four doors. Added weight made a 4.0-liter V-6 necessary, with 155 bhp.

▲ Ranger pickups, including this XLT Super-Cab, often had a 4.0-liter V-6; but a 145-bhp, 3.0-liter V-6 was a new option on 2WDs. A new Ranger Sport had unique bold tape striping.

▲ A Sport Appearance package, with graduated silver tape stripes and aluminum wheels, gave the F-150 pickup a rugged look. The option also added a black bar with off-road lamps.

▶ Aerostars needed little change to keep drawing buyers. Passenger wagons seated five or seven. A 3.0-liter V-6 was standard with 2WD, 4.0 V-6 with 4WD. Prices began at $13,131.

▲ This was the last outing for the boxy LTD Crown Victoria, on its long-lived rear-drive platform with 150-bhp V-8. Clearcoat paint was standard, but two-tones were out. Big rear-drive wagons were about to bite the dust.

Model Breakdown Chart

Escort—wb 98.4

		Wght	Price	Prod
10	Pony sdn 3d	2,287	7,976	
11	LX sdn 3d	2,312	8,667	
12	GT sdn 3d	2,458	11,484	304,127
14	LX sdn 5d	2,355	9,095	
15	LX wgn 5d	2,411	9,680	

Probe—wb 99.0

		Wght	Price	Prod
20	GL htchbk 3d	2,730	11,691	
21	LX htchbk 3d, V-6	2,970	13,229	93,814
22	GT htchbk 3d turbo	3,000	14,964	

Tempo—wb 99.9

		Wght	Price	Prod
30	L sdn 2d	—	8,306	
31	GL sdn 2d	2,529	9,541	
33	GLS sdn 2d	2,545	10,358	
35	L sdn 4d	—	8,449	
36	GL sdn 4d	2,587	9,691	218,197
37	LX sdn 4d	2,628	10,663	
38	GLS sdn 4d	2,603	10,506	
39	AWD (4WD) sdn 4d	2,808	11,390	

Taurus—wb 106.0

		Wght	Price	Prod
50	L sdn 4d, I-4/V-6	3,049	13,352	
52	GL sdn 4d, I-4/V-6	3,062	13,582	
53	LX sdn 4d, V-6	3,170	17,373	
54	SHO sdn 4d, V-6	3,463	22,071	302,577
55	L wgn 5d, V-6	3,276	14,784	
57	GL wgn 5d, V-6	3,283	14,990	
58	LX wgn 5d, V-6	3,345	18,963	

LTD Crown Victoria—wb 114.3

		Wght	Price	Prod
73	sdn 4d	3,822	18,227	
74	LX sdn 4d	3,841	18,863	
76	wgn 5d	4,028	18,083	
77	LX wgn 5d	4,021	18,833	85,532
78	Country Squire wgn 5d	4,047	18,335	
79	LX Country Squire wgn 5d	4,082	19,085	

Mustang—wb 100.5

		Wght	Price	Prod
40	LX cpe 2d, I-4	2,759	10,157	
40	LX 5.0L cpe 2d, V-8	3,037	13,270	
41	LX htchbk cpe 3d, I-4	2,824	10,663	
41	LX 5.0L 3d, V-8	3,102	14,055	
44	LX conv cpe, I-4	2,960	16,222	98,737
44	LX 5.0L conv cpe, V-8	3,238	19,242	
42	GT htchbk cpe, V-8	3,191	15,034	
45	GT conv cpe, V-8	3,327	19,864	

Thunderbird—wb 113.0

		Wght	Price	Prod
60	Coupe 2d, V-6/V-8	3,550	15,318	
62	LX cpe 2d, V-6/V-8	3,572	17,334	82,814
64	Super Coupe 2d	3,767	20,999	

▲ Available on regular-length Aerostar XL and XLT passenger models for $1285, the Sports Appearance package added silver-color accents, integral running boards, and aluminum wheels.

▲ Engines up to 7.5-liter size gave Club Wagons plenty of towing capacity. An inline six was standard. The short-wheelbase E-150 was dropped, and clearcoat paint became optional.

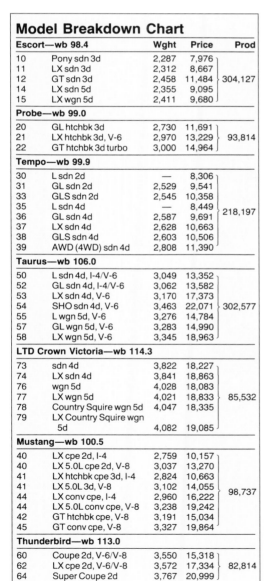

◀ Lincoln's Town Car was the first to receive Ford's new 4.6-liter overhead-cam V-8 engine. For its early '92 rounded restyling, however, the LTD Crown Victoria also would earn this modern 190-horsepower engine.

313

1992

Modernized Crown Victoria debuts, including Touring Sedan and police option

Passenger airbags available in Taurus and Crown Victoria

Tempos get V-6 option

Four-door sedan joins Escort line

Taurus drops four-cylinder engine choice

Econolines and Club Wagons restyled . . . F-Series facelifted up front

"One-price" sales program for Escort, T-Bird launched

Ford invests $1.2 billion to develop high-tech V-6

▲ Although the production version of the new Crown Victoria wasn't quite this slick and slippery, its basic shape is evident in this rendering. Despite the emergence of new full-size, rear-drive station wagons from GM, Ford planned no wagon version of the new Crown Vic. No longer using the "LTD" prefix, the '92 version rode a platform similar to its predecessor but looked far different at skin level.

▲ A restyled '92 Crown Victoria appeared in March 1991, joined in the fall by a Touring Sedan. Dual exhausts helped boost output of the 4.6-liter overhead-cam V-8 (automatic only) from the usual 190 to 210. The tourer also featured anti-lock braking, traction control, and a sport suspension.

▶ An inviting interior helped attract buyers to the Crown Victoria Touring Sedan. Not only was a driver's airbag standard in all three Crown Vic sedans, but a passenger airbag was optional. Also available: electronic gauges.

▼ During 1992, Ford launched a police package for its revamped Crown Victoria, including the 210-bhp V-8, calibrated 140-mph speedometer, and a host of toughened parts. Simulated ebony appliqués and special embossing decorated the Touring Sedan's door panel (right below).

▲ A four-door sedan joined the Escort line. The LX-E version carried the same 127-bhp, twin-cam four as the GT, plus all-disc brakes.

▲ Four-door Tempos wore new taillamps at the rear of a new monotone exterior. Four-wheel-drive models faded away due to weak sales.

▲ A 135-bhp, 3.0-liter V-6 went into the Tempo GLS, with its new sport suspension. Six-cylinder Tempos included a rear stabilizer.

◄ Subtly restyled Taurus sedans and wagons wore all-new sheetmetal (except doors), but didn't change dramatically. The potent but gentlemanly SHO (shown) got unique front-end styling for the first time. The modified Taurus dashboard had provision for a passenger airbag. Electronic gauges no longer were offered.

▲ Taurus wagons had a standard 3.8-liter V-6 and could get a remote liftgate release. The Insta-Clear windshield option was gone.

▲ Taurus taillamps sat higher and overall sedan length grew 3.6 inches, but wheelbase did not change. A 3.0-liter V-6 was now standard.

▲ Variable-assist power steering went into the Taurus LX, with less high-speed help. Spotting differences from 1986-91 models isn't easy.

▲ Keyless remote entry was a popular option, but Club Wagons could get a new twist. A Panic button caused headlights to flash and the horn to honk, to dissuade a would-be thief.

▲ Only the details changed in '92 Mustangs. LX models, like this $19,644 5.0L convertible, added color-keyed moldings and bumper strips. New option: a power four-way driver's seat.

315

▲ A new sport option package for the Probe LX coupe echoed the GT's appearance, including 205/60HR15 tires on alloy wheels. Certain formerly standard equipment on LX and GT models was now optional. Base GL Probes carried a 110-bhp, 2.2-liter four; LX, a 3.0-liter V-6; GT, the 145-horse-power turbo four.

▲ As usual, Mustang GTs had fog lamps, sill extensions, and a rear spoiler—plus the 225-bhp V-8 engine with 300 lbs/ft of torque. Wire wheel covers and whitewalls were extinct.

▲ A new Sport Option appearance group, including tape graphics and a rear roof-edge spoiler, added $341 to the price of a GL edition of the Korean-built mini Festiva.

◄ Identifying a Super Coupe got harder, as lesser Thunderbirds adopted its nose. Sport models had a 200-bhp V-8 and SC suspension.

1992 Engine Availability

Engines	bore × stroke	bhp	availability
I-4, 113.5	3.23 × 3.46	88	S-Escort
I-4, 109.0	3.27 × 3.35	127	S-Escort GT, LX-E
I-4, 133.0	3.39 × 3.70	110	S-Probe GL/LX
I-4T, 133.0	3.39 × 3.70	145	S-Probe GT
I-4, 140.0	3.78 × 3.13	105	S-Mustang LX
I-4, 140.0	3.70 × 3.30	96	S-Tempo
V-6, 182.0	3.50 × 3.15	135	O-Tempo
V-6, 182.0	3.50 × 3.15	140/145	S-Probe LX, Taurus
V-6, 182.0	3.50 × 3.15	220	S-Taurus SHO
V-6, 232.0	3.80 × 3.40	140	S-Taurus LX wgn, TBird; O-Taurus
V-6, 232.0	3.80 × 3.40	210	S-TBird Super Coupe (supercharged)
V-8, 281.0	3.60 × 3.60	190/210	S-Crown Vic
V-8, 302.0	4.00 × 3.00	200	S-TBird Sport; O-TBird
V-8, 302.0	4.00 × 3.00	225	S-Mustang GT, LX 5.0L

▲ Club Wagons and Econolines enjoyed their first restyle since 1975, with all-new metal.

▲ Facelifted big Broncos could get a new Nite appearance package, for an even bolder look.

▲ F-Series pickups got a new nose and the Flareside model was back, in F-150 form only.

▲ Regular-length Club Wagons and Econolines got a driver's airbag—first time in big vans.

Model Breakdown Chart

Escort—wb 98.4		Wght	Price	Prod
61/BM	Pony htchbk sdn 3d	2,287	8,355	36,568
61/AI	LX htchbk sdn 3d	2,312	9,055	
61/AX	GT htchbk sdn 3d	2,458	11,871	14,241
54/AI	LX sdn 4d	2,364	9,795	37,400
54/AX	LX-E sdn 4d	2,464	11,933	6,771
58/AI	LX htchbk sdn 5d	2,355	9,483	34,880
74/AI	LX wgn 5d	2,411	10,067	39,749

Probe—wb 99.0				
AF	GL htchbk 3d	2,730	12,257	50,517
AI	LX htchbk 3d	2,970	13,257	
AX	GT htchbk 3d turbo	3,000	14,857	

Taurus—wb 106.0				
FC/HVS	L sdn 4d	3,111	14,980	286,090
FC/HVD	GL sdn 4d	3,117	15,280	
FC/HVB	LX sdn 4d	3,193	17,775	
FC/HVE	SHO sdn 4d	3,309	23,889	8,000
FF/HVS	L wgn 5d	3,262	16,013	73,964
FF/HVD	GL wgn 5d	3,264	16,290	
FF/HVB	LX wgn 5d	3,388	19,464	

Tempo—wb 99.9				
66/HVB	GL sdn 2d	2,532	9,987	37,364
66/HVD	GLS sdn 2d	2,601	12,652	

		Wght	Price	Prod
54/HVB	GL sdn 4d	2,600	10,137	301,606
54/HVD	GLS sdn 4d	2,659	12,800	
54/HVC	LX sdn 4d	2,626	11,115	
AF	GL htchbk cpe 3d	2,730	12.257	50,517
AI	LX htchbk cpe 3d	3,000	13,257	
AX	GT htchbk cpe 3d	2,970	14,857	

Crown Victoria—wb 114.3				
FC/AB	sdn 4d	3,748	19,563	152,373
FC/AI	LX sdn 4d	3,769	20,887	
FC/A3	Touring Sedan 4d	3,850	23,832	

Mustang—wb 100.5				
66/HVS	LX cpe 2d	2,775	10,215	15,717
66/HVS	LX 5.0L cpe 2d	3,010	13,422	
61/HVS	LX cpe 3d	2,834	10,721	40,093
61/HVS	LX 5.0L cpe 3d	3,069	14,207	
61/HVB	GT cpe 3d	3,144	15,243	
66/HVS	LX conv cpe 2d	2,996	16,899	23,470
66/HVS	LX 5.0L conv cpe 2d	3,231	19,644	
66/HVS	GT conv cpe 2d	3,365	20,199	

Thunderbird—wb 113.0				
BA/VS-AB	cpe 2d	3,772	16,345	73,175
BA/VS	Sport cpe 2d	3,738	18,611	
BA/VS-AI	LX cpe 2d	3,719	18,778	
BA/VS-BB	SC cpe 2d	3,686	22,046	4,614

317

1993

Probe reworked with cab-forward teardrop styling

Right-hand-drive Probe tackles Japanese market

Mustang Cobra is announced along with F-150 Lightning pickup—both limited editions from Special Vehicle Team

Escort gains modest facelift

Alex Trotman named chairman and CEO

Goal for '90s: make the Ford ownership experience "as good as possible"

▲ Unveiled at Detroit's auto show in January 1992, the reworked '93 Probe featured cab-forward styling, a wider stance, and new powertrains. Mazda contributed the engineering; Ford's design staff (under Jack Telnack) the body and interior. The cowl sat three inches lower than on the prior Probe.

▲ A facelifted Escort went on sale in spring 1992 with a new grille and taillamps, and color-keyed moldings and bumpers. The GT added a new spoiler, rocker panels, and aluminum wheels. A CD player was optional. The 1.9-liter four had sequential fuel injection.

▲ Alex Trotman became chairman of the board and CEO of Ford Motor Company in November of 1993. He first worked for Ford of Britain.

▲ With a redesigned Mustang due for 1994, Ford ended the '93 model run with special White (shown) and Yellow "Feature Car Packages," here applied to an LX 5.0L convertible.

▲ Reviving a legendary name, Ford announced a limited-edition Mustang Cobra, created by its Special Vehicle Team. Modifications to the high-output 5.0-liter V-8 included GT40-spec heads and roller rockers. Jackie Stewart and Bob Bondurant contributed to suspension work.

▲ Thunderbird lost its base and Sport models, leaving the LX (shown) and Super Coupe. LX prices were trimmed significantly.

▲ In a bow to convention, the Crown Vic added a grille to its nose and cupholders to its interior, while the sporty Touring Sedan was dropped.

▲ With a replacement due for '94, the little Korean-built Festiva soldiered on with few changes.

▲ When the votes were counted, Taurus had become the most popular car in the U.S. for 1992. It led again in '93 despite the loss of the base L model.

▲ The high-performance Taurus SHO added an automatic transmission option for '93. It came with a 3.2-liter version of the 3.0-liter twin-cam V-6.

▲ A buckets-and-console interior was standard on the Taurus SHO and LX, and an option on the GL. Leather upholstery was optional across the board.

1993 Engine Availability

Engines	bore × stroke	bhp	availability
I4, 109.0	3.27 × 3.35	127	S-Escort GT (dohc)
I4, 114.0	3.23 × 3.46	88	S-Escort (ohc)
I4, 122.0	3.27 × 3.62	115	S-Probe (dohc)
I4, 140.0	3.78 × 3.12	105	S-Mustang LX (ohc)
I4, 141.0	3.70 × 3.30	96	S-Tempo
V6, 153.0	3.33 × 2.92	164	S-Probe GT (dohc)
V6, 182.0	3.50 × 3.15	140	S-Taurus
V6, 182.0	3.50 × 3.10	135	O-Tempo
V6, 182.0	3.50 × 3.15	220	S-Taurus SHO (manual) (dohc)
V6, 195.0	3.60 × 3.15	220	S-Taurus SHO (automatic)(dohc)
V6, 232.0	3.80 × 3.40	140	S-T-Bird, O-Taurus
V6, 232.0	3.80 × 3.40	210	S-T-Bird Super Coupe (S-charged)
V8, 281.0	3.60 × 3.60	190	S-Crown Victoria (ohc)
V8, 281.0	3.60 × 3.60	210	O-Crown Victoria (ohc)
V8, 302.0	4.00 × 3.00	200	O-T-Bird
V8, 302.0	4.00 × 3.00	205	S-Mustang LX 5.0, GT
V8, 302.0	4.00 × 3.00	235	S-Mustang Cobra

▲ The popular Explorer sport-utility gained 4-wheel anti-lock brakes for '93 that worked in both 2- and 4-wheel drive. Former versions had rear-only ABS that functioned only in 2-wheel drive. Otherwise a carryover, the Explorer racked up nearly 330,000 sales.

▲ Sometimes credited with instituting the "aero" look at Ford, John J. "Jack" Telnack became vice president of corporate design for Ford's global design team in 1993.

▲ Introduced for 1993 was the limited-edition F-150 Lightning. More than just an appearance package, the Lightning lived up to its name with a 240-bhp version of the 5.8-liter V-8 that made just 200 horses in other F-Series trucks. Available only in a regular-cab, Styleside, short-bed configuration, the Lightning also included special trim, lowered suspension, and 275/60HR17 tires on alloy wheels. Only about 10,000 were built.

Model Breakdown Chart

Escort—wb 98.4		Wght	Price	Prod
61/BM	Std. htchbk sdn 3d	2,285	8,355	
61/AI	LX htchbk sdn 3d	2,306	9,364	} 104,827
61/AX	GT htchbk sdn 3d	2,440	11,871	
54/AI	LX sdn 4d	2,359	10,041	} 78,905
54/AX	LX-E sdn 4d	2,440	11,933	
58/AI	LX htchbk sdn 5d	2,354	9,797	66,021
74/AI	LX wgn 5d	2,403	10,367	175,354
Probe—wb 102.9				
AB	htchbk cpe 3d	2,619	12,845	} 89,701
AX	GT htchbk cpe 3d	2,815	15,174	
Tempo—wb 99.9				
66/HVB	GL sdn 2d	2,511	10,267	56,250
54/HVB	GL sdn 4d	2,569	10,267	} 182,043
54/HVC	LX sdn 4d	2,613	12,135	
Taurus—106.0				
FC/HVD	GL sdn 4d	3,083	15,491	} 350,487
FC/HVB	LX sdn 4d	3,201	18,300	
FC/HVE	SHO sdn 4d	3,354	24,829	21,991

Taurus—wb 106.0		Wght	Price	Prod
FF/HVD	GL wgn 5d	3,255	16,656	} 86,231
FF/HVB	LX wgn 5d	3,368	19,989	
Crown Victoria—wb 114.4				
FC/AB	sdn 4d	3,793	19,972	} 108,201
FC/AI	LX sdn 4d	3,799	21,559	
Mustang—wb 100.5				
66/HVS	LX cpe 2d	2,751	10,719	} 24,851
66/HVS	LX 5.0L cpe 2d	3,035	13,926	
61/HVS	LX cpe 3d	2,812	11,224	} 56,978
61/HVS	LX 5.0L cpe 3d	3,096	14,710	
	Cobra cpe 3d	3,255	19,990	} 5,099
61/HVB	GT cpe 3d	3,144	15,747	
66/HVS (B2L)	LX conv cpe 2d	2,973	17,548	
66/HVS (B2I)	LX 5.0L conv cpe 2d	3,259	20,293	} 27,300
66/HVS (B2L)	GT conv cpe 2d	3,365	20,848	
Thunderbird—wb 113.0				
BA/VS-AI	LX cpe 2d	3,536	15,797	128,931
BA/VS-BB	SC cpe 2d	3,760	22,030	4,178

1994

Mustang is completely redesigned; only the powertrains are carried over

The boxy Festiva is replaced by the more rounded Aspire, both built by Kia in Korea

Crown Vic gains standard (rather than optional) passenger-side air bag and CFC-free air conditioning

Escort adds a standard driver-side air bag

Dual air bags are now standard on the Taurus

Thunderbird gets a redesigned dash and standard dual air bags

Splash decor package added to Ranger

Bronco sport-utility and full-size pickups get a driver-side air bag

Full-size vans gain 4-wheel anti-lock brakes

Both car and truck sales are up in the industry; total vehicle sales top 15 million

▲ Replacing the Festiva as Ford's entry-level offering was the new-for-'94 Aspire. Built by Kia in Korea (as was the Festiva), the Aspire came in 3- and 5-door hatchback body styles.

▲ At 93.9 inches, the 5-door Aspire's wheelbase was three inches longer than the 3-door's, and 3.5-inches longer than the departed Festiva's.

▲ Despite its position at the bottom of Ford's pecking order, the Aspire featured standard dual air bags and optional anti-lock brakes.

▲ Escort jumped two places in the new-car sales race, beating out the Toyota Camry and Chevrolet Cavalier to become the third best-selling car in America for 1994. A newly standard driver-side air bag no doubt helped its popularity.

◄ Taurus, the top-selling car in America since 1992, returned for '94 with few changes, though a passenger-side air bag was now standard instead of optional.

321

◄ Receiving its first major redesign since 1979, the new Mustang carried some styling cues from the 1965 original, notably its three-element taillights, side air scoops, "twin cove" dashboard layout, and galloping pony on the grille. Wheelbase grew by two inches, overall length by one. The former 3-door hatchback body style was dropped, leaving a 2-door coupe with steeply slanted backlight and a convertible. A base model replaced the former LX, while the GT moniker continued to grace the high-performance variant. The GT shown (foreground) is fitted with the optional 17-inch "twin spoke" alloy wheels.

▼Though the Mustang looked all-new from the outside, the platform underneath was little changed from before. However, four-wheel disc brakes were now standard across the board, with anti-lock brakes a new option.

▲ GTs kept their 5.0-liter V-8, which was now rated at 215 bhp. They also boasted fog lamps and a rear spoiler.

◄ Base Mustangs carried a new 145-bhp 3.8-liter V-6, which replaced a 2.3-liter four.

► Inside, the new model featured dual air bags.

▼ At midyear, a Cobra with a 240-bhp version of the 5.0 debuted, and was quickly chosen to pace that year's Indy 500. Five thousand coupes were built, along with 1000 convertibles. Only the drop-tops came with pace-car replica decals.

1994 Engine Availability

Engines	bore × stroke	bhp	availability
I4, 109.0	3.27×3.35	127	S-Escort GT (dohc)
I4, 114.0	3.23×3.46	88	S-Escort (ohc)
I4, 122.0	3.27×3.62	115	S-Probe (dohc)
I4, 141.0	3.70×3.30	96	S-Tempo
V6, 153.0	3.33×2.92	164	S-Probe GT (dohc)
V6, 182.0	3.50×3.15	140	S-Taurus
V6, 182.0	3.50×3.10	135	O-Tempo
V6, 182.0	3.50×3.15	220	S-Taurus SHO (manual) (dohc)
V6, 195.0	3.60×3.15	220	S-Taurus SHO (automatic) (dohc)
V6, 232.0	3.80×3.40	140	S-T-Bird, O-Taurus
V6, 232.0	3.80×3.40	145	S-Mustang
V6, 232.0	3.80×3.40	230	S-T-Bird Super Coupe (S-charged)
V8, 281.0	3.60×3.60	190	S-Crown Victoria (ohc)
V8, 281.0	3.60×3.60	205	O-T-Bird (ohc)
V8, 281.0	3.60×3.60	210	O-Crown Victoria (ohc)
V8, 302.0	4.00×3.00	215	S-Mustang GT
V8, 302.0	4.00×3.00	240	S-Mustang Cobra

▲ Convertibles could be ordered with a newly optional removable hardtop.

◄ An original '65 Mustang convertible shares the stage with '94 base (right) and GT (foreground) convertibles. The GT wears its standard 16-inch alloy wheels.

▲ Thunderbirds were freshened for 1994 with new front and rear facias. Newly optional on the LX was a 205-bhp 4.6-liter overhead-cam V-8.

▲ The Thunderbird Super Coupe returned with its 230-bhp supercharged 3.8-liter V-6. It still came standard with a 5-speed manual.

▲ Both T-Birds received a redesigned wraparound dashboard incorporating dual air bags.

▲ After being redesigned for 1993, the Probe returned for '94 little changed save for the addition of a standard passenger-side air bag to complement the existing driver-side air bag. Base and GT 3-door hatchbacks were again offered, the former with a 2.0-liter twin-cam four, the latter boasting a 2.5-liter twin-cam V-6, both courtesy of Mazda.

▲ The Tempo returned with few changes—something that could be said virtually every year since its 1983 introduction. This, however, would be its last; Ford was readying a new compact "world car" to replace it for '95. Minor changes included a manual driver's seatbelt to replace the hated motorized one on Tempos equipped with the optional driver-side air bag.

▲ A passenger-side air bag was standard rather than optional on the '94 Crown Victoria, which also got CFC-free air conditioning.

Model Breakdown Chart

Escort—wb 98.4		Wght	Price	Prod*
61/BM	Std. htchbk sdn 3d	2,304	9,035	96,434
61/AI	LX htchbk sdn 3d	2,325	9,890	
61/AX	GT htchbk sdn 3d	2,447	12,300	
54/AK	LX sdn 4d	2,371	10,550	50,786
61/AI	LX htchbk sdn 5d	2,419	10,325	116,321
74/AI	LX wgn 5d	2,419	10,880	47,278
Probe—wb 102.8				
AB	htchbk cpe 3d	2,690	13,685	115,951
AX	GT htchbk cpe 3d	2,921	16,015	
Tempo—wb 99.9				
66/HVB	GL sdn 2d	2,511	10,735	35,445
54/HVB	GL sdn 4d	2,569	10,735	145,625
54/HVC	LX sdn 4d	2,613	12,560	
Taurus—wb 106.0				
FC/HVD	GL sdn 4d	3,104	16,140	225,532
FC/HVB	LX sdn 4d	3,177	18,785	

Taurus—wb 106.0 (cont.)		Wght	Price	Prod*
FC/HVE	SHO sdn 4d	3,395	24,715	13,698
FF/HVD	GL wgn 5d	3,272	17,220	70,966
FF/HVB	LX wgn 5d	3,349	20,400	
Crown Victoria—wb 114.4				
FC/AB	sdn 4d	3,786	19,300	109,545
FC/AI	LX sdn 4d	3,794	20,715	
Mustang—wb 101.3				
63	cpe 2d	3,065	13,365	84,010
63	GT cpe 2d	3,276	17,280	
	Cobra cpe 2d	3,365	20,765	5,009
76	conv cpe 2d	3,245	20,160	47,055
76	GT conv cpe 2d	3,452	21,970	
	Cobra conv cpe 2d	3,567	23,535	1,000
Thunderbird—wb 113.0				
BA/VS-AI	LX cpe 2d	3,570	16,830	123,283
BA/VS-BB	SC cpe 2d	3,758	22,240	2,973
Includes production for export.				

▶ With the increase in interest—and sales—in the minivan market during the Nineties, Ford expanded its lineup midway through the 1994 model year with the early introduction of the '95 Windstar (foreground). Powered by a 155-bhp 3.8-liter V-6, the front-wheel-drive Windstar was a direct competitor to the immensely popular Chrysler Corporation minivans. Windstar joined the more truck-like rear-drive Aerostar (left), which sold in impressive numbers but wasn't a match for the Chrysler vans when it came to moving people. Ford Motor Company fired its first salvo in 1993 with the introduction of the smaller front-drive Villager minivan under the Mercury nameplate (right). Designed and built in conjunction with Nissan (which sold its own version as the Quest), Villager sold in relatively small volume, and Ford dealers had been clamoring for a front-drive minivan of their own. By 1994, Ford offered a van for virtually every need. The full-size rear-drive Club Wagon (background), which was redesigned for 1992, continued to lead its market segment. These big people-haulers got standard 4-wheel anti-lock brakes for 1994.

▲ Windstar rode a 120.7-inch wheelbase, the longest of any minivan. Only one body length was offered. It came standard with dual air bags and 4-wheel anti-lock brakes, and met all 1998 passenger-car safety standards.

▲ The Explorer compact sport-utility vehicle saw only minor changes for 1994, but continued to rack up big sales—which soared nearly 20 percent to over 390,000 units.

▲ Ford's F-Series pickups had been the best-selling vehicles in America since the early Eighties, and continued that streak for 1994. New that year was a driver-side air bag. The high-performance Lightning was dropped.

▲ Ranger continued to be America's most popular compact pickup, and Mazda began selling a rebadged version as the B-Series. New for '94 was a sporty Ranger Splash with flare-fender cargo box and monotone paint.

1995

Contour introduced to replace aging Tempo

Contour is a "world car," being based on the European Mondeo—developed at a cost of $6 billion

Escort gets new instrument panel; dual air bags are now standard, but motorized belts remain

Explorer is restyled with rounder contours; a new instrument panel contains a passenger-side air bag

A new full-time, automatic 4-wheel-drive system called Control Trac is standard on 4WD Explorers

Evergreen Crown Victoria gets front and rear freshening and revised instrument panel

▲ Ross H. Roberts took over as vice president and general manager of Ford Division in 1991 after holding the same post at Lincoln-Mercury.

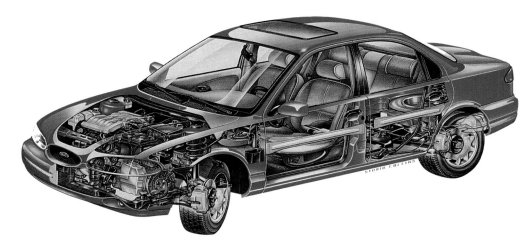

▲ Ghost view of the new Contour shows the side-guard door beams and MacPherson strut front and rear suspension. Three trim levels were offered; the V-6 engine and 4-wheel disc brakes mark this as the top-line SE model.

▲ Lowest-priced of the trio of Contours was the GL, which was powered by a 125-bhp 2.0-liter twin-cam 4-cylinder, as was the mid-level LX.

▲ Sporty SE had a 2.5-liter twin-cam 170-bhp V-6 that was optional on other Contours. Unique features included a rear spoiler and 15-inch wheels.

▲ With a wheelbase of 106.5 inches, the Contour stretched a half inch longer between the wheels than the mid-size Taurus, but the interior was sometimes criticized for having a cramped rear seat—something Ford would attempt to improve in later years. Dual air bags were standard

◄ Other standard features of the SE included fog lamps, sport suspension, 4-wheel disc brakes, and a leather-wrapped steering wheel. All Contours came standard with a 5-speed manual transmission, offering a 4-speed automatic and traction control as options. Also optional on all were anti-lock brakes and a power sunroof.

▲ For its final year in this design, the ever-popular Taurus returned with few changes, though an SE model (left) was added between the price-leading GL and mid-level LX that featured clear headlight lenses and some added standard equipment. Though an SHO model would reappear in the new generation, the '95 version (right) would be the last to offer a manual transmission. Taurus once again led the car sales hit parade, beating out the second-place Honda Accord.

▲ With the first major changes since its 1992 redesign, the Crown Vic got a revised grille, new bumper facias, and redesigned taillamps.

▲ Thunderbird returned for 1995 with only minor changes, most in the form of deleted standard or optional equipment.

▲ Early T-Bird stylists Alden "Gib" Giberson (left) and William Boyer (center) are pictured with current V.P. of design, Jack Telnack.

▲ A base Mustang convertible was a stylish ride. Little changed for 1995, though the power driver's seat was relegated to the options list.

▲ The GT (shown) also returned with few changes. A stripped-down GTS model debuted at midyear, but didn't last into '96.

▲ The mighty Cobra made an encore appearance for 1995. It again carried a 240-bhp 5.0-liter V-8.

1995 Engine Availability

Engines	bore × stroke	bhp	availability
I4, 109.0	3.27×3.35	127	S-Escort GT (dohc)
I4, 114.0	3.23×3.46	88	S-Escort (ohc)
I4, 121.0	3.34×3.46	125	S-Contour (dohc)
I4, 122.0	3.27×3.62	118	S-Probe (dohc)
V6, 153.0	3.33×2.92	164	S-Probe GT (dohc)
V6, 155.0	3.24×3.13	170	S-Contour SE (dohc)
V6, 182.0	3.50×3.15	140	S-Taurus
V6, 182.0	3.50×3.15	220	S-Taurus SHO (manual) (dohc)
V6, 195.0	3.60×3.15	220	S-Taurus SHO (automatic) (dohc)
V6, 232.0	3.80×3.40	140	S-T-Bird, O-Taurus
V6, 232.0	3.80×3.40	145	S-Mustang
V6, 232.0	3.80×3.40	230	S-T-Bird Super Coupe (S-charged)
V8, 281.0	3.60×3.60	190	S-Crown Victoria (ohc)
V8, 281.0	3.60×3.60	205	O-T-Bird (ohc)
V8, 281.0	3.60×3.60	210	O-Crown Victoria (ohc)
V8, 302.0	4.00×3.00	215	S-Mustang GT
V8, 302.0	4.00×3.00	240	S-Mustang Cobra

◀ America's best-selling sport utility underwent its first redesign since being introduced as a 1991 model. Contours were more rounded, and a redesigned interior featured standard dual air bags. Four-wheel disc brakes replaced the previous front disc/rear drum arrangement, also as standard. All four-wheel-drive models got a new 4WD system called Control Trac. Explorer's previous 4WD was a part-time, on-demand setup that was not for use on dry pavement. The new Control Trac allowed rear-wheel drive, along with 4WD that could be left engaged on dry roads—a much more sophisticated system than before. Also in '95, Ford no longer furnished Mazda with the 3-door version, which had been sold as the Navajo.

▲ Expedition and Eddie Bauer editions came with 16-inch wheels—a first for the Explorer. The standard and only powertrain was a 160-bhp 4.0-liter V-6 mated to a 4-speed automatic transmission. Some saw this as a drawback, feeling there was too much Explorer for too little power. The situation would soon change.

▲ Along with the Explorer's new standard dual air bags came some additional available features including a rear child seat on 5-door models; center console with rear air vents, cupholders, and headphone jacks; one-touch down feature for the driver's power window; a 6-disc CD changer; and a power moonroof.

▲ Introduced in the spring of 1994 as an early '95 model, the base Windstar GL adopted a 147-bhp 3.0-liter V-6 during the '95 model year. Windstar boasted a low 16-inch step-in height.

▲ Windstar featured a modern dash and an available electronic instrument cluster. It was praised for its car-like feel and low noise levels.

▲ Windstar options added at the start of the '95 model year included leather upholstery for the quad bucket seats, a child-safety seat, and a convertible seat/bed.

Model Breakdown Chart

Escort—wb 98.4		Wght	Price	Prod
P10	Std. htchbk sdn 3d	2,316	9,580	} 115,928
P11	LX htchbk sdn 3d	2,355	10,435	
P12	GT htchbk sdn 3d	2,459	12,720	
P13	LX sdn 4d	2,385	11,040	79,301
P14	LX htchbk sdn 5d	2,404	10,870	71,081
P15	LX wgn 5d	2,451	11,425	146,678
Probe—wb 102.8				
T20	htchbk cpe 3d	2,690	14,180	} 66,305
T22	GT htchbk cpe 3d	2,921	16,545	
Contour—wb 106.5				
P65	GL sdn 4d	2,769	13,310	} 194,240
P66	LX sdn 4d	NA	13,995	
P67	SE sdn 4d	3,040	15,695	
Taurus—wb 106.0				
P57	GL wgn 5d	3,285	18,680	} 65,497
P58	LX wgn 5d	NA	21,010	

Taurus—wb 106.0 (cont.)		Wght	Price	Prod
P52	GL sdn 4d	3,118	17,585	} 369,371
P52/SE	SE sdn 4d	NA	18,630	
P53	LX sdn 4d	NA	19,400	
P54	SHO sdn 4d	NA	25,140	
Crown Victoria—wb 114.4				
P73	sdn 4d	3,762	20,160	} 106,683
P74	LX sdn 4d	NA	21,970	
Mustang—wb 101.3				
P40	cpe 2d	3,077	14,330	} 167,880
P44	conv cpe 2d	3,257	20,795	
P42	GT cpe 2d	3,280	17,905	
P45	GT conv cpe 2d	3,451	22,595	
P42	Cobra cpe 2d	3,354	21,300	4,255
P45	Cobra conv cpe 2d	3,524	25,605	1,002
Thunderbird—wb 113.0				
P62	LX cpe 2d	3,536	17,400	} 115,165
P64	SC cpe 2d	NA	22,910	

1996

Taurus receives its first major redesign since being introduced in 1986

Ford's 5.0-liter ohv V-8 is offered in the Explorer

Mustang GT trades its 5.0-liter ohv V-8 for a new single-overhead-cam 4.6-liter V-8; high-performance Cobra gets a more potent dual-cam version

Thunderbird's supercharged Super Coupe is discontinued

Windstar's 3.8-liter V-6 gets a major power boost

Redesigned F-150/250 pickups are introduced in January 1996 as early '97 models, while heavier-duty versions continue with old design

Ford increases its stake in Mazda from 25 percent to 33 percent, giving Dearborn a controlling interest in the Japanese automaker

▲ Jacques A. "Jack" Nasser took over as executive vice president and president of Ford Automotive Operations in November of 1996.

▲ The SHO version of the new Taurus didn't show its face until midway through the '96 model year. Replacing the former Yamaha-built 3.0-liter twin-cam V-6 was a new 3.4-liter twin-cam V-8, also made by Yamaha. A 5-speed manual was no longer offered; a 4-speed automatic was standard.

▲ The new Taurus took the original "jelly bean" styling a step further, with prominent ovoid shapes inside and out. Wheelbase was stretched by 2.5 inches to 108.5, while overall length grew by five inches on the sedan, six on the wagon.

▲ Taurus was initially offered in GL and LX trim levels, but the SHO and a base G were added at midyear. G and GL had an overhead-valve 145-bhp 3.0-liter V-6. The LX got a double-overhead-cam 3.0-liter V-6 rated at 200 bhp.

▲ Taurus's ovoid styling theme carried over into the instrument panel and control layout for the radio and climate system. The car shown is equipped with the optional automatic climate controls; the standard setup used rotary knobs.

◀ Wagons returned, displaying an ovoid window treatment in the rear. Initial reaction to the Taurus's new styling was mixed, though it still managed to hold onto its number-one sales spot.

▲ Aspire changed little for '96, though it lost its sporty SE version along with the optional aluminum wheels and CD player.

▲ With a redesigned model due in the spring, the Escort had few changes for '96. Production was low due to the short selling season.

▲ A center horn pad replaced spoke-mounted buttons and the Towing Package was dropped on the Crown Vic for '96.

◀ A number of small styling alterations graced the Thunderbird for '96: new front and rear facias, "creased" hood, headlights with clear lenses and complex reflectors, a revised grille, and restyled taillights. The optional cruise control got a "tap" feature for one-mph speed changes, and there was a newly optional anti-theft system. The Super Coupe disappeared, along with its supercharged V-6 engine. That left the LX with a standard 145-bhp 3.8-liter V-6 or optional 205-bhp 4.6-liter V-8.

Model Breakdown Chart

Escort—wb 98.4		Wght	Price	Prod
P10	htchbk sdn 3d	2,323	10,065	
P11	LX htchbk sdn 3d	2,356	10,910	71,626
P12	GT htchbk sdn 3d	2,455	13,205	
P13	LX sdn 4d	2,378	11,515	17,019
P14	LX htchbk sdn 5d	2,398	11,345	15,056
P15	LX wgn 5d	2,444	11,900	42,708
Probe—wb 102.8				
T20	SE htchbk cpe 3d	2,690	13,930	38,618
T22	GT htchbk cpe 3d	2,921	16,450	
Contour—wb 106.5				
P65	GL sdn 4d	2,769	13,785	
P66	LX sdn 4d	NA	14,470	186,263
P67	SE sdn 4d	3,040	16,170	
Taurus—wb 108.5				
P51	G sdn 4d	NA	17,995	
P52	GL sdn 4d	3,326	18,600	378,577
P53	LX sdn 4d	3,358	20,980	
P54	SHO sdn 4d	NA	25,140	
P57	GL wgn 5d	3,480	19,680	60,672
P58	LX wgn 5d	NA	22,000	
Crown Victoria—wb 114.4				
P73	sdn 4d	3,780	20,955	115,547
P74	LX sdn 4d	NA	22,675	
Mustang—wb 101.3				
P40	cpe 2d	3,065	15,180	92,451
P42	GT cpe 2d	3,278	17,610	
P42	Cobra cpe 2d	3,393	24,810	7,496
P44	conv cpe 2d	3,264	21,060	33,127
P45	GT conv cpe 2d	3,471	23,495	
P45	Cobra conv cpe 2d	3,565	27,580	2,510
Thunderbird—wb 113.0				
P62	LX cpe 2d	3,536	17,485	86,549

▲ Mustang's age-old overhead-valve 5.0-liter V-8 was replaced by a pair of new 4.6-liter V-8s for 1996. The GT (shown) got a single-overhead-cam 4.6 with 215 bhp. Cobras received a dual-cam version with a rousing 305 bhp.

▲ Addressing what was perceived as one of Explorer's few shortcomings, Ford made its 5.0-liter 210-bhp V-8 available as an option.

► One of Ford's Indigo concept cars was a non-drivable display vehicle used only for "show," but a second was fitted with a drivetrain and was intended to "go." Power came from a 435-bhp 6.0-liter twin-cam V-12 (*below*). The engine was mated to a 6-speed transmission with an Indy-style, steering-wheel-mounted sequential shifter. Also reflecting a racing influence was the carbon fiber/aluminum body and double-wishbone suspension.

▲ Ford's compact pickup truck got an industry first for 1996: an optional passenger-side air bag with a disabling switch.

▲ Legendary race-car driver A. J. Foyt gives the "thumbs up" to Ford's GT90 concept car. Unveiled in time for the 1996 auto show season, the car was powered by a quad-turbocharged 6.0-liter V-12 rated at 720 bhp.

1996 Engine Availability

Engines	bore × stroke	bhp	availability
I4, 109.0	3.27 × 3.35	127	S-Escort GT (dohc)
I4, 114.0	3.23 × 3.46	88	S-Escort (ohc)
I4, 121.0	3.34 × 3.46	125	S-Contour
I4, 122.0	3.27 × 3.62	118	S-Probe
V6, 153.0	3.33 × 2.92	164	S-Probe GT
V6, 155.0	3.24 × 3.13	170	S-Contour SE
V6, 181.0	3.50 × 3.10	200	S-Taurus LX (dohc)
V6, 182.0	3.50 × 3.15	145	S-Taurus G, GL
V8, 207.0	3.20 × 3.10	240	S-Taurus SHO (dohc)
V6, 232.0	3.80 × 3.40	145	S-T-Bird
V6, 232.0	3.80 × 3.40	150	S-Mustang
V8, 281.0	3.60 × 3.60	190	S-Crown Victoria
V8, 281.0	3.60 × 3.60	205	O-T-Bird
V8, 281.0	3.60 × 3.60	210	O-Crown Victoria
V8, 281.0	3.60 × 3.60	215	S-Mustang GT
V8, 281.0	3.60 × 3.60	305	S-Mustang Cobra

▲ In an effort to appease those who felt the Windstar could use more power, Ford increased the output of the 3.8-liter V-6 to an even 200 bhp for 1996, up from 155. The engine was standard in the LX and optional in the GL, which came with a 150-bhp 3.0-liter V-6. Also new was the availability of rear disc brakes; they were included in the trailer towing package and with the optional traction control system.

► The rear-drive Aerostar, which had been slated for extinction after the 1995 model year, got a new lease on life but few changes for '96.

1997

Escort is redesigned, adopting the rounded, ovoid lines of the Taurus

Introduced in May of 1996, the Escort line arrives devoid of hatchbacks; only a 4-door sedan and wagon are offered

Full-size Expedition 4-door sport-ute replaces the 2-door Bronco

Expedition power comes from a pair of overhead-cam V-8s

Overhead-cam V-6 and 5-speed automatic join Explorer's options list

Aerostar also gains a 5-speed automatic transmission

Introduced in spring of '97, the 1998 Windstar boasts a longer driver-side door to ease access to the middle seats

Also introduced early is the 1998 Contour, carrying revised styling

▲ For what would turn out to be its final appearance, the Aspire got a slightly revised look front and rear.

▲ A GTS Sport Appearance group for the Probe GT included chrome wheels and a rear spoiler. Base models gained an optional moonroof.

▲ It would be a short selling season for the 1997 Contour. A new base model was added and traction control was deleted as an option.

▲ In addition to a twin-cam version of the 4.6-liter V-8 that produced 305 bhp (versus 215 for the single-cam version in the Mustang GT), Cobras boasted a distinct "bubbled" hood, round fog lamps, and 17-inch aluminum wheels. The only transmission offered was a 5-speed manual.

1997 Engine Availability

Engines	bore × stroke	bhp	availability
I4, 109.0	3.27 × 3.35	127	S-Escort GT (dohc)
I4, 121.0	3.34 × 3.46	110	S-Escort (ohc)
I4, 121.0	3.34 × 3.46	125	S-Contour (dohc)
I4, 122.0	3.27 × 3.62	118	S-Probe (dohc)
V6, 153.0	3.33 × 2.92	164	S-Probe GT (dohc)
V6, 155.0	3.24 × 3.13	170	S-Contour S (dohc)
V6, 181.0	3.50 × 3.10	200	S-Taurus LX (dohc)
V6, 182.0	3.50 × 3.15	145	S-Taurus G, GL
V8, 207.0	3.20 × 3.10	235	S-Taurus SHO (dohc)
V6, 232.0	3.80 × 3.40	145	S-T-Bird
V8, 281.0	3.60 × 3.60	190	S-Crown Victoria (ohc)
V8, 281.0	3.60 × 3.60	205	O-T-Bird (ohc)
V8, 281.0	3.60 × 3.60	210	O-Crown Victoria (ohc)
V8, 281.0	3.60 × 3.60	215	S-Mustang (ohc)
V8, 281.0	3.60 × 3.60	305	S-Mustang Cobra (dohc)

▲ After being redesigned for 1996, the Taurus returned for '97 with few changes. Once again, LX models got a 200-bhp twin-cam 3.0-liter V-6.

331

▲ A redesigned Escort went on sale in May of 1996 as an early '97 model. It rode the same 98.4-inch wheelbase as before but stretched nearly four inches longer overall. A larger 2.0-liter 110-bhp four resided underhood.

▲ Again developed with the help of Mazda, the Escort now came in only 4-door sedan and 5-door wagon body styles; the 3-door and 5-door hatchbacks were dropped. Styling took on the corporate "ovoid" look.

▲ The Escort was equally new inside, where dual air bags were standard equipment and two-tone color treatments were available.

▲ With its oval-shaped radio/heater control panel, the Escort mimicked the Taurus inside. Gone were the distained motorized seatbelts.

▲ At 63.4 cubic feet, Escort wagons were a bit smaller inside than before, but still larger than competitors such as the Saturn.

▲ Ford used the redesigned F-150 (left) and F-250 (right) as the basis for a full-size sport-utility vehicle. The Expedition (center) came only as a 5-door wagon. At 204.6 inches overall, it stretched about 16 inches longer than an Explorer. Replacing the 2-door Bronco in Ford's truck lineup, the Expedition could seat up to nine and targeted the Chevrolet Tahoe and Suburban.

▲ SuperCab truck interiors featured a 3-place rear bench seat that was split 60/40 and could be folded to create a flat cargo floor.

▲ A passenger-side rear door was standard on all SuperCab models. It could be opened only after the front door was opened.

▲ One of many Ford competitors in NASCAR's 1996 Craftsman Truck Series was the 1997 Ford number 98 entry driven by Butch Miller.

▲ Lariat was the top-line trim level for F-150s in 1997. Luxuries such as chrome wheels, two-tone paint, and leather interior were among its standard features.

▲ Both Flareside (shown) and flat-sided Styleside beds were offered on F150s. Flareside beds came only in 6.5-foot length, while Stylesides also offered an 8-foot bed.

▲ F-150s and 250s had a dash switch for deactivating the passenger-side air bag.

▲ The full-size 5-door Expedition SUV came with a 215-bhp 4.6-liter V-8 and either 2- or 4-wheel drive. A 230-bhp 5.4 V-8 was optional.

▲ Standard Expedition fare included dual air bags, height-adjustable shoulder belts, anti-lock brakes, and a 4-speed automatic transmission.

▲ Ford introduced a new overhead-cam V-10 based on the "modular" V-8. It produced 265 bhp from 6.8 liters and was offered on full-size vans.

▲ Club Wagons were treated to a new range of gasoline engines, a passenger-side air bag in a restyled dashboard, and a restyled grille for '97. An overhead-valve, 200-bhp 4.2-liter V-6 was standard. Optional were two overhead-cam V-8s, a 215-bhp 4.6-liter and a 235-bhp 5.4 liter. The new V-10 was also optional, along with the 210-bhp 7.3-liter turbodiesel V-8. Seating for up to 15 was available.

▲ The popular Explorer got a new overhead-cam V-6 and an equally new 5-speed automatic transmission added to its options list. The new engine displaced the same 4.0 liters as the standard overhead-valve V-6, but offered 205 bhp versus 160. The 5-speed automatic was available with either V-6, but not the optional 210-bhp 5.0-liter V-8. Four-wheel-drive buyers had a choice of Control Trac 4WD (with either V-6) or permanently engaged AWD.

Model Breakdown Chart

Escort—wb 98.4		Wght	Price	Prod*
P10	sdn 4d	2,457	11,015	
P13	LX sdn 4d	NA	11,795	
P15	LX wgn 5d	2,525	112,450	
Probe—wb 102.8				
T20	SE htchbk cpe 3d	2,690	14,280	
T22	GT htchbk cpe 3d	2,921	16,780	
Contour—wb 106.5				
P65	sdn 4d	2,769	13,460	
P65	GL sdn 4d	NA	14,285	
P66	LX sdn 4d	NA	14,915	
P67	SE sdn 4d	3,040	16,615	
Taurus—wb 108.5				
P51	G sdn 4d	3,326	17,995	
P52	GL sdn 4d	NA	18,985	
P53	LX sdn 4d	3,358	21,610	

Taurus—wb 108.5 (cont.)		Wght	Price	Prod*
P54	SHO sdn 4d	NA	26,460	
P57	GL wgn 5d	3,480	20,195	
P58	LX wgn 5d	NA	22,715	
Crown Victoria—wb 114.4				
P73	sdn 4d	3,776	21,475	
P74	LX sdn 4d	NA	23,195	
Mustang—wb 101.3				
P40	cpe 2d	3,084	15,355	
P44	conv cpe 2d	3,264	20,755	
P42	GT cpe 2d	3,288	18,000	
P45	GT conv cpe 2d	3,422	23,985	
P42	Cobra cpe 2d	3,404	25,335	
P45	Cobra conv cpe 2d	3,540	28,185	
Thunderbird—wb 113.0				
P62	LX cpe 2d	3,561	17,885	
Production figures not available				

1998

Sporty 2-door ZX2 added to Escort line in spring of 1997 as an early '98

ZX2 carries a twin-cam 2.0-liter 4-cylinder engine

Facelifted '98 Contour with chrome, oval grille and "cat's eye" headlights also arrives in the spring of 1997

Special limited-edition SVT version of the '98 Contour is offered; it carries a "tuned" 2.5-liter V-6 and sport suspension

New Limited model is added to the early de-buting '98 Windstar line

All '98 Windstars feature a new grille and wider driver-side door for easier access to the rear seat

Ranger-based electric vehicle debuts; shows off new grille

▲ Sharing many Escort mechanicals but boasting its own unique styling, the ZX2 2-door coupe effectively replaced the 3-door hatchback in the Escort line. Its standard 130-bhp twin-cam 2.0-liter Zetec four with variable camshaft timing boasted 20 more horses than the Escort's engine.

▲ Dimensions of the ZX2 were very similar to those of the Escort on which it was based. ZX2 features not offered on the Escort sedan and wagon included unique wheel covers, optional 15-inch aluminum wheels, and a power moonroof. Anti-lock brakes were optional.

▶ Inside, the ZX2 boasted a unique dashboard design. Dual air bags were standard, as was a split-folding rear seat. Options included an integrated child safety seat, 6-disc CD changer, remote keyless entry, and a Sport Package that included 15-inch aluminum wheels, a rear spoiler, fog lamps, and unique interior and exterior trim.

▲ All 1998 Contours got a freshened exterior appearance with a chrome-trimmed grille, large wrap-around headlights, and new taillights.

▲ Little changed inside the Contour, though the driver's armrest now moved with the driver's seat and a new console housed three cupholders.

◄ Ford's Special Vehicle Team (SVT), which was also responsible for the Mustang Cobra and past projects like the F-150 Lightning pickup of 1993, conjured up the Contour SVT. Equipped with a modified 2.5-liter twin-cam V-6 with 195 bhp—25 more than in the "standard issue" Contour SE—the SVT also boasted upgraded suspension and brakes, deeper front and side body cladding, and unique 16-inch aluminum wheels. A 5-speed manual was the only transmission offered. Interiors featured white-faced gauges (an SVT signature), leather-wrapped steering wheel, and ten-way power driver's seat. The sole interior color was dark blue, while exteriors came only in red, silver, or black.

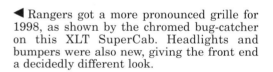

▲ The mid-line Contour LX came with a 125-bhp 2.0-liter four. Fog lamps were standard, and 8-spoke 15-inch cast wheels were optional.

◄ Rangers got a more pronounced grille for 1998, as shown by the chromed bug-catcher on this XLT SuperCab. Headlights and bumpers were also new, giving the front end a decidedly different look.

▼In an effort to combat the driver-side rear sliding doors offered on Chrysler and GM front-drive minivans, Ford extended the Windstar's driver-side door to allow easier access to the rear seat area. The door was six inches wider, and an available tip/sliding driver's seat further expanded the opening.

◄ Nineteen ninety-eight brought the U.S. Ford's first commercially available electric vehicle, the Ranger EV. Powered by 39 lead-acid batteries weighing 2000 pounds, the EV had an estimated range of 60 miles. It had a rear-mounted motor and transaxle, but looked very similar to a gas-powered Ranger save for a blocked-off grille panel and EV logos.

▶ Windstars got a revised front-end appearance courtesy of a new grille and lower facia. Joining the existing base (now 3.0L), GL, and LX models was a luxury-oriented Limited.

INDEX